Praise for *Refugee Law after 9/1*

"In *Refugee Law after 9/11*, Obi Okafor provides a meticulously detailed examination of the often-presented but rarely questioned assumption that the Canadian refugee regime is more generous than that of the United States. Highlighting continuities and disjunctures in the wake of the September 11, 2001, terrorist attacks, his comparative investigation of key questions enables a thoughtful, measured, and illuminating analysis of these neighbouring legal frameworks and their compliance with international human rights law."

– Jaya Ramji-Nogales, I. Herman Stern Research Professor,
Temple University, Beasley School of Law

"Okafor's intricate empirical work forces readers to come to terms with the security apparatus that surrounds refugee law. The unique US-Canada comparative setting compels Canadians to grapple with an uncomfortable truth about themselves and their immigration mythology."

– Catherine Dauvergne, Dean of Law,
University of British Columbia

Refugee Law after 9/11

LAW AND SOCIETY

Law and Society Series

W. Wesley Pue, Founding Editor

The Law and Society Series explores law as a socially embedded phenom-enon. It is premised on the understanding that the conventional division of law from society creates false dichotomies in thinking, scholarship, educational practice, and social life. Books in the series treat law and society as mutually constitutive and seek to bridge scholarship emer-ging from interdisciplinary engagement of law with disciplines such as politics, social theory, history, political economy, and gender studies.
Recent books in the series:

Trustees at Work: Financial Pressures, Emotional Labour, and Canadian Bankruptcy Law (2019)
Anna Jane Samis Lund

Crossing Law's Border: Canada's Refugee Resettlement Program (2019)
Shauna Labman

By the Court: Anonymous Judgments at the Supreme Court of Canada (2019)
Peter McCormick and Marc D. Zanoni

Seeking the Court's Advice: The Politics of the Canadian Reference Power (2019)
Kate Puddister

Ruling Out Art: Media Art Meets Law in Ontario's Censor Wars (2019)
Taryn Sirove

For a complete list of the titles in the series, see the UBC Press website, www.ubcpress.ca.

Refugee Law after 9/11

Sanctuary and Security in
Canada and the US

OBIORA CHINEDU OKAFOR

UBCPress · Vancouver · Toronto

29 28 27 26 25 24 23 22 21 20   5 4 3 2 1

Printed in Canada on FSC-certified ancient-forest-free paper (100% post-consumer recycled) that is processed chlorine- and acid-free.

Library and Archives Canada Cataloguing in Publication

Title: Refugee law after 9/11 : sanctuary and security in Canada and
   the US / Obiora Chinedu Okafor.
Names: Okafor, Obiora Chinedu, author.
Series: Law and society series (Vancouver, B.C.)
Description: Series statement: Law and society series | Includes bibliographical
   references and index.
Identifiers: Canadiana (print) 20190209380 | Canadiana (ebook) 20190209399 |
   ISBN 9780774861465 (hardcover) | ISBN 9780774861472 (softcover) |
   ISBN 9780774861489 (PDF) | ISBN 9780774861496 (EPUB) | ISBN 9780774861502
   (Kindle)
Subjects: LCSH: Refugees – Legal status, laws, etc. – Canada. | LCSH: Refugees –
   Legal status, laws, etc. – United States. | LCSH: National security – Canada. |
   LCSH: National security – United States.
Classification: LCC KE4472 .O43 2020 | LCC KF4483.I532 O43 2020 kfmod |
   DDC 342.7108/2 – dc23

Canadä

UBC Press gratefully acknowledges the financial support for our publishing program of the Government of Canada (through the Canada Book Fund), the Canada Council for the Arts, and the British Columbia Arts Council.

This book has been published with the help of a grant from the Canadian Federation for the Humanities and Social Sciences, through the Awards to Scholarly Publications Program, using funds provided by the Social Sciences and Humanities Research Council of Canada.

Printed and bound in Canada by Friesens
Set in Sabon Next LT Pro and Myriad Pro by Apex CoVantage, LLC
Copy editor: Frank Chow
Proofreader: Caitlin Gordon-Walker
Indexer: Noeline Bridge
Cover designer: Martyn Schmoll

UBC Press
The University of British Columbia
2029 West Mall
Vancouver, BC V6T 1Z2
www.ubcpress.ca

This book is dedicated to Atugonza
for her enduring love and dedication

Contents

Acknowledgments

I am deeply grateful to a great number of persons and institutions for their support during the nearly two decades it took to research and prepare this book. Although it is impossible to name all of them here, my family certainly comes to mind and deserves my deepest gratitude. I would therefore like to thank my amazing wife and partner, Atugonza, and our wonderful children, Ojiako, Mbabazi, and Kosi, for their untiring and enduring love and patience while I put in the long hours. My late father, Ichie F. Okwu-Okafor (Agundu n'Ukpo), and my mother, Lechi, have always been my primary sources of inspiration and strength. For these blessings, I remain eternally grateful. My siblings Ogo, Ofodile, Adaobi, Ojiugo, and Chibuzor deserve special mention as well, for their understanding, sacrifice, and support.

The ample financial assistance provided by the Canada-US Fulbright Program; the significant resources devoted to me by the Human Rights and Justice Program at the Massachusetts Institute of Technology (MIT) during my time as a Canada-US Fulbright Fellow; and the generous research funds awarded to me over many academic sessions by Osgoode Hall Law School and York University ensured that I could undertake the extensive research in Canada and the United States that grounds this book. Early versions of the ideas developed here were presented in late 2004 as part of the seminar series of the Human Rights and Justice Program at MIT. I am grateful to its director, Balakrishnan Rajagopal, for that opportunity.

I would also like to extend special thanks to Rebecca Pillai-Riddell (Associate Vice-President of Research) for inviting me to present the main ideas developed in this book at the York Circle Lectures at York University in November 2018; Susan McGrath for inviting me to present an early version of the Introduction at the Centre for Refugee Studies at York University in 2010; and Emily Carasco for inviting me to present parts of the book at a conference she organized at the Faculty of Law at the University of Windsor in 2005. I should also thank Sharyn Aiken, Ibrahim Awad, Reem Bahdi, Amar Bhatia, Sylvia Bawa, Bhupinder Chimni, James Gathii, Angus Grant, Barbara Jackman, Tavlin Kaur, Won Kidane, Zachary Lomo, Ikechi Mgbeoji, Usha Natarajan, Peter Penz, Kent Roach, Wes Pue, James Simeon, Lorne Waldman, and Sujith Xavier for the various ways in which they (consciously or unconsciously) facilitated the development of the thoughts expressed here.

During the many years it took to prepare this book, I was blessed to have the talented and dedicated assistance of a large number of student research assistants at the Osgoode Hall Law School of York University. Basema Al-Alami, Sasha Baglay, Ashley Barnbury, D'ette Bourchier, Sherifat Enikanolaiye, Chikeziri Igwe, Martin Jones, Cynthia Kwakyewah, Jennifer Yoon Lee, Pius Okoronkwo, Faustina Otchere, Udoka Owie, Dena Smith, Wudassie Tamrat, Kelly Tran, and Seeta Youll deserve my deep gratitude for their excellent work.

Last, but by no means the least, of those I would like to acknowledge are the staff at UBC Press, especially Randy Schmidt (my editor), for their dedication to the project, support throughout the process, and excellent editorial guidance. The anonymous reviewers of the manuscript also deserve my thanks.

Thank you one, thank you all!

Refugee Law after 9/11

Introduction: Refugee Law after 9/11: A Canada-US Comparison

In the days and years immediately following the September 11, 2001 (9/11), terrorist attacks on the United States, the mainstream wisdom, as Reg Whitaker has correctly noted, was that those tragic attacks changed everything and altered the world forever.[1] According to this view, the attacks triggered socio-political and legal rupture, a sharp departure from our social and legal "past," whatever that past was. While this view was, of course, not shared by every scholarly commentator and has since become less dominant, its resonance has not fully dissipated, necessitating the present inquiry. Does the available evidence of the responses of the Canadian and US refugee law regimes to the post-9/11 security vigil lend any significant weight to scholars (such as Whitaker, Kent Roach, and Reem Bahdi) who have suggested that 9/11 did not really change everything?[2] And given the lessons we ought to have learned from "earlier periods of panic ... and the cyclical process that swings along the security/humanitarian continuum,"[3] what are we to make of these post-9/11 refugee law developments in Canada and the United States?

To be sure, 9/11 did levy other kinds of important changes. It precipitated a renewed "war on terror," the overthrow of the Taliban regime in Afghanistan, a step-up in US interventionism in other countries, and the augmentation of the reconfiguration of government agendas/priorities in the United States and Canada.[4] The attacks of 9/11 also led to the invasion of Iraq (albeit on a false pretext),[5] and attracted renewed and even augmented interest in border/migration control.[6] Yet, one must keep in mind the fact that there is always "the danger of exaggerating" the extent and importance of these post-9/11 developments.[7]

Against this backdrop, the main purpose of this book is to determine *more precisely* the extent to which the heightened sense of security vulnerability that was produced by the 9/11 attacks did in fact trigger significant alterations in the refugee law regimes of Canada and the United States.[8] It is not, of course, in doubt that this heightened sense of vulnerability did trigger some changes to the form and content of the Canadian and US refugee law regimes.[9] The critical and challenging task is to map in as much detail as possible the extent of the alterations and stasis that may have occurred in this area of the law post-9/11.

Thus, on the broad level, the book is concerned with the relationship between refugee laws and national security – how such laws (mis)treat refugees under conditions of a felt national security emergency. More specifically, it is concerned with the relationship between a particular era of national security emergency (the post-9/11 era) and the law's (mis)treatment of refugees in Canada and the United States. This primary concern triggered two broadly related, if less central, conceptual preoccupations: 1) the precise extent to which a mentality styled "security relativism" helped shape the law's (mis)treatment of refugees in either Canada or the United States post-9/11; and 2) what the results of the first inquiry tell us about the cogency, coherence, and integrity of the dominant national self-images of both Canadians and Americans.

With this in mind, the book aims to do the following:

- Examine in a relatively comprehensive, more detailed, and systematic way the available legal evidence regarding the exact changes that were made or not made to refugee law in Canada and the United States after and/or because of 9/11. How precisely does each such change compare to the pre-9/11 refugee law regime in each country?
- Compare the post-9/11 refugee law regime in Canada (a country that was not directly attacked on 9/11) to the corresponding experience in the United States, which was directly targeted by those attacks.

Has it been better or worse in either country, or have they been similar?

- Explain the logics behind the changes (or lack thereof) observed in refugee law in Canada and the United States after 9/11, as well as the reasons for any differences in the respective characteristics or orientations of the post-9/11 refugee law regimes.
- Explain the relationship between refugee law and national security in each of the two countries after, and because of, 9/11. Was it undergirded by a mentality of security relativism?
- Tease out the logical inferences that can be drawn from the foregoing analyses regarding the cogency, coherence, and integrity of the national self-images of the two countries.

It should be emphasized the last two goals are less crucial than the first three.

This book offers the first overarching and detailed treatment to date of the situation of refugee law in Canada and the United States after 9/11, compared to the pre-9/11 situation in both countries. It is also the first book-length comparative study of the Canadian and US experiences, and the first broad-based study to probe this deeply into two important conceptual linkages: 1) the link between the law's (mis)treatment of refugee rights in Canada and the United States post-9/11 and the mentality of security relativism, as well as 2) the cogency, coherence, and integrity of the national self-images of Americans and Canadians.

The analyses contained here do not, however, run the entire gamut of refugee law. While they do deal with almost all of the key topics and themes regarding the law's (mis)treatment of refugee rights in our time in the context of national security fears (i.e., deportations to torture, detentions, terrorism-related inadmissibility, and safe third-country regimes), they do not treat each and every such issue. For example, they do not deal with the issue of how the Canadian and US refugee resettlement programs were affected by the pronounced security anxieties caused by the 9/11 attacks.[10] Neither do they treat the issue of the extent to which these post-9/11 security considerations affected the numbers of refugee claims processed and/or accepted by each country.[11] It should also be noted that the book is not really focused on a discussion of either the mentality of security relativism or the question of the cogency of the national self-images of Canadians and Americans. Rather, the treatment of these two issues flows logically from the execution of the main task here – namely, a comparative analysis of the extent to which the heightened post-9/11 security vigil can be viewed as causing a transformation of the refugee law regimes of the two countries.

In the light of the foregoing discussion, it is clear that a number of concepts and expressions are central to the analyses conducted in this book: refugee law regime, "after 9/11," security relativism, and national self-image. These require explanation at this point, even if only briefly in some cases. First, as used in this book, the expression "refugee law regime" refers to the set of laws, policies, norms, and procedures that govern the enjoyment or denial of refuge rights in a given national jurisdiction. This term "regime" is used here the way it is typically used in international relations theory. For example, Stephen Krasner defines a regime as a set of "principles, norms, rules, and decision-making procedures around which actors' expectations converge in a given issue area."[12]

Second, references in this book to "after 9/11" recognize that an event that was widely treated as exceptional and as causing a break in historical time occurred on that date, and that there is therefore in most of our minds a "before" and "after" in relation to that date. Nevertheless, it is still recognized that history hardly ever ruptures, that the "before" and "after" are almost always deeply connected, and that the "before" usually fades slowly into the "after."[13]

Third, since the concept of security relativism is discussed and defined in much greater detail in the Conclusion, suffice it to state here that

- [t]he term "security" within the expression "security relativism" refers to "national security."[14]
- [l]egally protected refugee rights would be viewed as having been treated in a security-relative way to the extent that they have been held to arise from, or have been viewed as determined by, or have been considered in some other sense to be dependent on security imperatives.[15]
- [a] useful distinction may be drawn between "strong" and "weak" security relativism.[16]

Finally, as it is used in this book, the expression "national self-image" refers to the complex composite of images of themselves as a group that the citizens of a country, the members of that national community, possess. This kind of composite image is usually held in relation to a number of different things, such as humanitarianism and diversity, and dominant national self-images invariably coexist with alternative self-identities.

In furtherance of these goals, the relevant refugee law–related statutes, regulations, processes, and procedures from Canada and the United States, as well as the relevant hard and soft international legal texts (and, to a lesser extent, jurisprudence) were identified and analyzed. Many relevant practices were also examined either through the facts of cases or through other sources to back up and illustrate the legal analyses that are the focus of this book. Clearly, the primarily legal methodology that informs the discussion imposes some limitations on the scope of the "data" that it is based on. Yet, while the greater deployment of socio-legal methodology might have yielded additional insight, enough of this approach has been integrated into the analysis – as a backup – to ensure that any such difference (if any) would not be all that significant. This having been said, it should also be remembered that the methodology adopted in the Conclusion is socio-legal. The book is therefore only primarily, and not totally, based on legal methodology.

The choice of Canada and the United States as the jurisdictions of focus was primarily due to the fact that the latter was the country that was attacked on 9/11 and Canada is its closest neighbour. This close neighbour status is ascribed to the two countries not just because they share a very long border but also because of their relative historical, social, cultural, political, and legal affinity. The United States, of course, shares a long border with Mexico and is also deeply interconnected with it culturally (largely because of its very large Hispanic population), but the dominant populations in these two countries are clearly not as close as the majority populations in Canada and the United States are to each other. For example, while the United States is a common law country, Mexico is not.[17] Furthermore, even other common law countries are, overall, not as close to the United States in the stated terms as Canada is. This significant closeness in socio-legal and other areas renders the two jurisdictions significantly more comparable for present purposes than, say, the United States and Mexico are. It is no wonder, then, that as Kent Roach has noted, "there is a long tradition of comparative studies of the politics, laws, and institutions of Canada and the United States."[18] Primarily based as it is on the study of Canada and US refugee laws, this book is part of this long tradition of North American comparativism.

It should also be acknowledged that the book has benefited much from the broader scholarly literature sets on "9/11 and its aftermath," national security, anti-terrorism legislation, and human rights. In this more general context, the work of scholars such as Kent Roach and Craig Forcese, as well as the separate volumes edited by Ron Daniels and colleagues, and by Niklaus Steiner and colleagues, have all been very helpful.[19] The same can be said of the Canada-US comparative work that has done in this connection by some of these same scholars. For example, Roach has done substantial work in comparing Canada's post-9/11 anti-terrorism laws and praxis to their US counterparts.[20] The book has also benefited to an even greater degree from the earlier work on the impact of national security and anti-terrorism legislation on refugee law/rights in Canada, the United States, and even globally by scholars such as Howard Adelman, Sharryn Aiken, Reem Bahdi, Muzaffar Chishti, David Cole, François Crépeau, Catherine Dauvergne, Joan Fitzpatrick, Regina Germain, Lawrence Lebowitz, Audrey Macklin, Ira Podheiser, and Reg Whitaker, and by eminent practitioners such as Volker Turk.[21] Nevertheless, systematic comparisons of the Canadian and US post-9/11 refugee law regimes have been quite rare. Reg Whitaker's early but shorter overview papers on this subject are one of the few exceptions.[22] And although focused more widely on four countries and limited to the indefinite detention area, Catherine Dauvergne's important contribution to this kind of comparative work also stands out in this respect.[23] Even rarer (if they exist at all) are book-length scholarly comparative analyses of the changes or lack thereof that were experienced post-9/11 in the Canadian and US refugee law regimes. It is against this backdrop that one of this book's contributions is to offer the first such work. The book also benefited from the earlier work of scholars such as Monica Juma and Peter Kagwanja, who have discussed the long-standing trend of sacrificing (refugee) rights at the altar of security;[24] as well as Catherine

Dauvergne's work on the intimate connection between migration law and national identity.[25] The book attempts to builds on the insights found in these writings.

Chapters 1 through 4 offer systematic and comparative analyses of the extent of stasis and change post-9/11 in the four key Canadian-US refugee law subregimes focused on in this book. Each chapter also assesses the validity under international law of the post-9/11 legal and other measures taken by each of the two focus countries. Chapter 1 considers the deportation to torture of refugees and other non-citizens; Chapter 2 examines the detention of refugees; Chapter 3 considers the application of terrorism-related inadmissibility to refugees; and Chapter 4 analyzes the Canada-US third safe country subregime. The Conclusion offers an overarching analysis of 1) the extent to which the mentality of security relativism was at play in shaping the developments and positions observed in Chapters 1 through 4, and 2) what the analyses in the preceding chapters teach us about the cogency, coherence, and integrity of the Canadian and US national self-images.

On the whole, the book, which is current up to March 2019, attempts to show that in many more respects than not, the pre-9/11 versions of these regimes looked much like their post-9/11 versions, "only more so."[26] In most respects, refugee law post-9/11 was refugee law pre-9/11, 2.0. The underlying point the book seeks to make is that in both countries, *things were already so bad with refugee law before 9/11 that there was significantly less room than many have supposed for them to get all that much worse*. It should be emphasized, however, that the argument here is *not* at all that nothing changed for refugee law after 9/11. The book also attempts to show that while there were significant differences in the post-9/11 refugees and in Canada and the US (especially in terms of the scale of their responses), *for the most part* the refugee law regimes in the two jurisdictions reacted in strikingly similar ways to the heightened security vigil triggered by the 9/11 attacks. This is interesting, even if only somewhat understandable, given that, unlike the United States, Canada was not directly attacked on that day. These points, separately and collectively raise equally interesting questions about the extent to which the mentality of security relativism has shaped refugee law in both countries (and why), and the accuracy of the national self-images of Canadians and Americans.

It is hoped that this book will add significantly to the broader debates about the precise impact of the heightened security vigil triggered by the 9/11 attacks, on law, politics, and institutions, both around the world in general and in Canada and the United States in particular. It is also hoped that the book will contribute significantly to the more *intra*-disciplinary debates on the actual impact (or otherwise) of this augmented security vigil on refugee law in the two countries as well as the world over. Such a contribution inevitably feeds into the debates on the age-old (if unwarranted) association between refugees and threats to national security,[27] a phenomenon that has become even more pronounced in the age of Donald Trump.

Deportations to Torture

1

Against the backdrop of the discussion in the Introduction of the much-diminished but persistent sense that the attacks in the United States on September 11, 2001 (9/11) "changed everything," this chapter has two principal objectives. The first is to assess the character of each of the refugee law regimes in Canada and the United States that seek to protect non-citizens (including refugees) from deportation to torture (D2T), with a view to ascertaining the nature and significance of the changes, if any, that have been made to either regime as a result of the heightened sense of security vulnerability that was fostered by the 9/11 attacks.[1] This entails analytical responses to some important questions. If, for instance, most of the observable denudation of the legal protection of this aspect of refugee rights had already occurred in either country before 9/11, to what extent can responsibility for the observed changes be attributed to the mass security hysteria fostered by those attacks?[2] Are there earlier dates in refugee law history that are equally or more significant as watersheds than 9/11? With respect to both regimes, was 9/11 not more of an accentuating event than a formative one?[3]

The other principal objective of the chapter is to compare the post-9/11 character of the Canadian and US deportation to torture regimes, in order to better understand the extent to which the 9/11 attacks can or cannot be considered responsible for the changes that have marked those regimes. If, for instance, the post-9/11 deportation to torture regime in the United States (the country that was attacked) turns out to be no less anti-refugee than its counterpart in Canada, would it still be reasonable to consider the post-9/11 heightened sense of security vulnerability as largely responsible for the negative orientation of this aspect of refugee law in either country? If the attacks of 9/11 are considered the key factor in explaining the denudation of protection against deportation to torture, would it not be reasonable to expect a greater weakening of such protection in the country that was directly attacked? What would the observance of significantly greater denudation in the country that was not attacked suggest about the role of other events and factors in explaining the impact of the post-9/11 mass security hysteria on this key aspect of refugee law in the two countries? What would it suggest about the comparative merits of the Canadian and US refugee regimes? What would it suggest about Canada's self-image as a country that pursues one of the most humanitarian refugee policies in the world? What would it suggest about the United States' self-image?

In order to achieve these objectives, the chapter has been divided into seven major sections, including this introduction. The chapter begins with an examination of the nature of the general prohibitions, in both the US and Canada, against deportations to torture. This is followed by a discussion of the character and impact of the many frontal assaults that have been launched in both countries against the continued absoluteness of the prohibition of such deportations. An analytical exposé of the numerous embedded loopholes in both regimes that permit the deportation of some non-citizens to torture despite the continued formal operation in both countries of the general bars against such deportations is then offered. Thereafter, the question of the national security challenge that is sometimes posed by the general bars, in both countries, against deportations to torture, is systematically raised. Following this discussion, an attempt is made to recalibrate this challenge in the light of alternative readings of the relevant legislation, cases, and social contexts. The objective here is to show that the national security challenge that is constituted by the prohibition of deportations to torture is not nearly as insurmountable within the limits established by international law as it is often made out by some states to seem. Lastly, a number of important analytical insights that are evident from a comparison of the US and Canadian regimes with respect to the prohibition of deportations to torture are offered in conclusion.

The General Bar against Deportations to Torture in Canada and the United States

The rule that no non-citizen (whether or not he or she is a refugee claimant) shall be returned from one state to a country where that person is at substantial risk of being subjected to torture is now well established in international law as absolute and permitting of no exceptions whatsoever. Article 3 of the *Convention against Torture (CAT)* clearly states this rule thus: "No State Party shall expel, return (*refouler*) or extradite a person to another State where there are substantial grounds for believing that he [or she] would be in danger of being subjected to torture."[4] This rule, which extends far more protection to non-citizens who qualify for protection under it than the contingent bar against *refoulement* to persecution that is prescribed in the 1951 Convention relating to the Status of Refugees (or *Refugee Convention*), is now so well established and fundamental that even though it is not explicitly stated in the *International Covenant on Civil and Political Rights (ICCPR)*,[5] the United Nations Human Rights Committee (the body charged with interpreting and applying that treaty's provisions) has in effect read it into the text of the treaty's prohibition, in Article 7, of the act of torture itself.[6] In its opinion in *Ahani v Canada*,[7] the committee excoriated Canada for deporting Mansour Ahani to Iran in spite of the committee's indication of interim measures; a request that such action be delayed until it had had an opportunity to consider Ahani's claim that, *inter alia*, his impending expulsion to Iran would expose him to torture in breach of Article 7 of the *ICCPR*. The committee stated that although it reserved its views as to whether Ahani actually faced a substantial risk of torture if deported to Iran, the expulsion of any person who faces such a risk would undermine the absolute prohibition of torture itself in Article 7.[8] What is more, the absolute and imperative character of the bar against such expulsions has also been affirmed and reiterated in a long line of opinions issued by both the Committee against Torture (the body charged with interpreting and applying the *Convention against Torture*) and the European Court of Human Rights.[9] Some commentators have even suggested that the rule now forms part of customary international law, and will therefore bind even those states that have not explicitly consented to the convention.[10]

In order to comply with their obligations under international law to outlaw and prevent deportations to torture, both Canada and the United States have established their respective domestic legal and institutional regimes for the assessment and adjudication of claims for relief from the prospect of such deportations. Although a general bar against these sorts of deportations constitutes the bedrock of these refugee regimes, the Canadian bar is couched in less than absolute terms, whereas its equivalent under the US regime is stated in flatly, absolute terms.

The General Bar under the US Refugee Law Regime

Although the United States signed the *Convention against Torture* in 1988, it was not until 1994 that it ratified that treaty and thus became a full party to it.[11] And it was not until Public Law No. 105-277 and the *Regulations Concerning the Convention against Torture of 1999* were enacted that an operational domestic regime designed to implement the requirements of the rule under international law against deportations to torture was put in place.[12] Section 2242(a) of this Act provides that (subject to the exceptions stated in the statute itself) "[i]t shall be the policy of the United States not to expel, extradite, or otherwise effect the involuntary return of any person to a country in which there are substantial grounds for believing the person would be in danger of being subjected to torture, regardless of whether the person is physically present in the United States." The clear intent of the relevant domestic legal instruments is to enact a general prohibition against the deportation by the United States of any non-citizen to a country where that person faces a sufficiently high risk of torture (as defined in the relevant domestic legislation and regulations). This point is so widely recognized in the relevant literature as to be beyond reasonable dispute.[13] In any case, the relevant regulations issued by the key government agency in the immigration enforcement area[14] makes it clear that even serious criminals and suspected or convicted terrorists shall not be deported to a place where they face a sufficiently high risk of torture.[15] The relevant operations memorandum issued by the Office of the Chief Immigration Judge in the United States to all Immigration Judges throughout that country support this position.[16] The jurisprudence of US appellate courts is fairly clear in prohibiting most such deportations of refugees (and other non-citizens) who meet the threshold, even in some cases when the person in question is shown to have committed an act that fits the definition of terrorism. For example, in the case of *Cheema v Ashcroft*, the US Court of Appeals for the Ninth Circuit interpreted an older version of the *Immigration and Nationality Act (INA)* in sustaining the Board of Immigration Review's grant to Harpal Singh Cheema of *CAT*-based *withholding* of removal even though he was shown to have committed a series of acts that fit the definition of terrorism under the US refugee law at the time.[17] The Court held that to prevail under the older version of the law, the government had to show, in addition, that there were reasonable grounds to believe that Cheema was a danger to the security of the United States, something that it had not been able to do.

Note, however, that a subsequent amendment to the *Immigration and Nationality Act* made terrorist activity on its own a sufficient ground for denying relief of withholding of removal under the *CAT*.[18] Thus in *Bellout v Ashcroft*, the same US Court of Appeals for the Ninth Circuit held that there was no longer a two-pronged test, and that mere terrorist activity was now sufficient grounds for denying such relief.[19]

Importantly, and by contrast, Cheema and Bellout were entitled to *deferral* of removal (a lesser benefit), regardless of the law concerning withholding of removal, and regardless of whether or not there were reasonable grounds to believe that they were terrorists or posed a danger to the United States, as long as they could show that they faced a substantial risk of torture on being returned to the places to which they were deportable.[20] Cheema was able to meet this test for a grant of deferral of removal in the eyes of the relevant court, but Bellout was unsuccessful.

This general prohibitionist stance is of course consistent with the general pre-9/11 tendency among the vocal section of the US elite to condemn, at least in public, the practice of torture.[21] It also accords with the US State Department's relentless and continuing annual condemnation of other states for practising torture.[22] And if the content of the bills that have been introduced or passed in that country are anything to go by, this sense of outrage and moral indignation against the practice of torture has – to a large extent – also been manifest, at least before 9/11, among most members of the US Congress.[23] It faded to some degree after 9/11 but revived, at least partially, after former president Barack Obama's victory in 2008.[24] President Donald Trump's successful campaign and his actions and statements since taking office in January 2017 appear to have again weakened this sense of outrage, especially on the right of the US political spectrum.[25]

The General Bar under the Canadian Refugee Law Regime

In January 2002, only a few months after the 9/11 attacks, the Supreme Court of Canada handed down two decisions concerning the legality of the federal government's attempts to deport two refugees on "national security grounds" to places where they alleged that they faced a substantial risk of torture.[26] The more important decision was rendered in *Suresh v Canada*.[27] In it, the Court established the general rule barring Canada from deporting non-citizens under its control to places where they faced a substantial risk of torture. The Court formulated this general (if less than absolute) Canadian bar against such deportations in the following way:

> We conclude that *generally* to deport a refugee, where there are grounds to believe that this would subject the refugee to a substantial risk of torture, would unconstitutionally violate the *Charter's* s. 7 guarantee of life, liberty and security of the person. This said, *we leave open the possibility that in an exceptional case such a deportation might be justified* either in the balancing approach under ss. 7 or 1 of the *Charter.*[28]

Thus, the Court left open the possibility that a non-citizen might be lawfully deported to torture from Canada, although it clearly realized that such deportations are absolutely barred by international law, and that even a person who is considered a national security risk can still be at risk of torture if deported to his or her country. That much is evident from a combined reading of the above statement and two other statements, that "the *Convention against Torture* absolutely prohibits deportations or expulsions to torture," and that "we find that Suresh made a *prima facie* showing that he might be tortured on return if expelled to Sri Lanka."[29]

The *Suresh* decision is all the more significant since, although Canadian domestic legislation has implemented Article 1 of the *Convention against Torture*, Canada has still not passed any domestic legislation that implements, in plenary form, the absolute bar against deportations to torture contained in Article 3 of the *Convention*. The "less than absolute bar" mandated in the *Suresh* case is all that protects prospective deportees to torture in Canada. This general bar is codified in Canada's 2001 *Immigration and Refugee Protection Act (IRPA)*, especially in its ss 113 and 115.[30] Section 115 formulates a principle of non-*refoulement* that applies to a new and broadened class of "protected persons" (an expression that now includes persons who would qualify as refugees under the 1951 *Refugee Convention*, persons who face a substantial risk of torture, and some other classes of non-citizens). Nevertheless, the section also allows (albeit in exceptional cases) the deportation of non-citizens who are either 1) deemed to be both serious criminals and dangers to the public in Canada, or 2) deemed to be both security risks and dangers to the security of Canada. Section 113 (relating to pre-removal risk assessments for qualified non-citizens) also allows the relevant Minister to do this kind of risk balancing – the risk of torture versus the risk to Canadian society – in reaching a conclusion as to whether a non-citizen should be expelled to a place where he or she faces a substantial risk of torture.[31]

Although the Supreme Court in *Suresh* makes much of the facts that torture is a despicable form of behaviour that is eminently illegal under Canadian law and that deportations to torture would be condemned by most Canadians,[32] the fact remains that in the end, Canadian law, as laid down in that case and reiterated in s 115 of the *IRPA*, does not contain an absolute formal bar against deportations to torture. Thus, the US formulation of the general bar is preferable to its Canadian counterpart, especially when both are viewed against the respective international law obligations assumed by Canada and the United States.[33]

Frontal Assaults on the US and Canadian Refugee Law Regimes before and after 9/11

Despite the very strong way in which the general rule prohibiting deportations to torture from the United States has been stated, frontal and direct assaults on this rule have not been uncommon within and outside that country's national legislature. Many such assaults were launched even before 9/11. In the case of Canada, the fact that its own Supreme Court has chosen to espouse a less-than-absolute formulation of the general prohibition of deportations to torture is most instructive, but the forces aligned against the enshrinement of an absolute prohibition extend far beyond the Court. The pre- and post-9/11 experiences of both countries will now be examined separately in order to illustrate the way in which tolerance for deportations to torture (and thus for torture itself) has both waxed and waned but gradually increased in both jurisdictions over time. This will lay the groundwork for understanding the dangers involved in maintaining the less obviously stated loopholes currently embedded in the anti-deportation to torture regimes of both countries.

The US Experience

The movement in the United States seeking to dismantle the very strong bar against deportations to torture dates back to well before 9/11. This is aptly illustrated by three congressional efforts. Between 1999 and April 2001, three bills were introduced in Congress that had a bearing on historical efforts to carve out at least one broad exception to the US *CAT*-relief regime with respect to convicted serious criminals and suspected terrorists. As Ellen Chung has correctly noted, all three bills were, to varying extents, attempts to "curtail United States obligations under the Torture Convention."[34] Although the first two bills (one relating to the proposed *Anti-Atrocity Act of 1999*[35] and the other relating to the proposed *Denying Safe Haven to International and War Criminals Act of 2000*[36]) did not explicitly seek to reformulate and weaken the absolute bar in the United States against deportations to torture, both bills gave vent to the fears of their *bipartisan* group of sponsors that the absolute bar would damage the ability of US immigration authorities to deport serious human rights abusers (including war crimes and terrorism suspects) to their own countries.[37] Much more harshly formulated, the third bill – the proposed *Serious Human Rights Abusers Accountability Act of 2000*[38] – explicitly sought to enable the United States to deport a certain class of serious human rights abusers to their own countries even when it has been proven in administrative or judicial proceedings that such persons would likely be tortured. Section 12 of the proposed act was a clear endorsement of the deportation to torture (and therefore torture) of at least some non-citizens in the United States.[39]

Since 9/11, there has also been much debate over the desirability of loosening the international and domestic prohibitions against torture and deportations to torture in the service of the "war against terror."[40] It became clearer after 9/11 that pro-torture and pro–deportation-to-torture views could in fact form the basis of polite conversation in the United States.[41] Even otherwise reasonable scholars espoused and defended their views as to the circumstances under which torture (and by implication deportation to torture) ought to be permitted in that country. Proponents of such views and practitioners involved in both cases were definitely emboldened by the post-9/11 mass security hysteria.

The most significant indication after 9/11 of the extent to which the policies and actions of the US government had swung in favour of the views of the pro-torture movement was the Abu Ghraib scandal.[42] This scandal involved the publication of shocking photographs documenting the severe ill treatment and torture of many Iraqi prisoners by US soldiers posted to the now-infamous Abu Ghraib prison. In a single-minded quest for intelligence, numerous criminal acts that clearly amounted to torture were committed against these prisoners in such a brazen way as to suggest a high level of official complicity or even authorization.[43] A Human Rights Watch report provided an analytical basis for such a conclusion, charging that the only thing that was exceptional about the incidents at Abu Ghraib were that they were photographed.[44] In the view of this organization, it was official (if secret) US government policy in the wake of 9/11 to allow the torture (or at least the serious ill treatment) of terrorist suspects and other prisoners in its custody in the quest for intelligence.[45] As is now public knowledge, the US Department of Justice under then Attorney General John Ashcroft had some months after 9/11 written a memo advising then White House Counsel Alberto Gonzales that the severe interrogation methods being employed by US soldiers in the war on terror (which were considered by many as tantamount to torture) were not prohibited under US and international law.[46] The memo warned that the international law prohibition against the use of torture by the United States might even be unconstitutional if it was applied to bar such interrogation tactics.[47] As Edward J. Markey stated on the floor of the US House of Representatives, the contents of this memo have resulted in much skepticism about the US government's commitment to the prohibition of torture.[48] The great reluctance on the part of many Bush Administration officials to acknowledge the full extent of their involvement in the practice of torture (or at least severe ill treatment) post-9/11 leaves even less room for doubt about the extent to which these practices received the mandate or acquiescence of high government officials.[49] The key point here is that this scandal showed quite clearly that after 9/11, the US government began to take a significantly more tolerant view of its own practice of torture directed against suspects in its custody considered important in the war against terror.

Another highly significant indication of the post-9/11 ascendancy of pro-torture and pro–deportation to torture views in the US government was the practice of so-called extraordinary rendition, exemplified by the Maher Arar scandal. As Joan Fitzpatrick noted: "US officials use the term 'rendition' to describe the Bush Administration's current policies regarding the forcible interstate transfer of suspected terrorists."[50] States, such as the United States, choose to "render" non-citizens in this way either because there is no extradition treaty between the two countries involved or in order to avoid the rigours of extradition.[51] Of particular interest here is the form of rendition that involves the transfer of a non-citizen from the United States itself to another country in order to obtain intelligence from that non-citizen through acts of torture that US officials fully expect officials of the foreign country to inflict on the non-citizen. This is the kind of rendition that was visited in October 2002 on Maher Arar, a Canadian engineer who had been born in Syria.[52] A dual citizen of Canada and Syria, Arar had lived in Canada for a very long time and had been travelling on a Canadian passport.[53] While changing planes in New York en route to Canada, he was arrested by US immigration officials.[54] He was accused of having links to al-Qaeda, interrogated, detained, severely mistreated for over a week in a US jail, and later deported to Syria for interrogation there.[55] He was deported to Syria despite his protestations that he wanted to be returned to his home in Canada.[56] As remarkably, US officials deported him with full knowledge that he faced a high risk of torture in a Syrian jail – a risk well documented in the annual reports on the human rights situation around the world issued by the State Department.[57] Arar subsequently alleged in a lawsuit against the US government that he was tortured in Syria.[58] A Canadian commission of inquiry investigated the incident, and its findings were part of the *Report on the Events Relating to Maher Arar*, also known as the *Arar Report*.[59] It is now apparent that the Arar case was hardly unique in recent US history.[60] Needless to say, such deportations to torture violate the absolute bar under international and even US law. Clearly, therefore, they are also likely to significantly undermine the normative authority of that bar.[61] The key point, however, is that the practice of extraordinary rendition, especially as highlighted by the Maher Arar scandal, is clear indication of the weakening, at least post-9/11, of the US government's public posture against deportation to torture. It is also evidence of the increased tolerance of such a practice in the post-9/11 United States with respect to non-citizens who are considered security risks.

The third development testifying to this increased tolerance is the significant though ultimately unsuccessful push by congressional Republicans to pass the *Securing America's Future through Enforcement Reform Act of 2003* (the so-called *SAFER Act*).[62] Section 433 of the proposed act contained almost the exact language found in s 12 of the *Serious Human Rights Abusers Accountability Act of 2000*, discussed above. Clearly, therefore, the *SAFER Act* aimed to gut the protection available under US law for a subset of the class of persons who show that they face a sufficiently high risk of being subjected to torture should they be deported. In this way did proposed legislation provide significant evidence of the renewal in the post-9/11 era of the movement that favoured the practice of deportation to torture, at least in the case of non-citizens who are considered threats to US national security.

The fourth and last development that will be offered here as evidence of this renewal is the push made in the context of unsuccessful efforts to gain passage of the House of Representatives' version of the so-called 9/11 Bill.[63] While the version of the bill that passed the House was far less harsh than the original proposal introduced on the House floor, and was quite unlike the proposed *Serious Human Rights Abusers Accountability Act of 2000* and the post-9/11 *SAFER Act* in not explicitly permitting the US government to deport to torture non-citizens considered serious human rights violators, national security risks, and terrorist suspects, s 3032 would have made it much easier for US officials to deport such persons even to countries where they would be at risk, as long as diplomatic assurances that they would not be tortured were sought from those countries. The unsuccessful bill also sought, in effect, to mandate the indefinite detention of non-citizens who were deemed "dangerous" by the Secretary of Homeland Security but whom the US for some reason (such as *CAT* relief) was unable to deport. To the extent that such diplomatic assurances were generally unreliable even when offered at all, and that detainees facing the prospect of permanent detention in the United States might actually "choose" to return to a high-risk torture-prone country, the bill would have, in effect, licensed a subversion of the prohibition in US law against deportations to torture. While these measures were omitted from the compromise legislation that passed both Houses of Congress in late 2004,[64] at the very least their inclusion in the bill clearly showed the continued vitality, three years after 9/11, of the movement that favoured the deportation to torture of some non-citizens. The power of this movement in Congress was indicated by the promise to reconsider the provisions in the 109th Congress that its leaders, such as Representative John Sensenbrenner, extracted from the House leadership.[65]

These four developments are evidence of the significant momentum enjoyed by the pro–deportation to torture elements within the US government following 9/11. They also evidence the concomitant increase in the tolerance for this practice on the part of a significant proportion of the relevant governmental actors. Viewed in the light of the relevant pre-9/11 developments, it is clear that a better explanation for the observed surge in pro–deportation to torture sentiments after 9/11 is that the tragic events of that day and the heightened security concerns expressed by most Americans accentuated and gave social cover to more vigorous expression of an already existing tendency within the US public and government.

However, the exposure of the incidents of torture at Abu Ghraib, and of the rendition to torture of Maher Arar and others, did trouble many in the US public and definitely caused sufficient embarrassment to many in the government, enough to produce a significant backlash against the pro-torture and pro–deportation to torture movement. The FBI rushed to reiterate to all its divisions its official policy against the practice of torture. In a priority marked message, the Bureau's General Counsel noted that "in the light of the widely publicized abuses at Abu Ghraib prison, Iraq, this EC reiterates and memorializes existing FBI policy,"[66] and warned that "FBI personnel may not obtain statements during interrogations by the use of force, threats, physical abuse, threats of such abuse or severe physical conditions."[67] Even more importantly, the White House itself issued a statement of policy that explicitly and "strongly opposed" the push by the pro–deportation to torture wing of the House of Representatives to pass s 3032 of the *9/11 Recommendations Implementation Bill* that would have made it significantly easier for the US to deport serious criminals and suspected terrorists to torture.[68]

Less important but still quite significant was the introduction in the 108th Congress of a bill,[69] sponsored by Representative Markey, that was designed to severely restrict the ability of the CIA or any other agency of the US government to deport or render any non-citizen to torture.[70] However, the bill did not bar legal, treaty-based extraditions, as long as the person to be extradited had the right to appeal to a US court that could block the proposed extradition based on the likelihood that the person would be tortured or ill-treated in the relevant country.[71] While commendable from an anti-deportation to torture perspective, the bill was nevertheless still open to abuse by pro-torture or overzealous officials. This is because s 2 would still have allowed deportations or renditions to torture to occur if the Secretary of State certified that the nation to which the non-citizen was to be sent had "made significant progress in human rights." The wording "made significant progress in human rights" is so vague and indeterminate as to provide very little, if any, real guidance to the Secretary of State in making such a determination. Given the long-standing and understandable US judicial tradition in favour of deference to the excecutive branch in the area of foreign relations, this may have been the intention of the drafters and supporters of the bill. Whether or not this was their intention, it seems clear from previous experience with US foreign policy in this regard that such determinations were likely to be highly politicized. For instance, based on past US behaviour, the Secretary of State was more likely to certify Pakistan than Zimbabwe.[72] There was little to commend Pakistan over Zimbabwe other than the fact that Pakistan was at the time considered an important ally in the war against terror, whereas Zimbabwe was not, and this did not detract from the reality of torture that many deportees might have had to face in Pakistan.[73] The issue is moot, however, since the bill was not passed into law by the 108th Congress.

In January 2009, President Obama's Executive Order 13491 called for a review of US transfer policies to ensure that they did not result in the transfer of individuals to nations where they might be subjected to torture, or cause transfers that would undermine or circumvent the United States' obligations to ensure the humane treatment of individuals in its custody or control.[74] This move indicated that in its efforts to close down Guantanamo Bay, the Obama Administration was taking into account the significant risk of torture that refugees (and other non-citizens) might face if returned to their countries. However, Manfred Nowak and colleagues argue that the Obama Administration eventually backed away to some extent from its rigorous adherence to the principle of non-*refoulement* to torture under increasing pressure to close the Guantanamo Bay detention facility, the reluctance of other countries to resettle more detainees, and "the strong political opposition by Congress and the American population to accept detainees in US territory."[75] Two examples of this shift can be seen in the cases of two Algerian Guantanamo detainees who were, at the Obama Administration's urging, cleared by the US Supreme Court to be sent back to their countries against their expressed claim that they faced a risk of torture. US authorities justified their return by citing diplomatic assurances received from Algeria that they would not be abused. The United Nations Special Rapporteurs on Torture and on Human Rights and Counter-Terrorism expressed concern with this decision, stating that the detainees "could be put in danger without a proper assessment of the risks." They rejected the reliance on diplomatic assurances. Despite this, the Obama Administration deported one of the detainees to Algeria on July 17, 2010.[76]

In summary, despite receiving a considerable boost from the 9/11 attacks, most of the pre- and post-9/11 frontal assaults against the absolute prohibition on deportations to torture in US law have in a formal legal sense failed. This is salutary in and of itself, as formal legal rules do retain significant protective power, despite the possibility of being violated in practice. The failure of all these measures is attributable in large part to the relative strength of the anti-torture movement in the United States, and to the fundamental and broadly normative character of the global prohibition against torture and deportations to torture. Nevertheless, as we shall see later in this chapter, this does not mean that refugees and other non-citizens in the US are free from the significant practical risk of being deported to torture through the utilization or operation of a number of subtle loopholes in the US *CAT*-relief regime.

The Canadian Experience

Despite Canada's ratification of the *Convention against Torture* in June 1987, the Canadian legal attitude toward the absoluteness of the bar against torture has not been as firm as it could be, at least at the formal level.[77] This is indicative of a certain comfort level within the relevant Canadian legal and institutional regimes with deportations to torture of non-citizens deemed to pose dangers to either Canadian society or national security. Thus, the frontal attacks launched in Canada against the absoluteness of the general prohibition of such deportations have been basically as successful at the formal level as similar attacks in the United States.

Important evidence of this is the very fact that Article 3 of the *Convention* had not been directly implemented in Canadian domestic law even at the time the *Suresh* and *Ahani* cases were filed in 1997 and 1999, respectively – at least one decade after Canada had ratified the *Convention!* – and Canadian law does not permit such unimplemented treaties to directly circumscribe executive action.

Second, it is noteworthy that under Canada's then operative *Immigration Act* (hereinafter "the old Act"), s 53(1)(b) permitted the relevant Minister(s) to order the deportation of even a person who has already been accepted as a Convention refugee 1) if an adjudicator has found that non-citizen to be a member of a terrorist organization; 2) if an s 40.1 (national security risk) certificate has been issued against that non-citizen and found reasonable by a judge of the Federal Court; and 3) if the Minister has issued an opinion declaring that non-citizen to be a danger to the security of Canada.[78] Nowhere in the old Act was the deportation of such a person to torture explicitly barred. As we have seen, in the end, both ss 113 and 115 of the 2001 *Immigration and Refugee Protection Act* (the currently operative legislation) adopt a similar, if less permissive, approach to the grant of *CAT* relief. While such deportations will generally be illegal under the new regime, they are still permitted in exceptional cases, and the current position is not as anti-torture as it could be. In *Almrei v Canada,* the Federal Court of Appeal laid out the internal contradiction found in the *IRPA* on the issue of deportation to torture, and stated that "on this issue of refoulement to a country where the deportee might be subject to torture, the Canadian position is not as conclusive" as that adopted by other jurisdictions, such as the English Courts.[79]

Third, it is incontrovertible that the relevant Minister did in fact exercise the discretion conferred on her by the old Act in a way that, but for the intervention of the Supreme Court of Canada, would have led to the deportation of Mr. Suresh to Sri Lanka, even though the Minister had also acknowledged that Suresh did indeed face a substantial risk of torture if sent there by Canada. A similar approach had been adopted by the immigration bureaucrats who actually make these kinds of assessments in the first instance, and who in reality tend to frame the boundaries within which such ministerial decisions are made.

Fourth, the two lower courts in *Suresh* – the Federal Court Trial Division and the Federal Court of Appeal – favoured the deportation of Suresh even though they were aware of the substantial risk of torture that he would face. According to McKeown J of the Federal Court Trial Division, given the risk posed by Suresh to Canadian national security, his deportation to a place where he was at risk of being tortured would not "shock the conscience" of Canadians. The Court therefore dismissed his application for judicial review.[80] The Federal Court of Appeal agreed with this decision.[81]

Needless to say, the Supreme Court of Canada has, while outlawing such deportations in general, explicitly left some room at that general level for such deportations to occur from Canada.[82] It is noteworthy that in 2004, the UN Human Rights Committee (the expert body established under the *International Covenant on Civil and Political Rights* to monitor the observance of that treaty by states) issued a rebuke to Canada concerning this indication of the Supreme Court of Canada's tolerance (albeit only in exceptional cases) of the deportation to torture of certain non-citizens.[83] More recently, the Committee against Torture raised concerns about the status of torture in Canadian law, stating that whereas "the law allowing deportation despite a risk of torture is merely theoretical ... the fact remains that it is the law in force at present."[84] In any case, it is unclear that that legal position is really "merely theoretical," since it can be misapplied in the hands of a less liberal-minded government. Despite these criticisms, Canada to this day has not taken any concrete measures toward reformulating its formal bar against such deportations in an absolute way. No bills to that effect are pending in Parliament, and no notable pronouncements have been made in Parliament in opposition to the current state of affairs. Other than academics, NGOs have been almost alone in denouncing the general loophole allowed by the *Suresh* case.[85]

The culpability of Canadian intelligence officers in the United States' rendition to torture of Maher Arar, a Canadian citizen, is also instructive in this regard.[86] For example, the *Arar Report* concluded that from October 2001 to the summer of 2002, the RCMP freely shared information with American officials without attaching caveats (restrictions that intelligence and law enforcement agencies generally place on shared information in order to maintain control over the information and ensure that it is not shared *or used for other purposes* without the consent of the agency that originally distributed the information). The RCMP also shared such materials without reviewing them for relevance or reliability (and some of the information shared was found to be inaccurate). Thus, by sharing materials in these problematic ways, the RCMP played some part in Arar's removal to torture while he was returning to Canada via the United States, since the American authorities very likely relied on these materials.[87] Just as importantly, the Iacobucci commission of inquiry found that Canadian officials were also indirectly responsible for the torture in Egypt of Ahmad Elmaati and in Syria of Abdullah Almalki, in both cases on suspicion of terrorism.[88]

This level of comfort within the Canadian government with the less than absolute formulation of the general bar against deportation to torture is significantly (though not exclusively) connected to the post-9/11 sense of heightened security vulnerability. This is illustrated, for example, by the copious references in the *Suresh* decision to "the global transport and money networks that feed terrorism" and to terrorism's "focus on a distant locale" not providing insurance against the fact that "the violent acts that support it" were "close at hand."[89] It is not unreasonable to suggest that a similar logic has permeated other parts of the Canadian government. This logic clearly existed before 9/11 but was accentuated by the comparative magnitude of what happened that day.

Overall, the key point here is that both before and after 9/11, Canada modified in a negative direction its international obligation to absolutely bar the deportation to torture of non-citizens. The frontal assaults on its fidelity to these obligations were successful to some extent, mirroring substantially (albeit not in a perfect way) the US experience.

The Embedded Loopholes in Both Regimes

Despite the absolute way in which the general prohibition on deportations to torture is couched in the United States, and the less than absolute way in which it is formulated in Canada, there are at least seven significant loopholes within each regime that portend varying levels of danger for those non-citizens who face a real risk of torture if they are expelled from either jurisdiction. Far less obvious to the untrained eye than the sort of explicitly stated exception to the general bar that figures prominently in the Canadian regime, these subtle loopholes are deeply embedded within the structures and operations of the two regimes.

The US Position

Definitional Loopholes

That one too many American officials felt the need to "have a less-cramped view of what torture is and is not" in the climate of heightened security consciousness following the 9/11 attacks is aptly illustrated by the following extract from Human Rights Watch's report on the Abu Ghraib scandal:

> According to the *Wall Street Journal*, a US official who helped prepare the report [in the Pentagon that advised that the US could legally practice torture as part of its "war on terror"] said "We'd been at this for a year-plus and got nothing out of them [certain Guantanamo detainees] ... *we need to have a less-cramped view of what torture is and is not.*" According to the official, interrogation techniques including drawing on prisoners' bodies, putting women's underwear on their heads, and threatening imminent harm to their families had not borne fruit and there was a need to "ratchet up the pressure."[90]

However, this kind of "narrow the definition to beat the prohibition" attitude on the part of relevant US officials did not emerge only after 9/11. It has been a part of the US refugee regime for a long time, albeit in more subtle ways.

For one, although the *Convention against Torture* adopts a more restrictive definition of *mental* torture than some other international instruments, both the US instruments ratifying that treaty and the *Regulations Concerning the Convention against Torture* contain an even more restrictive definition.[91] Article 1 of the *Convention* states that

> for the purposes of this Convention, torture means any act by which severe pain or suffering, whether physical or mental, is intentionally inflicted on a person for such purposes as obtaining from him or a third person information or a confession, punishing him for an act he or a third person has committed or is suspected of having committed, or intimidating or coercing him or a third person, or for any reason based on discrimination of any kind, when such pain or suffering is inflicted by or at the instigation of or with the consent or acquiescence of a public official or other person acting in an official capacity. It does not include pain or suffering arising only from, inherent in or incidental to lawful sanctions.

The text of the Resolution of Ratification adopted by the US Senate (on which the United States' instruments of ratification are based) further restricts the applicable definition of mental torture to only certain kinds of severe mental torture that have caused "*prolonged* mental harm."[92] The *Regulations Concerning the Convention against Torture* similarly provides that "in order to constitute torture, mental pain or suffering must be prolonged mental harm" caused by a specific and narrow range of factors.[93] The clear result is that if the non-citizen is able to prove that he or she faces a sufficiently high risk of mental torture, but cannot also show that such torture will cause him or her prolonged mental harm, he or she will not qualify for relief from deportation to torture. Clearly, it is a tall order to expect most such claimants to be able to predict the duration of the mental harm that may result from their prospective subjection to torture, or that any enduring harm will in fact result. Under the *Convention*, it suffices that the person will be subjected to severe mental pain or suffering.

Another instance of the United States' application of a definition of torture that is, arguably at least, significantly more restrictive than the *Convention*'s definition, is in its administrative interpretation of the *Convention*'s requirement for the relevant act of torture to be perpetrated "by or at the instigation of ... a public official or other person acting in an official capacity."[94] As Samuel David has convincingly shown, the US regime does not protect from deportations to torture those non-citizens who face a risk of torture at the hands of rebel forces or other non-governmental actors that are beyond the control of the relevant state.[95] I also agree with David that the US Board of Immigration Appeals (BIA) and the US Attorney General (who exercises overall control over the BIA and Immigration Judges) have tended to move too quickly to dispose of cases involving torture by non-state actors on the basis of a lack of proof of the "acquiescence by a public official," without first inquiring whether that non-state actor can be said to be so "state-like" as to satisfy the requirement that the torture be perpetrated by a "public official."[96] This was certainly the case in *In Re S-V*, as well as in Attorney General Ashcroft's opinion in *In Re Y-L, A-G, and R-S-R* (where the Attorney General overturned three BIA decisions granting *CAT* relief to three non-citizens who had claimed that they would be tortured by non-state actors if returned to their respective countries, and held that "violence committed by individuals over whom the government has no reasonable control does not implicate the treaty [i.e., the *CAT*]").[97]

The danger posed by this administrative posture to many non-citizens who face torture on deportation to their countries is aptly illustrated by a recently vacated BIA decision. In *Khouzam v Ashcroft*, the US Court of Appeals for the Second Circuit strongly disagreed with the decision of the BIA, which followed, in part, the Attorney General's opinion in *In Re Y-L, A-G, and R-S-R*.[98] The BIA had held that Khouzam did not qualify for *CAT* relief because the torture that he would likely face at the hands of the Egyptian police did not amount to torture (within the meaning of the *Convention*) because "the police will not be acting with the consent or approval of authoritative government officials."[99] As the Second Circuit suggested, it is difficult to fathom what persons can be more eminently described as "public officials" or as "acting in their official capacity" than police officers who commit torture in order to extract a confession.[100] The point, though, is that too many administrative decisions tend to adopt a narrow view of the definition of "public official," therefore allowing the possible deportation to torture of non-citizens who fear and can prove the likelihood of their being tortured by state-like non-state actors. When we consider that a large proportion of the torture that refugees have experienced, and are likely to experience, is perpetrated by rebel forces in *de facto* control of large portions of their country, we can better appreciate the extent of the danger posed by the narrow construction of the phrase "public official" and the consequent widening of the definitional loophole under consideration here. Thankfully, this danger is ameliorated, though not eliminated, in the United States by the possibility of judicial review.[101]

The last example of the tendency of some decision makers in the United States to apply a narrower definition than arguably permitted by international law relates to administrative and judicial interpretation of the phrase "with the acquiescence of a public official" in the *Convention* definition. Because the *Convention against Torture* does not provide much guidance as to the meaning of the phrase, the US instrument of ratification of the *Convention* entered an understanding to the treaty that restricts its meaning to situations in which the relevant public official

has "awareness" of the torture and thereafter breaches his legal responsibility to prevent it. This concept of "willful blindness" was reiterated
in similar language in the implementing *Regulations*.[102] Nevertheless,
this did not stop the BIA in *In Re S-V* and the Attorney General in *In
Re Y-L, A-G, and R-S-R* from adopting a test of "willful *acceptance*," a
somewhat more stringent test that had been explicitly rejected by the
US Senate during the ratification process. Clearly, a public official can
be aware of an act of torture and not *accept* it. Thankfully, the US Court
of Appeals for the Second Circuit rejected this view in *Khouzam*.[103] The
Ninth Circuit did likewise in *Zheng v Ashcroft,* and the Third Circuit
in *Silva-Rengifo v Attorney General of US*.[104] This last interpretation
was in keeping with the intention of the framers of the *Convention* to
adopt a liberal understanding of the meaning of "state acquiescence."[105]
However, since other Circuits are not necessarily bound by these two
decisions, the matter is not yet definitively settled. Thus, there is still a
small but significant loophole for the deportation to torture from the
United States of non-citizens who can show that a particular state will
more likely than not be aware of the practice of torture but be unable
to stop it, but who cannot go further to prove that that state is likely to
willfully *accept* such a practice.

As Irene Scharf has correctly noted, US courts have also tended to
interpret the definition of torture differently from the other signatories
of the *Convention* in at least one other way that is somewhat related to
the point made above: They have added the requirement that torture be
"specifically intended."[106] As Scharf has observed, decisions by the BIA
and several federal courts suggest that they have interpreted this specific
intent requirement even more narrowly than was initially intended in the
US domestic implementing legislation. The case of *Dalegrand v Attorney
General*[107] is a good example. In this case, Mr. Dalegrand's application for
CAT relief described his fears that, as a criminal deportee in Haiti, he
would be at risk of indefinite detention and would be denied access to his
medication for his psychotic condition. Dalegrand's lawyers argued that
without medication he would suffer a mental breakdown, which would
likely provide his jailers with justification to beat him or even torture him
by "electric shock" or burning by cigarettes.[108] The BIA held that while
his fears were substantiated, they did not rise to a level justifying *CAT*

protection.[109] Based on its narrow view of torture, the BIA stated that the requirement that the torturer must have had the specific intent to torture was not met in this case.[110] Rather, as Scharf points out, the BIA held that "these conditions of confinement would be considered merely a by-product of detention in the jails of an impoverished nation."[111] She states that while this interpretation of the term "specifically intended" as it was used in the *Regulations* was opposed vigorously even at the BIA by several of its own judges and has since been critiqued by numerous scholars and commentators, the ruling has been widely followed in the federal courts (albeit inconsistently).[112]

Overall, all four definitional loopholes show some of the subtle ways, some more egregious than others, in which deportations to torture can still be, and are still being, carried out despite the United States' formal commitment to an absolute ban on such deportations.

Deportations to "Failed States" (Such as Somalia)

In the wake of security concerns stemming from the threat posed by terrorism to the United States (concerns that were greatly intensified in the wake of 9/11), the Bush Administration "stepped up efforts to remove foreign nationals with orders of deportation, with an emphasis on those nations with links to terrorism."[113] The Administration feared that Somalia was one of these countries and included it in a group of states whose nationals were affected by "a series of directives from [then] Attorney General John Ashcroft" that indicated "a policy shift emphasizing removal of persons to suspect countries ... as expeditiously as possible."[114] Yet the very same Administration had also, under its Temporary Protected Status (TPS) program, designated Somalia as a country to which Somalis in the United States could not safely return. In the words of the then Secretary of Homeland Security, "fighting has continued throughout the county ... Interclan fighting throughout the country continues to *increase*."[115] This is a clear indication that, at the very least, deportees to Somalia faced a high risk of being subjected to acts amounting to torture, and at worst might even be killed there.

What is more, Somalia is considered so risky to the lives of immigration enforcement officers who normally escort deportees on their journey back "home" that such officers do not as a rule venture into the country themselves, preferring to stop en route in Dubai, where deportees are put on a plane to the Somali city of their choice.[116] It is therefore a matter of some concern (from the point of view of ensuring US compliance with its absolute obligations not to deport anyone to torture) that in the case of *Jama v INS*, the majority of the US Court of Appeals for the Eight Circuit [Bye J dissenting] overturned long-standing immigration practice as well as the decision of the district court below it, and ruled that s 241(b)(2) of the *Immigration and Nationality Act* did not necessarily require the consent of the destination country's government before a person could be deported there.[117] The case was appealed to the US Supreme Court, where Justice Antonin Scalia held that Somalia's inability to consent in advance to Jama's removal did not preclude his removal to that country.[118]

Before the Supreme Court's decision was announced, however, the US Court of Appeals for the Ninth Circuit, a court of coordinate jurisdiction with the Eighth Circuit, disagreed squarely with the Eighth Circuit's interpretation of the law and ordered a nationwide halt to such deportations.[119] Ominously, the Attorney General and the Secretary of Homeland Security issued a joint notice of proposed rule making that would toe the Eighth Circuit's line and reject the Ninth Circuit's decision.[120] Although the formal basis of these decisions was a question of interpretation of a slightly ambiguous legal provision, the fact that social considerations, including the high risk of harm to the possible deportees, played an important role is underlined by Justice Bye's dissenting opinion in the Eighth Circuit, in which he noted that the Court was duty-bound "not to interpret statutory text in a manner which leads to absurd [social] results" and went on to charge that "with this change in policy, we abandon a stateless person without a passport or travelling documents in a war-torn country victimized by battling warlords, and without a central government."[121] That a majority of the Supreme Court affirmed the Eighth Circuit Court of Appeals' view in *Jama* suggests that this loophole has been all but embedded in the US regime, and that Justice Bye's fears may have come to pass.

Diplomatic Assurances

US immigration regulations allow the Secretary of State to secure diplomatic assurances from a country to which a non-citizen is to be sent and where the non-citizen is likely to be tortured.[122] If such assurances are provided and are considered sufficiently reliable and verifiable, the person may be deported to that country despite the risk of torture that he or she faces there.[123] The *Convention* does not in general disallow the use of such assurances, and neither does the Committee against Torture. Section 3 of the *Convention* merely asks states to "take into account all relevant considerations including, where applicable, the existence in the State concerned of a consistent pattern of gross, flagrant or mass violations of human rights." For its part, the Committee has been prepared to accept such assurances as sufficient as long as they were offered in good faith by a high official and are capable of being monitored effectively.[124] I am, however, in agreement with the sense conveyed in a set of Human Rights Watch reports on this subject that the Committee's application of these principles to the facts before it has not been as coherent as might be expected.[125]

Instructively, however, both the Human Rights Committee and the UN Special Rapporteur on Torture have expressed serious doubts, especially in the absence of effective post-return monitoring mechanisms, regarding the efficacy of such assurances in ensuring that persons who are deported to torture-prone countries are not subjected to torture.[126] What is more, the Supreme Court of Canada has strongly warned, in *Suresh,* that such assurances are *by nature* significantly less reliable than assurances that the death penalty will not be carried out.[127] Similar logic has underlined the decision of the European Court of Human Rights in *Chahal v United Kingdom*.[128] Such reasoning is unassailable. Torture is rarely ever inflicted in public. It is also virtually impracticable for the United States or any other state to monitor adequately the treatment in secret of the person at risk, for American monitors cannot live with or follow the returnee 'round the clock in a foreign country. As Human Rights Watch has correctly noted, "the dangers of relying on diplomatic assurances as a safeguard against torture are apparent ... [in high-risk states] official assurances cannot be considered reliable."[129] It is therefore fair to conclude that, as with the "Maher Arar rendition to torture matter," where US government officials claimed that they relied on the "assurances" of the Syrian government that Arar would not be tortured,[130] the reliance on such assurances by the US government (given the lack of an opportunity for the non-citizen to challenge the reliability of such assurances in judicial proceedings) is more likely than not to result in the deportation to torture of non-citizens in the United States. This is yet another embedded loophole in the US refugee law regime's structural defence against such deportations.

A High Standard of Proof

Article 3 of the *Convention against Torture* prohibits the deportation of any person who shows that he or she has "substantial grounds for believing that he [or she] would be in danger of being subjected to torture." The US Supreme Court has interpreted similar wording in the UN *Convention Relating to the Status of Refugees* to require a standard of proof that is significantly *less* than the civil standard (of "a balance of probabilities" or "more likely than not," or "more than a 50% chance").[131] In the case of deportations to torture, however, it is this significantly higher civil standard of proof that is required by US law. One of the key "understandings" that was entered by the United States when it ratified the *Convention against Torture* was that "the United States understands the phrase 'where there are substantial grounds for believing that he [or she] would be in danger of being subjected to torture' as used in Article 3 of the Convention to mean 'if it is more likely than not that he [or she] would be tortured.'"[132] Although Public Law No.105-277 (which we have already seen) that implemented the *Convention* in the United States did not explicitly adopt this "more likely than not" wording, it did so by implication when it directed in s 1242(b) that the regulations to be enacted to further implement the *Convention* should be "subject to any reservations, understandings, declarations and provisos contained in the United States Senate Resolution ratifying the Convention." What is more, the case law is basically unanimous on the general point of the formulation of the standard of proof in cases where a non-citizen claims relief from deportation to torture. For example, in *Kamalthas v INS*, the Ninth Circuit Court of Appeals held that the petitioner for such relief has to show that "it is more likely than not that he or she would be tortured if removed to the proposed country of removal."[133]

In order to fully demonstrate why the existence of this higher standard within the US regime creates a gap in the wall of defence against deportations to torture, it is important to illustrate this point by reference to a number of actual cases. These cases illustrate how decision makers regularly differ as to whether the standard has been met, and/or how difficult it is to meet this seemingly low civil standard, especially in the case of refugees. In *In Re J-E,* a majority of the BIA *en banc* (13–6) held that a claimant for *Convention* relief who had introduced documentary evidence (including a US State Department Country Report for Haiti, an article in the *Miami Herald,* and a letter from an official of the State Department) had still not met the "more likely than not" standard of proof because those documents merely established that "isolated acts of torture occur in Haitian detention facilities."[134] After looking at the very same documents, the minority held that the defendants had "clearly" met the stated standard.[135] In their view, "the abuse documented in the record is extreme, deliberate, cruel, and intentionally inflicted to cause severe pain and suffering. It fits squarely within the regulatory definition of torture."[136] The minority then went on to warn that while "few, if any, prospective torture victims will be able to provide 'statistical proof' of a '50.001% chance' of torture," the information provided in this case "shows that torture of detainees in Haiti is routine, widespread, horrific, and officially tolerated."[137]

This kind of scenario also played out in *In Re M-B-A-,* where the BIA *en banc* split 13–6 on the question of whether a woman who was to be deported for drug offences in the United States and who had alleged that she would be immediately arrested and jailed and thereafter experience torture in detention if sent back to her home country had shown that such torture is "more likely than not."[138] The woman had tendered a copy of a law in operation in her country that mandated the detention of deported citizens who had been convicted of drug offences abroad.[139] She also provided affidavit and oral evidence to show that similarly situated persons had been subjected to torture in that country in the past.[140] The majority relied on the lack of further evidence about the manner of the enforcement of the said law, the lack of clarity with regard to whether the law was still on the books, and the relative freedom enjoyed by domestic human rights groups in that country to hold that she had not met the standard of proof.[141] After examining the very same evidence, the minority came to the opposite conclusion.[142] What is more, in *Antoine v US*, the judge felt compelled by what he referred to as the "rigid immigration laws" of the United States (largely the "more likely than not" standard of proof) to allow the deportation of a Haitian man with mild mental impairments who the judge agreed could not survive in Haiti on his own, even though the judge agreed with the man's counsel that this deportation "could" amount factually to torture.[143] In *Camara v Ashcroft*, the Fourth Circuit Court of Appeal berated the BIA and the Immigration Judge below it for, in part, grounding their decisions in speculation, and for failing to consider adequately the evidence for *Convention* relief provided by the claimant.[144]

More recently, in *Cole v Holder*, more evidence of the difficulty of applying this high standard of proof in real cases was provided.[145] The Ninth Circuit Court of Appeals considered the application of Mr. Cole, a citizen of Honduras, for deferral of removal under the *Convention against Torture*. The BIA had denied the application, concluding that Cole had not established that he would more likely than not be tortured if removed to Honduras. Cole made the argument that as a former member of the Crips gang, he would be tortured and killed by gangs, police, or death squads if he returned to Honduras. This would occur because of his race and his gang-related Crips tattoos, which would mark him as an outsider in that country. He also contended that he would be intentionally denied necessary medical care by Honduran public health officials because of his tattoos, and that the intentional denial of medical care also qualified as torture. The Court of Appeals held that because the BIA had failed to give reasoned consideration to potentially dispositive testimony by Cole's expert witnesses (an expert on the structure and dynamics of US and Central American gangs and an expert on gang members in Honduras) and did not address all of Cole's claims, the petition should be granted. The dissenting judge argued, however, that "the majority impermissibly (a) reweighs the evidence ... and (b) strings together a series of hypothetical events, related to Cole's claim that he will be misidentified as being a gang member and then tortured by rival gangs, police or death squads, none of which is more likely than not to occur."[146]

In an even more recent case, *Vinh Tan Nguyen v Holder*, the Ninth Circuit Court of Appeals again split on whether the evidence demonstrated that it was more likely than not that the applicant would be tortured if removed to Vietnam.[147] The majority held that contrary to the BIA's conclusion, the record compelled the conclusion that Nguyen would more likely than not be tortured. This was based on evidence in the record that the Vietnamese government was aware of Nguyen's activities on behalf of the Government of Free Vietnam (a US-based anti-communist political organization), country conditions evidence, and Nguyen's witness testimonies. The majority stated that "such documentary evidence of country conditions, alone, is sufficient to show that Nguyen is likely to be tortured in Vietnam ... But Nguyen does not rely on documentary evidence alone."[148] The dissenting judge, however, deferred to the BIA's conclusions, stating that "even if Vietnam is aware of Nguyen's opposition activities, the BIA provided several persuasive reasons why Nguyen failed to show that he would more likely than not be tortured."[149]

A Very High Level of Deference to Administrative Decision Makers

As the case law shows, the courts will not disturb the factual conclusions of administrative decision makers (such as Immigration Judges and the BIA) as long as these conclusions are grounded in "substantial evidence," or better still, "compelling evidence."[150] What this means is that the courts will allow these decisions to stand as long as a reasonable fact-finder would not be *compelled* to reach a different conclusion.[151] The evidence adduced by the claimant must not only suggest a conclusion favourable to him or her but also *compel* such a conclusion.[152] As the Third Circuit Court of Appeals noted in *Abdulrahman v Ashcroft*, the level of deference that this standard of review demands of the superior courts is *"extraordinarily* high."[153] Similarly, in *Laoye v Attorney General US*, the same court again stated that "such review is highly deferential, and the BIA's decision will not be disturbed unless it is 'arbitrary, irrational, or contrary to law' (quoting *Filja v Gonzales*, 447 F.3d 241, 251 (3d Cir. 2006))."[154] The Seventh Circuit has also described this standard of review as imposing a "highly deferential" attitude toward the factual conclusions of these administrative decision makers.[155] Yet, it is these factual conclusions that make or mar most claims for relief from deportation to torture. As a result, administrative decision makers enjoy a wide ambit of virtually non-reviewable discretion to make either correct or incorrect decisions. Even those decisions considered incorrect by a court will not be disturbed if there is substantial and cogent evidence on the record on which that decision can be founded. Unless the mistake made by the administrative decision maker rises close to the level of the egregious sort of error committed by the BIA in *Cheema v Ashcroft* (where the BIA had excluded the wife of a supporter of Sikh activists in India as inadmissible on grounds of terrorism because she had in essence sent money to widows and orphans in the Punjab region of India), it will be very difficult to get a US Court of Appeals to overturn a BIA decision.[156] Yet, the kind of error that the BIA can commit is indicated by the fact that the Ninth Circuit felt compelled to berate it for "stretch[ing] speculation to its breaking point."[157] Overall, the key point is that the very wide ambit given to administrative decision makers has tended to shield their factual conclusions from review to such an extent that there is a loophole for mistaken or even negligent deportations to occur, and that this occurs despite the absolute bar placed on such deportations in the United States.

The "Gatekeeping" Culture within the US Immigration Bureaucracy

The danger of deportation to torture (and subversion of the general bar) stemming from the broad scope of "very hard to review" discretion available to administrative decision makers and "immigration bureaucrats" under US law is significantly increased by the accentuation since 9/11 of the "gatekeeping" strain within the broad institutional cultures of the relevant bureaucracies.[158] Opposed to this gatekeeping strain is a more pro-refugee strain of decision making. That these two strains exist and compete within these bureaucracies is hardly controversial. That the gatekeeping strain is quite robust, even dominant, within the immigration bureaucracy is also not all that controversial. Many of the statements and actions of former US Attorney General John Ashcroft (whose office supervised much of the immigration bureaucracy) provide strong support for this last conclusion.[159] The conclusion is also illustrated, at least in part, by the diametrically opposed attitudes toward the relevant applicants for *CAT* relief displayed by the majority and minority of the BIA in *In Re M-B-A-* and *In Re J-E* (discussed above), and, to a lesser extent, by the vigour with which the former Immigration and Naturalization Service (INS) (whose functions were transferred to the newly constituted Citizenship and Immigration Services [CIS] and Immigration and Customs Enforcement [ICE]) has opposed the claims of most of the approximately 5 percent of claimants who were eventually granted relief from deportation to torture each year over the last several years.[160]

Needless to say, in none of those cases in which claimants have had to pass very stringent tests in order to satisfy the reviewing courts did the relevant bureaucrats agree with the obviously viable claims of these successful claimants. This is hardly surprising. Most such bureaucrats do not tend to see their main function as facilitating the admission of refugees to the United States. Rather, most tend to see themselves as gatekeepers who are primarily charged with keeping away undeserving non-citizens. As important, the fact that the events of 9/11 have accentuated, however slightly, the hold that anti-immigrant and gatekeeping sentiments have had on a significant percentage of US citizens (and the bureaucrats who are almost always chosen from among them) is also not really controversial. In this connection, Regina Germain is correct to suggest that "after the events of September 11, adjudicators [that is, the bureaucrats I am concerned with here] may feel compelled to *err on the side of caution* and exclude asylum seekers from protection [including *Convention* relief] if there is even the *smallest hint* of a tie to terrorist activity or a terrorist organization."[161] In the same vein, the transfer after 9/11 of the former INS to the new Department of Homeland Security (DHS), a larger bureaucratic environment whose first priority is national security, has led to "a larger institutional culture that emphasize[s] national security at the expense of refugee rights."[162]

The opposite result (the turn of these bureaucracies to a more pro-refugee approach) is also possible, but is highly improbable in the short run. Given the heightened sense of security vulnerability, no reasonable bureaucrat will want to be identified by his or her superiors and the public as the one who allowed into the United States a person who goes on to set off a bomb. Thus, in the aftermath of 9/11 and in light of these institutional changes, the gatekeeping tendency is likely to continue to prevail over the pro-refugee feelings of the more sympathetic bureaucrats, especially when they are faced with either borderline situations or claimants who give off even the slightest whiff of terrorism. This tendency is likely to be more pronounced when the claimant is either a Muslim or a person of Arab heritage. Although it has a long pedigree, going back to even before 9/11, anti-Muslim and anti-Arab animus in the United States appears to have grown since 9/11.[163] In this sense, the post-9/11 strengthening of the gatekeeping strain within the institutional culture of the relevant bureaucracies poses a real danger to those who face deportation to torture.

Expedited Removals and Interdictions

Although the dangers posed by expedited removal procedures in, and interdictions by, the United States are not discussed in any detail in this book, it is important to briefly discuss here the dangers posed by their use to persons who face the risk of expulsion to torture and who seek entry into the United States.[164] To the extent that the interdiction process allows the United States to intercept and turn back without further reason, persons caught on the high seas who are obviously headed to that country to claim refugee status, the process clearly poses a serious danger to those among the interdicted persons who face a significant risk of torture in their own countries. Similarly, to the extent that the expedited removal process allows "the removal of [many] ... arriving non-citizens from the United States without ever seeing a judge,"[165] based on the relatively hurried decisions of bureaucrats, that process also poses a real danger to non-citizens who are at risk of being tortured if removed to their own countries. While some of those placed in the expedited removal process do have a chance to contest their impending removal before a quasi-judicial administrative decision maker in the Executive Office of Immigration Review (especially if they have expressed a fear of being tortured if removed to their country), most will still be deported if they cannot convince the administrative decision maker that they have a "credible fear" of being tortured.[166]

To convince the decision maker of this credible fear, the non-citizen must show that his or her *CAT*-relief claim will *probably* (instead of *possibly*) succeed. This is a rather high standard to meet for a non-citizen who has just arrived at a port of entry. The standard is especially high given that at this point in the process the non-citizen will not have had the opportunity to consult legal counsel. In these ways, the US interdiction and expedited removal procedures constitute subtle loopholes through which the government can return non-citizens to torture. The negative impact of these procedures is likely to be exacerbated by, at the very least, the intensification of their use at least as intended by the Trump Administration.[167]

The Canadian Position

Definitional Loopholes

In terms of the presence of subtle definitional loopholes that might allow the deportation to torture of a non-citizen, the Canadian regime is similar to the US regime with regard to two subissues, and better than that regime in only one respect. This Canadian position is largely the result of the fact that the relevant Canadian judicial decisions and legislation and Canadian courts have either tended to adopt a definition similar to that contained in Article 1 of the *Convention against Torture* or simply adopted the *Convention* definition. The instrument with which Canada ratified the *Convention* does not enter any reservations to the treaty whatsoever. Similarly, s 269.1 of the *Criminal Code* defines torture in the following way:

> "torture" means any act or omission by which severe pain or suffering, whether physical or mental, is intentionally inflicted on a person
>
> (a) for a purpose including
>   (i) obtaining from the person or from a third person information or a statement,
>   (ii) punishing the person for an act that the person or a third person has committed or is suspected of having committed, and
>   (iii) intimidating or coercing the person or a third person, or
> (b) for any reason based on discrimination of any kind,
>
> but does not include any act or omission arising only from, inherent in or incidental to lawful sanctions.[168]

This provision goes on to state that "every official, or every person acting at the instigation of or with the consent or acquiescence of an official, who inflicts torture on any other person is guilty of an indictable offence and liable to imprisonment for a term not exceeding fourteen years."[169] In addition, torture is defined by reference to Article 1 of the *Convention* in s 97(1)(a) of the *Immigration and Refugee Protection Act of* 2000 as well as in all three court decisions in the *Suresh* case, namely, those of the Federal Court Trial Division, the Federal Court of Appeal, and the Supreme Court of Canada.[170]

With regard to the definition of the subissue of mental torture, the *Criminal Code,* Canada's *Convention against Torture* ratification instrument, and Canadian case law have all refrained from limiting the definition of mental torture to only those instances in which *prolonged* harm is caused to the victim.[171] It is chiefly in this way that the Canadian approach to the definition of mental torture is significantly better than its US counterpart.

With regard to the meaning of the phrase "a public official or person acting in an official capacity," the Canadian approach has been in keeping with the jurisprudence of the Committee against Torture.[172] Most of the Committee's decisions have not acknowledged the fact that many rebel groups do act in an official capacity in territory controlled by them, or in states without a central government. As we have seen, this has also been the dominant approach in the United States. Thus, with respect to this subissue, the Canadian position is virtually identical to the US position.

Regarding the definition of "with the acquiescence of a public official," Canadian law has also been closely in line with the jurisprudence of the Committee and with the US position.[173]

Deportations to "Failed States" (Such as Somalia)

The Canadian regime is no better and no worse in this respect than US law and practice. While the relevant Minister does have discretion under s 230 of the *Immigration and Refugee Protection Regulations* to bar removals to any "country or place where circumstances in that country or place pose a generalized risk to the entire civilian position" as a result of stated factors such as civil war, the Minister cannot exercise that discretion in favour of any non-citizen who is inadmissible on stated security or serious criminality grounds. Thus, non-citizens who are inadmissible on such grounds can in fact be removed to such places – including Somalia. In any case, Somalia has never been one of the countries designated in the exercise of the Minister's s 230 powers as a high-risk country to which no one would be removed.[174] It was only in 2011 that the Canadian authorities relented a little bit and declared an "administrative deferral of removal" to the Somali regions of Middle Shabelle, Afgoye, and Mogadishu.[175] This meant, however, that, at least in theory, Somalis could still be deported from Canada to almost all of Somalia. Thus, although the possibility of a favourable pre-removal risk assessment does exist, Canada can and does remove some non-citizens to Somalia despite the serious nature of the generalized risk of torture and death in that country.

Diplomatic Assurances

With respect to the legality and deployment of diplomatic assurances, the Canadian regime is significantly better than the corresponding US law and practice. This is so despite the fact that although the Supreme Court of Canada in *Suresh* did express very serious doubts about the utility of diplomatic assurances, it did not completely bar the executive branch from deporting non-citizens at risk of torture on the basis of such assurances.[176] Similarly, although US law does allow the relevant officials to rely on such assurances, the United States has developed a somewhat cautionary, if still inadequate, approach to its reliance on such assurances.[177] Unlike Canadian law, however, US law does not require that the prospective deportee to torture be given an opportunity to present evidence and make submissions as to the value of the particular diplomatic assurance at issue.[178] It is chiefly in this way that the Canadian regime has outpaced its US counterpart with respect to reliance on diplomatic assurances.

A High Standard of Proof

As clearly stated by the Supreme Court of Canada in *Suresh*, the standard of proof that a prospective deportee to torture has to meet in Canada is exactly the same as the standard set out in Article 3 of the *Convention against Torture*.[179] This standard simply requires the claimant to prove that there are "substantial grounds for believing that he [or she] would be in danger of being subjected to torture."[180] Put differently, the non-citizen must prove that he or she faces a substantial risk of torture.[181] As discussed earlier, the standard of proof under US law is a "clear probability" or "more likely than not" test that is significantly more difficult to meet than the test set forth in the *Convention*. Thus, the Canadian standard of proof is significantly better for prospective deportees to torture than the corresponding US standard.

A Very High Level of Deference to Administrative Decision Makers

The US and Canadian regimes are virtually identical regarding the degree of deference accorded to the factual findings and conclusions of politicians and immigration bureaucrats by the courts. Like the US regime, the Canadian regime allows a very broad ambit of "very hard to review" discretion to Canadian immigration bureaucrats.[182] For instance, in *Suresh*, the Supreme Court felt able to hold that the crucial "threshold finding" of whether refugees or other persons would face a substantial risk of torture if deported to the country to which they were deportable was the Minister's (read "bureaucrat's") to make, and that such decisions, once made by the Minister, should enjoy the highest possible level of deference.[183] In practice, the Minister's decision would be extremely difficult to overturn primarily because the Court found that the appropriate standard of review with regard to the Minister's decisions regarding the deportation of refugees or other persons at risk of torture was that the decision must not be disturbed unless it is shown to be *"patently unreasonable."* While this "patent unreasonableness" standard has now been collapsed into the "reasonableness" standard, it remains operative – at least in my view. The point, though, is that this is the standard of deference that allows the Minister the broadest possible discretion (short of absolutism). In such situations, the reviewing court cannot set the Minister's decision aside even "if it would have weighed the factors differently and arrived at a different conclusion."[184] The rationale offered by the Supreme Court was that the issues to be considered and factors to be weighed (by the Minister), such as the human rights record of the home state and the personal risk to the person to be deported, were "largely outside the realm of expertise of reviewing courts and possess a negligible legal dimension."[185] Acknowledging that the Court came to this conclusion after a thoughtful consideration of the issue of the "appropriate standard of deference," it would seem that given the extremely severe repercussions for a person at risk from a mistaken, negligent, or wrong decision, the Court allowed far too much discretion to a Canadian immigration bureaucracy that is hardly known for its pro-refugee behaviour.[186] On the whole therefore, it is fair to state that with respect to the deference shown by the courts to immigration bureaucrats, prospective deportees to torture are basically in the same situation in both Canada and the United States.

The "Gatekeeping" Culture within the Canadian Immigration Bureaucracy

The same kind of "gatekeeping" approach that is part of the US immigration bureaucracy's institutional culture also characterizes and inflects the operations of its Canadian counterpart. This is evident from incidents such as the latter's almost year-long resistance to a broad-based concrete implementation of the position adopted in a Supreme Court of Canada decision mandating that the "best interests of the child" be a key factor to be considered by the Minister (read "bureaucrats") in deciding whether a "humanitarian and compassionate" ground application for permanent residence in Canada should be approved.[187] It is also illustrated by that bureaucracy's dogged moves in the *Suresh* saga to deport to torture a *Convention* refugee who that very bureaucracy had conceded had actually proved that he faced a substantial risk of torture if returned to his country.[188] Thus, in this one regard at least, prospective deportees in the United States are no better off or worse off than those in Canada. This is a very important point given that it is the bureaucracy that *in practice* makes, without much prospect of successful review in the courts, virtually all the key factual findings and conclusions that ground decisions to deport non-citizens to places where they claim to be at risk of torture.

Expedited Removals and Interdictions

With respect to the system of expedited removals operating in the United States, suffice it to say that no comparable system operates in Canada today. Canadian Border Services guards, immigration officers, and superior bureaucrats do not make the same sorts of "credible fear" decisions that are routinely made by their US counterparts. And certainly Canadian officials do not make such key decisions in the hurried way they are apparently made under the US expedited removal system.[189] The Canadian regime is thus better than its US counterpart in this particular respect.

With regard to the interdiction of prospective refugee claimants and other non-citizens off the Canadian coast and abroad, the Canadian law and practice is not at all different. First, it is well known that Immigration, Refugees and Citizenship Canada (IRCC) and the rest of the Canadian immigration bureaucracy usually recommend and implement the imposition of travel visa restrictions on the citizens of a country as soon as that country begins to account for a significant number of refugee claimants in Canada.[190] The clear intention in such cases has always been to keep possible refugees from reaching Canada.[191] Second, it is also trite knowledge that this bureaucracy almost always makes strong efforts to prevent the arrival in Canada of refugee claimants who attempt to circumvent the visa requirement.[192] Such activities that have prompted two important Canadian refugee law scholars to point out the unfortunate, even tragic paradox in the fact that "although Canada is home to only about one-half of one percent of the world's refugees, it apparently sees no inconsistency between active participation in a program of deflection and its vaunted commitment to international burden sharing."[193] It is clear that Canada is not doing any better than the United States with regard to the negative effects of such interdictions on the access of prospective "deportees to torture" to processes that ensure that they are not sent back to places where they face a substantial risk of torture.

The General Prohibition against Deportations to Torture and "the National Security Challenge"

Despite the existence and operation of subtle loopholes in the *CAT*-relief regimes of both Canada and the United States, it is beyond serious dispute that the general prohibition on deportations to torture still poses a significant challenge to the removal from both countries of non-citizens deemed to be national security threats. This was well understood by both governments even at the time they ratified the *Convention against Torture*. The flat prohibition on deportations to torture in the text of Article 3 and the unequivocal statement in Article 2 that "no exceptional circumstances whatsoever" shall justify torture make this clear. In the United States, even as a strong prohibition on deportations to torture was enacted, s 2242 of the Public Law 105-277 that implemented the *Convention* still managed to express the discomfort of many in Congress with the absoluteness of this bar in international law. This is evident from the mandate to the relevant officials to ensure that

> *to the maximum extent consistent with the obligations of the United States under the Convention*, subject to any reservations, understandings, declarations, and provisos contained in the United States Senate resolution of ratification of the Convention, the regulations described in subsection (b) shall exclude from the protection of such regulations aliens described in section 241(b)(3)(B) of the Immigration and Nationality Act (8 U.S.C. 1231(b)(3)(B)) [that is, those who are inadmissible to the United States for having engaged in Nazi crimes or genocide, or those the Attorney General deems to be persecutors, serious criminals, or dangers to the security of the United States].[194]

Thus it is clear that while Congress clearly wanted to exclude from *CAT* relief the class of persons identified at the end of this provision, it knew that it could do so only within the limits set by the *Convention* itself. As it turned out, the framers of the regulations also realized this, for the said regulations did not exclude the stated class of serious criminals and national security risks from the possibility of an adequate measure of protection under the *Convention*.[195] What the regulations did was grant this class of non-citizens access to a lower form of relief – "deferral of removal" – rather than the "withholding of removal" to which other successful claimants for *CAT* relief are entitled.[196] The contents of this law and the provisions of these regulations are also clear evidence that Congress was well aware of the national security challenge that can sometimes be posed by the grant of *CAT* relief to the identified class of non-citizens.

The fact that the relevant government officials in Canada have always grappled with this kind of national security challenge is clear from the fact that Canada *chose* to ratify the *Convention* despite the absoluteness of the prohibition on deportations to torture prescribed by the treaty, and that Canada went on, nevertheless, to keep intact an immigration and refugee regime that allowed deportations to torture in exceptional cases.

The main ground for the expressed, if unevenly implemented, reluctance of the relevant officials in Canada and the United States to extend *CAT* protection to the class of non-citizens identified above is the notion that both countries could become safe havens for serious criminals, serious human rights abusers, and suspected terrorists if *CAT* relief were made available to them.[197] In the wake of the 9/11 attacks (and the understandable security hysteria that followed them), this "safe haven" argument gained even more currency and resonance. It even formed the basis of the post-9/11 decision of the Supreme Court of Canada, in *Suresh*, to allow a general exception to the bar on deportations to torture that it formulated.[198] In the United States, the safe haven argument has led to ongoing calls from powerful elements in Congress to soften the country's strong bar against deportations to torture.[199] What is more, as has already been shown, s 3032 of the defunct House version of the 9/11 bill contained at least one measure designed to achieve exactly that objective, albeit in an indirect way.

This challenge is complicated further by the understandable reluctance of the courts in both jurisdictions to endorse the indefinite (or, worse, permanent) detention of non-citizens who have not been convicted of any criminal offence or who have served their sentences in full.[200] This general reluctance can of course benefit those considered serious criminals and national security risks who have been held in detention for lengthy periods and who would surely have been deported but for their success in obtaining *CAT* relief. Such persons may have to be released from jail on such conditions as seem reasonable in the circumstances.

In the United States, the perception of this problem by opponents of an absolute bar against deportations to torture is captured by a news advisory issued by the Judiciary Committee of the House of Representatives that, in effect, explains the rationale for s 3032 of the defunct House 9/11 bill. According to the advisory, this provision helps address

> *a large problem* of criminal aliens *and possibly terrorists* being released onto US streets because of the Convention Against Torture (CAT) and US court rulings. Over 500 criminal aliens – including at least one murderer and one rapist – have been granted relief under CAT [the Convention] that they might be tortured in their home country. Because US courts have said criminal aliens *and possibly even terrorists* cannot be held indefinitely in the US, these criminal aliens – and possibly terrorists – have been released onto US streets.[201]

The "US court rulings" referred to in this statement are decisions that follow or reiterate the Supreme Court's decision in the famous case of *Zadvydas v Davis*, which laid down the general principle against indefinite detention of deportable non-citizens.[202] The Court found that the due process requirements of the US Constitution require only such a period of detention as is reasonably necessary to remove the non-citizen from the United States. If it becomes clear that the non-citizen cannot be removed within a foreseeable period after the approximately six months that the Court held was allowed under US law, then he or she must be released from detention and, if deemed necessary, placed under appropriate supervision. As shall become clear later, however, although this principle has been trumpeted (notably in the House Judiciary Committee statement discussed above) as a near-insurmountable bar to the lengthy detention of *even the most dangerous* among the serious criminals and suspected terrorists who have been granted *CAT* relief, the Zadvydas principle presents far less an obstacle than most of its opponents claim. Powerful reasons abound as to why the strong prohibition of deportations to torture should not be tampered with, even as part of the drive to deal appropriately with those non-citizens considered serious criminals or national security threats and who, as a result of *Zadvydas*, cannot be detained indefinitely. A range of alternatives do exist with which the relevant officials can manage cases of recipients of *CAT* relief in ethical and lawful ways, while avoiding both the subversion of the absolute bar on deportations to torture and the unfettered release of dangerous offenders.

Beyond the Zadvydas "Problem"

A number of arguments can be made against the logic of softening the strong prohibition on deportations to torture in order to help meet the presumed national security and anti-criminality objectives of Canada and the United States. In the case of the United States, these arguments would clearly be in favour of retaining the absolute nature of the general bar against such deportations. In the case of Canada, the same arguments clearly support the strengthening of that country's less than absolute general bar against such deportations, so as to make it flatly absolute. These arguments would clearly apply in spite of the exaggerated ideas about the actual effects of the *Zadvydas* case that have been disseminated by its opponents.

One such broad argument is simply that a careful examination of the *Zadvydas* case shows that the so-called Zadvydas problem poses far less of a national security problem than is commonly assumed by opponents of the absolute bar. For one, there is much less potential for a *CAT* relief–related Zadvydas-type scenario in Canada (that is, a situation where Canada is unable to deport a serious criminal or suspected terrorist because *CAT* relief has been granted to that person, and at the same time is also unable to detain that person indefinitely). This is because virtually anyone whom the Minister in Canada would seriously want to detain for such an indefinite period without first being tried and convicted for an offence would fall within one of the exceptions to the general bar stated in both ss 113 and 115 of the *IRPA*. Thus, despite its being a violation of international law, the Canadian legal position does give the relevant Minister discretion to deport non-citizens who are considered so dangerous that they should still be deported despite being able to demonstrate that they face a substantial risk of torture on return to the relevant country. In this event, there will be no Zadvydas "problem" at all, because the Minister will not be faced with the choice of either detaining indefinitely or releasing the non-citizen. The Minister will still have the admittedly extreme option of deporting the non-citizen to torture. In any case, s 84(2) of the *IRPA* allows the courts to refuse an application to release from detention certain persons who have been detained for over 120 days from the date that the court deemed the decision to label them as national security risks to be a reasonable one, even if such persons are unlikely to be removed from Canada within a reasonable time. The courts can refuse such an application if they are satisfied that the release of the non-citizen in question will pose a danger to national security or to the safety of any person. Thus, the *IRPA* also appears to allow the courts to order the lengthy, even indefinite, detention of those deportable non-citizens whom they view as particularly dangerous. This position is tempered to some extent by the Supreme Court of Canada's decision in *Charkaoui v Canada*, which established that while the detention of foreign nationals (including refugees) without a warrant does not infringe the *Canadian Charter of Rights and Freedoms*, the lack of review of such detentions until 120 days after the initial basis for detention has been confirmed as reasonable (a process that could last years) infringes the guarantee against arbitrary detention found in s 9 of the *Charter*.[203]

Even in the US context, where the relevant Cabinet secretary has no such explicitly stated exceptional option to deport a non-citizen to torture as long as he or she qualifies for deferral of removal, there are a number of reasons why the so-called Zadvydas problem is not nearly as formidable as is often charged. The foremost reason is that the US Supreme Court decision in that case clearly allows a loophole for the very lengthy detention of the most serious threats to national security, such as "say, suspected terrorists" (presumably until they can be tried and convicted of an offence).[204] And less serious criminals can be more safely released from prison under strict monitoring terms. What is more, the regulations issued by the US government to implement the Zadvydas principle clearly allow the relevant officials to detain, even indefinitely, the most "dangerous" of the deportable class of deemed serious criminals and national security threats.[205] Department of Homeland Security officials who implement these principles and rules on a day-to-day basis have acknowledged as much in a hearing before the House Subcommittee on Immigration and Border Security.[206] The March 2019 US Supreme Court decision in *Nielsen v Preap* does not appear to have altered the basic logic of *Zadvydas*.[207]

Furthermore, US practice clearly shows that the grant of relief from deportation to torture is the great exception rather than the rule.[208] Only a tiny fraction of those who seek such relief are successful. According to the 2015 Department of Justice *Statistical Yearbook*, the immigration courts adjudicated 30,116 *CAT*-related applications in 2015, of which only 625 applications (2.1 percent) were successful.[209] Another commentator's analysis of relevant statistics for some of the years before 2002 puts the figure at between 4 and 5 percent.[210] In real numbers, only about 1,700 claims were successful out of about 25,576 that were made in 2002.[211] Moreover, only about 500 (or about 2 percent) of all these claimants have been convicted criminals who have at the same time been granted *CAT* relief. Weighed against the millions of immigrants that live in the United States, these numbers are simply infinitesimal. It may of course be argued that one small terrorist cell, or even one "lone wolf" terrorist, can blow up thousands of people. While this is of course true, the lawful, credible, and ethical solution to that problem is not to gut further a fundamental rule of international law that protects thousands of deserving refugees around the world and promises to protect millions more, merely because of such an infinitesimal threat.

What is more, the Zadvydas principle did not originally extend so far as to protect those non-citizens (including refugees) who had not gained initial admission to the United States and who were then ordered detained and removed as a result of their inadmissibility under US law. It applied only where the alien had gained lawful admission into the country but was subsequently ordered detained and removed. This much was clear from the express language employed by the Supreme Court in its opinion.[212] This further reduced the scope of those who could benefit from this principle, but a subsequent decision, *Clark v Martinez*, extended the Zadvydas protections to non-citizens (including refugees) who had not yet been lawfully admitted, and were in fact inadmissible, to the United States.[213]

Just as importantly, as the US Supreme Court noted in *Zadvydas*, the choice is not between imprisonment and the non-citizen "living at large."[214] It is between imprisonment and supervision under release conditions that may not be violated.[215] Again, it is possible to prosecute and convict many of those detainees in the United States, or to deport them to another country where they will likely not be tortured, or to release them under strict conditions of supervision, as urged in the Court's decision.[216]

Moreover, there are several ethical and legal reasons for preferring the alternatives to deportation to torture. The first is that if the person who is considered a serious criminal had been born in the United States or Canada (for example, to a student who then left with the person and raised her in another country entirely), deportation would not be an option at all, and the government would probably have been able to deal with the person in an effective but humane way within the country itself, rather than by deportation to torture. Why, then, should the mere formalism of accident of birth determine whether one serious criminal is deliberately sent to torture whereas the other is not?[217] Second, to authorize the deportation to likely torture of even a suspected terrorist is to wittingly or unwittingly participate in torture and profess a benign view of that horrific crime. This is not just unethical; it is also absolutely illegal under international law.[218] Third, such facilitation of deportation to likely torture will also portray the United States or Canada as a country that harbours a weak image of international normative authority – the same international normative authority that it often urges other countries to adhere to.[219] Finally, it is important to remember, as former US Senator Patrick Leahy noted:

> We all know that if you make a couple of exceptions here and there for torture, then exceptions become the rule. If the United States [or for that matter Canada] is seen as complicit in torture, it makes it very difficult for ... [it] to articulate a moral position against torture, whether it takes place in China or Iraq or Chile or Pakistan or anywhere else.[220]

In summary, *Zadvydas* and similar Canadian cases do not present nearly as much of a problem to US and Canadian national security as their critics would like us to believe; thus, for this and other adduced reasons, it would not be legal, ethical, or appropriate to erode further either the absolute bar in the United States against deportation to torture or the less than absolute bar under Canadian law. Rather, efforts should be made to close as much as possible the loopholes that have been identified and discussed in this chapter.

Analytical Insights from a Comparison of the Two Regimes

As the analysis in the preceding sections clearly shows, Canada's law and practice in the area of deportations to torture are worse than those of the United States in one key identifiable area, better in five such areas, and similar to that of the United States in seven aspects. They are thus similar to or worse than their US counterparts in at least *eight of thirteen* aspects.

For one thing, although the general bar against deportation to torture is less than absolute in Canada, it is formulated in absolute terms in the United States. Canada's deportation to torture regime is similar to the corresponding US regime with respect to the presence of two definitional loopholes relating to the meanings of "public official" and "with the acquiescence of a public official" in Article 1 of the *Convention against Torture*. The two regimes are also very similar with respect to complicity in renditions to torture, deportations to failed states such as Somalia, the very high degree of deference shown to immigration officials by the courts, the dominance of a gatekeeping culture within the immigration bureaucracy, and interdictions. However, Canadian law and practice tend to be significantly better than the US regime in terms of the meaning of "mental torture," the standard of proof required for a claim against deportation to torture to succeed, the scale of the deportations to torture that have actually been carried out, the use of expedited removals, and reliance on diplomatic assurances. Thus, the *overall* Canada-US gap with regard to deportation to torture is relatively small, consistent with Reg Whitaker's general observation soon after 9/11.[221]

To the extent that the respective legal positions of the two countries have been shaped, at least in part, by the mass security hysteria that followed 9/11, most observers would expect to find the greater level of negative impact in the country that was directly attacked.[222] As Whitaker has correctly noted, "it is evident from 9/11 that America is the primary focus of terrorist wrath, and Canada is at best a secondary, peripheral target."[223] Thus, the fact that Canadian law and practice in the area of deportation to torture is not significantly better than the corresponding US regime is both intriguing and counter-stereotypical.

The comparative data discussed here suggests a multi-factorial (rather than a unitary or 9/11-focused) explanation for the comparative state of the Canadian and US *CAT*-relief regimes since 9/11. An adequate explanation for this counter-intuitive situation must reach into the past, to earlier (if less intense) periods of heightened security consciousness in both countries, and encompass other equally key factors, such as the pressure felt in Canada due to its very serious economic vulnerability to the United States; deeply felt public sympathy in post-9/11 Canada for its US neighbour; long-standing pro-immigration control sentiment in Canada; Canada's own home-grown national security worries; some direct US political pressure on its significantly less powerful Canadian neighbour; and the need on the part of most Canadians to see some distance between Canadian and American policies. This is an explanation that accords with Whitaker's well-formulated hypothesis regarding the extent of the overall impact of 9/11 on Canada's post-9/11 behaviour,[224] and is demonstrated empirically by the discussion in this chapter.

A more detailed discussion of this multi-factorial explanation is appropriate at this juncture. First, it is beyond dispute that most Canadians "instinctively sympathized with Americans," shared their pain and anger, and continue to support the idea of a war on terrorism (even while remaining deeply critical of the Bush administration's invasion of Iraq post-9/11).[225] Furthermore, 46.1 percent of Americans voted in 2016 for presidential candidate Donald Trump, who promised to be quite harsh on immigrants and refugees, and at least 37 percent of all Americans continued to support him by mid-2017.[226] Yet, as Howard Adelman and Kent Roach have correctly suggested, Canada's efforts to tighten its borders after 9/11 (including its efforts to deport suspected national security risks in spite of the danger of torture that they faced) has as much to do with its heavy economic dependence on cross-border trade with the United States.[227] The potential "collateral economic harm to Canadian interests" that could be caused by US overinterpretation of its security vulnerability on its Canada-US border and the consequent restriction of the movement of goods and people across that border is a key explanation for Canada's enhanced moves both before and after 9/11 to tighten its immigration and refugee regimes (for instance, by explicitly leaving some room for deportation to torture of non-citizens who are considered particularly dangerous).[228] This is underlined by the fact that most of Canada's exports are sent to the United States across the Canada-US border.[229]

Another key reason is Canada's own long-standing internal security anxieties, stemming principally from the public's fear for its own security, exacerbated by 9/11; the activities of some foreign rebel groups within Canada; relentless (usually US) press portrayals of Canada as a haven for terrorists; and the fact that Ahmed Ressam, who had planned to bomb Los Angeles International Airport before 9/11 had tried to cross into the United States from Canada.[230] Pressure was also exerted on Canada by the relentless finger-pointing of all-too-many US officials unhappy with what they saw as Canada's lax immigration laws and open borders.[231] For instance, even while expressing doubts about the efficacy of this approach to US security, former INS Commissioner Doris Meissner still predicted that "there will be far more focus on Canada. Canada as a gateway for terrorists is very much on the agenda."[232] She was correct: both the *PATRIOT Act* and the (defunct) *9/11 Bill* had lengthy provisions for measures designed to protect the United States from what their drafters saw as the vulnerable Canada-US border.[233]

Another reason for Canada's further tightening of its immigration/refugee policies after 9/11 (including its insistence on retaining an exceptional general loophole for deportation to torture) is the existence within the country itself of a deeply embedded tendency to control immigration. This tendency stems in part from a deeply entrenched ambivalence in sections of Canadian society about immigration and immigrants as well as from some fringe xenophobia, both of which have become more salient in recent years. As Adelman has noted, a poll conducted in the aftermath of 9/11 found that 80 percent of Canadians demanded stricter controls over immigration and refugee admissions to Canada.[234] The pre-9/11 evidence also shows that a significant, if smaller, percentage of Canadians had been demanding such controls for some time.[235] The factors discussed above help explain why Canadian law and practice in the area of deportation to torture are, despite important differences, on the whole as similar as they are to US policy. As important, however, is the fact that such Canadian law and practice have also been shaped in part by the need felt by many Canadians to maintain a distinct national identity, and therefore keep some limited distance between US and Canadian policy in this area.[236] To a limited extent, this may explain why Canadian policy is better than US policy in five identified respects but worse in one.

Finally, it is important to emphasize that in the area of deportation to torture, as in other areas of refugee law, as difficult as things seem to have been for refugees since 9/11, not all that much has changed in either the United States or Canada after 9/11. To be sure, in a very broad sense, things are worse today in terms of access of non-citizens to *CAT* relief in both countries. Fear of the potential harm that some foreigners can cause to the United States and the accession to power of the Trump Administration have led to a particularly aggressive attitude toward immigration policing that is more likely to increase the number of mistaken and even deliberate deportations to torture that occur in the United States and Canada. However, the extent of the deterioration that has actually occurred in each country since 9/11 is much less than might be imagined. This is because things were already pretty bad for refugees and prospective deportees to torture well before 9/11.[237] As Whitaker has suggested in the Canadian context, "refugee policies post–September 11 are *pretty much* like refugee policies pre–September 11, *but more so*."[238]

This situation is remarkable in view of the more or less extreme changes that have tended to mark and mar refugee law and practice during earlier periods of heightened security consciousness in both countries, including as recently as the period between 1993 and 1996.[239] In response to the bombing of the World Trade Center in 1993 and similar threats to US national security, the *Immigration and Nationality Act* was amended in 1996 by the *Illegal Immigration Reform and Immigrant Responsibility Act* and the *Anti-Terrorism and Effective Death Penalty Act* to substantially and sharply increase security controls over immigrants and refugees.[240] It is instructive that many have described these 1996 changes as the harshest US immigration/refugee control measures of the century. Remarkably, it is around the same period that a similar regime began emerging in Canada.[241] There is no reason to disagree with that characterization, even after the changes spawned by 9/11. Thus, the 9/11 attacks basically compressed and accentuated the stripping away of legal protection of refugee rights that had begun much earlier. More recently, the coming to power of the Trump Administration has added fuel to the fire.

Given these longitudinal and comparative insights, is Canada's refugee law regime as humane as it is widely reputed to be? Is it really more humane than the corresponding US regime? These questions also animate the discussion in the rest of the book.

The Detention of Asylum Seekers and Refugees   **2**

One major area of concern involves the mass arrests and secret detentions that followed the September 11 attacks. Columnist Stuart Taylor referred to it as the Administration's truly alarming and utterly unnecessary abuses of its detention powers. Earlier this year, the Department of Justice's own Inspector General reported critically on the department's handling of immigration detainees swept up in the 9/11 investigation.

> – US senator Patrick Leahy

In that respect ... Mr. Zogby certainly is justified, to focus on the 80,000 number [of persons registered under NSEERS] and the 13,000 deportations [and entailed detentions]. But to put it into context, every year the immigration authorities initiate proceedings against approximately one million persons who are illegally or unlawfully in this country.

> – Professor Viet Dinh

Immigration detention is one of the areas of refugee law most negatively affected by the response in both Canada and the United States to the 9/11 attacks. In quantitative terms, the use and misuse of immigration detention in relation to non-citizens (including refugees) rose quite significantly in the United States. Other indicators confirm a trend toward more and more refugee detention in that country. Examples include: 1) the fact that detention is one of the "primary refugee protection concerns for UNHCR [Office of the United Nations High Commissioner for Refugees] in the United States" and "accounts for a large portion" of its activities in that country;[1] 2) the authorization by Congress in 2004 of the construction of up to 40,000 additional immigration detention bed spaces over five years;[2] 3) President George W. Bush's request of US$90 million in fiscal year 2006 for the provision of as high a number of additional bed spaces;[3] 4) the dramatic 19 percent (US$176 million) increase in the budget allocation to the Detention and Removal Office (DRO) within the Immigration and Customs Enforcement (ICE) unit of the Department of Homeland Security (DHS) that same year;[4] and 5) the recent authorization in an executive order issued by President Donald Trump of the increased construction of detention facilities at or near the US border with Mexico.[5] While the number of detention beds and the budget allocation for detention and removal have fluctuated between 2004 and 2016, there is still clear indication that refugee detention is occurring at an increasing scale. The budget for fiscal year 2016 allocated US$3.3 billion for the detention of non-citizens held in government custody because they present a risk of flight or a risk to public safety, or are subject to mandatory detention,[6] compared with US$1.8 billion in fiscal year 2015.[7] The Trump Administration allocated money in its subsequent budgets to increase, or at least maintain, a high number of detention beds and the numbers of refugees (and other non-citizens) who are put in immigration detention.[8]

Although on a much smaller scale, the post-9/11 trend in Canada has been similar. This is broadly indicated by both quantitative and qualitative measures. Sharp rises in the numbers of detained refugees and other non-citizens were recorded in the years immediately following 9/11.[9] Significant increases in the security and detention budgets were announced by the federal government.[10] After 9/11, the government devoted additional financial and other resources for immigration enforcement and screening. A budget tabled in December 2001 provided an additional Cdn$7.7 billion for public security and anti-terrorist measures for 2001–07, out of which the department in charge of immigration enforcement got Cdn$639.4 million.[11] The relevant enforcement agencies also began to pay increased attention to the task of removing undocumented or otherwise inadmissible non-citizens from Canada.[12] Such removals are usually preceded by the detention of the affected individual(s). This trend continued unabated until 2009, then declined by about 20 percent between 2009 and 2011.[13] Although disaggregated statistics are not readily available for the period 2011–16, there is some indication that the numbers during this period may have remained around the 2009–11 levels.[14]

Yet, as this chapter shows, this rise in the use of detention was not entirely a post-9/11 phenomenon. In the United States and Canada, the period beginning in the mid-1990s and ending just before the tragic events of September 11, 2001, was an era of remarkably negative developments in the use of detention in the refugee context. Indeed, as will become clear, in the US context, the year 1996 is nearly as important to the present discussion as 2001, and in the Canadian context, the 1990s are just as important as the 2000s.[15] The number of those in immigration detention in Canada had been climbing steadily for very many years before 9/11.[16]

One of the main tasks at hand is to carefully analyze the available evidence relating to several discrete aspects of the refugee detention story in order to assess more precisely the extent to which 9/11 has affected the use and misuse of this process in both countries. A related and equally important task is to tease out the insights that can be gained from a comparison of the extent of the changes in the United States – the country that was directly attacked on 9/11 – to the position in post-9/11 Canada.

To this end, the rest of the chapter is organized in the following way. The section that follows this introduction is devoted to a discussion of the use of refugee detention as a deterrent – as a way of dissuading similarly situated persons from attempting to seek refugee status in Canada or the United States. Thereafter, the use of identity-based detentions in both countries before and after the events of 9/11 is examined. Following this discussion, the detention of refugees in the two countries on grounds of security-related inadmissibility is analyzed. This discussion deals with such subquestions as the utilization of racial/ethnic profiling tactics, preventive detention, mandatory detention, material witness detentions, longer or indefinite detentions, and secret detentions. The next section considers the legal norms and practices relating to the conditions under which many refugees were detained in both countries. Thereafter, the social and institutional context in which the detention of refugees has proceeded in both countries is considered, with a view to appreciating the ways in which these have helped shape the pre- and post-9/11 refugee detention regimes in each country. This discussion is followed by an analysis of the extent of the congruence or lack thereof, in each country of focus, between its refugee detention regime and the relevant international standards. The last section discusses the main analytical conclusions that stem from the preceding comparison of the detention regimes in both countries, and concludes the chapter.

Detention as Migration Deterrent

The US Position

Although immigration (including refugee) detention seems increasingly normal in the United States, the relatively high tolerance for and rates of detention that now characterize its refugee laws and practices is a fairly modern construction. Ellis Island, the country's most famous historical immigration detention facility, was established only in 1892.[17] Only a small portion of the immigrants of the time were ever detained, and the vast majority of these were released within days or weeks.[18] Today, many "people languish in immigration detention for [months] and years."[19] Indeed, the Immigration and Naturalization Service (INS) or its successor, the Department of Homeland Security, budgeted about US$1 billion for detention and removal in fiscal year 2001, US$1.1 billion in 2003, US$1.59 billion in 2005, US$2.49 billion in 2007, US$2.45 billion in 2009, US$1.1 billion in 2011, US$2.6 billion in 2013, and about US$3 billion in 2015.[20] It should be noted, however, that in 2011 the Obama Administration instituted immigration detention reforms that were meant to reduce the average length of stay in detention, reduce the number of detention facilities, and draft new detention standards.[21] Nonetheless, the United States is still widely believed to have the largest immigration detention population in the world.[22] For example, it detained approximately 478,000 foreign nationals in 2012.[23] Of that number, 6–14 percent tended to be refugees.[24] From the mass roundups of immigrants that followed the "communist scare" and the Second World War, to the mass interdictions, detentions, and expulsions that followed the so-called Central American refugee crisis of the 1980s, immigration detention has been employed by the US government or powerful elements within it in response to prevalent or loudly expressed national security, economic, social identity, and/or xenophobic fears in society.[25] As we have noted, the Trump Administration is set to expand the utilization of this approach even more.

Starting with President Ronald Reagan's handling of the Central American refugee crisis of the 1980s, such detention has also been used by the US government as a way of deterring similarly situated persons from particular countries or regions from attempting to seek refugee status in the United States.[26] During this same period, thousands of Haitians were interdicted and/or detained at the now infamous detention facility in Krome, Florida.[27] Their number has been estimated at about 25,000.[28] Since that time, there have been other periods of relative intensity in the attempts by some people from the Caribbean and Central America to reach the United States by boat or raft. One such period was between 1991 and 1994, when tens of thousands of Cubans and Haitians left their countries for the United States in order to claim refuge there.[29] Thousands more were interdicted and detained at the US military base at Guantanamo Bay, Cuba.

One key policy motivation for these actions was to deter more Haitians and Cubans from embarking on a journey to the United States to seek refuge. It was thought that this would contribute to the realization of the stated aims of the United States in the immigration detention context, which were allegedly to "quell this influx of migrants" and "save the rafters' lives."[30] Thus, in the hope of deterring potential migrants from that country, the United States has been interdicting and detaining Haitian refugees since the early 1980s.[31] As Olga Velez has correctly noted:

> Under this [long-standing] policy 210 people were held indefinitely from the 1980s and others who had been released but committed minor offenses while on parole were re-detained on an indefinite basis ... Only in 2005 did the Supreme Court rule that the statute used to detain the group was subject to temporary limits in *Clark v*

Martinez, and this allowed the supervised release of the detainees after some 25 years in indefinite detention.[32]

The passage of the *Illegal Immigration Reform and Immigrant Responsibility Act (IIRIRA)* in 1996 helped ensure that those Haitians (read, the vast majority of them) who did not arrive in the United States with proper immigration documents were kept in detention, at least until their case was referred to an Immigration Judge.[33] The current phase of the story of the interdiction and detention of Haitians is but one part of a long-standing US government policy. This phase began on October 29, 2002, when approximately 220 Haitian refugees washed ashore in Biscayne Bay, Florida, and 167 of them were apprehended and detained by the Coast Guard.[34]

Note that this policy of indefinite detention stretched into the post-9/11 era.

What most distinguishes the post-9/11 phase of the Haitian migration saga, however, is the explicit designation in late 2002 of those Haitian refugees who arrive in the United States by boat as national security threats, ostensibly because they "divert Coast Guard and other resources from their homeland security duties."[35] As noted in an ICE policy statement, it is clearly official US policy that "aliens who arrive by boat are subject to a national policy of continued detention [even] post-credible fear [when they have been adjudged to have a *prima facie* valid refugee claim] *in order to deter others* from taking the life threatening boat trip and ensure our maritime defense assets are not diverted from their national security mission."[36] This policy was reinforced by a Department of Justice order to INS field operatives to ensure that "none of them [Haitians] should be paroled [released] without the approval of INS headquarters."[37]

As if this INS/DHS policy was not sufficiently controversial, the decision of then Attorney General John Ashcroft in *In Re D-J* to exercise his powers under US law and overrule the parole from detention granted a young Haitian refugee by both an Immigration Judge and the Board of Immigration Appeals (BIA) fuelled the firestorm of debate that has raged over the appropriateness of the Haitian detention policy.[38] The decision mandated detention without bond for the young Haitian and "similarly situated undocumented seagoing migrants," and in effect directed

Immigration Judges to refuse to release from detention all future Haitian refugees who arrive in the United States by boat. The Attorney General basically agreed with INS arguments that 1) because a few Haitian boat people could be dangerous, all of them had to be detained, 2) Pakistanis were now using Haiti as a staging ground to enter the United States, and (c) releasing these Haitians would encourage a deluge of Haitians and divert valuable Coast Guard resources from counter-terrorism. Yet, other than being framed in 9/11-sensitive language, these claims were essentially recycled from earlier US government justifications for inter- dicting and detaining Haitians during more intense periods of Haitian seafaring migration to the United States. The Attorney General's key justification for issuing this harsh and highly consequential directive was that "national security interests [are] implicated by the encouragement of further unlawful mass migrations."[39] The deterrence of potential refugees (at best to save them from drowning at sea) was, in effect, portrayed as a national security imperative.[40]

It is hardly plausible that helping save the lives of some Haitians is the key reason why hundreds of those who arrive in the United States safely, who are not flight risks, who clearly do not pose any direct national security risk, and who have been preliminarily determined to have a credible fear of persecution,[41] are punished by being kept in detention for months or years.[42] This is especially clear when contrasted with the fact that most Cuban boat people who arrive in the country under similar circumstances are not similarly detained. Similarly situated refugees of other nationalities are routinely released.[43] For example, "Cuban migrants receive more generous treatment under US law than Haitians or foreign nationals from any other country."[44]

The deployment of refugee detention to deter similarly situated persons from attempting to come to the United States as refugees has been condemned by many US legislators and academics, as well as by the Office of the UN High Commissioner for Refugees (UNHCR). Senator Edward Kennedy, then chair of the Senate Sub-committee on Immigration, declared that "many of us are troubled by the detention policy of the Department of Justice" (which was responsible for refugee detention at the time).[45] Representative John Conyers agreed and warned that in keeping Haitians who have no possible connections to terror in detention even after they had demonstrated at least a credible fear, the government was abusing the authority granted to it in the wake of 9/11 to combat terror.[46] The objections expressed by David Cole are similar.[47] For its part, the UNHCR has roundly criticized, as contrary to international law and the very idea of a right to seek asylum, the use of detention as a means of deterring refugee migrations to the United States and any other country.[48]

So, did 9/11 and public reaction to it change anything in the United States in terms of the use of detention to deter mass migration from certain neighbouring countries? Yes, it did, although not as much as may be commonly assumed. Although many were rounded up and detained after 9/11 and alterations of legal texts were pushed through, huge changes did not occur in the US refugee "detention for deterrence" regime, in part because, even before 9/11, things were already quite bad under US law and practice for most seafaring refugees. We have already seen that the government's use of detention to deter mass migration dates back to the 1980s and earlier. The introduction in 1996 of the expedited removal process ensured that even before 9/11, undocumented as they mostly were, the vast majority of Haitian and other seafaring refugees were routinely detained for some period on their arrival in the United States.[49] As Bill Frelick shows, detentions of refugees had increased steadily between 1999 and 2001.[50] After 9/11, with public opinion more prepared than ever to support arguments phrased in national security terms, the tendency among government officials to deploy such arguments to trump opposing arguments and justify otherwise implausible policies was accentuated, leading to the detention of many more refugees than would have been possible before 9/11, licensing the non-release of a significant number of even those refugees who had been adjudged to possess a credible fear of persecution, and increasing the average length of jail time for refugees.[51]

The Canadian Position

Although Canada detains (largely on security grounds) a comparatively smaller number of people with active refugee claims who have no criminal history, it does not engage in the blanket detention of either all refugee claimants or all such claimants who hail from a particular country or group of countries.[52] As such, direct evidence of the practice of detaining refugees within Canadian territory as a migration deterrent, while certainly much more available in more recent times (at least from 2010), is comparatively more difficult to find. In addition, unlike in the United States, Canadian immigration authorities almost never admit the existence of such a policy, and tend to disguise it within more general policies.[53]

Nevertheless, the Canadian Council for Refugees (CCR), a knowledgeable observer of Canadian immigration practice, has alleged that the relatively prolonged detention of many of the 599 asylum seekers who over the course of 1999 arrived on four ships on the shores of British Columbia was in part "deterrence practice."[54] To them, the significant public attention garnered by such mass arrivals by boat put pressure on the government to increase the use of detention to secure the removal of the "boat people" and discourage similar future arrivals. The government's acknowledgment in 1998 that detention could be used as a migration deterrent given that "there are few consequences to discourage undocumented arrivals, since they receive the same benefits as those who arrive with genuine documents" does lend some weight to these allegations.[55]

Since 9/11, there have been a number of examples of this practice in Canada. In August 2010, 492 Sri Lankan Tamils arrived in British Columbia aboard the MV *Sun Sea*.[56] Of these, 443 were detained.[57] In most cases where release was ordered, Canadian authorities stridently opposed this and applied for judicial review of the administrative decision to release them.[58] Although the government offered various reasons for this course of action, including security considerations and a lack of identification, the palpable strategy it deployed was to ensure that these refugees were held in detention, probably to deter other Tamils in Sri Lanka who might nurse the ambition of travelling to Canada to seek asylum.[59] The government had reacted similarly to the seventy-six Sri Lankans who arrived in Canada in October 2009 aboard the *Ocean Lady*.[60] Based on the reaction of the relevant governments to these and other incidents, Alex Neve and Tiisetso Russell have argued, quite correctly, that the policy and practice of the Canadian government since 2010 has favoured the utilization of detention to deter migration.[61] They note that amid the frenzy of concern about boatloads of migrants viewed as poised to swamp Canada's immigration system, Bill C-49, the *Preventing Human Smugglers from Abusing Canada's Immigration System Act,* was tabled in Parliament on October 21, 2010, and enacted soon after.[62] This law did not explicitly go after those arriving by boat, and legislates only generically about "irregular arrivals" of "groups of persons."[63] Its intent, however, was to deter such arrivals by boat.[64] The *Act* also provided for the indefinite detention of persons who are part of such "irregular arrivals."[65]

The foregoing discussion shows that while Canada's use of the "detention as migration deterrent policy" has not been as widespread or intense as its deployment in the United States, this does not mean that Canada does not make robust attempts to deter the arrival of refugees on its territory. The evidence discussed above is clear on this, and Canada certainly does engage in interdiction of potential refugees at major airports abroad and on the high seas.[66] This is not the same, however, as detaining those who have already arrived safely in Canada largely as a way of sending a signal to similarly situated persons about the harsh fate that awaits them should they eventually reach this country.

Identity-Based Detentions

The US Position

Even well before 9/11, most refugees who sought to enter the United States in order to claim refugee status were placed into the expedited removal process that has been in operation since April 1997.[67] This was so because the *Illegal Immigration Reform and Immigrant Responsibility Act of 1996* mandated the routine detention of almost all of these refugees.[68] Virtually all of them must be automatically detained if they are determined by the relevant INS or DHS officials to have sought to enter the United States by fraud or misrepresentation, or without proper documentation. In this chapter, detention for these reasons will be referred to collectively as identity-based detention.[69] Such mandatory detention is prescribed by the *IIRIRA* despite the fact that these refugees have claimed refugee status in the United States and have been referred to a credible-fear determination hearing before an Immigration Judge.[70] What is more, virtually all such refugees are detained unless and until they receive a positive credible-fear decision from an Immigration Judge.[71] Under the same statute, parole (i.e., release from detention) of these refugees at this pre-credible-fear stage is at the non-reviewable discretion of the DHS (formerly INS) District Director (or other equivalent officer) at the relevant port of entry.[72] In December 2009, ICE issued new parole guidelines for refugees in Expedited Removal, under which individuals found to have a credible fear of persecution are automatically considered for parole.[73] Parole may be granted once refugees establish a credible fear, their identity, community ties, and that they are not security risks, unless there are "exceptional overriding factors."[74] In any case, it is important to keep in mind that in conformity with the *IIRIRA*, almost all of these refugees are detained for a significant period before their actual asylum hearing. While credible-fear interviews have been required to take place within ten days to two weeks since June 2012, ICE reported that it was taking up to three months at the Karnes County Civil Detention Center.[75] Although it has since been reduced to three weeks,[76] this is nonetheless a long time for a *prima facie* non-criminal asylum seeker to be detained.

What is more, the tendency to subject refugees to the expedited removal process and place them in identity-based detention as a result was quite troubling even before 9/11, given that the determinations that a particular refugee was seeking to enter the country by fraud or misrepresentation or did not have the proper immigration documents, or that that person merited detention, were not always reached in a manner that inspired confidence in the system's fairness or accuracy. For example, although 99 percent of the refugees in the sample on which the 2005 US Commission on International Religious Freedom (USCIRF) Asylum Report was based established their identity to a reasonable degree of certainty, 75 percent were still placed in the expedited removal process and detained as a consequence.[77] This type of situation pre-dated the Report and went back to at least 1999, even before 9/11.[78] Again, 20 percent of the refugees for whom the DHS had recorded information on both their identities and community ties were nevertheless detained up to and until the final determination of the merits of their asylum claim.[79] Six percent of refugees in the USCIRF sample who had valid passports and visas were still marked for expedited removal and detained as a result.[80]

It would be fair to conclude that the experience of the vast majority of refugees subjected to identity-based detention in the United States was already quite harsh well before 9/11. In this context, the passage in 1996 of the *IIRIRA* and the *Anti-Terrorism and Effective Death Penalty Act (AEDPA)* is as significant as the 9/11 attacks in the construction of the harsh identity-based refugee detention regime in the United States. As the American Immigration Lawyers Association (AILA) has noted, "the 1996 laws are merciless."[81] Regrettably, attempts in the 107th and 108th Congresses and since then to ameliorate the harmful effects of these laws have been unsuccessful on the whole.[82] The 9/11 attacks and the consequent sense of mass security vulnerability, and later on the election of President Trump, have all but sealed the fate of these reform efforts (at least for now).

The important influence of the 9/11 attacks on the character of the subsequent identity-based refugee detention regime is underlined by the USCIRF Asylum Report's finding of a highly significant drop in the rate of release after 9/11 of refugees who had received a positive credible-fear decision: from 78 percent paroled at that stage in fiscal year 2002 to 62.5 percent by fiscal year 2003, a drop of 27 percent.[83] A 2007 USCIRF "report card" stated that although the DHS had by then established national criteria to determine when asylum seekers in the expedited removal process should be released from detention pending their asylum hearing, there was no evidence that such criteria were actually being implemented.[84]

As important, the identity-based refugee detention regime has been marked and marred by certain post-9/11 changes in its governing socio-legal framework. In the exercise of their lawful discretion, immigration authorities have significantly expanded the application of the expedited removal process, adding even more bite to the ability of the relevant agencies to apprehend and detain refugees and other non-citizens for identity-based reasons. For example, on November 13, 2002 (just over one year and two months after 9/11), expedited removal and identity-based detention was extended to apply to undocumented non-Cubans who entered the United States by sea within the prior two years.[85] On August 11, 2004, the DHS further extended authority for such detention to the Border Patrol for undocumented non-citizens apprehended within fourteen days after entry and within 100 miles of the border in the Tucson and Laredo Border Patrol sectors.[86] That same year, the ill-fated *9/11 Recommendations Implementation Act* (Bill HR 10) was introduced in the House of Representatives.[87] Had it passed, its s 3007 would have expanded the applicability of expedited removal (and the detention that usually precedes it) to undocumented non-citizens who had been in the country for less than five years. A counterpart but substantively very different bill, the *Intelligence Reform and Terrorism Prevention Act* (S 2845), was passed by the Senate around the same time.[88] After lengthy negotiations, the Senate bill, which did not contain the s 3007 provision, also passed the House in December of the same year, and became law.[89]

In the end, the greatest danger faced by refugees subject to expedited removal and identity-based detention, both before and after 9/11, is "the possibility that individuals with a genuine asylum claim may not be identified by the screening procedures and will erroneously be returned to their native countries, possibly facing further danger or death."[90] The post-9/11 climate in the United States has only exacerbated this real danger of mistaken, negligent, or even fully intentional *refoulement* to persecution, torture, or even death. After all, as has been shown, all too many Haitian boat people continue to be sent back or forced to return to very dangerous conditions in their country, despite the fact that the dangers they face are crystal-clear.

The Canadian Position

Long before 9/11, the now-defunct *Immigration Act* of 1976 authorized the detention of any person (including a refugee) seeking entry into Canada who was unable to satisfy an immigration officer as to her or his identity.[91] The *Act* was in force until June 2002, when it was replaced by the *Immigration and Refugee Protection Act (IRPA)*, a statute that had been drafted in full before 9/11 and received Royal Assent in November 2001, after 9/11.[92] The *IRPA* contains similar provisions authorizing the detention without a warrant of a foreign national where an officer is not "satisfied as to the identity" of that person.[93] Unlike under the 1976 *Act*, this authorization in the *IRPA* applies whether or not the relevant foreign national is seeking to come into Canada. What is noteworthy here is that immigration statutes either in force or already set in content before 9/11 authorized the identity-based detention of many refugees and other foreign nationals.[94]

As significant is the fact that well before 9/11 proposals for greater resort to identity-based detention were advanced by the relevant parliamentary committee. In 1998, the Standing Committee on Citizenship and Immigration recommended the detention of all non-citizens whose identity could not be established.[95] However, the government disagreed with this proposal on the basis that "[t]he legality, cost and effectiveness of this approach would be of significant concern. While the legality of imposing detention in matters related to danger or flight has been upheld by the courts, to impose detention indefinitely for failing to establish identity may not be consistent with the Charter."[96] This attests to the more moderate approach to identity-based detention followed in Canada in the 1990s, compared to the United States.

Yet, the fact remains that the use of identity-based detention did intensify and become "much more prominent" in Canada after 9/11.[97] For example, soon after 9/11, immigration authorities launched "Project Identity," which aimed to detain people whose credibility was in doubt, who were evasive or uncooperative, or who had no identity documents.[98] This focus on detaining people whose identity is in doubt has not waned significantly in subsequent years.

Given that refugees tend to lack the requisite identification documents when they arrive at a Canadian port of entry, the heightened focus on identity-based detention has also tended to have a disproportionate impact on them.[99] Indeed, roughly 60 percent arrive either with false documents or without proper documentation.[100] For example, for the approximately two-year period between June 15, 2003, and March 31, 2005, refugee claimants represented 43 percent of all those in immigration detention, though not all of them were detained on identity grounds.[101] Failed refugee claimants represented another 10 percent of detainees.[102] A more recent study by the Canadian Council for Refugees found that in 2015 refugee claimants made up about the same percentage of total immigration detainees.[103] Another study found that the vast majority (93 percent) of refugee claimants detained in 2015 were detained on grounds of identity or of their being flight risks, without allegations that they represented a danger to the public or a security risk.[104]

Detention on Grounds of Security-Related Inadmissibility

Of Profiles, Dragnets, and Roundups

The US Position

With regard to the profiling and rounding up of Muslim and Arab male non-citizens in the United States (including many refugees), the pre-9/11 situation was far less troubling than after 9/11. For sure, in the present connection, the year 1996 is widely regarded as, at the very least, nearly as significant as, if not on par with, 9/11 as a marker of the commencement of the harsher treatment of Arab and Muslim non-citizens under US immigration and refugee laws. As noted in a 2004 report: "For the last seven years, the 1996 laws have torn apart families, ruined lives, and even led to people's deaths. Sometimes, intervention by courts and the press have saved a few individuals from permanent banishment from their loved ones, but the majority of immigrants caught in the laws' web find no reprieve."[105] However, although there have always been periods and instances of relatively intense focus on and unease about their presence in the country, and despite the fact that the excessive use of detention was not unknown to the US immigration and refugee regimes before 9/11,[106] there were no massive roundups of Muslim and Arab males before that date. Indeed, as David Martin has correctly concluded, "before September 11, 2001, our [US] system had evolved over many decades to a point where [immigration and refugee] detention during proceedings became [more or less] the exception, not the rule."[107]

All that changed immediately after the 9/11 attacks. Within hours, the process that led to at least one thousand Muslim and Arab males being racially/ethnically profiled, hunted down, rounded up, and clamped into detention was initiated.[108] That these roundups occurred is no longer all that controversial.[109] Indeed, such roundups continued to occur for many years after 9/11, albeit less intensively.[110] For example, over 500 people were rounded up between 2003 and 2005.[111]

In their various forms, these roundups received the fullest sanction at the highest echelons of the Justice Department (and later at the DHS as well). This is confirmed by the statement of a top DHS official that immigration/refugee-centred roundups were key to the overall success of the US anti-terrorism campaign.[112] In describing the nature of "Operation

Liberty Shield" (a comprehensive national plan to increase protections for US citizens and infrastructure), the DHS noted that a key element of the plan was that

> asylum applicants from nations where al-Qaeda sympathizers, and other terrorist groups are known to have operated will be detained during the duration of their processing period [i.e., even after they have established a credible fear of persecution]. This reasonable and prudent temporary action allows authorities to maintain contact with asylum seekers while we determine the validity of their claim. DHS and the Department of State will coordinate exceptions to this policy.[113]

This point drew judicial notice, for example, in a 2003 decision of the US District Court for the Western District of Washington, Seattle Division.[114]

There were two major approaches to casting a dragnet for young male Muslims and Arabs, rounding them up, and detaining most of those caught in the net: 1) immigration charges were laid against young male non-citizens of Muslim and Arab descent, many of them refugees, as a proxy for anti-terrorism enforcement; and 2) a special registration process was instituted for nationals of a large number of Muslim and Arab countries.

Concerning the first approach, a senior official declared that such use of immigration enforcement was "an incredibly important piece of the terrorism response."[115] With respect to the second one, on September 11, 2002 – exactly one year after 9/11 – a substantial expansion in the registration requirements for non-citizens in the United States was instituted by Attorney General John Ashcroft.[116] This new rule established a broader system of non-citizen registration – referred to as the National Security Entry-Exit Registration System (NSEERS) – that was much more onerous and discriminatory than the pre-9/11 rule. Before the rule came into force, most non-permanent residents in the United States were simply deemed to have registered by virtue of their visa application, and most others simply by being issued an I-94 arrival/departure document or waiver under the regulations.[117] Two classes of non-citizens became subject to this new system of special registration (over and above the standard registration requirements for all non-citizens).[118] The first class consisted of young male citizens of certain designated countries and persons who "share[d] ties" with any of those countries.[119] North Koreans aside, persons from Muslim- or Arab-majority countries were the specific targets of this measure, that is, young male citizens or descendants of Iran, Iraq, Libya, Sudan, Syria, Pakistan, Saudi Arabia, Yemen, Afghanistan, Algeria, Bahrain, Bangladesh, Egypt, Eritrea, Indonesia, Kuwait, Lebanon, Morocco, North Korea, Oman, Qatar, and so on.[120] The other class was made up of persons so tagged by a US visa officer or by an INS inspector taking into consideration the national security interests of the United States.[121] In practice, young males who were from or who had made trips to the Muslim and Arab countries listed above and some others were the key targets of this second class.[122] Of the over 85,000 people who complied with this regulation and registered, more than 13,000 were detained for various, often technical, immigration violations.[123] In 2011, a decade after 9/11, following input from community groups and advocacy organizations as well as advances in several automated systems that capture arrival and/or exit information, the DHS officially ended the NSEERS registration process.[124]

Other measures were also taken, including the so-called Voluntary Interview Project (initiated in November 2001), under which the Justice Department directed the FBI and other agencies to conduct interviews with 5,000 non-permanent residents in the United States from countries in which al-Qaeda had had a presence.[125] Another measure was the Absconder Apprehension Initiative (launched in January 2002), which, though aimed in general at locating about 314,000 persons who had violated their deportation orders and remained in the country, focused on 6,000 men from the so-called al-Qaeda countries of operation.[126] The last comprised interviews, in preparation for the US invasion of Iraq, of 11,000 Iraqi-Americans and Iraqis living in the United States.[127] More recently, following a lull in intensity in the implementation of such measures during the Obama era, the Trump Administration issued executive orders on immigration and refugees, one of which authorizes the DHS to enter into agreements with municipalities and local law enforcement services to arrest and detain certain types of immigrants, including many refugees. An important justification offered for this was the need to protect public safety in the United States, but all of this was done against the backdrop of President Trump's dramatic and often controversial pledges to take troubling measures to improve US national and economic security.[128]

That all of these measures were substantially grounded in the "racial/ ethnic/country profiling"[129] of persons who were detained as part of the mass roundups that followed 9/11 is now beyond reasonable doubt.[130] The evidence of this is simply overwhelming. For one, it is noteworthy that even the US Department of Justice Guidance on Racial Profiling,[131] developed after 9/11, did not impose its greater restrictions on officials involved in national security and the protection of US borders.[132] It is as interesting to note that one report found that although profiling may or may not have been systematic, many ordinary US citizens profiled Muslims and Arabs, and law enforcement agents selectively followed up on such tips from private citizens based on a profile targeting young male Muslims and Arabs.[133] US Senator James Durbin spoke at a Senate hearing on what he referred to as a proactive effort by the US government to focus on and target Muslims and Arabs.[134] For its part, one US-based NGO concluded that "our research suggests that the 'indications' that triggered [the] questioning [that led to the detentions] in many cases may have been little more than nationality, religion, and [male] gender."[135] Other than the fact that all too many arrests and detentions occurred arbitrarily and without probable cause,[136] almost all the persons arrested were young males from Muslim and Arab countries.[137] The largest group of detainees was from Pakistan, followed by Egypt and then Turkey.[138] More specifically, of the 762 national security detainees held on immigration-related charges in 2003, 254 (about 33 percent) were Pakistani and 111 (15 percent) were Egyptian.[139] In total, nearly half were from these two Muslim-majority countries. The fact that large numbers of persons of Pakistani origin fled the country in the years immediately after 9/11 and sought refuge in Canada, and that many of them pointed at the implementation of NSEERS as the reason for their flight, only bears out the aforementioned data.[140] Thus, the ascription of probable guilt on the basis of racial/country-based/religious identification formed a significant motivation for the roundups of Muslim and Arab men that occurred in the United States after 9/11.[141]

It is partly for this reason that all the measures discussed earlier in this section (be it the special registration program or the use of immigration detention as a proxy for anti-terrorism enforcement) have been roundly condemned by a range of commentators. For example, some members of Congress condemned the special registration program as anti–civil liberties and discriminatory.[142] One NGO characterized it as "a discriminatory and poorly implemented plan."[143] A former INS general counsel denounced it in similar terms.[144] However, an attempt to get a US District Court to order the temporary suspension of this program was unsuccessful.[145] President Trump's executive orders on immigration and refugees have also been widely condemned.[146]

It is important, however, to emphasize – even at this stage – that the sense of fear that arose out of the tragic events of 9/11 merely accentuated an already well-established tendency in the United States to stereotype and view Muslims and Arabs with suspicion and treat them in the ways outlined here.[147] This historical circumstance led in part to the high level of tolerance for the abuse of the rights of Arab and Muslim non-citizens (and even of some citizens) displayed by far too many ordinary Americans in the wake of 9/11.[148] As Elaine Hagopian has noted, "although the process [of the denudation of their rights] began earlier, it gathered speed as a result of the climate following September 11, 2001."[149]

The Canadian Position

Unlike the United States, Canada did *in general* resist the post-9/11 temptation to round up and detain in near blanket fashion young Muslim and Arab males.[150] It has also consistently refused, at least officially, to sanction the utilization of racial profiling measures in its use of immigration control as a proxy for anti-terrorism enforcement. The government's official position that its anti-terrorism efforts have never singled out any religion or targeted any nationality is, however, not entirely accurate.[151] There is much direct and indirect evidence that the response of the Canadian government and its immigration enforcement agencies to the post-9/11 heightened sense of security vulnerability was characterized, at least in part, by the combined deployment of racial profiling, dragnets, and roundups of young Muslim and Arab males.

For one, "without a doubt, 9/11 generated a hitherto unmarked interest in racial profiling on the part of legislators, the media, and scholars."[152] As important, in the months after 9/11, about 48 percent of Canadians signified support of such profiling.[153] In a survey taken in 2007, nearly half of all Canadians admitted that they were at least a bit racist, and (partly as a result of the 9/11 attacks) about the same percentage had a "very bad" or "somewhat bad" impression of the Arab community in Canada.[154] This reality did not change all that significantly between 2001 and 2017, to the point that even in 2017, about 25 percent of all Canadians would ban Muslim immigration to Canada – even Trump-style.[155] It is no wonder, then, that the racial profiling of Arabs and Muslims does seem to have flourished in Canada in the years following 9/11, albeit mostly under cover.[156] Indeed, as Professor Reem Bahdi has shown, even government lawyers have at least on one occasion conceded that law enforcement authorities do employ some form of racial profiling in their work.[157] She has also shown that after 9/11, the focus of such profiling shifted to a significant extent from African Canadians to Arab and Muslim Canadians.[158]

This profiling of Muslims and Arabs in Canada has led to something akin to a narrower net being cast for them. For instance, soon after 9/11, the then Premier of Ontario announced the formation of a special police unit to track down, detain, and deport illegal immigrants as a way of preventing terrorism.[159] This measure was neutral on its face, but, given that the 9/11 attackers were all Muslim Arabs, and in light of the backlash against Arabs and Muslims that occurred in Canada after 9/11, the main targets of this special unit were not in doubt.[160] Speaking more bluntly, Major-General Lewis MacKenzie, sometime security adviser to this same premier, argued that airport staff ought to conduct more thorough checks on passengers arriving from Arab countries.[161] Many Arabs and Muslims reported "being subjected to higher scrutiny at Canadian airports and elsewhere in Canada.[162] And perhaps one of the most damning pieces of evidence of a dragnet, however narrow, was a leaked internal bulletin suggesting that Canada Customs officers (now Canada Border Services agents) were being directed to intensify their questioning of men who had spent time in any of sixteen named "Muslim" countries.[163] This policy was confirmed by the Canada Border

Services Agency (CBSA), which denied that the practice amounted to racial profiling.[164]

This dragnet resulted in the immigration-related roundups of many Arabs and Muslims in Canada, albeit on a much smaller scale than in the United States. The best-known example of this was the case of twenty-three Pakistani and Indian men who were arrested, publicly identified, and detained by the police and immigration authorities as suspected terrorists. As the Canadian Council for Refugees observed, however, "it soon became clear that the suspicions were based on the flimsiest of evidence, some of which consisted of little more than stereotypes."[165] And while the allegations against these mostly Muslim men were soon quietly dropped,[166] the authorities still pursued minor immigration violations against them.[167] Other cases, such as Canada's complicity in the secret detention and rendition of Maher Arar to torture in Syria on apparently flimsy grounds,[168] and the similar treatment meted out to a number of other Arabs and Muslims such as Benamar Benatta, only reinforce the conclusion that a roundup of some kind did take place in Canada after 9/11, however small its proportions were compared to those in the United States.

It is important to emphasize, however, that, as in the United States, the Canadian deployment of racial profiling, dragnets, and roundups pre-dated the 9/11 attacks. Controversies over racial profiling in Canada are not new.[169] The only difference before 9/11 was that they targeted mainly African Canadians.[170] As significant, for years before 9/11 the security agencies did, to some extent, target certain communities, including Arab and Muslim communities, for greater surveillance. This is indicated by the fact that before 9/11, three Arab Muslims were detained in Canada as a result of their being named in security certificates as suspected national security threats.[171] The principal difference between the pre- and post-9/11 situations is one of scale. The targeting of Arabs and Muslims was done on a much smaller scale before 9/11 than after 9/11.

Overall, it is also fair to say that while there have been qualitative differences between Canadian and US actions after 9/11 regarding the deployment of racial profiling, dragnets, and roundups targeted at Arabs and Muslims (for example, racial profiling in the United States was done more openly or closer to the surface as part of explicitly stated official policy), the single most important difference lies in the much smaller scale of the Canadian roundups. While the United States profiled Arabs and Muslims in the thousands and rounded up nearly a thousand of them on national security grounds, only a tiny fraction of that number experienced similar treatment in Canada. Then again, it is trite knowledge that the United States hosts a much larger population of immigrants and Arabs/Muslims than Canada, even as a percentage of their total populations.

Preventive Detentions for Security Reasons

The US Position

Although the passage in 1996 of both the *Anti-Terrorism and Effective Death Penalty Act* and the *Illegal Immigration Reform and Immigrant Responsibility Act* greatly expanded the number of non-citizens (including refugees) ineligible for release on bond or parole while deportation or exclusion proceedings were pending against them,[172] and despite the fact that (since the US immigration bureaucracy has no punitive power and can only detain "in aid of removal")[173] most immigration detention is by definition preventive in nature, it is correct to say that before 9/11, US immigration/refugee laws (in keeping with the country's criminal and constitutional law provisions) rarely permitted preventive detentions for investigative purposes.[174] Before 9/11, there was a near-universal understanding that no one would be jailed without conviction for a specific offence unless they met the strict conditions specified later in this paragraph.[175] Under the regime that was operative between 1996 and 9/11, however, refugees and other non-citizens considered by immigration enforcement officials to be deportable on "security-related grounds," but who had not been ordered removed from the country on such grounds, were by law denied access to the judicial procedure for review of the validity of the decision to detain them.[176] This class of persons could be released on bail only under a set of very strict and narrow conditions.[177] This was in effect preventive detention par excellence. Nevertheless, the decision to detain was not in this case necessarily designed to facilitate a broader national security investigation as much as it was to ensure that the specific detainee did not threaten US security in the meantime. During this period in the process of assessing a person's refugee claim, preventive detention was permissible only if the person was a flight risk, was dangerous because of mental illness, or was an enemy non-citizen during a declared war.[178] The first two situations demanded an individualized risk assessment, while the latter obviously does not apply to almost all of those detained on security-related grounds in the post-9/11 period.

This is one major difference between the US refugee preventive detention regime before 9/11 and the equivalent socio-legal order after 9/11. A key government strategy to prevent further attacks after 9/11 was the preventive detention of even those against whom it had *no* specific evidence linking them to terrorism at the time they were taken into custody.[179] This has been alluded to in our earlier discussion of the roundups of young Muslim and Arab men. This much was stated in the 2003 report of the Justice Department's Inspector General (hereafter the OIG Report) and was implicitly admitted in the Department's response to that document.[180] The strategy was authorized by the passage of legislation and regulations and the issuance of informal high-level orders. In this case, though, preventive detention was used mostly for investigative purposes.

Under the *PATRIOT Act* and some of the regulations and orders that grounded the detention activities of the immigration bureaucracy, preventive detention was decreed for refugees and other non-citizens loosely suspected of having some vague link to the national security threat that the United States faced after 9/11 (hereafter the "9/11 detainees"), even when these persons could not on any reasonable interpretation of the evidence be viewed either as dangerous or as flight risks.[181] Thus, the *PATRIOT Act* gave the US government new authority it had long sought to detain for investigative purposes non-citizens loosely suspected of posing national security threats.[182] Under s 412 of the *PATRIOT Act*, which added a new s 236A to the *Immigration and Nationality Act (INA)*, the executive branch of the US government can certify and detain any non-citizen, including a refugee, for a potentially indefinite period, based on mere suspicion that the non-citizen is engaged in "terrorist activity" or "any other activity that endangers the national security of the US."[183] However, although the Bush Administration had asked Congress to grant it almost unlimited power to detain non-citizens suspected of constituting security threats, the final version of the *Act* contains significant limitations on the detention power of the US government in this respect.[184] Under s 412, the certification that precedes detention of non-citizens must be personally done by the Attorney General or his or her deputy, and cannot be delegated. Once the certification is issued, the Attorney General must also review its continuing validity or necessity at least once every six months, and immigration or criminal charges must be filed against detainees within seven days of their detention. Despite the protections embedded within the *Act*, however, the regime it created still allows the government significantly more latitude to detain certain non-citizens than it had under the pre-9/11 regime. The relevant pre-9/11 immigration regulation allowed the government only twenty-four hours within which to charge security detainees with immigration or criminal offences.[185]

Interestingly, it was not the *PATRIOT Act* that the immigration bureaucracy relied on in arresting the vast majority of the 9/11 detainees. Section 412 of the *Act* appears never to have been invoked between 2001 and 2017.[186] Almost all 9/11 detainees were detained pursuant to an INS regulation that was hastily amended on September 20, 2001, to allow immigration enforcement agents to hold 9/11 detainees for forty-eight hours or, in the event of an emergency, for a longer indeterminate period.[187] This regulation thus provided a loophole that allowed agents to hold the detainees far longer than the forty-eight-hour period that was ordinarily allowed.[188]

A similar US government delay tactic was the issuance and deployment of a regulation by the Justice Department that, in effect, allowed INS/DHS immigration lawyers in security-related cases to automatically stay the release order of an Immigration Judge without having to first obtain an emergency stay of that order from the appellate Board of Immigration Appeals (BIA).[189] Although this authority did not exist in this form before 1997, much of the substantive grant of power involved pre-dates 9/11. Whereas the post-1996 and pre-9/11 regime applied only to non-citizens suspected of being removable on grounds of serious criminality or terrorism and who met certain other requirements, the post-9/11 regime applies to *all* non-citizens who meet those other requirements.[190] There was thus a post-9/11 expansion in the range of non-citizens subject to what is in fact an extraordinary preventive detention power conferred on INS/DHS lawyers. The extraordinariness of this power is rendered even more remarkable by the fact that, as a former INS general counsel has observed, it is now being used routinely in cases involving 9/11 detainees.[191] Although a US District Court in *Zavala v Ridge* held that the regulation that conferred this power was invalid in that it went beyond the authority of the statutory framework of 8 USC s 1226(a) by eliminating the discretionary authority of Immigration Judges to determine whether an individual may be released, both the US Court of Appeals and the Supreme Court upheld it.[192]

As important, the DHS policy of automatically detaining all asylum applicants who are nationals of countries in which, in its view, al-Qaeda sympathizers and other terrorist groups have operated, is worthy of reiteration here. This policy, made public on March 18, 2003, was part of the overall strategy of preventive detention employed by the US government in the aftermath of the 9/11 attacks. This has already been discussed in detail elsewhere in this chapter.

Under the informal and unwritten operating procedures that originated from the top echelons of the Department of Justice in the aftermath of 9/11, US immigration enforcement officials and their FBI counterparts understood that they were to apply a "hold until cleared by FBI policy" to 9/11 detainees, and they did apply this policy.[193] The *PATRIOT Act* and the *INA* certainly permitted the detention without bond of non-citizens suspected of being national security threats if a link to terror could be established *before* the detention.[194] Nevertheless, the "hold until cleared by the FBI policy" exceeded the legal authority granted by these two laws. This is because, as Margaret Taylor has correctly shown, in the case of the 9/11 detainees, Muslim and Arab non-citizens were rounded up before any link to terrorism could be established and were detained while the FBI essentially fished for any such link.[195] For the most part, this was certainly a post-9/11 innovation in US immigration and refugee law.

Another informal policy implemented by the immigration bureaucracy after 9/11 was to oppose the release of all 9/11 detainees using general template affidavits and documents that recited the facts surrounding 9/11 and the security threats the US faced as a result, but that contained little information about the justifiability of the particular detention decision at issue.[196] Taylor has described this practice as using "boilerplate memos" as a tactic to delay the release of these 9/11 detainees until the FBI might find something with which to craft a charge against them.[197]

Officials also used multiple requests for continuances (adjournments) in such cases, to buy time for investigation of the 9/11 detainees in question.[198] Time was needed to see whether they could find something with which to charge detainees and/or remove them from the United States. These were largely fishing expeditions buoyed by the detention of non-citizens of Muslim and Arab heritage.

Of more minor significance in this regard is the fact that the Department of Justice's own Office of the Inspector General found that in at least one case, a 9/11 detainee was held for three days without any valid immigration charge, despite being rounded up for an immigration violation that he had supposedly committed.[199] In fact, his detention for this period was designed to facilitate the FBI's fishing expedition for some inkling of a national security–related violation that would render him deportable from the United States.

That the use of all of these tactics was the explicit policy of the US government is clear from the admission of then Deputy Attorney General Larry Thompson to the OIG that "my staff understood that the immigration authorities of the Department should be used to keep such people [9/11 detainees] in custody until we could satisfy ourselves – by the FBI clearance process – that they did not mean to do us harm."[200] Taken together with the Bush Administration's efforts in the immediate aftermath of 9/11 to secure virtually unlimited detention powers under the *PATRIOT Act*, the subsequent attempt to pass an even harsher law often referred to as *PATRIOT II*,[201] and the substantial post-9/11 increase in the number of non-citizens detained by US immigration enforcement authorities,[202] it is clear that the US government relied heavily on the preventive detention of non-citizens of Muslim and Arab descent for investigative purposes as a key element of its post-9/11 national security strategy. Yet, there was near-unanimous agreement before 9/11 that the government could not simply round up people and lock them up without a good reason *specific to the detained individuals*.[203]

That this sort of investigation-centred preventive detention regime is almost always problematic is underscored by the fact that, as David Cole has found, "virtually all of the 1,500–2,000 persons detained in the government's investigation of September 11 have turned out to be innocent of any involvement in terrorism."[204] Thus, the end result of the government's approach in this respect has been the unnecessary (and perhaps illegal) detention of thousands of Muslims and Arabs. Even scholars like David Martin who suggest that the use of immigration detention as a part of the government's post-9/11 strategy was justified in theory have also concluded that not all uses of such detention were appropriate.[205]

The Canadian Position

Although it has been customary to focus on the much higher profile security certificate (SC) cases when thinking about preventive detentions on security grounds in Canada, this is not necessarily the best way to proceed. As the Canadian Council for Refugees has correctly urged, "it may in fact be necessary to consider not only the security certificate cases, but also immigration security [detention] provisions more broadly, since security certificates are relatively rare, while other extremely problematic security [detention] provisions of the Immigration and Refugee Protection Act (IRPA) are routinely employed."[206] Some of these have already been examined in this chapter. Three interrelated sets of preventive detention provisions will be considered here: SC detentions, non-SC immigration detentions, and detentions of refugees under the 2001 *Anti-terrorism Act (ATA)*. All three will be examined in terms of the situation before 9/11 and after 9/11.

Before 9/11, the main law governing the preventive detention of refugees in Canada was the 1976 *Immigration Act (IA)*.[207] Under ss 39, 40, and 40.1, the Minister of Immigration and the Solicitor General of Canada (as the position was then known) could jointly issue SCs against persons who might be refugees or refugee claimants (together referred to as refugees in this book). Subject to certain strictures, they could do so if each had *reasonable grounds* to believe that the person had committed or would commit certain specified acts, and was thus a threat to the national security of Canada. In the case of permanent resident refugees, once proposed, the SC had to be referred to the Security

Intelligence Review Committee (SIRC). The purpose of the referral was for the SIRC to determine whether issuance of the SC would be warranted on the evidence. Based on SIRC's report, the Governor in Council might direct the Minister of Immigration to issue the SC. In the case of foreign national refugees, SCs had to be directly referred to a designated judge of the Federal Court, who determined whether the issuance of the SC was reasonable. If the SC was deemed unreasonable, it was quashed by that court. Thus, permanent resident refugees enjoyed greater procedural protections under the *IA* regime than their foreign national counterparts. In addition, as we shall see later, the issuance of an SC could, depending on a person's immigration status, lead to the person's mandatory detention.[208] As importantly, foreign national refugees were detained for at least 120 days before their very first detention reviews.[209] In Davies Bagambiire's view, the government had to make its case on the civil standard of a balance of probabilities.[210] This view is likely incorrect, however, as another highly regarded scholar has noted in another context that the wording "reasonable grounds to believe" implies a lower standard of proof than the civil standard.[211] In any case, as we shall see, subsequent case law strongly supported the latter view. Thus, the threshold for showing "reasonable grounds to believe" was remarkably low. Besides not needing to produce evidence that could convict the person in a court of law, the government did not even need to show that it was more likely than not that the person named in the SC had done or would commit the feared act.

Regarding the broader subcategory of non-SC preventive detention before 9/11, note that under the defunct *Immigration Act,* only senior immigration officers (SIO) and the Deputy Minister enjoyed the power to issue warrants for the arrest and detention of refugees if there were "reasonable grounds" to believe that they were inadmissible and either represented a danger to the public or constituted a flight risk.[212] This significantly restricted the number of officers who could issue such warrants.

As important, it has always been trite law in Canada that the *Criminal Code* does authorize the preventive detention of anyone, including refugees, on stated grounds, such as a reasonable belief that the person is about to commit a serious offence.[213] This was so even before 9/11, and such preventive detention powers could, of course, be deployed against refugees if any relevant official were to hold the kind of reasonable belief required in relation to any of them.

Just as significantly, the detention statistics for the period before 9/11 show, among other things, that (in part as a result of concerns over serious crime and security vulnerability) the rate of detention of immigration detainees (including many refugees) had been steadily increasing since 1996, long before 9/11.[214] These statistics also show that three of the seven persons who were being detained on security certificates as at 2002–03 had been detained before, not after, 9/11.[215] This is not at all surprising given that, as former Minister of Public Safety Anne McLellan, noted, Canada's pre-9/11 policies and practices in the immigration and national security area were shaped significantly by "the solid foundation and experience gained through many years of engagement on the issue of terrorism."[216]

Since 9/11, the primary source of law relating to this area has been the *Immigration and Refugee Protection Act,* a statute that was more or less set in its current form in the one-year period before 9/11 but only came into force in its entirety in June 2002. Sections 77 to 87.2 authorize the preventive detention of a refugee if the Minister of Public Safety and the Minister of Citizenship and Immigration jointly sign a security certificate stating that the person named in it is inadmissible, *inter alia,* on grounds of security, and if the two ministers also have reasonable grounds to believe that the person is either a danger to national security or the safety of any person, or a flight risk. However, such a certificate has to be referred to a designated judge of the Federal Court alongside the information and other evidence on which the SC is based.[217] The judge determines whether or not the SC is reasonable.[218] If the SC is declared unreasonable, it is quashed by the judge.[219]

As we shall see, before amendments in 2008, the *IRPA* did authorize the mandatory detention of some refugees who were named in such SCs.[220] In any case, the point is that from its very beginnings up to the present, the *IRPA* has always authorized the preventive detention of refugees named in SCs, whether or not that detention was automatic. Again, before 2008, foreign national refugees had to wait for at least 120 days after a judge had found SCs issued against them to be reasonable before their very first detention reviews could be held.[221] In practice, this could mean the detention of such refugees for years on end.[222] By contrast, although they have often been detained for prolonged periods as well, under the pre-2008 *IRPA* regime, permanent resident refugees named in SCs were guaranteed their first detention review within forty-eight hours of their arrest.[223] Since 2008, both categories of refugees have been entitled to this forty-eight-hour detention review.[224] There is no doubt whatsoever that the standard of proof that the government has to meet under the current *IRPA* provisions – the "reasonable grounds to believe" standard – in order to justify the detention of a refugee on a security certificate is "something more than mere suspicion, but less than the standard applicable in civil matters."[225] Thus, the standard of proof that the government must meet before naming a refugee in a security clearance or detaining him or her is as low after 9/11 as it was before 9/11.

Concerning other types of security-based preventive detentions of refugees, in effect, s 55(1) of the *IRPA* empowers any CBSA officer to issue a warrant of arrest against a refugee whom the officer has reasonable grounds to believe is inadmissible (including on security grounds) and is, in addition, either a flight risk or a danger to the public.[226] As we saw above, before 9/11 this specific power was restricted to senior enforcement officers and the Deputy Minister; thus, the *IRPA* did expand the arrest powers of junior enforcement officers, broadening the scope for mistakes and even abuse to occur. Section 58(1) of the *IRPA* is also novel in prescribing that a refugee's lack of cooperation in establishing his or her identity will be one of the main factors that can preclude release from preventive detention. This places one more obstacle in the path to freedom of detained refugees, and enhances the ability of enforcement officers to hold them in detention.

It must also not be forgotten that the *Anti-terrorism Act*, which was prepared after 9/11 and became law on December 18, 2001, confers some preventive detention powers on law enforcement agents.[227] Like everyone in Canada, refugees are subject to the exercise of these powers. Indeed, in practice, as the focus of Canada's anti-terrorism lens has largely been on immigrants, these powers are more likely than not to affect refugees.[228] Among other measures, the *ATA* introduced new procedures for preventive detention and investigative hearings into the *Criminal*

Code. Sections 83.3 and 83.3(4) of the *Criminal Code* allow peace officers to make arrests with a warrant where there are reasonable grounds to believe that a person will commit a terrorist act, or in exceptional cases to make an arrest without a warrant when it is believed that a terrorist act is about to occur and it is impractical to obtain the necessary warrant in time.[229] In addition, ss 83.28 and 83.29 allow a peace officer, for the purpose of investigation of a terrorism offence, to apply *ex parte* to a judge for an order to gather information relevant to that investigation, and this may lead to the examination of a person as a material witness (discussed in more detail below).[230] Clearly, many such material witnesses could be placed in preventive detention, especially if they are considered flight risks.

Some of the ways in which these *ATA* powers differ from similar powers under the pre-existing *Criminal Code* are discussed below. Suffice it to note here that by the time these provisions were abolished in 2007, some of the new *ATA* measures had not been utilized to a significant extent, and certainly not with respect to refugees.[231] Between 2002 and 2007, no arrests to prevent terrorist acts in Canada were made specifically under s 83.3(4) of the *Criminal Code*,[232] although a number of arrests were made subsequently under that provision.[233] There was also an attempt in 2016 to arrest one Aaron Driver, who was suspected of being about to carry out a terrorist attack imminently, but he was killed in the confrontation with police officers.[234] Similarly, very few applications were made for investigative hearings under ss 83.28 and 83.29 of the *Criminal Code*, or for a recognizance (which may involve detention for up to twelve months) under s 83.31.[235]

The turn to, and much greater utilization of, the strategy of "front-end screening" of refugees as they arrive in Canada, announced in the wake of the 9/11 attacks by the then Immigration Minister, is another measure that expanded the scope of and increased the opportunities for the preventive detention of refugees.[236] It increased the likelihood that a refugee would be held in detention on arrival, at least for some time, until any suspicion that the person posed a threat to national security was investigated and proved invalid.

Data on the government's expenses in the area of "managing access to Canada" (including interception, detention, and removal) demonstrates a significant decrease in expenditure between 1995 and 1999, followed by a gradual rise in 1999–2001, and a rapid hike of almost 75 percent in 2001–02, in the immediate aftermath of 9/11. After that date, the government allocated additional resources for immigration enforcement and screening proceedings. A budget tabled in December 2001 provided for an additional Cdn $7.7 billion for public security and anti-terrorist measures for 2001–07, out of which the former Citizenship and Immigration Canada (CIC) got $639.4 million.[237] After a hike between 2013 and 2015, the budget for this immigration enforcement item began to fall and remained relatively stable until 2018.[238] This budget line increased greatly thereafter, however, and in 2019 it amounted to about $1 billion under the government's strategy to deal with irregular asylum seekers.[239] What is more, in terms of the rate of detention of refugees, the difference between the pre-9/11 and post-9/11 periods may lie not necessarily in the numbers per se but in the underlying reasons for the use of detention. Given that it was most frequently applied in response to particular boat arrivals, much of the non-criminality-based immigration detention that occurred in Canada before 9/11 can be viewed as largely designed for deterrence. After 9/11, identification and containment of security threats began assuming a more prominent role in the preventive detention of those refugees who were not viewed as potential or actual criminal threats. Regarding SC-based detentions, as of 2015 such certificates had been issued against twenty-seven persons.[240] Three certificates were current as of December 2009,[241] and almost all the persons named in, and detained as a result of the issuance of, the last five certificates were refugees. As of 2017, all three SC detainees had been released from detention and subjected to some form of house arrest and/or electronic monitoring.[242]

As is evident from the above discussion, while the post-9/11 security vigil led to some changes in the character of the law relating to the preventive detention of refugees in Canada, there was at the very least as much continuity with, as there was change from, the period before 9/11. Canadian-issued SCs are hardly a post-9/11 innovation, having been used in Canada since 1978.[243] For example, far more SCs were issued in the ten years before 9/11 than in the eighteen years since. The fact that permanent resident refugees who were named in SCs enjoyed more procedural protections before 9/11 was clearly not due to the post-9/11 heightened security consciousness, but to provisions of the *IRPA*, the content of which had been settled before 9/11. Foreign national refugees named in SCs have actually enjoyed better detention rights at least since 2008 than they did before 9/11, as a result of the *Charkaoui v Canada* decision and the consequent amendment of the *IRPA*.[244] The very low standard of proof for the issuance of SCs and the detention of refugees under them pre-dates 9/11. Also, the expansion of the general detention powers of junior immigration enforcement officers wrought by the *IRPA* was clearly not a post-9/11 development. Even the "new" detention powers authorized by the *ATA* were already substantially authorized under the pre-9/11 version of the *Criminal Code*. And despite a significant hike after 9/11, the rate of preventive detention of non-citizens (including refugees) had been rising steadily since 1996, long before the 9/11 attacks.

This is not to say, however, that there were no changes in the preventive detention regime as it applied to refugees after 9/11. The turn to front-end security screening, and its vastly increased use, was largely a post-9/11 innovation. Undoubtedly, some aspects of the investigative hearings powers provided for under the *ATA* were new, such as the power to detain a person considered a material witness *before* criminal proceedings had been commenced against someone in connection with that investigation, and the power to detain such a witness even when no offence had yet been committed.[245] There was also a post-9/11 spike in the funding allocated by the government for immigration detention and other such enforcement measures, and a more moderate increase in the numbers of those preventively detained by the immigration authorities, including refugees. As important, 9/11 led to the allocation of a greater share of the overall detention pie to those subject to preventive detention. On the whole, therefore, as new as some of the relevant legal provisions and practices were, with regard to this specific aspect of the detention regime, 9/11 appears to have initiated a process of intensification rather than one of innovation. The post-9/11 preventive immigration detention situation was much like that before 9/11, only more so.

The Anti-terrorism Act 2015 (Bill C-51), which is different from the one passed soon after 9/11, was another post-9/11 development in the law that fortified the anti-terror legislative framework in Canada even more, in a way that can, of course, affect refugees. Among other things, it expanded the preventive detention and peace bond powers of the law enforcement agencies, and lessened the evidentiary thresholds (thereby expanding the utility of some of their law enforcement powers).[246] The Act amended the relevant statutes so that, when seeking to obtain a "recognizance with conditions" order, which would theoretically be used to detain a suspect linked to a threat of terrorism, law enforcement officers would no longer be required to prove to a judge that a terrorism offence "will be carried out," but need only establish that it "may be carried out." It also replaced the requirement that the recognizance order must be "necessary to prevent" the offence with the less stringent "is likely to prevent." Finally, Bill C-51 increased the maximum time a terrorism suspect could be held from three days to seven days.[247]

The Canadian situation in this area is not as different from the US situation as some might expect. For one, unlike the US security certificate regime, which was basically introduced after 9/11, the Canadian equivalent (the basis of the preventive detention of many refugees and other non-citizens) was already in place long before 9/11. The Canadian situation was thus actually worse on this score. Both countries apply rather loose standards in determining the appropriateness of both the certification of refugees and other non-citizens as security threats and their preventive detention as a result. The United States simply applied this already loose standard with slightly less restraint and greater frequency. After 9/11, both countries expanded the preventive detention powers of law enforcement officers in a way that is relevant to refugees, but although the *IRPA* did expand the detention powers of CBSA officers, this was not a post-9/11 innovation. It was the *ATA*'s grant of these broader powers to law enforcement agents in general that was in some senses innovative. As important, in line with a similar spike in the United States, there was a steep spike in the national totals of persons subject to immigration detention in Canada in 2002–03 (within months of 9/11).[248] Since 9/11, however, Canada has continued to place in preventive detention far fewer refugees and other non-citizens than the United States,[249] both in terms of their absolute numbers and as a percentage of their respective total immigrant populations.[250] One general indication of this fact is that, as we saw earlier in this chapter, there have not been any mass roundups in Canada on anything close to the scale in the United States. The US immigration bureaucracy has also relied on a wider range of administrative memos, policies, procedures, and regulations than its Canadian counterparts in justifying the preventive detention of refugees and other non-citizens. This has created a somewhat looser legal framework for preventive immigration detentions in that country. On the whole, however, there has been as much similarity as difference in the nature of, and changes made to, the post-9/11 preventive detention regimes of both countries. The difference has been largely in the scale of preventive detentions.

Mandatory/Automatic Detentions for Security Reasons

The US Position

Prior to the passage of the *Illegal Immigration Reform and Immigrant Responsibility Act* in 1996, "most asylum seekers were released" before any assessment of whether or not they posed a security threat to the United States.[251] However, public reports of some abuses of this process led to the inclusion of language in the *IIRIRA* that made "the detention of asylum applicants the norm rather than the exception."[252] This was a pre-9/11 development.

In any case, although the more general requirement that any refugee or other non-citizen who is suspected of constituting a security threat to the United States must be detained by immigration enforcement authorities is not altogether novel under US law, before 9/11 most such detainees were eligible for a bond hearing before an Immigration Judge.[253] The INS also had the discretion to grant or refuse bail to these suspects.[254] In addition, before 9/11 and in spite of the passage into law of the *Anti-Terrorism and Effective Death Penalty Act* and the *Illegal Immigration Reform and Immigrant Responsibility Act*, the federal courts retained relatively broad jurisdiction to review the Attorney General's decision to detain a non-citizen, whether or not that person was classified as a security threat.[255] These key procedural protections were eroded almost overnight, however, by the passage of the *PATRIOT Act* in the immediate aftermath of 9/11.

The *PATRIOT Act* was rushed through both chambers of Congress ostensibly in order to, *inter alia,* authorize the detention of suspected terrorists and other perceived threats to US national security.[256] It was introduced just over one week after the attacks and was signed into law by President Bush about a month later, on October 26, 2001.[257] For present purposes, s 412 of the *Act* is the operative provision. The revised, post–*PATRIOT Act Immigration and Nationality Act* thus reads similarly.[258] As noted earlier, this amended provision prescribes the mandatory detention until removal from the United States of any non-citizen who is certified in accordance with the rest of the provision. The *INA* now clearly states that the "Attorney General *shall* take into custody any alien who is certified under [the above-discussed] paragraph (3)."[259] It may be of historical interest to some that similar certification and mandatory detention powers would have been granted to the Attorney General by s 3142 of the defunct House version of the *9/11 Recommendations Implementation Act.* This *Act* would have modified s 3142 of Title 18 of the *United States Code* to mandate the automatic pre-trial detention of all suspected terrorists certified in accordance with that provision.

As the revised *INA* provision states, prior to certification of any person under this section, the Attorney General must have "reasonable grounds to believe" that the person meets the requirements stated therein. This statutory test for certification has been described by one commentator as "an extremely low standard."[260] However, although Lofgren notes that this test has generally been considered lower than the "probable cause" test for lawful searches in the United States, another commentator has cited one BIA decision in 2000 that interpreted "reasonable grounds to believe" to mean the same thing as probable cause.[261] One thing is certain: in refugee law, wording similar to that of the test for certification has been widely interpreted by the courts as denoting a lower standard than the "balance of probabilities" (or "more likely than not") test used in civil proceedings.[262] This is trite knowledge.

Also worthy of note is the fact that when read as a whole, ss 212(a)(3)(B) and 237(a)(4)(B) of the *INA* may also require the detention of the spouses and children of persons certified and detained under the *PATRIOT Act,* whether or not these spouses and children are themselves refugees.[263]

Importantly, especially in contradistinction to the pre-9/11 situation, there is no discretion given to either the immigration enforcement authorities or the immigration courts (not the regular federal courts) to grant bail to those certified suspects who neither pose a danger to the community nor constitute a flight risk.[264] The provision is thus overbroad in this respect.[265] What is more, the Attorney General is in effect permitted by the *PATRIOT Act* to rely on little more than suspicion and the non-citizen status of a person in order to certify and detain that person.[266] As a result, the detention of some certified non-citizens under s 412 of the *PATRIOT Act* may, under certain conditions, likely constitute an unreasonable exercise of the US government's detention powers, and thus violate the substantive due process rights of many detained non-citizens.

However, if the decision of the US Supreme Court in *Carlson v Landon* over fifty-five years ago is to control the outcome of a court challenge on the validity of this provision, the prospects of the impugned provision of s 412 being struck down by the courts will be dim.[267] In that case, the Court declined to find a violation of substantive due process in a case involving the mandatory detention under the then-operative *Internal Security Act* of non-citizens in the United States who were considered members of the Communist Party. The chief reason for the Court's decision to uphold the challenged law was that, although the law allowed the Attorney General to do so, statistics showed that the Attorney General had refrained from detaining every single member of this class of non-citizens who had been arrested.[268] We must remember, however, that the key difference between this case and a case that could be made against s 412 of the *PATRIOT Act* is that under the old law the Attorney General had some discretion not to detain persons identified as suspected communists, whereas the new regime wrought by the *PATRIOT Act* allows no such discretion. Under the current *INA*, once the Attorney General certifies a person as a suspected security threat, detention of the suspect is automatic/mandatory.

Nevertheless, it is doubtful that the US Supreme Court would have been, or will in the future be, prepared to strike down s 412 and the new *INA* regime. The Court has much more recently ruled in favour of the mandatory detention of non-citizens just because they fit a predetermined category – that is, when such detention is based on what the Court referred to as "reasonable presumptions and generic rules."[269] In so doing, it parted ways with the US Court of Appeals for the Ninth Circuit, and held that substantive due process does *not* always require that individualized determinations be made before "someone is locked away." In other words, even when certified suspects neither pose a danger to the community nor constitute a flight risk, they can be detained, potentially indefinitely, without a prior individualized risk assessment. The procedural due process protections (contained in the due process clause of the Fifth Amendment to the US Constitution) enjoyed by some non-citizens in the United States are also threatened by the fact that under the *PATRIOT Act,* the decision to certify, and thus to detain, is not made by a judicial officer at a hearing, and the non-citizen is not afforded an adequate opportunity to present evidence at a hearing in rebuttal of the government's case against her or him.[270] The non-citizen may present only written submissions and evidence to the Attorney General requesting reconsideration of the certification.[271] The accentuation of the denial of procedural due process that is involved in both decisions to certify and detain is, to a significant extent, a post-9/11 innovation in US non-citizen law.

Furthermore, post-9/11, the federal courts no longer enjoy the virtually unrestricted jurisdiction that they previously possessed to review and hear appeals from the Attorney General's decision to detain a non-citizen. Section 412 of the *PATRIOT Act* and the new *INA* s 236A(b)(3) have brought about some slight changes in the nature of the pre-9/11 regime. While any competent federal District Court can still review the certification decision in itself (including by implication the decision to detain), such a review can be done only by way of the specific writ of *habeas corpus,* with all of its particular strictures and requirements.[272] And while the decision of any such federal court can still be appealed, such appeals now lie exclusively within the jurisdiction of only one circuit of the US Court of Appeals, the District of Columbia Circuit.[273]

It must be noted, however, that some due process protections were built into the new regime. Aside from the fact that the detained non-citizen may request the Attorney General for reconsideration, the Attorney General must review the certification every six months and may release the detained person if he or she deems that to be the appropriate course of action.[274] Note that, limited as it is, certified persons still enjoy a right to apply for judicial review of the Attorney General's decision not to release them from detention.

In February 2017, the Trump Administration issued three executive orders on immigration/refugees. Together they constituted a dramatic push toward "a new regime of large-scale detention" of refugees (and other non-citizens).[275] As one study correctly observes: "The Border Enforcement Order [in particular] calls for a massive expansion of the existing system, greatly increasing the number of refugees and other migrants subject to detention. There are no exceptions made in any of its provisions for asylum seekers."[276]

The Canadian Position

Aspects of the nature of the Canadian security certificate regime have already been discussed, if only in outline. The discussion here will be limited to the issue of the mandatory or automatic detention of refugees and other non-citizens who have been named in such SCs.

Section 40.1(2) of the 1976 *Immigration Act*, which was in force until June 2002, provided for the mandatory detention of any foreign national (FN) refugee named in a security certificate. The person would remain in detention until removed, unless the Minister of Immigration or a designated judge ordered that person's release.[277] By contrast, permanent resident (PR) refugees named in security certificates were not automatically detained.[278] Thus, in a formal sense, PR refugees enjoyed more protections during this era in this regard than their FN counterparts. In reality, many PR and FN refugees were detained under the *Immigration Act*'s SC regime. It did not seem to make all that much difference for PRs that their detention under such circumstances was not mandatory. Virtually all PRs against whom security certificates were issued were detained anyway.[279]

Under the pre-2008 form of the *Immigration and Refugee Protection Act*, which replaced the *Immigration Act* in June 2002, this legal position continued. The old s 82(2) of the *IRPA*, "Mandatory Detention," had provided that a foreign national named in a security certificate should be detained without the issuance of a warrant. The two ministers (i.e., the Minister of Immigration and the Minister of Public Safety) had no discretion in the matter: named FNs had to be detained on the issuance of the certificate. They could, however, be released by the Minister, or failing that, by a designated judge at their detention review. As we have seen, however, the first such review took place within 120 days after the SC had been deemed reasonable by a designated judge. By contrast, under this same regime, permanent residents named in a security certificate were to be detained only if the two ministers had "reasonable grounds to believe" that they were a national security threat, a danger to any person, or a flight risk. Thus, unlike for FN refugees, no mandatory detention procedure was prescribed for PR refugees under this regime. The two ministers had discretion to decide whether or not to detain them. In practice, however, it did not make a difference under the pre-2008 *IRPA* whether persons named in security certificates were permanent residents or foreign nationals. All were detained anyway.[280]

Under the current, post-2008 version of the *IRPA*, s 81 eliminated the distinction between permanent residents and foreign nationals for the purposes of the detention of those named in security certificates. More importantly, it abolished the mandatory detention procedure for all persons named in SCs, meaning that neither FNs nor PRs named in SCs would be detained automatically. The ministers now have broad discretion whether or not to detain a named refugee, be they FNs or PRs. What is more, both kinds of named persons now enjoy the same kind of speedy detention review. The first such review must take place within forty-eight hours after the start of detention.[281]

The elimination of mandatory detention under this new security certificate detention regime was partly in response to the overall tone (though not the actual reasoning) of the Supreme Court of Canada decision in *Charkaoui* and partly in response to pressure from pro-immigrant groups and the relevant parliamentary committee.[282] In *Charkaoui*, the Supreme Court, *inter alia*, struck down the system in place for the use of secret evidence in the security certificate process, and held that the lack of review for foreign nationals until 120 days after the reasonableness of a certificate had been judicially determined violated the constitutional guarantee against arbitrary detention.[283] In the same decision, however, the Supreme Court rejected the argument that the mandatory detention of foreign nationals was arbitrary because it was effected without regard to the personal circumstances of detainees.[284] According to the Supreme Court:

> Detention is not arbitrary where there are "standards rationally re-lated to the purpose of the power of detention" ... The triggering event for the detention of a foreign national is the signing of a cer-tificate stating that the foreign national is inadmissible on grounds of security ... The security ground is based on the danger posed by the named person, and therefore provides a rational foundation for the detention.[285]

The Supreme Court also rejected the argument that this regime violated the rule of law, holding that "the rule of law does not categorically prohibit automatic detention."[286] By contrast, the Canadian Council for Refugees had long argued that the rules relating to the detention of those subject to a security certificate, including mandatory detention of those who were not permanent residents, did lead to violations of basic rights.[287] Similarly, a Special Senate Committee had recommended the elimination of the mandatory detention scheme even before the *Charkaoui* decision was handed down.[288] To its credit, the government accepted these contrary arguments and eliminated the mandatory deten-tion procedure from the *IRPA*'s SC detention regime, even though the Supreme Court of Canada had upheld it.

It is clear, however, that the mandatory detention regime in Canada in relation to security certificates was much the same before and after 9/11. The *Immigration Act* continued in force well after 9/11, and the *IRPA* basically maintained the pre-9/11 position. The situation did not worsen in this respect as a result of 9/11. When change occurred about seven years after 9/11, it was not really because of the post-9/11 security vigil, and in fact brought about significant improvement compared with the pre-9/11 regime.

In contrast, the position in the United States did deteriorate signifi-cantly after and as a result of the events of 9/11. Although mandatory detention of refugees did exist under the *IIRIRA* regime before 9/11, the post-9/11 *PATRIOT Act* significantly expanded the possibility and practice of such mandatory detention. It should be noted, however, that the negative post-9/11 changes in the United States merely brought US laws and practices on par (in most respects) with the bad pre-2008 Canadian situation, so that, a few years after 9/11, both the Canadian and US legal positions looked similar. The key difference before 2008 was that, unlike in the United States, the mandatory security certificate detention regime in Canada did not apply to permanent resident refugees. Since 2008, however, the two relevant national non-citizen detention regimes have diverged in an important way: mandatory SC detentions no longer exist in Canada, whereas that procedure still applies in the United States.

Material Witness Detentions

The US Position

Prior to 9/11, the relevant US federal government authorities possessed lawful authority to detain persons considered by a court to be material witnesses in criminal investigations should the court reasonably suspect that they pose a flight risk.[289] This power was granted to these authorities by the *Bail Reform Act of 1984*.[290] To be sure, it was sometimes used by the US government in the years between the passage of the *Act* and 9/11, primarily in the immigration and refugee law area. Indeed, before 9/11, 94 percent of all those detained as material witnesses were held by the former INS.[291]

In the immediate aftermath of the 9/11 attacks, however, there was a "dramatic rise" in the number of material witness arrests and detentions involving non-citizens, many of whom were refugees.[292] The government initially did not reveal how many persons were detained on material witness warrants, but subsequently admitted to holding forty to fifty material witnesses as of 2004.[293] At least seventy individuals were detained as material witnesses after 9/11.[294] A significant number were refugees awaiting review of their applications for asylum.[295] That this increase was largely attributable to the sense of heightened security vulnerability as a result of 9/11 is underscored by the manner in which the incidence of such detentions tapered off in subsequent months and years.[296] As important, as Heidee Stoller and colleagues have noted, much credible suspicion exists that these detentions were used after 9/11 for reasons other than to secure testimony, and more as preventive detention.[297] Indeed, although this power of detention was conferred on the US government in order to secure the testimony of witnesses, about one-third to one-half of all those detained after 9/11 never testified before their release.[298]

The Canadian Position

As Martin Friedland has noted, the Canadian *Criminal Code* has historically allowed the detention of material witnesses as a way of compelling their testimony, but only if they had failed to obey a subpoena and only after the commencement of the relevant criminal proceedings.[299] This power was already in existence well before 9/11. Soon after 9/11, however, law enforcement was given additional power. As we have seen, ss 83.28 and 83.29 of the *Criminal Code,* which were added to it by the post-9/11 adoption of the *Anti-terrorism Act,* ultimately allow for the arrest and detention of a person as a material witness even before a charge has been filed against anyone, i.e., before the relevant criminal proceedings have even commenced. This is basically an investigative power, and, as the government itself has acknowledged, "it authorizes the [relevant] judge to order the examination of a material witness who may possess information regarding a terrorist offence that has been, or may be, committed."[300] This significant expansion of law enforcement's power immediately after 9/11 had great potential to affect refugees in Canada, but the power expired in March 2007, when the "sunset clause" that had been built into the relevant provisions of the *ATA* took effect.[301]

Until 2007, the Canadian legal position after 9/11 was not all that different from the US situation. Non-citizens (including refugees) could be, and were, detained as material witnesses in the United States even before the criminal proceedings at which they were supposedly going to testify had been commenced against anyone.[302] In Canada, refugees could also be detained on the same basis. Before 2007, the main difference between the two regimes lay in their implementation. Although a large number of non-citizens in the United States were in effect placed in preventive detention as material witnesses after and as a result of the 9/11 attacks, only one person was ever explicitly detained as a material witness in Canada under ss 83.28 and 83.29 of the *Criminal Code* (i.e., under the *ATA*), and this was not done because of 9/11 or post-911 terrorist plots or actions.[303] Rather, the person was detained as a result of the Air India case – a matter concerning events that took place in 1985.

Since 2007, however, the situations in the two countries have diverged widely. In Canada, the pre-9/11 positions on material witness detention are operative once again: unlike in the United States, a refugee or other person can no longer be arrested as a material witness *before* the commencement of the relevant criminal proceedings. There is also much less scope in Canada for using material witness detentions for preventive purposes under ss 83.28 and 83.29 of the *Criminal Code*.

Prolonged and/or Indefinite Detentions

The US Position
In the cases of both mandatory detention under the *PATRIOT Act* and the use of material witness detention, the length of time that 9/11 detainees have spent in detention is as relevant to the present discussion as the nature of the legal authorities invoked for such detentions. In many cases, refugees and other non-citizens have been kept in lengthy or even indefinite detention while awaiting resolution of their immigration matters, including review of their applications for refuge in the United States.

Although before 9/11 the incidence of lengthy or indefinite detention of non-citizens was not as salient an issue as it currently is, it was nevertheless a matter of serious concern. Clearly, immigration authorities had the power to hold in custody any non-citizen who was the subject of an immigration charge, as long as that person was considered a flight risk or a national security threat.[304] From 1996 onward, these authorities were also mandated by the *IIRIRA* regime to detain *any* non-citizen against whom a removal order had been issued.[305] Such a person could lawfully be held by immigration authorities during a ninety-day removal period.[306] More controversially, the Attorney General could order the continued detention, well past the ninety-day removal period, of any such non-citizen suspected of being inadmissible either for national security reasons or on certain grounds of serious criminality – as long as that person was first determined by the Attorney General to constitute a serious risk to the community or to be unlikely to comply with the removal order.[307] As we have seen in the Introduction, when we considered the so-called Zadvydas problem, this extraordinary detention power directly challenged the due process rights that the US Supreme Court had held were to be enjoyed by even non-citizens who have already been ordered removed from the United States.[308]

As has already been discussed at length in the Introduction, the decision in *Zadvydas v Davis* was handed down on June 18, 2001, a few months before the 9/11 attacks. In it, the Supreme Court held that 8 USC s 1231(a)(6), the *IIRIRA* provision that authorized the lengthy detention past the ninety-day removal period of removable non-citizens, did not also authorize their indefinite detention.[309] However, this same decision allowed at least a couple of loopholes. The first involved the indefinite detention of especially dangerous persons and those considered to be serious national security risks (such as terrorist suspects); the second was the case of those non-citizens who had not yet been lawfully admitted into the United States. However, the latter was unexpectedly closed off by the Supreme Court in January 2005 in *Clark v Martinez*, leaving immigration authorities with less scope to detain non-citizens indefinitely.[310]

It was the "national security" loophole that was exploited by Attorney General John Ashcroft when he issued in November 2001 a regulation that basically allowed, *inter alia*, the indefinite detention of non-citizens against whom a final removal order had been issued and who were either deemed to be national security risks, determined to be especially dangerous, or detained on account of the adverse foreign policy consequences of their being released – if no country could be found to which they could be removed.[311] Thus, after 9/11, the Attorney General could, under certain conditions, still certify a non-citizen as a national security threat and detain the person indefinitely, subject to recertification every six months.[312] This detention power is reinforced by s 412 of the *PATRIOT Act*, which introduced a new s 236(A)(a) into the text of the *Immigration and Nationality Act*.[313]

In practice, indefinite detention has continued to be imposed by US authorities on far too many 9/11 detainees, many of them refugees. A survey conducted in 2002 by the *New Jersey Law Journal* found that twelve of eighty-five such detainees had been "stuck in detention with no cnd in sight."[314] In a few cases, detainees waited as long as five months for immigration authorities to lay an initial charge against them.[315] And despite *Zadvydas*, even those 9/11 detainees who had already been ordered removed (often for minor immigration violations) were too often kept in detention by immigration enforcement authorities after removal orders had been issued against them, just so the FBI could investigate and clear them of any involvement in terrorism.[316] Although this practice was ended in January 2002, it had important implications until that date for the overall length of time that 9/11 detainees were kept in detention.[317]

Similarly, unduly prolonged stays in detention have been the lot of too many of the Muslims and Arabs who were rounded up in the aftermath of the 9/11 attacks. As David Cole has shown, a large number of these detainees who had agreed to leave the country voluntarily and who had been given voluntary departure orders were still held in detention thereafter, not because the authorities had any reasonable grounds to suspect that they were involved in terrorism or posed a national security risk or were especially dangerous, but basically to facilitate the FBI's investigation of the 9/11 attacks.[318] The average length of time that a 9/11 detainee spent in detention until being cleared by the FBI was eighty days – nearly three months.[319] And only about 3 percent of these detainees were cleared within three *weeks* of being placed in detention.[320] As the OIG Report found, the FBI clearance process was inefficient, resulting in undue delays that kept detainees in detention far longer than necessary.[321] In any case, another study found that, overall, refugees in the United States often spent a similarly lengthy period in detention. Fifteen percent were detained for longer than six months, while the mean length of detention overall was sixty-nine days (over two months).[322] Overall, a majority were released within one month but, as we saw earlier, the length of detention of refugees who were also national security suspects was much longer.

Overall, the post-9/11 immigration detention practices of the United States have been described in the OIG Report as marked and marred by too many instances of unnecessary initial or continued detention, leading to unduly lengthy or even indefinite stays in detention by refuges and other non-citizens.[323] As David Martin has put it, the Department of Justice often "did not follow through with needed measures to file charges in a timely fashion, to keep detention to a minimum, or to release or deport promptly those whose continued detention should not have been seen as justifiable."[324] Most remarkably, the main thrust of this criticism was not denied in the responses of the Departments of Homeland Security and Justice to the OIG Report.[325]

The Canadian Position

The indefinite and even unduly prolonged detention of refugees and other non-citizens who have not been convicted of any crime and sentenced to imprisonment has long been abhorred in Canadian law – at least on paper. For example, the *Guidelines on Detention* issued by the Immigration and Refugee Board (IRB), in force since March 12, 1998, notes that "Canadian Law regards preventive detention [which is what immigration detention is] as an exceptional measure. This general principle stems from statute and case law, and is enshrined in the Canadian Charter of Rights and Freedoms ... International law ... respects the same principle."[326] Yet there is no hard and fast rule, no firm measure, by which detention is viewed as unduly prolonged or even indefinite. It is settled law in Canada that as long as the initial decision to detain the person was lawful and the specific length of time at issue is deemed by the relevant judge to be reasonable "given all the circumstances," even detention for a prolonged period will be upheld as lawful.[327] Thus, whatever the legal position regarding indefinite detentions, exceptions to the general prohibition on prolonged detentions do exist. The law has sought to guard against the illegal, unduly prolonged, or indefinite detentions of refugee and other non-citizens through the institution of timely detention reviews. The nature of these reviews will be outlined below as part of our more general consideration of the law and practice in Canada relating to prolonged or indefinite detentions before and after 9/11.

The incidence of prolonged detention of refugees and other non-citizens was less salient in public consciousness before 9/11, but even during this era Canadian immigration and other law enforcement authorities could, under the 1976 *Immigration Act,* hold refugees for prolonged periods. Under this *Act,* this could be done either 1) under the more general power to detain non-citizens until their identities are proven, or as inadmissible on security or other grounds while being flight risks or dangers to the public; or 2) under the security certificate process.[328] Nevertheless, the *Immigration Act* did prescribe that in type 1 situations, detention reviews must be held within forty-eight hours after the initial detention, and thereafter within 7 days, and if necessary thereafter within every 30-day period.[329] The same *Act* also provided that in type 2 situations, the timing of such reviews depended on the immigration status of the person named in the security certificate. Permanent residents were entitled to a detention review within forty-eight hours of their initial detention, and thereafter at least once within every six-month period.[330] Foreign nationals were entitled to the first such review within 120 days after the decision to name them in a security certificate was deemed reasonable – a provision that in practice meant that such persons tended to spend several years in detention. One main reason for this was that it often took a very long time for their SC cases to get to the point where the designated judge would rule on its reasonableness.

Significantly prolonged and even indefinite detentions did result from both type 1 and type 2 detentions. For example, the courts in *Lin v Canada (Minister of Citizenship and Immigration)* and *Canada (Minister of Citizenship and Immigration) v Liang* decried type 1 detentions – even when justified or lasting only a few months – as usually taking a heavy toll on the detained refugees.[331] The judge in *Lin* also pointed out that it took almost two years to release all of those who had arrived by boat in 1999 on Canada's west coast.[332] In *Liang*, the judge noted that the refugee had been detained for about one and a half years by the time of this decision to release him.[333] With regard to type 2 (i.e., security certificate) cases, it is important to note that Mansour Ahani was detained for about nine years before his deportation in 2002; Mahmoud Jaballah was detained for the second time between August 2001 and April 2007 (five and a half years), initially under the *Immigration Act;* and Mohammad Mahjoub was detained between June 2000 and February 2007 (six and a half years).[334] In all three cases, the detention was clearly prolonged; more controversial is whether they were unduly prolonged, and even more controversial is whether they were indefinite at some point. These issues will be dealt with in more detail below.

The basic legal position under the *Immigration and Refugee Protection Act* (which, it is important to re-emphasize, was drafted before 9/11 but came into effect in June 2002) is not all that different. Legal authorities (1) and (2) outlined above continue to apply to this day.[335] The law relating to the entitlement of detained non-citizens to detention reviews remains largely the same as well.[336] The main difference between the legal position under the defunct *Immigration Act* and the position under the current version of the *IRPA* is that, as we have seen, since the recent amendments to the latter came into effect in 2008, there is no longer a distinction between permanent residents and foreign nationals who are subject to a security certificate with regard to the timing of their detention reviews. Both types of refugees are now entitled to a detention review within forty-eight hours of their initial detention, and to the subsequent minimum six-monthly reviews.[337]

In practice, a significant (if perhaps not all that massive) increase in the incidence of prolonged detention in Canada occurred after 9/11. There was a noticeable, though not huge, jump in the number of days spent in detention by refugees and other non-citizens detained on the type 1 grounds outlined above.[338] Similarly, some refugees who were named in security certificates after 9/11 have suffered prolonged (and, more arguably, indefinite) detention. The case of Hassan Almrei, a Syrian national and refugee in Canada aptly illustrates this. Detained in October 2001, he was released only on January 2, 2009, over seven years later.[339] He could not be deported until the Minister of Citizenship and Immigration issued a "danger opinion," yet two such opinions had been quashed by the Federal Court. It was clear that his removal from Canada was not a "done deal" and would not occur within a reasonable time. The time he spent in detention became so lengthy partly because the relevant judges found that his release would pose a danger to national security and so refused to release him for years, and partly because of delays occasioned by his understandable decision to challenge in the courts the issuance of the security certificate against him. Less favourably compared with persons in a similar position, it has also been suggested that the delay was due in large part to Almrei's decision in 2003 to recant some of his previous testimony.[340]

There is no doubt whatsoever that Almrei's detention for over seven years was prolonged; the question is whether it was unduly so. Was it indefinite? And if so, was it illegal? In *Charkaoui*, the Supreme Court of Canada took the view that while "the IRPA in principle imposes detention only pending deportation, it may in fact permit lengthy and indeterminate detention or lengthy periods subject to onerous release conditions."[341] In the end, the Court reasoned that the prolonged detention suffered by Almrei and others did not violate the *Canadian Charter of Rights and Freedoms*.[342] According to the Supreme Court:

> The IRPA interpreted in conformity with the *Charter*, permits robust ongoing judicial review of the continued need for and justice of the detainee's detention pending deportation. On this basis, I conclude that extended periods of detention pending deportation under the certificate provisions of the IRPA do not violate s.7 or s.12 of the *Charter*, provided that reviewing courts adhere to the guidelines set out above [relating to the reasons for detention, length of time detained, which party is responsible for the delay, and the availability of alternatives to detention].[343]

Thus, to the Supreme Court, although prolonged and/or indefinite detention is to be abhorred in general, depending on the circumstances, immigration detention on security grounds may still be legal in Canada, even when it is either prolonged or indefinite, or both. While indefinite detention would hardly ever be sanctioned by the courts, with respect to national security cases, it would in practice be permissible under the language used by the Supreme Court, so long as it is based on a formal system of robust periodic review.[344]

Thus, despite one or two differences, the formal legal position with regard to the use of prolonged and/or indefinite detention in Canada was much the same before and after 9/11. It is true that with the 2008 amendments, there is on paper much less scope for such detention of foreign nationals named in security certificates. In practice, however, prolonged and/or indefinite detention of refugees was as possible before 9/11 as it has been thereafter. The key difference seems to be in the way in which the relevant legal norms have been implemented since

9/11 – with more intensity after 9/11, so that overall, more refugees and other non-citizens have spent longer in immigration detention than before 9/11. This trend was confirmed in 2017 by the Federal Court decision in *Alvin John Brown v Canada*.[345] Although the case did not concern a refugee as such, the Court held that once the detention and its continuation have been subjected to a fair process, the Canadian state can detain people for significant periods of time. And by refusing to specify any upper time limit to the length of time a refugee or other non-citizen may be detained in the process of being removed from the country, the Court also affirmed that such lengthy detentions are not illegal merely because of the prolonged periods involved, or their indefiniteness.[346]

Compared with the US position, the Canadian situation is not all that different in terms of the nature of the relevant formal legal provisions. While US immigration authorities have always enjoyed broader powers to detain a wider class of refugees for longer periods than their Canadian equivalents, the difference was not all that great before 9/11. Indeed, some may argue, not without some justification, that factoring in the existence of a security certificate system in Canada before 9/11, a process that was not introduced in the United States until after 9/11, means that the Canadian position was at best at par with the US one – at least on paper. The key difference between the two jurisdictions after 9/11 is that while both countries gave their law enforcement agents similar legal powers to issue security certificates, the US agencies were more explicit in claiming the right to detain refugees and other non-citizens suspected of being national security threats for prolonged and/or indefinite periods. In Canada, while prolonged detentions were noted and justified by the relevant authorities, indefinite detentions tended to occur without the relevant officials claiming legal powers to keep non-citizens so detained, and without such detentions being explicitly acknowledged as such. On a practical level, overall, the practice of prolonged and/or indefinite detention has occurred on a much broader scale in the United States. Thus, the main difference between the two countries was not in the nature of the relevant formal legal texts but in the way those texts were implemented after 9/11.

Secret Detentions

The US Position
In the wake of the 9/11 attacks, and despite opposition from some members of Congress, civil liberties groups, and the media, the US government concealed the names, citizenship status, locations, legal counsel, reasons for detention, and other such information concerning a large number of the more than one thousand Muslims and Arabs rounded up and detained as part of the domestic response to those attacks, many of them refugees.[347] Although the government willingly released some of this information with respect to some of the detainees, the names and locations of arrest and detention of a large number of others were kept secret.[348] The implementation of this policy, especially through denial of the freedom of information requests filed by a number of groups, led to a lawsuit, *Center for National Security Studies, et al v United States Department of Justice*, in which the plaintiffs asked the US District Court for the District of Columbia to order the public disclosure of this information.[349] Other such suits were brought,[350] but because this case became the most well known, we will focus on it here.

In its attempt to justify the secret jailing for investigative purposes of these 9/11 detainees, the government argued that, *inter alia*, Exemption 7A in the US *Freedom of Information Act (FOIA)*, "which protects from disclosure any information 'compiled for law enforcement purposes' whenever it 'could reasonably be expected to interfere with enforcement proceedings,'" allows the sorts of secret detentions that it had practised against most of the 9/11 detainees.[351] It offered three main reasons in support of its contention that release of the requested information was likely to prejudice its 9/11 investigations:

1.   On learning of the detention of a member of their organization, terrorist groups may refuse to deal further with this member, or may threaten them, thereby eliminating a valuable source of information.[352]

2.   The public release of this information would allow terrorist organizations to map the progress of the investigation and thereby develop means to impede them.[353]

3.   The public release of the names of the 9/11 detainees could allow terrorist organizations and others to interfere with pending proceedings by creating false or misleading evidence.

The plaintiffs disagreed with these arguments for the reasons offered in the Court's decision and discussed below.

The Court concluded that the government must release the identities (names) of all of its 9/11 detainees and of the legal counsel representing them. However, it declined to order the government to disclose the dates and locations of detention of these detainees. With regard to the release of the identities of the detainees and their lawyers, the court reasoned that the government's first argument was unpersuasive and undemonstrated because 1) it assumed that terrorists did not already know which of their members were detained, yet the government acknowledged that terrorists were free to contact whomever they wanted; 2) the government had contradicted itself by making extensive disclosures of the same kind of information it wanted to keep secret; and 3) the government had not discharged its burden of establishing a "rational link" between release of the names and the alleged harms – its affidavits merely assumed this link and did not come close to demonstrating it.[354] The Court also rejected the government's second and third arguments based on similar logic.[355]

The government's co-reliance on Exemptions 7C and 7F of the *FOIA* (protecting privacy interests and personal safety) was also rejected by the Court. The government had argued that release of the information would forever connect these detainees to the 9/11 attacks, causing them "embarrassment, humiliation, risk of retaliation, harassment, and possibly even physical harm."[356] The Court held that although the detainees did have the kind of substantial privacy interests that the government argued for, these interests must be balanced against the strong public interest in disclosure regarding the nature of the exercise of the government's extraordinary power of detention.[357] In the end, the Court concluded that "detainees wishing to keep their names confidential may opt out of public disclosure by submitting a signed statement to that effect."[358]

However, with regard to the government's refusal to release the dates and locations of arrest, detention, and release of the 9/11 detainees, the

Court found for the government, holding that based on the evidence before it, and the logic presented to it by the government, Exemptions 7A and 7F justified this policy/action. In particular, the Court agreed with the government that it was reasonable to conclude that these "dates and locations would be particularly useful to anyone attempting to discern patterns in the Government's investigation and strategy" and that the disclosure of such information could also make detention facilities vulnerable to retaliatory attacks.[359]

This mixed-outcome decision was appealed by both sides. The majority of the US Court of Appeals for the District of Columbia Circuit found for the government on all the issues.[360] In their view, the government had made a reasonable argument that would allow them to invoke the relevant exemptions in the *FOIA*.[361] Indeed, the Court accepted the government's arguments virtually in their totality, and made absolutely clear that its decision was based on its deference to the government because of what the Court saw as the government's comparative advantage in the matter of predicting what terrorist organizations might do in the future.[362] Tatel J dissented, however, holding that the government had failed to show that the feared harm could reasonably be expected to occur if public disclosure of the information occurred.[363] He chided the majority for "disregarding settled principles" and lamented what he saw as "the court's uncritical deference to the government's vague, poorly explained arguments."[364] His warning that "before accepting the government's argument, this court must insist on knowing whether these harms 'could reasonably be expected to' result from disclosure – the standard Congress prescribed for exemption under 7(A)," is particularly noteworthy in the present connection.[365]

Given the split nature of this Court of Appeals decision, the powerful dissent of Tatel J, and the importance of the issues involved, it would have greatly advanced the jurisprudence in this area had the US Supreme Court intervened and settled the matter. Regrettably, the Court denied *certiorari* in the case, refusing to hear the appeal from the judgment of the Court of Appeals.[366]

The Supreme Court's refusal to hear this appeal is all the more troubling given attempts in the unsuccessful efforts to introduce a bill for a *PATRIOT II Act* to give law enforcement agents even more authority to engage in secret detention of persons considered national security threats.[367]

The Canadian Position

In general, there have not been any secret detentions of refugees and other non-citizens on Canadian soil after or as a result of the 9/11 attacks. Neither does the law allow immigration or other officials to detain a refugee in secret. However, at least one secret rendition of a refugee from a Canadian to a US jail did occur after 9/11. On September 5, 2001, Benamar Benatta, an Algerian citizen and former Algerian Air Force engineer, crossed into Canada from the United States and sought political asylum.[368] He had escaped in April 2001 from a training program in new aircraft technology in Baltimore to which he had been sent by the Algerian government.[369] He was detained at the time he made his refugee claim in Canada, pending investigation into his identity.[370] The 9/11 attacks occurred while he was in detention, and Canadian officials alerted US law enforcement to his presence in Canada and apparently identified him as someone who may have had something to do with the attacks.[371] On September 12, he was driven to a US-Canada border post and handed over to US law enforcement agents.[372] Although the FBI had cleared him of any link to terrorism soon after his arrest, he was still held for five years in horrible conditions, incommunicado for much of that time.[373] As US Federal Magistrate H. Kenneth Schroeder Jr. noted: "As a result of the horrific events of Sept. 11, 2001, the Canadian authorities alerted United States authorities of defendant's presence and profile ... and returned him to the United States ... To accept the [US] government's arguments would be to join in the charade that has been perpetrated."[374] It should be noted in passing that Canada also facilitated and cooperated in the initially secret detention in the United States and Syria of a racialized Canadian citizen.[375]

Thus, the position in the United States with regard to secret detentions was far worse than the Canadian one, at least after 9/11. US courts sanctioned and licensed the secret detention for at least some period of scores, if not hundreds, of 9/11 detainees. By contrast, as far as we know, only two or so incidents can be considered remotely similar in Canada. Here again, the difference was one of scale and intensity.

Conditions of Detention

The US Position

The fact that some abusive detention practices were experienced by 9/11 detainees in the United States, including by many refugees, is well documented in the reports that have been produced on the treatment of non-citizens in that country after 9/11.[376] Credible reports that the many 9/11 detainees were too often "treated like criminals" have come from a number of organizations.[377] This assessment received ample support in the OIG Report of April 2003.[378] Indeed, this practice is of long standing. The bipartisan Commission on International Religious Freedom came to the same conclusion in its 2005 study of the pre- and post-9/11 treatment of refugees in the United States.[379] In its view, the detention practices applied to refugees before the report was issued embodied a "correctional system approach to the housing and treatment of post-credible fear asylum-seekers."[380] The USCIRF study found that all but one of the detention facilities operated just like jails.[381] This was so despite the fact that the detention standards that guided the work of immigration enforcement authorities in the United States since the year 2000 and that were revised and reissued in 2003 appear to contemplate the possibility of alternatives to the standard jailhouse approach to the detention of refugees.[382] The need for such alternatives in the refugee detention area is further recognized in both the 2003 DHS report *Endgame*[383] and a 2013 USCIRF Special Report.[384]

In particular, both before and after 9/11, detained refugees were too often housed or mixed in with convicted criminals.[385] Indeed, the 2004/2005 USCIRF study found that, at least after 9/11, it was only in one detention facility that the guards were explicitly told which detainees were convicted or suspected criminals and which were refugees.[386] Interestingly, the 2013 USCIRF Special Report found that although US authorities had made some progress toward the elimination of this abusive practice, all too many refugees continued to be detained under such conditions.[387] Similarly, many 9/11 detainees, about 12 percent of them, a substantial number of whom were refugees, were held in solitary confinement, and too often in jail cells that were lit for twenty-four hours a day, seven days a week.[388] When not held in solitary confinement, some 9/11 detainees were – without any individualized assessment of the danger they posed – detained in the highest-security sections of regular jails.[389] Yet, these spaces were meant to hold the most dangerous offenders. Detainees held there were locked down twenty-three hours a day, seven days a week.[390] The physical abuse of 9/11 detainees, leading in at least one case to the death of an inmate, was also reported by the relevant studies.[391] Noteworthy here is the fact that the OIG Report concluded that "we believe the evidence indicates a pattern of physical and verbal abuse against some September 11 detainees held at the MDC [the Metropolitan Detention Center in Brooklyn, where most of the 9/11 detainees referred to in the OIG Report were held] by some correctional officers, particularly during the first months after the terrorist attacks."[392] Verbal abuse of 9/11 detainees was not uncommon.[393] As important, too many detainees at the MDC were not permitted to make social and legal calls at least until late September 2001.[394] Many lawyers have recounted their difficulties in trying to locate and/or obtain access to their detained clients.[395] It appears that these particular difficulties were for the most part created by instructions handed down to the director of the US Bureau of Prisons from the highest levels of the Justice Department to delay, as much as possible within the law, the social and legal calls of 9/11 detainees.[396] Although the 2013 USCIRF Special Report did find that some improvements had been made by US authorities in this respect, it still concluded that such changes were not nearly enough to correct the situation. Refugees were still being held in "inappropriate conditions."[397]

It should be noted, however, that not all detainees suffered these indignities and abuses. For instance, 9/11 detainees held at the Passaic County Jail in New Jersey reportedly had a less harsh experience overall.[398] This may have been because most of them were not categorized as of "high interest" to the FBI's 9/11 investigation.[399]

Overall, it appears that the heightened sense of security vulnerability that followed the 9/11 attacks led to the significant augmentation and accentuation of a pre-existing pattern of at times harsh detention of persons who were linked to or suspected of being national security threats.

The Canadian Position

The occurrence of significant abusive immigration detention practices in Canada (much of which affected refugees) long pre-dated the 9/11 attacks. Long before 9/11, immigration detention in Canada, despite its many commendable features, was a "distinctly carceral experience."[400] The 9/11 attacks had little to do with the fact that in far too many respects immigration detention facilities in Canada operated much like regular jails.[401] As Anna Pratt has shown, things were already known to be relatively rough within these facilities as far back as 1995.[402] And this was so despite the 2000 report of the Inter-American Commission on Human Rights that concluded that the Toronto West and Laval Detention Centres, two of the major immigration detention locations in Canada, "appeared to comport with reasonable standards of cleanliness, organization and safety."[403] In contrast, in that same year, the decision in *Gao v Canada* portrayed "troubling" conditions of detention of Chinese minor asylum seekers (fifteen to eighteen years old) at two major immigration detention centres in Canada.[404] Historically, two major types of concerns have continued to dog immigration detention practice in Canada: the mixing of immigration detainees with the criminal population, and their inadequate access to basic services/necessities. As far back as 1998, the Standing Committee on Citizenship and Immigration had recommended that refugees about whom there was no suggestion of criminality should not be detained with persons convicted of criminal offences.[405] In response, Citizenship and Immigration Canada promised to make efforts to minimize contact between detained refugee claimants and persons awaiting trial or serving sentences.[406] In the same year, the inadequacy of access to basic services/necessities was also noted by the Canadian Council for Refugees.[407] A 2011 study found that these problems have persisted.[408]

That these problems have persisted through the years and continue to occur is underlined by the fact that two years after 9/11, then Immigration Minister Denis Coderre publicly rejected concerns about the mixing of immigration detainees with the general prison population, claiming that it conformed with the standard practice pertaining to other carceral situations.[409] In practice, the tendency to hold immigration detainees in provincial penitentiaries has too often led to a lack of proper accommodation of their needs. For example, individuals with minor criminal records are often held on "immigration hold" in a maximum-security prison in Lindsay, Ontario, with restricted phone access and infrequent contact with lawyers.[410]

Especially since 9/11, these kinds of inadequacies have been particularly evident in the case of long-term detainees held on security certificates. Most were initially detained at the Toronto West Detention Centre (TWDC) and later moved to a special facility built for that purpose in Kingston, Ontario. At least two were held in solitary confinement for several years, allegedly for their own safety.[411] One was initially mixed with the general accused/criminal detainee population at the TWDC.[412] At that time, the TWDC lacked facilities and programs normally available to long-term detainees, such as family "touch" visitations and exercise. In *Almrei v Canada* (2004) and *Jaballah v Canada*, Hassan Almrei and Mahmoud Jaballah (two of the three SC detainees long after 9/11) made highly plausible allegations that the conditions in which they were held amounted to cruel and unusual punishment.[413] Whatever the merits of these claims, in another case brought by Almrei in 2003, the court found that the refusal of detention authorities to allow him to wear footwear in his cell, despite the fact that the cell area was particularly cold in winter, was unlawful.[414]

Thus, the problem of abusive and/or inadequate detention conditions existed in Canada even before 9/11. It appears, however, that 9/11 led to increased ill-treatment in detention of a certain category of detainees, those held on national security grounds, nearly all of whom were Muslim male non-citizens. Mohammad, who was already in detention before 9/11, testified that his experience worsened markedly after 9/11, especially in terms of the verbal abuse he endured from some detention officers and fellow detainees.[415]

Compared with the United States, conditions in Canada were milder but not by a large margin. The real difference was one of scale. More non-citizens were rounded up in the United States after 9/11, so more of them were subjected to abusive conditions there than in Canada.

The Social and Institutional Context

The US Position

There is no doubt that the social and institutional contexts in which laws and practices relevant to the detention of refugees were formed and implemented, and which shaped their content and character, were on the balance already unfavourable to refugees before 9/11. For example, it was partly as a result of the prevailing anti-immigrant sentiment at the time that, effective September 30, 1996, Congress tightened the standard of parole for non-citizens (including refugees) who were detained while seeking entry into the United States.[416] As important, after 1996, the institution of the expedited review system and greater detention funding did more to increase the number of non-citizens detained than tightening of the standard of parole.[417]

As we saw in the Introduction, even before 9/11, the courts and Congress had always shown a high level of deference to administrative decision makers. For example, as one author put it, although some courts did challenge this attitude, in the past judicial deference had broadly insulated the executive from accountability in matters of national security.[418] This situation was heightened after 9/11. As Muzaffar Chishti has argued, in the context of the post-9/11 US situation, "Congress has shown extraordinary deference to the executive branch on immigration measures."[419] Also telling is the fact that the American Immigration Lawyers Association (AILA) does not see the immigration courts and the Board of Immigration Appeals as sufficiently independent from executive branch (i.e., political) interference.[420]

As we also saw in the Introduction, a gatekeeping culture exists within the US immigration bureaucracy. It did not begin after 9/11, of course, but in the area of detention of refugees and other non-citizens, the post-9/11 security vigil appears to have deepened and broadened this culture. As one author has put it: "With the media criticism and congressional scrutiny that led to the dismantling of the INS itself in the aftermath of the terrorist attacks, the trend of decreasing ICE [Immigration and Customs Enforcement] decisions granting parole [i.e., release from detention] to asylum seekers is understandable, yet is still inimical to the proper exercise of the agency's discretion."[421] After 9/11, the immigration bureaucracy more than ever before began to see its role as largely one of homeland security, of keeping out undesirable non-citizens – hence the greater tendency to detain them.[422] And some have argued that too many courts also fell victim to this sort of exclusionary mindset, and not merely after or because of 9/11.[423] This trend has not waned significantly before and during the Trump Administration.

The extraordinary security vigil in the United States after 9/11 exacerbated the situation, in part by accentuating the deference shown by the courts to the immigration bureaucracy and by intensifying the gatekeeping culture within the relevant bodies. As we have seen, this post-9/11 security vigil was largely directed at Muslims and Arabs. After 9/11, there was a dramatic surge in hate crimes targeting people who were Muslim or Middle Eastern or who "look foreign."[424] Such hate crimes rose over 1,500 percent in the immediate aftermath of 9/11.[425] There has also been much employment and airline discrimination against Muslims and Arabs.[426] Approximately 28 percent of the largely Muslim/Arab detainees were arrested as a result of tips by private citizens.[427] Thus, it is only correct to conclude that after 9/11 there was a significant change in perspective in Washington.[428] The atmosphere became significantly harsher.[429] This change in turn affected appreciably the detention decision making of the relevant authorities. At least as of 2007, nearly six years after the 9/11 attacks, this trend had not abated.[430] Whatever relief was experienced as a result of the Obama Administration's milder attitude toward Arabs and Muslims in the United States appears to have been reversed in great measure by the Trump Administration in January 2017.[431]

The Canadian Position

It is safe to say that even in the Canadian context, the social atmosphere and the relevant institutional contexts were already relatively harsh for refugees and other non-citizens well before 9/11. One important and telling (though subtle) indicator of this is the fact that when Bill C-86 for an Immigration Act was enacted in 1992, "a defiantly 'law and order' federal government had moved the entire immigration bureaucracy to a newly created Department of Public Security."[432] In a similar move after 9/11, a key part of this same bureaucracy was moved to an equally new Department of Public Safety and Emergency Preparedness.[433]

As shown in the Introduction, the Canadian courts have historically tended to show a very high level of deference to the executive branch in matters of national security, and the post-9/11 position has not been any different. This was shown comprehensively in the previous chapter and so will not be discussed in any detail here. Suffice it to say that this tendency to defer to the executive has had an appreciably negative impact on the detention of refugees and other non-citizens.

As also shown extensively in the Introduction, the Canadian immigration bureaucracy does suffer from a gatekeeping culture. Suffice it to note here that this kind of institutional culture has led to a more exclusionary mindset within that bureaucracy than should be the case, and that this mindset has in turn had negative consequences for all too many refugees and non-citizens.

On the whole, the post-9/11 social and institutional context in the United States was significantly less favourable to Arab/Muslim refugees and other non-citizens who were the principal targets of the security agencies than it was in Canada. This is not surprising given that it was in the United States that the 9/11 attacks took place, yet, at least until recently, Canada's response tended to track US policies and actions, albeit often on a significantly narrower scale and with much less intensity.

International Legal Standards and the Post-9/11 Detention Regimes in Canada and the United States

The Relevant International Standards

In Anna Pratt's view, the international legal standards that govern the detention of refugees and other non-citizens include 1) the *United Nations High Commissioner for Refugees (UNHCR) Guidelines on the Detention of Asylum Seekers* (hereinafter "the Guidelines"); 2) *Executive Committee Conclusion 44 (XXXVII) of 1986* ("ECC 44"); 3) the *United Nations Body of Principles for the Protection of all People under Any Form of Detention or Imprisonment;* and 4) the *United Nations Standard Minimum Rules for the Treatment of Prisoners.* Whereas the first two mostly set standards regarding the appropriateness or otherwise of detaining refugees, the last two focus on the nature of the conditions under which detainees of all kinds are held. Other legal standards are also applicable, notably: 1) the *1951 Convention Relating to the Status of Refugees* itself ("the *Refugee Convention*"); the *International Covenant on Civil and Political Rights (ICCPR);* and the *American Declaration on the Rights and Duties of Man* ("the American Declaration").[434] For the sake of brevity, only some of these will be discussed here. The greatest emphasis will be placed on the Guidelines and ECC 44 (the most directly relevant to the specific situation of refugees).

Various international human rights monitoring bodies and mechanisms have also issued persuasive statements that embody hortatory international legal standards that are relevant to the refugee detention context. These include the UNHCR Executive Committee, the UN Human Rights Committee, the Inter-American Commission on Human Rights, the UN Working Group on Arbitrary Detention, the UN Committee on the Elimination of Racial Discrimination, and the International Commission of Jurists. A few illustrative examples of the relevant observations of these mechanisms are discussed below.

It remains to assess, albeit not in great detail, how closely or otherwise the post-9/11 laws and practices of the United States and Canada have complied with these international legal standards. It is recognized that some of the relevant international standards are soft-law standards, and as such are only hortatory. They are, however, still important standards against which the conduct of all states in the area of refugee law can be assessed. Here, discussion of the conformity or non-conformity with international law of some US and Canadian detention practices will suffice to provide the general picture.

The US Position

There is little doubt that the well-documented US practice of detaining refugees from certain countries (especially Haiti), mainly as a way of deterring them from seeking asylum, is illegal under international law.

Article 31(1) of the *Refugee Convention* states that parties thereto

> [s]hall not impose penalties, on account of their illegal entry or presence, on refugees who, coming directly from a territory where their life or freedom was threatened in the sense of Article 1, enter or are present in their territory without authorization, provided they present

themselves without delay to the authorities and show good cause for
their illegal entry or presence.

This is supplemented by the Guidelines. Guideline 3 explicitly prohibits
the detention of refugees seeking entry into a state "as part of a policy
to deter future asylum-seekers." The Advisory Opinion of the UNHCR
on the US practice of deterring (mostly) Haitian refugees from making
the treacherous ocean journey from their country by detaining them
in mass on their arrival in the United States clearly regard that practice
as illegal under international law.[435]

As important, though identity-based detention can be permissible
under international law, the automatic detention of all undocumented
refugees at the point of seeking entry into the United States is almost
certainly unlawful under international law. Guideline 3(i) and (iii) and
ECC 44 do permit the detention of a refugee for a limited period where
the refugee's "identity may be undetermined or in dispute," but only
"when there is an intention to mislead or a refusal to cooperate with
the authorities" or such detention is otherwise necessary. But, as they
clearly say, these guidelines do not justify the US practice of detaining
a refugee who has merely arrived without the proper documentation or
did not have any at all.

There is also no question that virtually all decisions to detain a refugee
based largely on their state of origin or race are illegal under international
law. Thus, the utilization of blatant racial profiling in conducting the
mass roundups of Muslims and Arabs in the United States after 9/11
hardly conforms to the relevant international standards. For example,
Article 3 of the 1951 *Refugee Convention* states that "the Contracting
States shall apply the provisions of this Convention to refugees without
discrimination as to race, religion or country of origin." The Guidelines
also provide that even when it becomes a necessity, the detention of
refugees "must be exercised in a non-discriminatory manner."[436] It is
on this basis that the near-blanket deployment of racial profiling by US
Homeland Security officials, especially in the years immediately after
9/11, was most probably illegal.[437]

Racial profiling aside, the mass roundups themselves were of questionable international legality. ECC 44 notes that the detention of refugees

should normally be avoided.[438] The Introduction to the Guidelines provides that "the detention of asylum-seekers is, in the view of the UNHCR inherently undesirable ... Freedom from arbitrary detention is a fundamental human right and the use of detention is, in many instances, contrary to the norms and principles of international law."[439] Guidelines 3–4 support this position. Detention, especially the detention of refugees, is therefore an exceptional measure, to be applied sparingly. Clearly, the mass roundups of Arab and Muslim males after 9/11 did not respect this principle. A wide net was simply cast.

As important, the practice of mandatory or automatic detention of refugees is implicitly condemned in the Guidelines. Paragraphs 2–3 of the Introduction to the Guidelines make clear that "detention should only be resorted to in cases of necessity." Guideline 3 supports this provision. Thus, detention may not be legal under these Guidelines if a particular refugee (even one who has been identified as a national security risk) is detained without an individualized assessment of the necessity for such detention. And yet, as we have seen, that is the very nature of the practice of the mandatory detention of refugees in the United States.

Although the preventive detention of refugees on national security grounds is generally allowed, it can be applied only to the extent necessitated by the evidence.[440] In addition, such detention must occur in humane conditions and be accompanied by due process protections.[441] Alternatives to detention must also be applied where appropriate.[442] There is little doubt that such US practices as using boilerplate memos with little specific evidence about particular detainees to oppose their release, and the "hold until cleared policy" of detaining non-citizens even before any evidence against them has been found, violate the relevant international legal standards.

In all cases involving detention of refugees, their prolonged or indefinite detention is frowned on by international law. For example, according to Guideline 3, even when adjudged necessary, the detention of a refugee should be imposed only for "a minimal period." This is hardly a controversial statement. What is less certain and far more controversial is whether there is an exact maximum length of time beyond which a refugee may not be detained. It all depends on the specific circumstances of each detention. Yet most observers agree that too many Arabs and

Muslims were detained in the United States for far too long, and too often with no end in sight, in the months and years after 9/11.

However long a refugee's detention lasts, Guideline 10 requires that the conditions be "humane with respect shown to the inherent dignity of the person." In particular, this guideline requires "the use of separate detention facilities" to accommodate refugees, and mandates that in the cases where separate detention facilities are not used, refugees "should be accommodated separately from convicted criminals or prisoners on remand." There is no doubt that aspects of the conditions of the detention of refugees in the United States after 9/11 do not conform to the relevant international standards. For example, as has been shown earlier in this chapter, refugees are all too often mixed in with convicted criminals in the regular US jails, a clear violation of Guideline 10.

The Canadian Position

At the outset it is important to note that although unincorporated treaties are generally not directly applicable in Canada, the *Immigration and Refugee Protection Act* provides that its interpretation and application should comply with the international human rights instruments that Canada is party to.[443] What is more, as the discussions in cases like *Suresh* and *Baker* show, even treaties that Canada has not ratified can still be applied in a largely hortatory way to interpret relevant Canadian legislation.[444] While actual practice sometimes belies these worthy principles,[445] the latter nevertheless provide a basis for assessing Canada's laws and practices against the relevant international legal standards.

As shown above, the practice of detaining refugees so as to deter persons in similar circumstances from making their way to the relevant country is illegal in international law. Thus, the Canadian near-blanket policy/practice of detaining, at least for a time, almost all refugees who form part of "irregular arrivals" is problematic, and probably illegal in international law.

As we also saw above, the practice of detaining refugees only because they lack documentation is not covered by the broad authority that states enjoy under international law to detain refuges who are deceptive or uncooperative about establishing their true identity. Thus, the Canadian practice of detaining, albeit for varying periods, all refugees who are unable to satisfy an officer as to their identity is at least questionable from an international law perspective. While Canada does not tend to detain for all that long those who cooperate and are not deceptive, the fact remains that even those refugees who are cooperative but who lack identity documents may be detained in Canada for some length of time. Although the appropriateness of such a practice will turn on the specific circumstances of each case, the practice, *prima facie*, clashes with Guideline 3(i) and (iii) and ECC 44. Indeed, the UN Committee on the Elimination of Racial Discrimination (CERD) has expressed concern about identity-based detention in Canada and the adverse effects it may have on refugees.[446] What is more, the UN Working Group on Arbitrary Detention (UNWGAD), which visited Canada in June 2005, expressed concerns about what it saw as the unchecked discretion of immigration officers to detain non-citizens on identity grounds.[447]

Although there were no mass roundups on the same scale as in the United States after 9/11, there were nevertheless some roundups of Arabs and Muslims in Canada. A narrower net was cast for "suspect" Arabs and Muslims. The CERD has noted its concern about the heightened risks of racial/ethnic profiling and discrimination in the context of increased national security measures after 9/11.[448] And as we have seen, roundups of the sort that occurred in Canada violate the "detention as exceptional measure" norm found in the Guidelines and ECC 44.

As has been shown, the international law norms do, in general, allow the preventive detention of refugees on national security grounds. Yet, this detention practice can be applied only to the extent necessitated by the evidence, and such detention must be accompanied by due process protections. Like the United States, Canada has rather loose standards for detaining refugees and other non-citizens on security certificates. Thus, a person can be detained for half a decade on one of these certificates with evidence that does not even make one reasonably confident that it is more likely than not that the person committed the specified act or offence. And once the two relevant ministers have met this very low standard, there is little the reviewing courts can do about it. For example, the UNWGAD has criticized the fact that the designated judges of the Federal Court have no jurisdiction to assess a security certificate on its merits, but merely enjoy the power to decide whether the decision to issue the certificate was "reasonable."[449] It should be noted, though, that

Federal Courts in Canada have sometimes declared the issuance of such certificates to have been unreasonable.[450]

Similarly, the mandatory detention scheme that applied until recently to foreign national refugees who were detained in Canada under security certificates was unlawful under international law. For example, a report by the International Commission of Jurists (ICJ) concluded that any detention process, and individual detention decisions, should be properly grounded in the evidence and subject to regular and effective review by a judicial body.[451] Mandatory detentions are almost by definition not grounded in any individualized assessment of the evidence but on a general notion that all foreign nationals (but not permanent residents) against whom such certificates are issued ought to be detained. Furthermore, in 2000, the Inter-American Commission on Human Rights specifically found this mandatory detention scheme to be in violation of the international human rights obligation to provide detained persons with prompt detention reviews, since the legality and appropriateness of the detention was reviewed for the very first time only within 120 days of the security certificates' being found reasonable.[452]

With regard to prolonged or indefinite detention, the Commission has also observed that detention pending deportation must be time-limited and has to cease when deportation is no longer a realistic prospect.[453] For its part, the UN Human Rights Committee has expressed concern that Canada's SC detention scheme leads to the unduly prolonged detention of those named in the certificates, and urged Canada to institute a maximum length of such detention.[454] This view is supported by the CERD.[455]

Regarding the conditions of detention of refugees, although Canada's detention institutions have often won relatively mild praise from international monitors,[456] there are still areas where they do not measure up to the relevant international legal standards. For example, many detained refugees are still accommodated in regular jails, and some are mixed in with convicted criminals in violation of Guideline 10.

Analytical Insights from a Comparison of the Two Regimes

As we have seen, Canadian law and practice regarding the detention of refugees and other non-citizens after 9/11 has been more or less similar – at least for most of the relevant period – to that of the United States in *six of eleven* key identifiable aspects: identity-based detention, preventive detention, mandatory detention, prolonged/indefinite detention, secret evidence, and conditions of detention subareas. The only caveat that must be added here is that since 2008, the mandatory detention and secret evidence laws and practices in Canada as they relate to the treatment of refugees have become better than the counterpart regimes in the United States. Impressively, regarding the post-9/11 era, Canada's law and practice has been significantly better for the duration of the relevant period than the US equivalent in *five of the eleven* identified aspects. Until the Conservative Harper government took office in 2006, Canada hardly used the detention of refugees as a migration deterrent;[457] it has rounded up Arabs and Muslims far less frequently and to a lesser extent; it has not tended to use material witness detentions against refugees; it has rarely detained refugees in secret; and it has not tended to utilize closed hearings. As important, Canada has not performed significantly worse than the United States in even one such aspect.

Yet, the key difference between the US and Canadian refugee detention regimes after 9/11 has been the much larger *scale* of the utilization of the impugned laws and practices in the United States. Even in the six cases in which the Canadian and US positions have been characterized in this chapter as more or less similar, the scale of activities in the United States has been broader. Given that the 9/11 attacks occurred on US soil and that the United States has remained the primary target of al-Qaeda–type terrorism, this is not surprising.

In the detention subregimes of both countries (as opposed, for example, to the deportation to torture area), the heightened security vigil following the 9/11 attacks triggered and fostered considerable changes relative to their respective pre-9/11 regimes, especially in the sense of the "living" law. For example, although Cherif Bassiouni's conclusion that "the [US] nation has never before seen a more systematic erosion of civil rights than after 9/11" may have overstated the point to some extent, the significant effect of 9/11 on the refugee detention regime in the United States is captured in Human Rights Watch's considered view that after 9/11, "immigration arrests and detention was used as a way of rounding up Muslim non-citizens and detaining them. Before 9/11 most would not have been detained (other than briefly) for the immigration violations for which they were now being held."[458] This is corroborated by the OIG Report, which declared, among other things, that "fear of additional terrorist attacks ... changed the way aliens detained in connection with the investigation of the September 11 attacks were treated."[459]

As was suggested at the end of the Introduction, however, the fact that even though the 9/11 attacks did not occur on its territory Canada's positions with regard to six of the eleven identified subareas of the refugee detention regime have been so similar to those of the United States suggests that much more than the events of 9/11 were responsible for the observed changes in the refugee regimes of both countries. A multifactorial (rather than unitary) explanation is clearly suggested. Again, as argued at the end of the Introduction, with respect to Canada the other factors in play were the sympathy/empathy of many Canadians with their US neighbours (or kith and kin); Canada's deep economic dependence on trade and other similar relations with the United States; Canada's long-standing internal security anxieties (e.g., over the Tamil Tigers, al-Qaeda "sleeper cells," and the like); some US socio-political pressure on Canada (e.g., by pointing to the Canada-US border as a chink in the American armour); and a long-standing pro-immigration control element within Canadian society (with some on the xenophobic fringe). While these factors tended to push Canadian refugee law and practice in a negative direction, others helped push it toward the positive end, including the deeply felt need among millions of Canadians for a distinct national identity from the Americans, and the humanitarian instinct that is deeply embedded in Canadian society.

Given the comparative and other insights discussed above, to what extent can Canada's overall refugee regime be validly described as humane in fact? Is it actually more humane than that of the United States? What, if anything, does this tell us about the nature of each country's adherence to a mentality that elsewhere in this book I have styled "security relativism"? What, if anything, does this tell us about the cogency and coherence of the national self-images of each country? These and related questions will be tackled in the Conclusion, following further comparative analysis of the refugee laws of both countries in the next two chapters.

Terrorism-Related Inadmissibility   **3**

> After 9/11, our laws were modified in the interest of protecting national security. No one wants terrorists or their supporters to come here as refugees. But the Congress cast the net so widely that we are now denying asylum to legitimate refugees.
>
> – US Senator Patrick Leahy

Before turning to the substantive discussion in this chapter, it should be pointed out that much, though not all, of the Attorney General's power under the *INA* (in regard to immigration detention) was delegated by him to the Secretary of Homeland Security in March 2003.[1] The main tasks at hand in this chapter are to carefully analyze the available evidence regarding to the terrorism-related inadmissibility (TRI) regimes in the United States and Canada as they relate to refugees and asylum seekers, in order to assess the extent to which 9/11 has affected their character in each country and compared with each other.[2] A related and equally important task is to tease out the analytical insights, if any, that can be gained from comparing the extent of the changes that occurred in the United States (the country that was directly attacked on 9/11) to the post-9/11 state of affairs in Canada (which was not attacked directly on that fateful day).

To these ends, the rest of the chapter is organized in the following way. It begins with a discussion of the changes that occurred or did not occur, after and because of 9/11, in the character and scope of the TRI regimes in the United States and Canada. Several discrete aspects of these separate regimes are discussed in this vein before the relationship (if any) between the interactive functioning of scope, threshold, context, and racial profiling (on the one hand) and the possibility of error/injustice in the implementation of the TRI regime (on the other hand) are considered. Following this discussion, the effect or otherwise of the nature of the emergent TRI regimes on certain forms of dissent is examined. Thereafter, the extent of the harmony or lack thereof in each country between its TRI regime and the relevant international standards is examined. The chapter ends with a discussion of the main analytical conclusions stemming from the comparisons between the US and Canadian TRI regimes.

A number of caveats and clarifications are in order. First, as used in this chapter, the term "inadmissibility" refers both to the rules regarding the denial of entry to non-citizens seeking entry and to the rules concerning the removal from the relevant jurisdiction of those who have already entered it. This clarification is crucial given the very particular technical meaning of "inadmissibility" in US immigration and refugee law. In that country, the grounds of inadmissibility are carefully distinguished from those that require removal, and the two concepts are in some cases governed by different (if sometimes overlapping) rules.[3] However, this distinction is not nearly as important in contemporary Canadian immigration and refugee law.

It must also be noted though that the focus of this chapter on TRI rather than on the much more expansive and far more vague concept of "national security–related inadmissibility" is a deliberate one.[4] The main reason is that TRI appears to be the more relevant of the two to this book's focus on the extent of possible changes to refugee law after and because of the events of 9/11. It appears that it is within the specific TRI subarea (within the much broader security inadmissibility field) that the most significant changes did occur after 9/11. As Won Kidane has correctly noted, "terrorism is likely the most significant and most controversial statutory bar to asylum, currently."[5]

As importantly, the discussion in this chapter deliberately does not include a section on the use of closed hearings and/or secret evidence in TRI proceedings and the effects thereof. This is because a similar discussion appears extensively in Chapter 1, and there is very little significant difference in character between the use of closed hearings and/or secret evidence in the security detention context and their utilization in TRI proceedings. It is for this same reason that this chapter does not contain a section on the social and institutional context in which TRI has functioned since 9/11.

On another note, there is of course a sense in which being impugned for some form of suspected or proven involvement in terrorism may preclude one from being conceived of and recognized as a refugee at all.[6] This is a result of the effect of the provisions of Article 1(F) of the 1951 *Convention Relating to the Status of Refugees* (the *Refugee Convention*) and the various equivalent provisions in the relevant domestic jurisdictions.[7] There is also another sense in which a person may, despite recognition as a refugee and being entitled to the benefit of the principle of non-return (or non-*refoulement*), be turned away or removed from a country on the basis of being inadmissible as a result of suspected or proven involvement in terrorism. This can come about as a result of the effects of the Article 33(2) exception to the non-*refoulement* principle and the equivalent provisions in the relevant domestic jurisdictions.[8] In the first instance, the person is not considered a refugee at all, but is clearly an asylum seeker or refugee claimant. In the second case, the person is recognized as a refugee but is still bereft of the basic protection that every refugee ought to enjoy, i.e., non-*refoulement*. It is important to acknowledge, of course, that a person who has already been recognized as a refugee will enjoy more legal protection from removal from the given jurisdiction than one who has not received such protection. Yet, in both cases, as long as the relevant definitional thresholds are met (including, in the case of the recognized refugee, an additional finding that he or she is a serious danger to the community), the affected person can in practice be effectively excluded from being protected as a refugee as a result of involvement with terrorism. It is for this reason that, for the most part, no distinction will be made in this chapter between the differing situations discussed above. It is more practical to concentrate here on the character of the basic definitions of TRI that can function to render inadmissible in the United States and Canada both recognized and unrecognized refugees.

As such, this chapter will focus on the following: 1) deciphering and comparing the expansions (if any) of the *definitional scope* of TRI in the two countries; 2) exposing some of the socio-legal effects of these changes; 3) considering the conformity of the current TRI regime in each country to the relevant international legal standards; and 4) teasing out some analytical insights from the preceding discussions.

The Scope of Terrorism-Related Inadmissibility

The US Position

The highly consequential 1996 changes to US immigration and refugee law are relevant to the discussion here. As has been emphasized in previous chapters, it was in that year that the *Illegal Immigration Reform and Immigrant Responsibility Act (IIRIRA)* and the *Anti-Terrorism and Effective Death Penalty Act (AEDPA)* were enacted into law, leading to the introduction of several significant changes both to the *Immigration and Nationality Act (INA)* in particular and to the US refugee law regime in general.[9] Prior to the *IIRIRA*, "no provision in the INA required a threat assessment of asylum applicants before being released into society."[10] Thus, the pre-9/11 TRI regime in the United States was shaped appreciably by both the *IIRIRA* and the *AEDPA*.

As important as the 1996 changes may have been to the area of TRI, the post-9/11 era saw a flurry of legislative activity that imposed even greater change. Although some of the proposed legislation was not ultimately enacted,[11] the *USA PATRIOT Act* and the *Real ID Act* (which followed it a few years later) introduced significant change to the TRI regime.[12]

Terrorist Activity

Well before 9/11, and perhaps as far back as 1798,[13] the US TRI regime directly or indirectly mandated the inadmissibility (including removability) from US territory of individuals who engage in terrorist or similar activity.[14] There was no explicit terrorism-related ground for exclusion prior to the early 1990s, but this changed with the passage of the *Immigration Act of 1990*.[15] In the years immediately preceding 9/11, the combined effect of *INA* ss 208(b)(2)(A)(v) and 212(a)(3)(B)(i) barred anyone if there were reasonable grounds for regarding that person as a danger to the security of the United States or as having been involved in the specified ways in terrorist activity.[16]

For our purposes, the TRI of a person hinges on whether the conduct in question fits the definition of "terrorist activity" under the relevant statutes. Yet the expression "terrorism" and even "terrorist activity" have been notoriously difficult to define with sufficient precision.[17] Some have even suggested that terrorism is more appropriately considered a political rather than a legal term.[18]

Nevertheless, in the case of the United States, this phrase was defined in a particular way in the version of the *INA* that was operative during the pre-9/11 period. The then operative section 212(a)(3)(B)(ii) defined it in much the same way as the current s 212(a)(3)(B)(iii).[19] The only change in the wording of this definition seems to be the addition of the expression "or other weapon or dangerous device" to segment (v)(bb) of the current provision (which details one of the substances, the use of which would combine with other factors to constitute a terrorist act) so that it now reads "explosive, firearm, or other weapon or dangerous device (other than for personal monetary gain)." Thus, there does not seem to have been all that much change in the content of this provision as a result of the heightened security vigil following 9/11. Whatever changes have been introduced do not appear to have *transformed* the overall character of the definition.

Still, it is noteworthy that a careful student of this provision has concluded that "Congress chose to define these terms [i.e., terrorism and terrorist activity] very broadly."[20]

Providing Material Support to Terrorists

Long before 9/11, s 301(b) of the *AEDPA* had sought to prevent persons within the United States or subject to its jurisdiction from providing material support or resources to foreign organizations that engage in terrorist activities.[21] Thus, the basic idea of deploying the TRI regime to stem the provision of support to organizations viewed as terrorist by the relevant authorities is not new at all.

Not surprisingly, the then operative version of s 212(a)(3)(B)(iii) of the *INA* had defined the phrase "engaging in terrorist activity" to include the provision of material support to a group or individual that is constructed by the relevant statutes as terrorist.[22] According to this section, to "engage in terrorist activity" includes doing any of the following either in an individual capacity or as part of the group, while knowing or being deemed on reasonable ground to have known that it affords material support to any individual, organization, or government in conducting a terrorist activity, namely: "The providing of ... material support including a safe house, transportation, communications, funds, false documentation or identification, weapons, explosives, or training."[23]

Only weeks after 9/11, s 411 of the *PATRIOT Act* effectively expanded this definition and did so in significant measure.[24] In effect, with a narrow exception for groups that had not yet been designated as terrorist, and a possibility of waiver (which will be discussed in more detail later), giving funds to any organization that had been explicitly deemed by the relevant authorities to be a terrorist group was in itself "engaging in terrorist activity," even if the donor did not know or could not reasonably have known of the terrorist nature of that organization. As such, the built-in safety net in the pre-9/11 definition was eliminated with respect to designated terrorist groups. Thus, to be clear, under the *PATRIOT Act* regime, a non-citizen who provided material support to a designated group was automatically inadmissible regardless of that person's knowledge of the organization's terrorist activities.[25] A non-citizen who provided such support to a non-designated group that had engaged in terrorism was inadmissible only if he or she supported the group's terrorist activity.[26]

It is no wonder, then, that a number of critics have, not without some justification, charged that the *PATRIOT Act* excessively expanded the definition of "engaging in terrorist activity" and the aspect of it that impugned those who provided "material support" to terrorists, to the extent of permitting refugees and other non-citizens "to be deported for the kind of wholly nonviolent associational activity protected by the First Amendment."[27]

Four years after the enactment of the *PATRIOT Act*, the *REAL ID Act* effectively abolished the agreement brokered in Congress (during the debate over the bill to enact the *PATRIOT Act*) to maintain a significant "knowledge requirement" in the case of the provision of material support to non-designated groups.[28] Just to be clear, the current s 212(a)(3)(B)(iv)(IV) of the *INA* includes within the definition of engaging in

terrorist activity soliciting funds or other things of value for a terrorist activity, a designated terrorist group, or a non-designated terrorist
organization.[29] In addition, s 212(a)(3)(B)(iv)(VI) of the *INA* provides that
to engage in terrorist activity is to, among other things, "commit an
act that the actor knows, or reasonably should know, affords material
support, including a safe house, transportation, communications,
funds, transfer of funds or other material financial benefit, false documentation or identification, weapons (including chemical, biological,
or radiological weapons), explosives, or training" to an individual or
group for the purpose of terrorist activity, or as otherwise stated in the
INA.[30] Under the post–*REAL ID Act* regime, non-citizens who provide
such support to a non-designated group that has committed a terrorist act are inadmissible unless they can prove by clear and convincing
evidence that they neither knew nor should have known that the group
was a terrorist organization.[31] The latter is obviously more expansive
than the pre–*REAL ID Act* definition.

Again, it is not surprising that critics have claimed that the current definition of material support in the *INA* is so broad as to catch
even US allies, for example, many of those who provided support to
the United States in its war against Saddam Hussein's Iraq and in
its subsequent anti-insurgent struggle in that country.[32] Making a
somewhat similar charge in his separate opinion in *In Re S-K-*, Juan
Osuna, a sometime chair of the Board of Immigration Appeals (BIA),
warned that "the statutory language is breathtaking in its scope."[33]
Indeed, this has been the case – hence the necessity for congressional
intervention in passing legislation specifically exempting certain
actions (and the persons who commit them) from the operation of
this overly expansive definition.

Others have also correctly argued that "the US government has
concluded that these statutory provisions taken together preclude any
exception for material support provided under duress."[34] Thus, even
those who had been captured by Maoist rebels in Nepal and forced to
provide certain services to them, or from whom FARC rebels in Columbia had exacted a form of protection money, have all too often been
subjected to the TRI provisions of the *INA*.[35] The effect has been that
the TRI regime has too often "defined terrorism's victims as terrorists."[36]

Those who should be protected as refugees have in practice tended to be excluded as terrorists. As one study of the situation of Colombian refugees has found, this definition has also tended to exclude them from the United States.[37]

Critics have also accurately charged that the US government has concluded that "the purposes of the individual providing the support [i.e., whether the person intended the support to go to terrorist activity or some other purpose], or [the goal of] the group being supported, [or] the amount of support [for example, whether it is a large amount], [or] the nature of the support, and when it occurred[,] are irrelevant."[38] For example, in *In Re S-K-*, a donation of 1,100 Singapore dollars over an eleven-month period (amounting to about US$71 per month) to the Chin National Front fighting against the Burmese junta was held to suffice as material support.[39] Although the BIA decided not to conclusively resolve the question of the exact meaning of the term "material," it is clear that relatively modest amounts of support may bring a non-citizen within the scope of this aspect of TRI.[40] This reading is confirmed by the decision in *Alturo v US Attorney General*.[41] In that case, the US Court of Appeals for the Eleventh Circuit held that the BIA reasonably concluded that annual payments of about $300 over a period of six years were not so insignificant as to fall outside the definition. The Court also cited *Singh-Kaur v Ashcroft*, in which it was noted "that 'material support' is a broad concept" and that the court would defer to "the BIA's conclusion in an earlier iteration of that case that the 'provision of food and setting up tents' qualified as such support."[42]

The Definition of "Terrorist Organization"

The scheme for designating foreign terrorist organizations (FTOs) was created by the *AEDPA* in 1996, partly as a result of the heightened security vigil that followed the Oklahoma City and World Trade Center bombings.[43] The then s 219 authorized the Secretary of State (in consultation with the Secretary of the Treasury and the Attorney General) to designate any organization (by publication in the *Federal Register*) as an FTO if he or she found that 1) it was a foreign organization; 2) it engaged in terrorist activity; and 3) such activity threatened the security of the United States.[44] The finding that US national security was threatened was to be made by the Secretary of State in his or her non-reviewable discretion.[45]

As has been well acknowledged, s 411 of the *PATRIOT Act* effectively expanded the definition of "terrorist organization" beyond the scope set out in s 219 of the *INA* (which referred, and continues to refer, only to the ability of the Secretary of State to designate organizations as terrorist, pursuant to the definition in s 212(a)(3)(B) of the *INA*.[46] Section 411 amended *INA* s 212 (which, among other things, mandates the inadmissibility of non-citizens who have provided material support to terrorists). This *PATRIOT Act* provision introduced within the FTO concept two types of organizations: 1) organizations that have been otherwise designated by the Secretary of State in the *Federal Register* in consultation with or on the request of the Attorney General and the Secretary of Homeland Security as engaging in the specified forms of terrorist activity; and 2) organizations that have not been designated at all as terrorist under either s 219 or s 212(a)(3)(B)(vi) of the *INA* if the Secretary of State finds that the organization of any of its subgroups engages in the specified forms of terrorist activity. Thus, as Margaret Stock has noted, currently, "an organization can be deemed a foreign terrorist organization ... even if the Secretary of State has not published notice of its designation in the Federal Register."[47] In addition, the *PATRIOT Act* added the words "or retains the capability and intent to engage in terrorist activity" to item (b) of the above definition of an organization that may be designated as an FTO under s 219 of the *INA*, so that item (b) now reads "engages in terrorist activity or retains the capability and intent to engage in terrorist activity." This was clearly an expansion of the scope of the definition in s 219 to include even some of those organizations that do not currently engage in terrorist activities.

Section 103(c) of the *REAL ID Act* further expanded the scope of the post–*PATRIOT Act* definition of an FTO to broaden the specified forms of terrorist activity to include all of the activities listed in s 212(a)(3)(B) (iv) (I–VI) of the *INA*, rather than just items I–III.

With much justification, the current definition of "terrorist organization" in the *INA* has been criticized by some as framed as a "catch-all," as a provision that is "so broad as to include those who fought alongside the US like the Montagnards in Vietnam and members of the Northern

Alliance in Afghanistan."[48] This overbroad nature of the definition is even more troubling when viewed in light of the issue of the use and abuse of various terror watch lists by the United States to identify terrorist organizations (discussed later in this chapter, under the heading "International Legal Standards and the Post-9/11 Terrorism-Related Inadmissibility Regimes in Canada and the United States").

Mere Membership in Terrorist Organizations

Before 9/11, the mere membership of a person in a terrorist organization was not per se a bar to either asylum or withholding of removal, unless the person's actions or inaction had in some way furthered the persecution of another.[49] As Regina Germain has reported, the US immigration authorities had taken the view in 1996 that as long as a non-citizen had not engaged in terrorist activities, the non-citizen was not necessarily barred from asylum – that is, from being considered as someone who fit the definition of a refugee.[50]

The question of fitting the refugee definition is conceptually distinct, however, from that of being inadmissible in the United States. As Germain recognizes, mere membership in a terrorist organization could suffice to render a non-citizen inadmissible and lead to removal from that country, as long as the specific threshold and other requirements for removing a refugee (as opposed to other non-citizens) are met.[51] Before 9/11, it was membership in a foreign terrorist organization that the Secretary of State had designated as such under s 219 of the *INA*, and that the non-citizen knew or should have known was a terrorist organization, that led to TRI. However, s 411 of the *PATRIOT Act* expanded the scope of TRI on grounds of mere membership in a terrorist organization. It did so by amending s 212(a)(3)(B)(i)(V) of the *INA* so as to render inadmissible a non-citizen who is a member either of a designated terrorist organization or of any group that the non-citizen knows or should have known is such an organization.

For its part, s 103 of the *REAL ID Act* amended s 212(a)(3)(B)(i) to provide in two new or modified clauses within that section – i.e., the current s 212(a)(3)(B)(i)(V–VI) – that non-citizens will be inadmissible if they are members of a group designated as such under s 219 of the *INA*, or of an otherwise designated group, or even of an entirely non-designated group that engages in terrorism. Membership in a non-designated group will not suffice to lead to TRI if they can show that they did not know and should not reasonably have known that the organization is a terrorist organization.[52] It is unclear what if any significant difference exists between the *PATRIOT Act* and the (current) *REAL ID Act* versions of this ground of TRI. Clearly, therefore, the issue of the use and abuse of various terror watch lists, referred to earlier, is as relevant here.

Receipt of Military Training from a Terrorist Organization

Section 103(a)(i)(VIII) of the *REAL ID Act* introduced into the *INA* a new ground of TRI based on the receipt of military-style training, as defined in s 2339D(c)(1) of Title 18, *United States Code Act*, from or on behalf of any organization that, at the time the training was received, was deemed to be a terrorist organization by or under the *INA*.[53] This was clearly a post-9/11 innovation that was also attributed to the heightened sense of security vulnerability produced by the events of that day.

Endorsing Terrorist Activity

Section 411 of the *PATRIOT Act* significantly expanded the categories of TRI by creating new subcategories relating to the endorsement of terrorism.[54] In the first case, s 212(a)(3)(B)(i)(IV)(bb) of the *INA* now provides that any person who is a representative of a political, social, or other group that endorses or espouses terrorism (i.e., any officer, official, or spokesperson of that organization, or who directs, counsels, commands, or induces its terrorist activity) is inadmissible in the United States.[55]

Similarly, under s 411 of the *PATRIOT Act*, a non-citizen in a position of prominence who had endorsed terrorism was inadmissible after 9/11.[56] According to the operative version of s 212(a)(3)(B)(i)(VII) of the *INA* of the time,[57] any non-citizen who had used his "position of prominence within any country to endorse or espouse terrorist activity, or to persuade others to support terrorist activity or a terrorist organization, in any way that the Secretary of State has determined undermines United States efforts to reduce or eliminate terrorist activities" was inadmissible. Section 103 of the *REAL ID Act* amended this provision to state more simply (albeit slightly more expansively) that any non-citizen who "endorses or espouses terrorist activity, or persuades others to *endorse or* support terrorist activity or a terrorist organization" is inadmissible. Thus, following the *REAL ID Act,* if a non-citizen persuades anyone to endorse (but not necessarily to support) terrorist activity, that non-citizen would be inadmissible. This would not necessarily have been the case before the passage of this statute. However, this difference between the defunct and current regimes does not seem major.

Spouses and Children

Section 411 of the *PATRIOT Act* broadened the *INA* to render inadmissible even the spouse and children of a person who is deemed removable on grounds of terrorism, as long as the activities for which that person is removable occurred within the previous five years.[58] This was a post-9/11 innovation. However, this exclusion would not apply: 1) if the spouse or child can show that she did not know or should not reasonably have known of the terrorist activity of the relevant person; or 2) a consular officer or the Attorney General has reasonable grounds to believe that the spouse or child has renounced the terrorist activity that caused the relevant person to be inadmissible.[59] This expansion in the legal position was introduced through amendments to s 212(a)(3)(B) of the *INA* that were made by the *REAL ID Act* of 2005. The change in legal text here does not appear to make an exception for refugees.

Expanded Ability to Remove Those Already Admitted

Prior to the passage of the *REAL ID Act* in 2005, the scope of the grounds for deporting a refugee or other non-citizen for TRI after they had been admitted to the United States was "considerably less broad" than the TRI grounds for refusing entry to a person who had not yet been admitted.[60] The then s 237(a)(4)(B) of the *INA* (concerning already admitted non-citizens),[61] differed significantly from s 212(a)(3)(B) (concerning non-admitted non-citizens).[62] For example, before that time, membership in or association with a terrorist organization, or the espousal or endorsement of terrorist activity, *inter alia,* did not appear to be sufficient grounds for deporting an already admitted refugee.[63]

Bill HR10, the House of Representatives' defunct version of the *Intelligence Reform and Terrorism Prevention Act of 2004,* would have altered this situation.[64] However, as a result of significant opposition in the Senate and the conferencing process in Congress, the relevant provision of HR 10 was removed from the final version of the *Act*.[65]

Section 104 of the *REAL ID Act* resurrected these HR10 provisions and harmonized the grounds of TRI as they applied before and after a non-citizen's admission into the United States. The current s 237(a)(4)(B) of the *INA* provides in effect that any non-citizen who has already been admitted into the country and who would have been inadmissible (in terms of the narrower US use of that term) under s 212(a)(3)(B) or (F) is removable.

Blanket Travel Bans

Soon after he was sworn into office in January 2017, President Donald Trump signed and issued an executive order (soon to be replaced by a revised one) that, among other things, banned for a ninety-day period the entry into the United States of the nationals of a number of designated Muslim-majority countries.[66] The ban was explicitly justified on the basis of the Trump Administration's felt need to protect the US homeland from a perceived threat of terrorism from nationals of these countries. The order also explicitly mentioned the September 11 attacks and subsequent acts of terrorism in the United States as part of its justification. This measure imposed administratively an additional kind of terrorism-related inadmissibility.

To be sure, the revised executive order did waive this ban for some categories of foreign nationals from affected countries, including those who had already received refugee status or relief under the *Convention against Torture* in the United States; those the appropriate authority had determined would be subjected to undue hardship as a result; US or Canadian permanent residents; those holding study or work visas or authorized to enter to pursue other long-term activity in the United States; persons needing urgent medical care; infants; young children; those entering to reside with or visit close family members who are US citizens or permanent residents; those authorized to enter to conduct business; diplomats accredited to the United States; and those who work for international organizations.[67]

The first ban was struck down by the courts, and despite the exemptions it included, the second ban was also struck down initially.[68] Soon after, however, the US Supreme Court partially restored the ban pending the Court's consideration of the Trump Administration's appeal in this matter in October 2017, when the bans would likely have expired, and exempted persons (including refugees) who already had a family, business, educational, or other such close connection to the United States from the ban.[69] In June 2018, the Supreme Court ruled in favour of the Trump Administration in a split five-to-four decision, and fully restored the ban.[70]

The Possibility of Waivers

Perhaps conscious of the very broad scope covered by the TRI provisions both before and after the enactment of the *PATRIOT Act* and the *REAL ID Act,* Congress had consistently introduced a number of statutory provisions that either authorized various executive branch officials or staff to, at their discretion, waive a non-citizen's TRI, or granted such waivers in themselves. Discussion of a few of these will serve to illustrate and buttress this point, but note that the situations in these cases were similar before and after 9/11.

Waiver by executive discretion – As was shown above, a consular officer or the Attorney General may waive the inadmissibility of a spouse or child of a person who is subject to TRI if the relevant decision maker has reasonable grounds to believe that the targeted spouse or child has renounced the terrorist activity that caused the relevant person to be inadmissible.[71] This waiver was introduced by s 412 of the *PATRIOT Act.* Under the *Act,* the Attorney General or the Secretary of State can (after consulting the other) choose, in their non-reviewable discretion, not to apply TRI to anyone who comes within the material support to terrorism bar discussed earlier, as defined by s 212(a)(3)(B)(iv) of the *INA.*[72] Section 104 of the *REAL ID Act* modified this waiver process slightly to require that both the Attorney General and the Secretary of State must, in addition, consult the Secretary of Homeland Security before granting this waiver.[73] For example, on June 3, 2008, the Secretaries of Homeland Security and State exercised their discretion under the *INA* to exempt persons belonging to certain listed groups from most aspects of TRI.[74] This authority was exercised under the *Consolidated Appropriations Act of 2008.*[75] This exercise of discretion allows lower officials of the Department of Homeland Security to exempt persons associated with the listed groups from most TRI grounds. Again, this was a post-9/11 development. However, it was not the first time this kind of authority was exercised after 9/11.[76] There is authority in s 212(d)(3)(B)(i) of the *INA* for the Attorney General, the Secretary of Homeland Security, and the Secretary of State to decide not to apply certain TRI grounds to a non-citizen.[77] This authority continues to be exercised to this day.

Waiver by legislation – In addition to the discretionary waivers provided for in certain statutes, in rarer cases the statute itself has directly mandated the waiver of the TRI of a person or group. For example, s 691(b) of the *Consolidated Appropriations Act of 2008* provides that the ten groups listed in it should no longer be considered "terrorist organizations" under the *INA* based on their activities before December 26, 2007. These include key Burmese rebel groups who had been fighting to remove the notorious military junta in that country for many years, a goal that seems to be broadly shared by the US government. Thus, for example, a person who provided material support to the African National Congress (ANC) or the Karen National Union is no longer subject to TRI.[78]

The Possibility of Error or Injustice

As shown above, while the situation was definitely grim before 9/11, post-9/11 statutes have expanded to a significant degree the scope of TRI in the United States. For instance, as Juan Osuna has noted, the definition of a terrorist organization

> includes groups and organizations that are not normally thought of as "terrorists" per se. Read literally, the definition includes, for example, a group of individuals discharging a weapon in an abandoned house, thus causing "substantial damage to property ... This may constitute inappropriate or even criminal behavior, but it is not what we normally think of as "terrorist" activity.[79]

Similarly, as we have seen, the definition of engaging in terrorist activity encompasses even many of those who have been victimized by terrorist groups abroad and who have been forced to contribute funds to the activities of such organizations.

This expansion in the scope of TRI is problematic given the remarkably low standard of proof that the authorities must meet before denying persons admission into the country or removing them on TRI grounds, and considering the charged post-9/11 social and institutional contexts in which the TRI regime must operate. The mix of these three factors (a definitional expansion, a low standard of proof, and a charged context) will, it is argued, increase the immigration bureaucracy's capacity for error or injustice.

As is well recognized in the literature and jurisprudence, in almost all cases the authorities need not show an actual conviction for the impugned "terrorist" conduct.[80] All they need show in most cases is that they have "reasonable grounds" to believe that the non-citizen has behaved in such a way.[81] Clearly this does not require proof beyond a reasonable doubt.[82] It is unclear whether the civil standard of proof on a balance of probabilities must be met.[83] In *In Re U-H-*, the BIA held that "the reasonable ground to believe standard is akin to the familiar 'probable cause' standard ... [and] that a reasonable belief may be formed if the evidence 'is sufficient to justify a reasonable person in the belief that an alien falls within the proscribed category.'"[84] Thus, not all that much evidence needs to be produced before a non-citizen is labelled a terrorist or supporter of terrorism and excluded from the United States.

When this is mixed with the current harsh social and institutional climate (as portrayed in detail in previous chapters), especially the intensified gatekeeping culture within the immigration bureaucracy and the heightened fear and suspicion of Arabs and Muslims that pervade the land, the likelihood of error or injustice is even greater.[85]

This is not a speculative argument, for there is already evidence that this has happened on several occasions. For example, in the Maher Arar case, the findings of a commission of inquiry showed clearly that a Canadian *citizen* of Syrian descent was detained with little if any justification in the United States, summarily deported, and rendered to many months of torture in Syria on the mistaken suspicion of being a member of al-Qaeda.[86] If this could happen to a Canadian citizen, what would be the fate of citizens of other countries, especially those seeking or who have already been granted refuge in the United States?

Human Rights First has reported numerous cases of foreign nationals caught within the broad net cast by the redefinition of TRI.[87] Jamshid, a refugee from Afghanistan, was a young child in 1979 when the Soviet Union invaded his country. Two of his brothers joined the rebellion against the new regime. His father, who had been a member of parliament under a former government, was jailed and tortured by the secret police of the new Soviet-backed regime. In 1983, Jamshid and his family fled to Pakistan as refugees. He carried supplies between Pakistan and Afghanistan for the National Islamic Front of Afghanistan (NIFA), acting at the behest of his older brothers, who were fighting with the group inside Afghanistan. Fearing for his safety, his family sent Jamshid to the United States in 1988, where he arrived as an unaccompanied minor at the age of sixteen and applied for asylum the following year. Due to extreme administrative delays, he was finally granted asylum in 1998. In 1999, he applied for permanent residence. In February 2008, his application was denied, on the basis of his statement (made at age seventeen) that when he was twelve years old he had helped to carry supplies such as weapons, ammunition, flour, and sugar from Pakistan to the soldiers fighting in Afghanistan. The denial letter stated that the Mujahideen "meets the current definition of an undesignated terrorist organization." Notably, the particular group that Jamshid had helped, the NIFA, was generally viewed as the most moderate of the numerous groups that fought politically and militarily against the Soviet occupation of Afghanistan, and the United States itself provided support to the NIFA and other Afghan Mujahideen groups in the 1980s. At the time of Jamshid's application for permanent residence in 1999, the NIFA had effectively ceased to exist even as a political entity, and was no longer functioning as a military force. Its former leaders had assumed an active political role in exile during the last years of Taliban rule, and went on to assume high positions in government and Afghan civil society under President Hamid Karzai. Yet even as of 2009, Jamshid remained in legal limbo, caught by the definition of TRI.[88]

Salih was a member of the democratic opposition in Sudan after the 1989 military coup that brought the current president, Omar Al-Bashir, to power. Specifically, he was a member of the Democratic Unionist Party (DUP), one of the two largest and oldest political parties in Sudan. The DUP was part of the democratically elected coalition government over-thrown by the 1989 coup, and has been in opposition since then. When the coup was followed by a major crackdown on all forms of peaceful political activity, Salih fled to the United States in 1993. He was granted asylum in 1997 and subsequently applied for permanent residence. In early 2008, US Citizenship and Immigration Services (CIS) denied his application on the grounds that his membership in the DUP made him a "member of a terrorist organization." The denial letter noted that he had engaged in such activities as "participat[ing] in a conference organized by the Fund for Peace for the DUP" in 1992 and being "very active within the activities of the DUP" in the late 1980s and early 1990s. The letter then quoted from a variety of Internet sources – all referring to periods of time *after* Salih's arrival in the United States – describing how the Sudan People's Liberation Army (SPLA), a South Sudanese rebel group, had joined the National Democratic Alliance (the opposition umbrella coalition of which the DUP was already a leading member) in the mid-1990s, such that "the DUP and other members of the NDA meet the current definition of an undesignated terrorist organization." However, the letter failed to take chronology into account, overlooking the fact that Salih was already in the United States by the time the SPLA joined the DUP as part of the National Democratic Alliance, and the fact that by the time Salih's application for permanent residence was denied, the SPLA itself had laid down its arms. Salih's application was later reopened, but remained on hold as of 2009.[89]

Such cases, among others, raise serious questions about how much the judgment of the immigration and security bureaucracy can be trusted not to commit such brazen errors or injustice.[90] Some have found the Attorney General's lack of accountability in facilitating such errors or injustices, despite enjoying a huge amount of power, "disturbing."[91] To this one can add that this lack of accountability does nothing to discourage the perpetration of such errors or injustice.

In the end, the fact that there is in reality very little chance of positive judicial review makes this possibility of administrative error and injustice in TRI matters even more worrisome. For example, in refusing to set aside the designation of the People's Mojahedin Organization of Iran and the now defunct Liberation Tigers of Tamil Eelam (LTTE) as FTOs, the US Court of Appeals for the DC Circuit held that the Secretary of State's decision to designate a group as an FTO was a "political judgment," and "decisions of a kind for which the judiciary has neither aptitude, facilities nor responsibilities and have been long held to belong in the domain of political power not subject to judicial intrusion or inquiry."[92] Speaking more broadly, it is fair to say that US courts tend to defer to the executive in the area of immigration law.[93]

Whither Dissent?

It appears that the net effect of the post-9/11 changes to provisions in the *INA* with regard to the provision of material support to terrorists is that any non-citizen who provides support to any group fighting against an established government would *by definition* be engaging in terrorist activity.[94] In the view of Margaret Stock, "the language [deployed under the current TRI regime] is so broad that it punishes 'people who fought for freedom from apartheid in South Africa, Jews who resisted persecution in Germany and Vietnamese and Hmong who aided the United States forces during the Vietnam War.'"[95]

In one case, the BIA found that "[c]ontrary to the respondent's assertions ... there is no exception in the Act [i.e., the *INA*] to the bar to relief in cases involving the use of justifiable force to repel attacks by forces of an *illegitimate* regime."[96] This is the crux of the matter here – that there is no "freedom fighter exception" to TRI in US law, and that this can be problematic.[97]

The troubling character of the suppression of dissent, intended or otherwise, that is facilitated by the expansiveness of the definition of engaging in terrorist activity in the United States is illustrated by reference to a few examples – one historical, the others more contemporary. Former US Secretary of State Condoleezza Rice correctly described as "embarrassing" the fact that until recently Nelson Mandela and ANC leaders were inadmissible to the United States and required a waiver in order to enter it, having been branded terrorists for forcibly resisting the brutal apartheid regime, something for which they are now honoured the world over.[98] It was only in July 2008 that then President George W.

Bush signed a bill into law that remedied this situation.[99] Again, in *In Re S-K-*, the BIA chair declared in frustration that

> we are finding that a Christian member of the ethnic Chin minority in Burma, who clearly has a well-founded fear of being persecuted by one of the more repressive governments in the world, one that the United States Government views as illegitimate, is ineligible to avail herself of asylum in the United States despite posing no threat to the security of this country. It may be, as the majority states, that Congress intended the material support bar to apply very broadly. However, when the bar is applied to cases such as this, it is difficult to concede that this is what Congress intended.[100]

What happened to the case of Luis Posada Carriles, the Cuban exile who led a violent anti-Castro movement and sought asylum in the United States further illustrates this point. In 2005, Carriles requested political asylum in the United States and in May that year, the Venezuelan Supreme Court approved an extradition request for him. He withdrew his asylum appeal and was attempting to leave the country when he was arrested by the DHS. On September 28, 2005, a US immigration judge ruled that he could not be deported because he faced the threat of torture in Venezuela.[101] He was released from jail after paying bond on April 19, 2007. The US Fifth Circuit Court of Appeals in New Orleans rejected a Justice Department request that Carriles be refused bail for entering the US illegally.[102] He was escorted by federal agents to Miami, where "members of the Cuban community welcomed him as a patriot. He was required to remain under 24-hour house arrest until trial, with permission to leave only to meet with attorneys or for doctor's appointments. On May 8, 2007, the court dismissed seven counts of immigration fraud that had been filed against him and ordered his electronic bracelet removed.[103] This ruling was overturned in September 2008 by the US Court of Appeals for the Fifth Circuit, which ruled that Carriles should be tried for the alleged immigration violation.[104] In the 2010 trial, he was found *not* guilty on all charges.[105] Many would see this as a rather curious result. Here, a person who was reasonably believed to have committed acts of violence (even terrorism) but who was ideologically akin to the majority in the US establishment was somehow able to secure his stay and freedom in the United States – in sharp contrast to the negative experiences of even victims of terrorism such as the person in *In Re S-K-.*

There is of course a possibility of administrative waiver, but this is complicated and difficult to get.[106] For example, the US government did not make any exemptions for persons who had been forced to provide material support to terrorist groups for the two years preceding 2006.[107] It appears that in practice the structure of this particular waiver provision tends to – at the very least – require the cooperation of three executive departments (State, Homeland Security, and Justice).[108] As one study concluded, "this is a heavy burden and administratively difficult."[109] This is in part why the US Congress had to legislate much more recently in favour of the exemption from TRI of certain Burmese and other rebel/resistance groups from the material support aspect of TRI.[110] It is thus clear that the waiver authority conferred on certain executive branch officials does not appear to provide an adequate safety valve.[111]

The Canadian Position

There is very little doubt that the TRI provisions of Canadian immigration/refugee law do not owe their character entirely to post-9/11 executive, legislative, and judicial developments. Long before 9/11, the Canadian state had directly or indirectly legislated one form or another of TRI since at least the early 1900s, even though not usually explicitly labelled as such.[112] As long ago as 1919, national security exclusion was introduced into Canada's body of immigration/refugee laws.[113] And although this provision was not expressly stated as a TRI provision, it could definitely accommodate that form of exclusion. However, it was not until 1992 that Bill C-86 introduced explicitly stated TRI clauses into the *Immigration Act* of 1978.[114] What is more, as we have seen, the statute from which the bulk of Canadian immigration/refugee law is currently sourced, the *Immigration and Refugee Protection Act (IRPA)* of 2001, as well as the regulations made under it, basically pre-date 9/11.[115] This is not to say, however, that certain post-9/11 executive, legislative, and judicial developments have not significantly affected the current character of Canada's TRI regime. These developments will be examined below, as part of our focused examination of the definitional changes to that TRI regime after and as a result of 9/11.

Terrorist Activity

First, it must be acknowledged that, as has been suggested earlier and as the Supreme Court of Canada has observed in *Suresh v Canada,* the task of defining terrorism is a notoriously difficult endeavour.[116] In the Court's words, "one searches in vain for an authoritative definition of 'terrorism.'"[117] It is no wonder, then, that although it features prominently in Canada's refugee law regime, the term "terrorism" as it is used in s 34 of the *IRPA* (excluding from Canada all non-citizens who are impugned in the stated ways for terrorism) is not defined either in that statute or in its regulations.[118] The largely interchangeable phrase "terrorist activity" is similarly left undefined by the *IRPA.*

Thus, in order to understand more fully the meaning of these similar expressions in Canadian immigration/refugee law, the *IRPA* must be read alongside the *Anti-terrorism Act (ATA),*[119] and the major cases that have grappled with this question in the last several years (especially the *Suresh* and *Khawaja* cases).[120] Significantly, these are all post-9/11 statutory and judicial interventions. Indeed, there was no definition of terrorist activity in Canada before 9/11.[121]

As summarized by government lawyers, s 4 of the *ATA* defined "terrorist activity" as including

> an act or omission undertaken, inside or outside Canada, [for a political, religious or ideological purpose] that is intended to intimidate the public with respect to its security, including economic security, or to compel a person, government or organization (whether inside or outside Canada) from doing or refraining from to do any act, and that intentionally causes one of a number of specified forms of serious harm. These harms include causing death or serious bodily harm, endangering life, causing a serious risk to health or safety, causing substantial property damage where it would also cause one of the other harms listed above, and in certain circumstances, causing serious interference or disruption of an essential service, facility or system, whether public or private. As well, that aspect of the definition

that relates to seriously interfering with or disrupting an essential service contains an exception for advocacy, protest, dissent and stoppage of work, providing this is not intended to cause most of the other forms of harm referred to in the definition. This exception recognizes that even unlawful protests and strikes that could lead to the disruption of an essential service are not the same thing as terrorist activity under the ATA.[122]

The definition also includes the offences provided for in a long list of international treaties, if committed in Canada, as specified in s 4 of the *ATA*. These offences mostly relate to the prevention of aircraft hijacking, defence of internationally protected persons, protection of nuclear material, safety of maritime transport and structures, and suppression of terrorist bombings and financing. The statutory effect of the *ATA* in this respect was to introduce this definition into the *Criminal Code*. Thus, s 83.01 of the *Criminal Code* (as amended by the *ATA*) creates a statutory definition of "terrorist activity" that embraces a wide range of acts committed both in and outside Canada.[123]

Critics of this definition have, among other things, charged that it is rather too broad in scope. A leading authority on the *ATA*, has characterized it as broader in scope than any other related definition in the history of attempts to curb and punish political violence in Canada.[124] Others have argued that the definition "catches a potentially wide sphere of human activity."[125] These scholars even go as far as to claim that the definitions of terrorism in the US *PATRIOT Act* and the British *Terrorism Act* are tighter and less expansive than that of the *ATA*.[126] It is no wonder, then, that they also describe the *ATA* definition as "extremely broad."[127]

However, the courts have thus far not tended to share this view. For example, in the *Khawaja* case, the Ontario Superior Court held that as expansive as the definition or aspects of it are, they are neither overbroad nor unconstitutionally vague.[128] Similarly, in *United States of America v Nadarajah*, the Ontario Superior Court expressly held that the definition of "terrorist activity" in s 83.01(1)(b) of the *Criminal Code* was neither vague nor overbroad and did not constitute an infringement of the freedoms in ss 2(a) and 2(b) of the *Canadian Charter of Rights and Freedoms*.[129]

The Court in *Khawaja* also addressed head-on the question of the novel inclusion of "motive" as an element of the *ATA* definition of terrorist activity. Section 83.01(1)(b)(i)(A) had made "proof under that part of the definition of 'terrorist activity' ... dependent on showing that the specified activity was undertaken *in whole or in part* for a political, religious or ideological objective or cause."[130] The Court reasoned that

> it seems to me that the inevitable impact to flow from the inclusion of the "political, religious or ideological purpose" requirement in the definition of "terrorist activity" will be to focus investigative and prosecutorial scrutiny on the political, religious and ideological beliefs, opinions and expressions of persons and groups in Canada and abroad. Equally inevitable will be the chilling effect Webb predicts. There will also be an indirect or rebound effect of the sort Professor Stribopoulos described, as individuals' and authorities' attitudes and conduct reflect the shadow of suspicion and anger falling over all who appear ... to have any connection with the religious, political or ideological grouping identified with specific terrorist acts. This in my view amounts to a prima facie infringement or limitation of freedoms of conscience, religion, thought, belief, expression, and association such that would have to be justified with reference to s.1 of the Charter.[131]

The Court went on later to hold that this infringement of the *Charter* was not saved by s 1 of that document.[132] In reaching this conclusion, the Court found it significant that the definition of terrorist activity in the United States and many other "Western" countries "contains no definitional element of motive resembling that in the Canadian statute [i.e., the *ATA*]."[133] In the end, rather than strike down the entire definition, the Court chose to sever the offending clause from it and save the rest of the definition.[134]

The *Suresh* case provides an alternative definition, although only of the term "terrorism" (as opposed to "terrorist activity") as it should be used in understanding the TRI regime established in the *IRPA*. While agreeing that no single definition of terrorism is accepted the world over or even in Canada, the Supreme Court of Canada declared that it "was not persuaded, however, that the term 'terrorism' is so unsettled that it cannot set the proper boundaries of legal adjudication."[135] It then went on to hold that the definition of "terrorism" in the *International Convention for the Suppression of the Financing of Terrorism* forms the core of meaning to be attributed to the word "terrorism" as used in the then *Immigration Act* (and by analogy the *IRPA*), and declared that "this definition catches the essence of what the world understands by 'terrorism.'"[136] The definition adopted by the Court from the aforementioned treaty provides that "terrorism" includes "any act intended to cause death or serious bodily injury to a civilian, or to any other person not taking an active part in the hostilities in a situation of armed conflict, when the purpose of such act, by its nature or context, is to intimidate a population, or to compel a government or an international organization to do or to abstain from doing any act."[137] Remarkably, with minor departures, it is does not seem to be all that different from the core of the definition provided in the *ATA*, less the portion struck down by the judge in the *Khawaja* case.

Compared with the US position, the Canadian definition of "terrorist activity" (as opposed to "engaging in terrorist activity") seems to be different in some respects. While the US definition of terrorist activity in s 212(a)(3)(B)(iii) of the *INA* is clearly limited by the requirement that if committed abroad the act must be unlawful in the place where it was committed, the Canadian one is not so circumscribed, at least not in an explicit way. In addition, while the *ATA* definition initially included "motive" as an element of the definition before that aspect was struck down by the Canadian courts, the US equivalent never did include this element, at least not explicitly.

Also noteworthy is that, as we have also seen, while there has been quite a lot of change to the state of affairs regarding the definition of terrorist activity/terrorism in Canada after 9/11, there was relatively little significant change in this regard in the pre- and post-9/11 situations in the United States. This is not to say, of course, that there were no significant changes to other aspects of the TRI regime in the United States after 9/11.

Providing Material Support to Terrorists

Although s 19 of the *Immigration Act* of 1976 did not explicitly define terrorism or make the provision of material support to terrorists a ground for TRI, it is quite clear that the provision of such support was a ground for TRI long before 9/11. The fact that those who were believed on reasonable grounds to have provided material support to terrorists came within the purview of the terrorism bar to admission to Canada as provided for in s 19 was put well beyond doubt by the reasoning of the Supreme Court of Canada in the *Suresh* case. One of the grounds on which Mr. Suresh was held to be inadmissible in Canada (though he could not be removed as he faced a substantial risk of torture in Sri Lanka) was the fact that he was a fundraiser for the World Tamil Movement, an organization that at the very least provided support to the Liberation Tigers of Tamil Eelam (LTTE), a group that was viewed as terrorist.[138] As the Supreme Court stated, Suresh had not been "involved in actual terrorist activity in Canada, but merely in fundraising and support activities that may, in some part, contribute to the civil war efforts of Tamils in Sri Lanka."[139] It concluded that "persons associated with terrorism or terrorist organizations" in this and other ways are inadmissible under section 19 of the then effective *Immigration Act*, and their exclusion from Canada is not unconstitutional.[140]

It is also clear that the Supreme Court's reasoning in *Suresh* will apply by analogy to the current, post-9/11 TRI regime, such that the provision of material support to terrorists continues to be a ground for TRI in Canada. In any case, the definition of terrorist activity introduced into the *Criminal Code* by the *ATA*, and the provisions of that statute relating to the financing of terrorism, have placed beyond reasonable doubt the fact that provision of material support to terrorists renders the offender culpable for terrorism. Significantly, the new s 83.01 of the *Criminal Code* includes within the definition of terrorist activity those involved in a conspiracy to commit terrorism or who are accessories after the fact. These two concepts are broad enough to accommodate some of those who provide material support to terrorists. Sections 83.02 and 83.03 are more explicit in outlawing the provision of property "intending that it will be used or knowing that it will be used" to commit terrorism. And since the *ATA*'s provisions as to who can be indicted for terrorism must surely inform future decisions as to TRI, it is fair to conclude that refugees who come within the purview of any of the abovementioned *ATA*-generated *Criminal Code* provisions (for, in effect, providing material support to terrorists) will also fit within the TRI provisions in s 34 of the *IRPA* and be ordinarily removable from Canada, as long as they also constitute a danger to the security of Canada.

Like their US equivalents, these provisions are troubled, however, by "problems of sheer breadth."[141] They may catch even those who fight against brutal regimes to which Canada itself is opposed, and certainly threaten to render inadmissible in Canada very many widely acknowledged and even venerated freedom fighters. The danger posed by the expansive scope of these provisions is, as in the United States, exacerbated by the fact that, given that the *ATA* effectively leaves much discretion to interpret and implement its provisions in the hands of law enforcement officers, and in view of the nature of the current social context in Canada, the ill effects of implementing them will disproportionately affect members of specific ethno-cultural groups.[142]

Unlike in the United States, where the only way a person who provided material support to a terrorist group under duress can escape TRI is by a grant of ministerial or statutory waiver, the very wording of s 83.02 of the *Criminal Code*, one of the "financing of terrorism" provisions of the *ATA*, explicitly absolves from the charge of terrorism those who have "lawful justification or excuse" for providing property to a terrorist group. It follows therefore that a refugee who has been coerced to pay protection money or the like to a terrorist group would not be caught by this provision, and would most likely not be viewed as inadmissible merely on this basis. As such, the question of the grant of a waiver does not even arise. However, inexplicably in my view, s 83.03 does not explicitly save this class of persons from being charged with terrorism.

Unlike in the United States as well, the person who provides the material support must in virtually all cases "subjectively know" that it will be used for terrorism. The knowledge requirement is thus central in the Canadian case.[143] In *Suresh*, the Supreme Court of Canada concluded that

> it was not the intention of Parliament to include in the s.19 [read s 34 *IRPA*] class of suspect persons those who innocently contribute to ...

terrorist organizations. This is supported by the provision found at the end of s.19, which exempts "persons who have satisfied the Minister that their admission would not be detrimental to the national interest." Section 19 must therefore be read as permitting a refugee to establish that his or her continued residence in Canada will not be detrimental to Canada, notwithstanding proof that the person is associated with ... a terrorist organization. This permits a refugee to establish that the alleged association with the terrorist group was innocent.[144]

Yet, in both countries once an organization has been listed as a terrorist group, it will be extremely difficult for one to show ignorance that it possessed this character.[145] Again, as the Supreme Court of Canada reasoning shows, the Canadian material support TRI scheme relies on the same kind of "exclude in broad terms then allow for executive waiver" scheme found in the United States.

More recent cases illustrate and buttress the argument regarding the Canadian position. For example, in *Toronto Coalition to Stop the War v Canada (Minister of Public Safety and Emergency Preparedness)*, a motion was brought by the applicants (the Toronto Coalition to Stop the War, the British Member of Parliament George Galloway, and others) praying the court to grant them an interim injunction permitting Galloway to enter Canada.[146] The Coalition and the other applicants scheduled anti-war public forums over a series of days in different Canadian cities. Galloway was scheduled to speak at the forums and sought to ensure that he would not be detained on entry on grounds of inadmissibility related to security. Galloway had no criminal record and no prior problems with entry. His personal views and open sympathy for the Palestinian cause was a matter of public record. Media reported that he was part of a convoy that delivered financial and material assistance to Gaza. The Hamas government in Gaza delivered a Palestinian passport to Galloway. Hamas was listed as a terrorist organization in Canada. An official of the immigration section of the High Commission of Canada in Britain advised Galloway as a matter of courtesy that he was inadmissible to Canada on security grounds based on a preliminary assessment. The letter stated:

> Hamas is a listed terrorist organization in Canada. There are reasonable grounds to believe you have provided financial support for

Hamas. Specifically, we have information that indicates you organized a convoy worth over one million British pounds in aid and vehicles, and personally donated vehicles and financing to Hamas Prime Minister Ismail Haniya. Your material support for this organization makes you inadmissible to Canada.

The assessment invited Galloway to make submissions, failing which a final determination on inadmissibility would be made at the point of entry. Galloway made submissions, stating that he had never engaged in terrorism, nor had he ever been a member of a terrorist organization. He characterized the allegations in the preliminary assessment as unreasonable and defamatory; however, he did not receive any assurances that he would be allowed entry. The court dismissed the motion for an interim injunction that would allow Galloway to enter Canada, on the basis that the refusal to grant the relief sought would not result in irreparable harm, nor did the balance of convenience favour the applicants. The court held that technology existed that would provide Galloway with the opportunity to present his views to the anti-war forums from outside of Canada. Immigration officers were conferred exclusive legal authority to determine the admissibility of a foreign national, and no final determination had yet been made in that regard with respect to the admission of Galloway.

The Definition of a "Terrorist Organization"

Prior to 9/11, there was no authoritative statutory definition of "terrorist group" in Canada. After 9/11, s 83.01 of the *Criminal Code* (as amended by the *ATA*) created a statutory definition of that expression. According to that provision, the phrase "terrorist group" means "(a) an entity that has as one of its purposes or activities facilitating or carrying out any terrorist activity, or (b) a listed entity."

According to s 83.05(1) of the *Criminal Code*, on the recommendation of the Minister of Public Safety, the Governor-in-Council may list an entity if satisfied that there are reasonable grounds to believe that the group has knowingly carried out, attempted to carry out, participated in, or facilitated a terrorist activity, or is knowingly acting on behalf of, at the direction of, or in association with a terrorist group.[147] Once a decision is made, the name of the group is published in the *Canada*

Gazette as being on the "list of entities."[148] As at June 21, 2017, there were fifty-four entities on this list (though some as listed under their different names), and as at June 21, 2019, the number of entities on this list had grown to sixty.[149]

On the whole, there seems to be very little, if any, significant practical difference between the Canadian concept of a "terrorist group" as discussed here and the US definition of a "terrorist organization" analyzed earlier in this chapter.

The *IRPA* does not define the term "organization," hence there has been litigation in Canada concerning when a group is an "organization." However, this litigation has mostly focused on whether a group is a "criminal organization" pursuant to s 37 of the *IRPA*, and has not generally been directed at determining when a group is a "terrorist organization."[150] The reason for this is that since groups considered "terrorist organizations" are generally listed by the government in the list of entities, there is usually not all that much to argue about in this regard. Exceptions do occur, however. For instance, in *United States of America v Nadarajah*,[151] a Canadian court discussed the question of when there is "sufficient evidence that a group was a 'terrorist group'" for the purposes of s 83.01 of the *Criminal Code*. In that case, the Record of the Case specifically indicated that an expert would be called to testify about the background, structure, leadership, methods of operation, and worldwide support system of the LTTE (the group at issue), and the court held that such expert testimony was sufficient to establish the LTTE as a terrorist group. The court further noted that

> in addition to the evidence in the Record of the Case being sufficient to establish that the LTTE is a terrorist group, it is also established, in my view, by the fact that on April 8, 2006, the Canadian Government listed the LTTE as a listed entity under s. 83.05 of the *Criminal Code* ... Section 83.01 of the *Criminal Code* defines a terrorist group as being, among other things, a "listed entity." Accordingly, as of April 8, 2006, which was before the Authorities to Proceed in this proceeding were first issued against either Mr. Nadarajah or Mr. Sriskandarajah, the LTTE was a terrorist group as defined in s. 83.01 of the *Criminal Code*.

I am therefore satisfied that there is evidence in the Record of the Case, which if accepted, establishes that the LTTE is a terrorist group.

Mere Membership in Foreign Terrorist Organizations

Well before 9/11, s 19 of the defunct *Immigration Act* of 1976 had included "membership" in an organization regarded as terrorist by the Canadian authorities as a ground for TRI. That provision clearly rendered inadmissible in Canada those refugees with respect of whom there were reasonable grounds to believe that they were members of an organization that there were reasonable grounds to believe had engaged or would engage in terrorism.[152] During this pre-9/11 era, although the Federal Court Trial Division tended to "accord a broad and unrestricted interpretation" to the concept of "membership" in a terrorist group, it suggested in *Al Yamani v Canada* that the provision in this section that a non-citizen was not inadmissible in Canada merely because of membership in an organization that is likely to engage in acts of violence was unconstitutional, being an infringement on the person's right to freedom of association under the *Charter*.[153]

After 9/11, however, the reasoning of the Supreme Court of Canada in *Suresh* suggests that the logic of *Al Yamani* is no longer good law. In *Suresh,* the Court explicitly stated that the provisions of s 19 of the old *Immigration Act* relating to mere membership in a terrorist organization as a ground for inadmissibility were not unconstitutional. In the Court's view, these provisions did not violate the rights to free association and expression guaranteed by the *Charter* because the Constitution does not protect violent forms of expression and association; in any case, s 1 of the *Charter* would justify such restrictions.[154]

As such, the current position is that since the reasoning in *Suresh* does apply (with any necessary modifications) to the interpretation of s 34 of the *IRPA*, the mere membership of a refugee in a terrorist group suffices to render that person inadmissible in Canada, for s 34(1) (f) is couched in very similar terms to the defunct s 19 that was the subject of interpretation in *Suresh*. The courts tend to agree that the term "membership" here should be given "an unrestricted and broad interpretation."[155]

Notably, there is no definition of the term "member" in the *IRPA*, and the courts have not established a precise and exhaustive definition.[156] In interpreting the term "member" in the former *Immigration Act*,[157] the court in *Canada v Singh* stated that the term was to be given an "unrestricted and broad interpretation."[158] Subsequently, in *Poshteh v Canada*, the court held that the same considerations apply to s 34(1)(f) of the *IRPA*.[159] The court held that a refugee claimant who had handed out flyers for a terrorist organization for two years while he was a minor was a "member" of that organization, despite never having attended any meetings, or participated in any way beyond giving out leaflets in his local community, and despite being a minor at the time.[160] This limited "membership" alone was sufficient to render Mr. Poshteh inadmissible. Moreover, in *Jahazi v Canada*, Mr. Jahazi, a long-time Canadian temporary resident, was denied permanent residence on the basis of s 34(1)(f) for being a "member of a terrorist organization," but was never informed of the name of the terrorist group of which he was allegedly a member.[161] The judge held that this did not prejudice him, stating that "the knowledge of the specific organization of which he was eventually found to belong could not have materially modified the substance of his answers, especially since he denied any involvement with a subversive or terrorist organization."[162] Jahazi was thus deemed to be inadmissible simply on the basis of membership in an alleged terrorist organization whose name was never even disclosed to him.

This broad conception of membership in terrorist organizations was sustained in *Ismael v Canada*.[163] This case concerned an application for judicial review of a decision of the Immigration Division of the Immigration and Refugee Board of Canada (IRB) in which the Board found the applicant inadmissible to Canada under s 34(1)(f) of the *IRPA*. The thirty-seven-year-old refugee claimant was a citizen of Ethiopia. In his Personal Information Form (PIF), he described himself as a supporter of the Oromo Liberation Front (OLF) who recruited people to work for the OLF and collected/donated money for/to the organization. In an interview with the Canadian Security Intelligence Service (CSIS), he explained that he had become a supporter of the OLF in 1991, when he was twenty years old, as the new regime did not favour the Oromo people. He explained that his activities consisted of collecting money to support the OLF, and he agreed that this money was presumably used to help fighters in the hills, although he was never sure what it was used for. The applicant also donated some money himself. In late 1997, he was arrested and detained by the Ethiopian authorities as a suspected supporter of the OLF. Shortly after being released from prison, he fled Ethiopia and came to Canada. In his PIF, he alleged that he was "targeted because of [his] activities in support of the O.L.F." and that he would face imprisonment or death if he returned to Ethiopia because of his involvement with the OLF. He indicated that he had been a supporter of the OLF from 1991 until 1998. The issue was whether he was a "member" of the OLF under s 34(1)(f) of the *IRPA*. The court held that the Board's finding that the applicant was a member was not unreasonable, noting at para 21: "Among other things, for a period of seven years (1991–98), the applicant raised funds for the organization, voluntarily engaged in recruiting other members/supporters, and left the organization only when he was forced to leave the country."

An even looser conception of membership was adopted more recently in *Kanagendran v Canada*.[164] This judicial review matter turned on whether it was reasonable for the Immigration Division to find that membership in the Tamil National Alliance (TNA), a political party, was tantamount to being a member of the Liberation Tigers of Tamil Eelam. The applicant admitted to having been a member of the TNA, but he argued that while the TNA was collaborating with the LTTE, the two were operating in parallel and that the TNA was not a proxy for the LTTE. He testified that at no time in his service as a member of parliament did he ever receive directives from the LTTE, nor did the TNA have any involvement in the activities of the LTTE. While he supported the same end goal of the liberation of Tamils, he never considered himself a member of the LTTE, and had never raised support, either financial or otherwise, for the LTTE. He stated that he had never endorsed their use of violence to forward their agenda. However, the court found that there was sufficient documentary evidence to indicate that the TNA was subservient to the LTTE and "explicitly served as the proxy of the LTTE." The Immigration Division's conclusion was therefore held to be reasonable.

It should be noted, however, that although the Supreme Court of Canada was interpreting another provision in *Ezokola v Canada*,[165] its decision in this case ought to cast significant doubt on the wisdom of the approach taken so far by the Canadian courts on this question.[166] In that case, the Court held that mere membership in a government (an organization) was not enough to render a junior diplomat complicit in any international crimes committed by the government.[167] At least one lower court has already raised this question.[168]

Comparatively, the main difference between the positions of Canada and the United States is that the *IRPA* does not make any distinctions between membership in a designated/listed terrorist group and membership in non-designated ones. On its own, however, this distinction is not really significant. If anything, the US provision appears to be a little more lenient here, since in the case of non-designated terrorist groups, it allows impugned non-citizens the escape route of showing, before even getting to the point of having to seek an executive waiver, that they did not know, and could not reasonably have known, that the organization to which they belonged was a terrorist group. There is no such leeway in the Canadian provision. The common escape route from this kind of TRI is, in all cases and regardless of whether the group is designated, to seek and obtain a waiver from the relevant minister.

It should also be emphasized that the use and abuse of at least two terror watch lists for individuals (under the Passenger Protect program and Tuscan) interacts with and facilitates the operation of the TRI regime in Canada. This issue is discussed below under the heading "International Legal Standards and the Post-9/11 Terrorism-Related Inadmissibility Regimes in Canada and the United States."

Receipt of Military Training from a Terrorist Organization

Both before and after 9/11, there does not appear to have been any explicit provision in Canadian law for TRI merely for receiving military training from a terrorist organization. However, given the broad scope of the definitions of terrorist activity, membership in a terrorist group, and so on, a person who is shown to have received such training could presumably be declared inadmissible on such other subgrounds of TRI.

Endorsing Terrorist Activity

Both before and after 9/11, there has not been any direct equivalent in Canadian law of the US ground of TRI that bars from that country representatives of groups that endorse or espouse (as opposed to committing) terrorism. There is also no direct equivalent in Canada of the US ground of TRI that renders inadmissible non-citizens in a position of prominence in another country who use their position there to espouse or endorse terrorism. The closest analogy to these two grounds of TRI in Canadian law is the post-9/11 inclusion within the *ATA*'s definition of terrorist activity (i.e., in the new s 83.01(1)(b)(ii)(E) of the *Criminal Code*) of the act of "counseling" terrorist activity. Given this fact, any non-citizen who counsels terrorist activity (which may include many who espouse or endorse it) would very likely be seen by the courts as coming within the purview of the TRI provisions in s 34 of the *IRPA*. Although, as in the United States, this particular form is a post-9/11 innovation, its content does not differ significantly from the pre-9/11 prohibitions on intentional mass murder in the *Criminal Code*.[169]

Spouses and Children

Ordinarily, s 42 of the *IRPA*, which has been in force since 2002, would render inadmissible a family member of a person who has been determined to be inadmissible on grounds of terrorism. This provision does not apply to already accepted refugees, however – refugees (as opposed to refugee claimants) are not rendered inadmissible merely because their family member is inadmissible, including on grounds of TRI. It is important to reiterate that in post-9/11 Canada, refugee claimants themselves can still be found inadmissible for terrorism under s 42 because of the TRI of family members. In *Tareen v Canada*, the refugee claimants (principal claimant and his family members) were all found to be inadmissible due to the principal claimant's TRI.[170] The court found that the principal claimant's having been a senior official in the Afghan government during a period of overlap with Taliban rule made him inadmissible. The family members were then found inadmissible pursuant to s 42.

Before 9/11, there was no explicit exception carved out for refugees by the equivalent provision in s 19(2)(c) of the defunct *Immigration Act* of 1976.[171] One case in which the entire family was rendered inadmissible due to the TRI of one member is *Khalil v Canada*.[172] While this was actually a tort case, the facts are relevant. Ms. Haj Khalil and her two children were granted Convention refugee status shortly after their arrival in Canada in 1994. Ms. Khalil then applied for permanent residence, and included her children and her husband (who was abroad) as dependents. In late 1999, she was found to be inadmissible on security grounds pursuant to s 34(1)(f) of the *IRPA*, because of her husband's involvement with the Palestine Liberation Organization. In February 2000, she was notified that her application had been refused. Due to various administrative delays, a decision with respect to her application remained outstanding in 2008. (The two children were granted permanent residence in late 2006 and early 2007, after their applications were severed from their mother's.) Ms. Khalil sued the Crown for negligence due to unreasonable delay, which caused her personal loss. The court dismissed her action, claiming that there was insufficient proximity to ground a private law duty of care. In *Khalil v Canada*, the Federal Court of Appeal dismissed her appeal.[173]

Here, the post-9/11 Canadian position is, on the whole, better than the US equivalent with regard to those refugees who would ordinarily be inadmissible as a result of a family member's inadmissibility. As we have seen, many (albeit not all) such persons would be inadmissible in the United States. In Canada, no accepted refugee at all can be excluded merely on this basis.

Expanded Ability to Remove Those Already Admitted to Canada

There was virtually no discrepancy in Canada on or immediately before 9/11 between the scope of the grounds for rendering inadmissible a non-citizen seeking entry and the grounds for inadmissibility of non-citizens already admitted here. Thus, there have been no changes in this respect after and because of 9/11.

Blanket Travel Bans

Both during the period between the Second World War and September 11, 2001, and in the post-911 era, Canada never imposed a blanket travel ban of the kind instituted by the Trump Administration. Indeed, the Trudeau government appears to be opposed to the US approach to this matter.[174] At the very least, Prime Minister Justin Trudeau is reported to hold a "different view of the issue."[175]

The Possibility of Waivers

Conscious of the expansiveness of its TRI provisions and the fact that the legislation catches within its net a potentially huge swath of non-citizens, many of them not necessarily culpable for terrorism, the drafters of the *IRPA* included a built-in safety or escape hatch. Initially, s 34(2) was this escape hatch, but it later became s 42.1 of the *IRPA*. This clause provides that any person who would otherwise be caught by many of the TRI grounds set out in s 34(1) would escape being so impugned if the person "satisfies the Minister" that his or her presence in Canada would not be detrimental to the national interest. For example, although mere membership in a proscribed organization can make a person liable for TRI in Canada, persons who did not know of the violent character of the organization may possibly use the s 34(2) exception.[176] To be clear, this provision applies to all the grounds of TRI discussed above.

This concept of empowering Ministers to, in their discretion, grant waivers to those who would ordinarily be caught by a TRI provision is hardly a post-9/11 invention. It has existed in one form or another in Canadian law since at least the enactment of s 19 of the defunct *Immigration Act* of 1976.[177] Subsection 19(1)(e) of that *Act* contains the same kind of waiver provision as s 34(2) of the *IRPA*.

It is also noteworthy that, at its core, the Canadian TRI waiver scheme outlined above is not significantly different from its US equivalent. Canadian waivers are, at the very least, as difficult to obtain as their US equivalents. Below are three examples of cases in which applicants accused of terrorism have unsuccessfully sought such waivers, and have thus applied for judicial review of the Minister's denials of their waiver applications. In all three cases, the court upheld the Minister's exercise of discretion (which is almost always the result in such cases, since the standard of review is the "reasonableness" of the Minister's decision and not its "correctness").

The first example is *Kablawi v Canada*.[178] Mr. Kablawi and his family came to Canada in 1998 and were found to be Convention refugees, based on Kablawi's membership in the Syrian Socialist Nationalist Party. He claimed that attempts had been made on his life because he was trying to root out corruption in the Party. Kablawi was later found inadmissible to Canada because he had been a member for twenty-three years of a political organization believed to engage in acts of violence. He then tried to convince the Minister that his presence in Canada would not be detrimental to the public interest, pursuant to the exemption under s 34(2) of the *IRPA*. He submitted that his existence in Canada had been peaceful and productive and that he had severed his ties with the Party, and he claimed to have had no knowledge of any violence perpetrated by the Party while he was a member. However, the Canadian Border Services Agency concluded that this denial of knowledge was improbable, and recommended that the Minister refuse Kablawi's request for relief, despite the significant humanitarian and compassionate grounds to consider. The Minister dismissed Kablawi's application for waiver, and he applied to the Federal Court for judicial review, claiming that the Minister had breached the duty of fairness. The Court dismissed his application, holding that the Minister had breached no duty of fairness to Kablawi. He had a leadership role in the Party for too many years not to know what was going on. The Agency's report to the Minister was fair and balanced in its consideration of the humanitarian and compassionate factors applicable to the case.

In *Chogolzadeh v Canada*, the Mujahedin-e-Khalq (MEK) was listed as a terrorist entity by the government of Canada.[179] Mr. Chogolzadeh had been involved with the MEK in the 1980s, distributing literature and gathering medicine, arms, food, and petrol. In 1991, the MEK arranged for his four children to come to Canada. Later that year, Chogolzadeh stopped supporting the MEK when it announced it would fight with the government of Saddam Hussein against the Iraqi Kurds. He was detained by the MEK in March 1991, but escaped on October 30. He came to Canada on January 26, 1993, and was granted a Convention Refugee Minister's Permit. Subsequent to an interview on September 13, 2000, an immigration officer considered the applicant inadmissible to Canada due to his involvement with the MEK. Chogolzadeh applied to the

Minister for a waiver under s 34(2), claiming that his presence in Canada would not be detrimental to the national interest. The Minister denied his application, determining that Chogolzadeh had furthered the goals of the MEK and had been aware of its activities, including bombings, killings, and assassinations. The Minister concluded that Chogolzadeh had had a level of trust with the MEK, since the MEK had arranged for his children to come to Canada, that his activities indicated a strong allegiance to an organization committed to the use of violence, of which the applicant was aware, and that such considerations outweighed any national interest that would enable the Minister to approve the application. Chogolzadeh then applied for judicial review of the Minister's decision. The application was dismissed, with the court holding that decisions of the Minister under s 34(2) were to be upheld unless they were unreasonable, and it was open to the Minister to conclude that evidence favourable to an exemption did not outweigh the impact of the applicant's long-standing past membership in a terrorist organization.

The third example is *Soe v Canada*.[180] Mr. Soe was denied a waiver in Canada despite the fact that a US judge had found his presence in the United States not to be detrimental, and the fact that his "terrorist" activities had been for the cause of democracy, in an attempt to raise awareness of the situation in Burma.

The Possibility of Error or Injustice

As a similar argument has been made with respect to the US position, the discussion of several points made here will be relatively brief.

First, there is little disagreement in the literature and jurisprudence that the TRI provisions of Canadian law have a very wide scope, and potentially impugn a broad range of non-citizens, some much more appropriately than others. It is only reasonable to expect that the potential for the Canadian TRI regime to result in error or injustice has been significantly augmented in the post-9/11 era, given the breadth of these provisions; considering the fact that the relevant authorities are, in virtually all TRI cases, merely required to show "reasonable grounds to believe" that the non-citizen has engaged or will engage in terrorism (a remarkably low standard of proof that is even lower than the civil standard of proof on a balance of probabilities);[181] and in the light of the indisputably harsh character of the post-9/11 social and institutional climate (especially against Arabs and Muslims in Canada).[182]

Indeed, just as we saw in our discussion of the equivalent US position, there is evidence to suggest that this is already the case in Canada. In June 2009, CSIS admitted to the Federal Court of Canada that it had failed to disclose evidence that one of its confidential informants in the TRI and security certificate case against a Syrian refugee named Hassan Almrei was deceptive in answering questions and that another such witness had not been subjected to a lie detector test as the agency had earlier claimed.[183] One month earlier, the same agency had been forced to admit that it had also withheld evidence from another judge of the same court regarding polygraph tests that had cast doubt on the reliability of one of its key witnesses in a similar case against Moham-med Harkat, a Syrian refugee who had been accepted as a Convention refugee in 2000, after entering Canada on a fake passport in 1993.[184] The post-9/11 unjust (or at best mistaken) treatment of Maher Arar, in part as a result of the actions of members of the Canadian security/police establishment who suspected him of ties to terrorism, only supports the claim that the expansive scope of the TRI provisions in the *IRPA* would likely combine with other factors to increase significantly the chances of error or injustice in the implementation of those provisions.[185]

On the whole, it is important to note that there is not much qualitative difference between the Canadian and US situations in this regard, with the key difference between the two being one of scale.

Whither Dissent?

Again, given the discussion earlier of this question in the US context, the discussion here will be brief. As we have seen, the definitional breadth of the TRI regime is quite vast. Some have argued, with some justification, that the definition of terrorism in the *ATA* makes no distinction between activities against a democratic government and activities against a dictatorship.[186] Others have suggested that the definition of terrorist activity in the *ATA* could catch "individuals and groups engaged in unlawful advocacy, protest, dissent or stoppage of work."[187] Indeed, it is hardly controversial that this all-embracing posture tends to characterize the approach of the Canadian immigration/security authorities to the application of the *IRPA*'s TRI provisions to the real world. The evidence for this is very solid in terms of both quantity and quality.

For example, in the *Suresh* case, the court implicitly accepted that the potential scope of a provision similar to s 34(1) of the *IRPA* was very broad, but argued that the built-in authority of the relevant minister to waive a person's inadmissibility under that provision saved it from being so broad as to catch persons "who innocently contribute to or become members of terrorist organizations."[188] Yet, the very fact that Mr. Suresh himself (a non-citizen who supported an organization, the LTTE, in its fight against another country entirely and who clearly did not pose any direct threat to Canada) was still caught firmly by the definitional scope of the Canadian TRI regime illustrates the point at hand. Another example is the exclusion from permanent residence in Canada of Ms. Nawal Haj Khalil, a Palestinian refugee who had worked as a magazine writer for the Palestine Liberation Organization (PLO).[189] Similarly, in 2008, a senior Eritrean government official (the foreign minister) was barred from entering Canada because he was a member of the ruling party in that country, a group that had violently overthrown the brutal Mengistu-led "Derg" junta in the old Ethiopia.[190] At the time of his alleged activities, Eritrea was still part of Ethiopia. And in March 2009, prominent left-wing British MP George Galloway was ruled inadmissible allegedly because of his contrary views on Canada's role in Afghanistan and his financial support for the people of Gaza (which was construed by the Conservative government of the time as support for Hamas).[191] Galloway had been scheduled to give a couple of talks in and around Toronto on "resisting war."[192]

The unmistakable signal sent by all of the above TRI decisions is that (perhaps depending on the nature of their politics) many of those who fight or support groups that fight against brutal or repressive regimes are liable to TRI in Canada. This tendency has grown to some extent since 9/11. It is mainly in this way that the expansive definitional scope of the Canadian TRI regime facilitates the suppression of some forms of dissent.

It is of course possible for affected refugees to apply to the relevant minister to waive their TRI, thereby enabling them to either enter or remain in Canada, or to become a Canadian permanent resident. In practice, however, such waivers are difficult to obtain, are as politically determined as most other TRI decisions, and may take years to materialize, if at all. For example, Ms. Khalil's application for such a waiver languished for many years in the bureaucracy.[193] In another *Khalil v Canada* case, she had applied for judicial review of the decision denying her permanent residence, as well as a review of the denial of ministerial relief from her inadmissibility finding.[194] While the court found that she had been treated fairly by the officer who found her to be inadmissible, it did allow the application for judicial review of ministerial relief and ordered the Minister to reconsider her request for a waiver of her inadmissibility. This decision was reversed on appeal, however.[195] The Federal Court of Appeal held that in determining whether a person's continued presence in Canada would not be detrimental to the national interest, the Minister must consider more than just national security and whether the applicant was a danger to the public or to the safety of any person. The Court held that the Minister had flexibility in determining whether a person's presence in Canada would be detrimental to the national interest, and that the Minister had considered both positive and negative factors highlighted in the CBSA assessment. Thus, the Minister's decision not to grant the waiver to Khalil was held to be reasonable. In the same vein, when asked whether the Minister of Immigration would exempt George Galloway from TRI in March 2009, a spokesperson declared that the Minister "would decline to exercise that discretion."[196]

International Legal Standards and the Post-9/11 Terrorism-Related Inadmissibility Regimes in Canada and the United States

General

Before a step-by-step consideration of how well aspects of the TRI regimes in Canada and the United States conform to the relevant international standards, a number of general points must be made.[197] First, it is noteworthy that although the 1951 *Convention Relating to the Status of Refugees* does not explicitly require that refugees who commit or are suspected of terrorism be barred or excluded from a country of refuge (though not necessarily from refugeehood), it clearly does permit their exclusion if there are reasonable grounds to believe that they pose a danger to the country's security.[198] This authority is contained in Articles 33(2) and 32 of the *Convention*. The terrorism bar is, by implication, subsumed in this provision.[199]

One general problem with the implementation of the authority to bar refugees on grounds of terrorism is that states tend to take an unduly broad view of what constitutes an undeserving refugee, and this attitude also characterizes their consideration of who is liable for TRI and who is not.[200] Yet, it is now a rather trite proposition that the permission to expel some refugees under certain conditions, granted to states by Articles 33(2) and 32, must be applied "restrictively."[201] Indeed, for Article 33(2) to apply, the refugee must pose "an extremely serious [actual or future] threat to the country of asylum."[202]

It is no wonder, then, that some have warned that many of the post-9/11 anti-terrorism measures adopted in the United States and Canada, including some of the expansions or modifications of the two countries' TRI regimes mapped earlier, have violated the relevant international standards.[203] This has been so despite the fact that "a key part of States obligations [in relation to the fight against terrorism] is precisely to ensure that counter-terrorism measures are not inconsistent with international refugee law" and other relevant international standards.[204]

It should also be noted that the *Convention* does not offer all that many definitions that are relevant to the task at hand. For example, neither the term "terrorism" nor the expression "terrorist activity" is defined in that treaty. The relevant international standards must therefore be sought elsewhere.

Terrorist Activity

As the UN Special Rapporteur on the Promotion and Protection of Human Rights and Fundamental Freedoms while Countering Terrorism (SPHRT) has noted, "vague or broad definitions of terrorism are extremely problematic" as they tend to include many who are not, and ought not to be, ordinarily regarded by most as terrorists.[205] In this light, the SPHRT has warned that "in the absence of a universally agreed definition of terrorist acts, some states have included in their national counter-terrorism legislation a broad range of acts which do not, in terms of severity, purpose or aim, reach the threshold of objectively being considered terrorist acts, or the threshold required for exclusion from refugee status."[206] In my view, given the orientation of the discussion earlier in this chapter, this charge definitely implicates aspects of the definition of terrorism in both the United States and Canada. The breadth of the definitions of "terrorist activity" in both countries suggests that they would (albeit to different degrees) be viewed somewhat unfavourably by the SPHRT, a key – if merely persuasive – interpreter of the international standards in this area.

Material Support

At least one advisory opinion issued by the Office of the United Nations High Commissioner for Refugees (UNHCR) has suggested, correctly in my view, that a refugee ought not be subjected to TRI for providing material support to a group that is viewed as terrorist unless that person in addition poses a present or future danger to the security of the country of refuge.[207] It bears emphasis here to note that this danger must be posed to the country "in which he [or she] is."[208] These views are consistent with the clear wording of Article 33(2) of the *Refugee Convention*.

More broadly, the SPHRT has decried the fact that the material support bar in US law has "caused grave difficulties" for refugees in that country, and that "such provisions may, in fact, even lead to situations where persons who are victims of terrorism will be excluded from protection."[209] This is one of the main problems, from the perspective of the provisions of the relevant international standards, with the US position in this respect. The fact that the relevant US rules can lead to the TRI of even those refugees who have been coerced to provide such material support is highly problematic, more so as the waivers that could allow such persons to escape TRI are in far too many cases scarcely forthcoming. As we have seen, the equivalent Canadian scheme is less restrictive and more likely to avoid catching this class of refugees.

The Definition of a Terrorist Organization

The UNHCR has suggested that rather than the current practice of individual states drawing up their own lists of terrorist organizations, one centralized such list should be drawn up at the international level.[210] The "Consolidated United Nations Security Council Sanctions List," which includes all individuals and entities subject to sanctions measures imposed by the Security Council, partly satisfies this desire.[211]

Canada and the United States, however, continue to draw up their own lists of terrorist organizations (and suspects), and although deeply interdependent and interconnected, the two lists do not always match.[212] For example, as at June 21, 2017, the US list of terrorist organizations contained sixty different entities, whereas the Canadian list contained only fifty-four, and as at June 21, a similar discrepancy continued to exist.[213] Besides their different lengths, the lists also contained several different groups. Among those on the US but not the Canadian list were the Communist Party of the Philippines/New People's Army (CPP/NPA), Continuity Irish Republican Army, Harakat ul-Jihad-i-Islami/Bangladesh (HUJI-B), Libyan Islamic Fighting Group (LIFG), Real IRA, and Revolutionary Organization 17 November, to name a few. Three groups on the Canadian list were not found on the US list: the World Tamil Movement (WTM), Vanguards of Conquest (VOC), and Islamic Army of Aden (IAA).

Concerns have been raised about the extent to which such lists violate the rights to privacy and due process of persons associated with the listed entities, or of persons who are themselves placed on a terrorism watch list.[214] It has also been rightly emphasized that such lists too often contain "false positives," that is, individuals or groups who are incorrectly listed.[215] It is unclear, however, whether such national lists – in and of themselves – necessarily contravene international law. In my view, the mere fact that a list is drawn up does not *intrinsically* do so but may violate international law if created or administered in a way that unjustifiably infringes on due process, privacy, or other human rights.[216]

Mere Membership in a Terrorist Organization

It seems clear enough from the language used in Article 33(2) of the *Refugee Convention* that mere membership in an organization that is deemed "terrorist" by the country of refuge does not per se render a refugee liable to *refoulement* under this provision. The refugee must, in addition, be deemed to be a danger to the security of that particular country. Thus, membership in a group engaged in a violent struggle for national secession in another country ought not on its own lead to TRI for a person who poses no danger to the country of refuge itself.

Commendably, s 115 of the *IRPA* ensures that no refugee can be deported from Canada for mere membership in a terrorist group unless that person is also deemed a danger to the security of Canada. The Canadian position here is thus in conformity with the applicable international standards. It appears that the US position – that while mere membership in a terrorist group may make a person inadmissible, it does not necessarily make the person ineligible for asylum or to remain in the United States, unless the person is found to be a danger to the security of the United States) – is also consistent with the relevant international standards.[217]

It is noteworthy, however, that in both countries a refugee can still be inadmissible if he or she is a member of a terrorist group that targets its activities entirely at another country (and not at the United States or Canada). For example, in the *Suresh* case, the Supreme Court of Canada deployed the concept of "security interdependence," the link between events in other countries and the safety of Canadians, to argue and hold that Mr. Suresh, who was found to be a member of a group that was focused entirely on armed struggle with the government of Sri Lanka and posed no direct danger to Canada, was still liable to TRI in Canada.[218] Some members of the PLO have also been removed as dangers to the United States on the basis of that organization's armed struggle against Israeli occupation.[219]

Receipt of Military Training from a Terrorist Organization

Reasonable as this kind of TRI provision would ordinarily appear, suffice it to say that the Canadian and US positions in this respect (explicit or implied) will likely run afoul of the SPHRT's warning against the inclusion of broad and vague formulations of anti-terrorist bars in the immigration and refugee laws of states.

Endorsing Terrorist Activity

Again, this provision appears to be a reasonable one, but it also appears to be the type of provision that the SPHRT had in mind in warning that "broad definitions [of terrorism] have in many instances been used to suppress legitimate activities which fall within the ambit of freedom of opinion, expression, or association enshrined in the International Covenant on Civil and Political Rights."[220] As such, this kind of TRI exclusion might also run afoul of this soft international law guidance.

Spouses and Children

Since, in Canada, an already accepted refugee cannot be inadmissible for being an inadmissible person's spouse or child, there is little or no possibility or potential of a violation of the relevant international standards. However, the spouses and children of refugee claimants and asylum seekers can be excluded from Canada. In the United States, moreover, the inadmissibility, under the stated circumstances, of such a refugee is likely to be viewed by those who set and interpret international standards as having pushed that country's definition of terrorism beyond the limits allowed by international refugee and human rights law.

Analytical Insights from a Comparison of the Two Regimes

Canadian law and practice regarding the TRI of refugees and other non-citizens since 9/11 has been more or less similar to, albeit not exactly the same as, that of the United States in at least *eight of twelve* key identifiable aspects, including: the definition of terrorist activity (though this is more arguable); the definition of terrorist organizations/groups; the question of TRI for mere membership in a terrorist organization; TRI for the receipt of military training from a terrorist organization; TRI for endorsing terrorism; and waivers for TRI. The Canadian position is also similar to the US equivalent with regard to the potential for its TRI regime to produce error or injustice, and to the treatment of dissent. Canada's law and practice has been significantly better than the US equivalent in only *three of the twelve* identifiable aspects: the scale of implementation of TRI; the law concerning the provision of material support to terrorists; and the treatment of the spouses and children of accepted refugees who are inadmissible on grounds of terrorism. In not a single aspect, however, has the US regime been superior to the Canadian. On the whole, it bears emphasizing here that the key difference between the two regimes since 9/11 appears to have been the much larger *scale* of the implementation of the changes made to the relevant legal texts by the United States after 9/11.

As we have seen, however, neither country changed its own relevant texts and practices after 9/11 as much as might have been expected, or as radically as suggested in some quarters. Overall, the law reads much the same years after 9/11 as it did in the years immediately before 9/11. This is not to suggest that the reaction to 9/11 in both countries was somehow benign. Rather, the fact is that relatively little further change could be made to the TRI regime without establishing an authoritarian regime in this area because – in terms of the relevant legal norms – things were already quite bad for refugees and other non-citizens well before 9/11.

Yet, as we have also seen, the heightened security vigil triggered in both countries by the 9/11 attacks led to significant changes to the nature of the overall TRI regime as it was experienced by refugees and other non-citizens. One high official testified in 2006: "It is clear that the [US refugee admissions] program has felt the impact of post September 11 expansions in the scope of terrorism-related inadmissibility provisions of the Immigration and Nationality Act (INA)."[221] In Canada, there was a marked increase in security surveillance of refugees and other non-citizens and in the classification of non-citizens as subject to TRI.[222] Many people were labelled as "security concerns," generally without being named in security certificates. And although such certificates are "rarely used" in Canada, their use did increase between 2001 and 2004.[223] In November 2001, Citizenship and Immigration Canada (now Immigration, Refugees and Citizenship Canada) reported that three people were detained under security certificates.[224] Two years later, six men were known to be held on security certificates, a 100 percent increase.[225]

The substantial similarity between the Canadian and US TRI regimes (despite the fact that only one of them was attacked on 9/11) suggests that much more than 9/11 was at play in bringing about the observed changes to both regimes. Factors that tended to push post-9/11 Canadian refugee law and practices in the TRI area in a negative direction have been discussed elsewhere: the sympathy/empathy of many Canadians with their US "cousins" and neighbours; Canada's deep economic dependence on the United States; its own long-standing internal security anxieties; some US socio-political pressure on Canada; and a long-standing pro-immigration control element within Canadian society. Other factors helped, however, in pushing Canada's TRI laws/practices in a positive direction, such as the deeply felt need among millions of Canadians for a distinct national identity (separate from the Americans), and the humanitarian instinct within much of Canadian society. The resulting Canadian TRI regime is a product of this constant push and pull.

Following the discussion in the next chapter, the insights outlined above will, in the Conclusion, be pressed into service. Together with the other findings of this book, they will develop an understanding of the conclusions reached in Chapters 1 to 4 to tell us about the nature of security relativism and national self-image in Canada and the United States.

The Canada-US Safe Third
Country Measure

4

The "safe third country" concept emerged in international refugee law over the last three decades or so to address the concerns of Western European states about the sharp increases in the number of refugee claimants arriving at their borders.[1] This concept is usually embodied in treaties and other international agreements. As Andrew Moore has put it:

> Essentially, a safe third country agreement provides that once a person fleeing persecution crosses through the territory of a country [which is] party to the agreement, that [third] country is responsible for assessing [the person's] refugee status. If an individual attempts to enter another country party to the agreement (the second country), he or she may be summarily returned to the third country. The second country does not make any determination as to whether the person fleeing deserves refugee protection because the safe third country agreement assigns responsibility to the third country to assess refugee status.[2]

The coherence of these agreements is dependent, however, on the third country's being considered "safe" by the other countries, and designated as such.[3]

The principal goals of this chapter are to: 1) analyze the nature of the safe third country measure that was established under the *Canada–United States Safe Third Country Agreement*,[4] something that more or less occurred after 9/11; 2) consider the general implications of the evidence that has emerged since then regarding the practical implication of the separate but intimately connected safe third country regimes in Canada and the US; 3) evaluate the extent to which these regimes align or comply with the relevant international legal standards; 4) assess the extent to which 9/11 has or has not affected their character; and 5) tease out the analytical insights, if any, that can be gained from comparing changes in this area of refugee law in the United States after 9/11 to the situation in Canada in the same period.

To these ends, the rest of the chapter is organized as follows. In the section that follows, the historical development and nature of the *Agreement* are outlined. Thereafter, the nature of each of the "twin" domestic legal regimes established under the *Agreement* in both Canada and the United States are analyzed and compared. Folowing this discussion, the main criticisms that have been levelled against the *Agreement* and the two regimes are considered. This analysis is followed by a discussion of a number of important issues concerning the practical implementation of the regime. In a subsequent section, the issue of the conformity or otherwise of the *Agreement* and regimes with international legal standards is examined. Thereafter, the chapter ends with a section dedicated to teasing out some of the analytical conclusions that are suggested by the preceding discussion.

History, Rationale, and Outline of the *Canada-US Safe Third Country Agreement*

Historical Backdrop to and Development of the Agreement

As widely understood, the practice of removing asylum seekers to so-called safe third countries (STCs) is basically a European invention.[5] Following Denmark's lead in 1986, virtually every Western European country had introduced STC measures by the end of the 1990s.[6] For example, it was during this period that STC clauses appeared in the much-debated *Dublin Convention* and *Schengen Agreement*.[7] The official rationale among European states for the introduction of such measures tended to centre on the felt need of these states to more efficiently share the "burden" of processing the rising but uneven numbers of refugee claimants who approached their borders.[8]

It was against this European backdrop that a safe third country clause first appeared in Canadian law in 1988 amendments to the *Immigration Act* of 1976, and an attempt was made by the Canadian and US governments in the mid-1990s to introduce an STC measure between the two countries.[9] Due to US reluctance, the negotiation of this proposed accord, something that was primarily pushed by Canada, was aborted.[10] Canada's eagerness to enter into this type of agreement with the United States stemmed from its desire to reduce the population of refugee claimants that it processed, a large percentage of whom have always entered its territory from the United States.[11] Until fairly recently, US resistance to such an agreement stemmed from the fact that relatively few of the claimants who approached it for protection entered the country from Canada.[12]

In the wake of the 9/11 attacks, however, the United States became willing to accept Canada's proposed agreement, perhaps in order to secure much-needed Canadian cooperation in other areas, in order to realize its high-priority counter-terrorism measures.[13] This did not mean, however, that both countries were of the same mind regarding the national security value of concluding such an agreement. To be sure, as Audrey Macklin has shown, the proposed agreement was linked to national security by then Canadian Immigration Minister Denis Coderre, who alluded to it as one of several measures taken to help ensure the safety of Canadians in the fight against terrorism that his ministry was pursuing in collaboration with its US partners.[14] The United States did not, however, really see the conclusion of the agreement as necessarily connected to its counter-terrorism efforts, and signed the agreement only to appease the Canadians.[15]

Whatever the nature of the give and take between the two countries, the fact remains that following the 9/11 attacks, Canada-US cooperation in this area became a reality. Indeed, less than three months after 9/11, then Canadian Immigration Minister Elinor Caplan and US Attorney General John Ashcroft announced that both governments had agreed to pursue discussions on concluding a safe third country agreement.[16] This joint commitment was reaffirmed just days later when then Canadian Foreign Minister John Manley and the US Homeland Security Advisor Tom Ridge at the time announced the *Smart Border Declaration* and associated action plan.[17] The *Canada-US Safe Third Country Agreement* was signed on December 5, 2002, and entered into force on December 29, 2004.[18] Ongoing border control cooperation between the two countries continues under the Security and Prosperity Partnership of North America, launched on March 23, 2005.[19]

Rationale for the Agreement

A number of rationales have been offered by both countries for adoption of the *Agreement:* the need for "responsibility sharing" with respect to the movement of asylum seekers across their shared border; the necessity of "managing the flow" of these persons across that border; and the imperative of limiting "forum shopping" by refugee claimants.[20] Perhaps the least mentioned rationale in the official public discourse is Canada's desire to reduce the number of refugee claims that it has to process, for while this is somewhat implied in the "responsibility sharing" rationale, it is not coterminous with it. Most refugee advocates believe, however, that the true purpose of the *Agreement* is to sharply depress the numbers of refugee claimants that have to be processed by Canada.[21] In this they are not off the mark since it is a matter of record that Canadian immigration officials did tell a parliamentary committee that the purpose of the *Agreement* was to "reduce the number of refugee claims being referred to the IRB [the Immigration and Refugee Board]."[22]

A Broad Outline of the Main Contents of the Agreement

Ostensibly designed to facilitate "responsibility sharing" between the two jurisdictions (or, more accurately, the deflection of refugee claimants from Canada), "the Agreement is founded on the belief that both Canada and the US maintain refugee protection programs that meet international standards and both have mature legal systems that offer procedural standards [and are thus 'safe']."[23] According to the Preamble, in crafting and adopting that treaty, the two states parties were also mindful of their non-*refoulement* obligations under the 1951 *Refugee Convention,* their obligations under the *Convention against Torture,* and their duties to promote and protect human rights and fundamental freedoms.[24] Both the official narrative of the two states parties and the Preamble state that their commitment to international refugee and human rights standards, as well as their fidelity to certain policy objectives (such as family unity, the best interests of children, and the discretionary authority of each county to take responsibility for any application where it would be in the public interest to do so), must be balanced against the need to "strengthen the integrity" of the institution of the international protection of refugees and "the public support on which it depends."[25]

The crux of the *Agreement* is Article 4(1), which states that "the country of last presence shall examine, in accordance with its refugee determination system, the refugee status claim of any person who arrives at a land border port of entry on or after the effective date of this Agreement and makes a refugee status claim."[26] Thus, in general, a person who arrives at a Canadian port of entry (border post) from the United States and makes a refugee claim there will be returned by the Canadian authorities to the United States so that the person's claim may be determined there, and vice versa.

This general measure is subject to a number of limitations and exceptions, however. It applies only at the officially designated land border posts, and therefore does not apply to claims made either inland or at air or sea ports.[27] Neither does it apply to the following categories of refugee claimants:

- citizens of Canada or the United States, or persons who are stateless habitual residents of either country[28]
- claimants who hold a validly issued visa to enter the country in which they seek to lodge their refugee claims[29]
- claimants who do not require a visa to enter that country[30]
- many claimants who are unaccompanied minors[31]
- many claimants who have at least one family member in the country they seek to enter (as defined in the *Agreement* and the implementing domestic laws)[32]
- certain other claimants who may – at the discretion of one of the states parties – be permitted to enter and lodge their refugee claims in the relevant country in the public interest.[33]

In order to significantly reduce the intimately related risks of the chain *refoulement* of refugee claimants or the sending of such claimants into "orbit," Article 3 provides that neither state party shall return or remove to another country a refugee claimant referred to it by the other party or returned from that other state (other than Canada and the United States) until "an adjudication of that person's refugee claim has been made." It also provides that such a return or removal would not be allowable even if authorized under another safe third country agreement or regulatory designation. In chain *refoulement* situations, "asylum seekers are deflected from one country to another, either informally or pursuant to successive 'readmission agreements,' until they are eventually returned to their country of origin without ever accessing a refugee determination process."[34] A related "refugee in orbit" situation is constituted when

> country A designates country B as a safe third country, thereby entitling country A to refuse to adjudicate the claim of an asylum seeker who arrived in country A via country B. However, in the absence of a readmission agreement, country B may refuse to re-admit the asylum seeker, and send the person to country C, who may in turn bounce the person concerned to country D, and so on.[35]

As such, Article 3 is, subject to its limitations, a commendable provision.

The Nature of the Domestic Legal Regimes That Implement the Agreement

The Canadian Regime

In an attempt to implement domestically its international obligations under the *Agreement*, Canada issued the relevant regulations in October 2004.[36] Following the issuance and coming into force of corresponding regulations in the United States, both the *Agreement* and the Canadian regulations came into force on December 29, 2004.[37]

Even before these specific regulations were issued and became effective, however, under Canadian law an immigration officer would not refer a refugee claim for determination by the Refugee Protection Division of the IRB unless the person who made the claim was eligible to do so under s 101 of the *Immigration and Refugee Protection Act* of 2001 (*IRPA*).[38] This section sets out the conditions under which claimants will not be eligible to have their claim referred to the IRB. Section 101(1)(e), in particular, makes a refugee claim ineligible to be so referred if the claimant came directly or indirectly to Canada from a country designated by the *Immigration and Refugee Protection Regulations* as a "safe third country." Under s 102(2), a country will be designated as such if it is determined by the Governor-in-Council that, *inter alia*, it respects its international obligations not to return persons to places where they are at risk of being persecuted, tortured, or subjected to certain forms of ill-treatment. From Canada's perspective, the *Agreement* basically mandates the designation of the United States as a safe third country for the purposes of s 101(1)(e). The implementing regulations made under the *Agreement* and the *IRPA* have, in compliance with the *Agreement*, designated the United States as such a country.[39]

The obvious effect of such a designation is that, in general, refugee claimants who arrive at a Canadian land border post from the United States will not be eligible to have their claims referred to and determined by the IRB. These claimants will be immediately removed to the United States, where their claims will be processed. And since access to Canada's pre-removal risk assessment process is also denied to these refugee claimants under s 112(2)(b) of the *IRPA*, which cross-referenced s 101(1)(e) of that *Act*, their removal to the United States will in these cases be far swifter and much more immediate than is usual within the Canadian refugee determination system.[40]

In line with the letter and spirit of the *Agreement*, however, not every refugee claimant who arrives at a port of entry in Canada from the United States will be deemed ineligible to have his or her case referred to the IRB, and be removed from Canada as a result of such ineligibility.[41] As we have seen, the *Agreement* contains a number of explicit and implied exemptions to the general rule. As a result, the Canadian *Regulations* do exempt the following categories of persons:

- unaccompanied minors who have no parent or guardian in Canada or the United States; such minors must be under eighteen years of age, without spouse or common law partner, and not accompanied by a parent or legal guardian[42]

- claimants who have at least one family member (spouse, common law partner, legal guardian, parent, sibling, child, grandparent, aunt, uncle, niece, or nephew) who is a Canadian citizen or permanent resident, a protected person in Canada, or a person "in favour of whom a removal order has been stayed" because the Minister of Immigration is of the opinion that humanitarian, compassionate, or public policy grounds exist that warrant further consideration of his or her application for permanent residence in Canada based on such grounds[43]
- claimants who have at least one adult family member who is in Canada and has had his or her refugee claim referred to the IRB[44]
- claimants who have at least one adult family member who is in Canada and holds a valid work or study permit (other than a work permit issued to an indigent foreign national in Canada who is not a refugee claimant but is subject to an unenforceable removal order)[45]
- claimants who nevertheless hold valid Canadian permanent or temporary residence visas or other stated documents (except visas or documents held "for the sole purpose of transit through Canada")[46]
- claimants who do not require a visa to enter Canada but would need one to enter the United States[47]
- claimants who are foreign nationals previously resident in Canada, who are seeking to re-enter Canada after having been refused entry to the United States without having their claims adjudicated there[48]
- claimants who are permanent residents of Canada and have been ordered removed from the United States and are being returned to Canada[49]
- claimants who are stateless persons and who came to Canada directly or indirectly from a designated country that is their country of former habitual residence[50]
- claimants facing the death penalty in the United States or in any other country, as evidenced by a charge or conviction with regard to a capital offence[51]
- claimants who are US nationals (since the rule that persons who arrive in Canada from a designated country are ineligible to have

their refugee claims processed there does not apply to persons who are nationals of such countries, and the United States is the only designated country under the *IRPA* and the *Regulations*).[52]

What is more, not everyone who cannot benefit from one of these exemptions will be ineligible to have their claims referred to the IRB. The *Regulations* also specify that, in general, only those claimants who arrive at a land border port of entry will fall under the general rule.[53] The only categories of persons who will be subject to the general rule despite making a refugee claim at other than a land border post are those who are in transit at a Canadian airport either because they are in the process of being removed from the United States or because they are leaving that country after making an unsuccessful refugee claim there.[54]

Until July 22, 2009, claimants who were nationals of any of a handful of countries to which Canada would not – for the time being – remove anyone (as designated by the Minister of Immigration under s 230 of the *Regulations*) were also exempted from the general rule of exclusion from eligibility to make a refugee claim in Canada. Effective July 23, 2009, however, this exemption was abolished by the Canadian government.[55] Remarkably, according to the Canadian immigration authorities themselves, this was done precisely because the exemption had provided succour to the most number of refugee claimants caught by the safe third country measure.[56]

In terms of the relevant procedural requirements, it is important to note that Canadian law places squarely on the shoulders of refugee claimants the burden of proving that they are covered by one or more of the exemptions discussed above.[57] This is clear from a combined reading of the first paragraph of s 159.5 of the *Regulations* and s 100(4) of the *IRPA*. While the former requires claimants to satisfy the relevant official "in accordance with subsection 100(4) of the Act" that they fall under any of these exemptions, the latter makes it clear that the burden of proving that a claim is eligible rests on the claimant.[58] The standard of proof required to determine whether a claimant qualifies for one of the stated exemptions is that of a "balance of probabilities."[59] It appears that, in the absence of documentary records or computer records, credible oral testimony may suffice to meet this burden.[60]

The "Statement of Principles on the Procedural Issues Associated with the Implementation of the Agreement" binds both countries to provide "at a minimum ... an opportunity for the applicant to have a separate decision maker, who was not involved in preparing the proposed determination [to the effect that the claimant is or is not eligible to have the claim processed in the relevant country], review any proposed determination before it is finally made," and Canada has indeed instituted an administrative process to give effect to this principle.[61] While claimants who are aggrieved by a determination that they do not fall under one of the exemptions to the general rule, or who are declared otherwise ineligible to have their claim processed in Canada, may also apply for leave of the Federal Court of Canada to commence judicial review of the relevant determination, it should be noted that this process would in practice be virtually unavailable to most persons returned to the United States under the *Agreement*.[62]

The US Regime

The United States finalized its implementing regulations on November 29, 2004, leading to the entry into force of the *Agreement* one month later.[63] The effect of these regulations in US refugee law is similar to that of their Canadian equivalents in Canadian law. As in Canada, the broad statutory authority to implement the Canada-US safe third country measure and other such agreements pre-dated the issuance of the relevant US regulations. The *Immigration and Nationality Act (INA)* had long provided that aliens physically present in the United States may not apply for asylum

> if the Attorney General determines that the alien may be removed, pursuant to a bi-lateral or multilateral agreement, to a country ... in which the alien's life or freedom would not be threatened ... and where the alien would have access to a full and fair procedure for determining a claim to asylum or equivalent temporary protection, unless the Attorney General finds that it is in the public interest for the alien to receive asylum in the United States.[64]

It should be noted that this legislative provision was introduced into the *INA* by s 604 of the *Illegal Immigration Reform and Immigrant Responsibility Act of 1996 (IIRIRA),*[65] an enactment that was obviously made long before 9/11.

In line with this provision and the terms of the *Agreement,* the regulations establish a general rule that persons who arrive at a relevant US border post from Canada and make a refugee claim there will be declared ineligible to have their claims processed in the United States and will be returned to Canada to pursue their protection claims there (whether based on persecution or torture).[66] Among other things, these regulations amend s 208 of the US *Code of Federal Regulations* to provide for the conduct of newly instituted "threshold screening interviews" by US Citizenship and Immigration Services (USCIS) asylum officers, in order to determine whether an alien is ineligible to apply for asylum under s 208(a)(2)(A) of the *INA* by operation of the *Canada-US Safe Third Country Agreement.*[67] The authority so conferred on asylum officers pertains to their functions within the expedited removal process, which is the broader socio-legal context in which the *Agreement* is usually applied in the United States.[68] As the US government has noted, in general the *Agreement* will be applied to aliens who are subject to expedited removal provisions under s 235(b) of the *INA,* which provides a specific removal mechanism for aliens who are inadmissible for fraud, willful misrepresentation, or failure to possess proper documents when seeking entry into the United States.[69] Thus, in most cases, if an alien arrives at a US border post from Canada and makes a refugee claim there, a USCIS asylum officer determines whether the *Agreement* or US law excludes the alien from making a claim in that country.[70] Aliens who are not excluded either because the *Agreement* does not apply to them or because they fit one of the exempt categories are placed in the standard expedited removal proceedings, and are allowed access to a "credible fear interview" (at which point an asylum officer determines whether they have a credible fear of persecution or torture).[71] Those excluded by the *Agreement* are returned to Canada.[72]

In certain cases, however, the Department of Homeland Security (DHS) may decide to place an arriving alien in general removal proceedings before an Immigration Judge under s 240 of the *INA* (rather than in expedited proceedings under s 235 of the same statute).[73] In such cases, the task of applying the *Agreement* basically falls on the Immigration Judge.[74] The judge may determine whether or not the claimant falls within the scope of the *Agreement* and is thereby barred from making a protection claim in the United States, including one for withholding of removal either on persecution grounds or under the *Convention against Torture*.[75] Claimants who fall within the purview of the general rule and do not meet any of the exceptions permitted under the US regime may be ordered by the judge to be removed to Canada to have their claims adjudicated there.[76]

The exceptions to the general rule that persons who enter the United States from Canada are barred from claiming refugee status in the former country are codified at 8 CFR, s 208.30(e)(6)(iii). As in Canada, these US regulations provide that the following categories of refugee claimants are exempt from the application of the *Agreement*, as long as they are not being removed from Canada in transit through the United States:

- Canadian citizens and those stateless persons who habitually reside in Canada
- unaccompanied minors who have no parent or guardian in Canada or the United States. Such minors must be below eighteen years of age, and be without spouse or common law partner. At first blush, this provision appears to be broader in scope than the equivalent Canadian one, which explicitly requires that the minor not be accompanied by a parent or legal guardian. It appears, however, that this US formulation merely eschews stating the grammatically obvious, while the Canadian one strains to state the equally obvious requirement that an unaccompanied minor is by definition a child who is not accompanied by a parent or legal guardian
- claimants who have at least one family member (defined in the same way as in Canada) who has been granted asylum, refugee, or other lawful status in the United States (with the exception of family members who are visiting the United States temporarily for business or pleasure).[77] As in Canada, this provision should cover claimants whose family members enjoy permanent resident status in the United States (including permanent residents who have been ordered

removed from Canada) or hold valid work or study permits in that country. It should also cover claimants whose family members hold a range of other lawful statuses in the United States. This provision appears, however, to be slightly narrower than the corresponding Canadian one, which includes even claimants who have family members there against whom removal orders may be pending but who have applied for permanent residence on humanitarian and compassionate grounds and have received a positive step one (albeit not final) determination. It is not readily apparent whether this category of persons would be covered by the phrase "other lawful status" above

- claimants who have at least one adult family member who is in the United States and has a pending asylum claim
- claimants who do not require a visa to enter the United States but would need one to enter Canada
- claimants who arrive in the United States with a valid US visa or other admission document (other than one issued for transit purposes)
- claimants in favour of whom the USCIS Director or designate determines in his or her unreviewable discretion that it is in the public interest to allow the protection claim to be lodged in the United States.[78] Significantly, Canadian law does not contain any such broad fail-safe "public interest" exception.

The following are exceptions allowed under the Canadian regime but not specifically and explicitly provided for under US law: 1) claimants facing the death penalty in Canada or in any other country; and 2) claimants who are foreign national claimants previously resident in the United States who are seeking to re-enter that country after having been refused entry to Canada without having their claims adjudicated there.[79] If claimants who fit these last two categories do not have some other exemption to the safe third country measure, they will be subjected to its rigours and barred from having their claims adjudicated in the United States. In addition, unlike the Canadian position between December 2004 and July 2009, the United States has never at any time made an exception in favour of claimants who are nationals or former habitual residents of a country to which it would not remove anyone.[80]

A significant point to note is that while there are no exceptions allowed under the US regime that are not also permitted by Canadian law, the reverse is not the case. This may, at first blush, suggest that the Canadian safe third country regime is the more generous of the two. The general implications of these differences in the two regimes will be considered more fully in all the sections that follow.

To be clear, in general, determinations in the United States as to whether or not a refugee claimant meets any of the exceptions to the general exclusionary rule are made either by USCIS asylum officers at threshold screening interviews (for claimants in expedited removal) or by Immigration Judges (for those referred by DHS to "ordinary" removal proceedings). However, the determination of whether a claimant meets the public interest exception cannot be made by an Immigration Judge, but is made by the Director of the USCIS or designate.[81]

Importantly, in terms of the relevant procedural issues, US law also places squarely on the shoulders of refugee claimants the burden of establishing that they meet an exception to the safe third country measure.[82] They must meet this burden by showing that a "preponderance of the evidence" supports their case.[83] Significantly, both US and Canadian authorities agree that this standard of proof is functionally equivalent to the Canadian standard of proof on a balance of probabilities.[84] Another important procedural point is that, as in Canada, the US regime clearly provides an internal mechanism for the review of an asylum officer's determination at a threshold screening interview that a claimant does not qualify for an exception to the safe third country measure under the terms of the *Agreement* or is barred from having his or her claim adjudicated in the United States. A supervisory asylum officer must concur in the written and reasoned determination of an asylum officer to the aforementioned effect, and the latter's determination does not become final until this condition has been satisfied.[85] A senior manager at DHS headquarters must in turn review the supervisor's determination.[86]

Unlike in Canada, a negative eligibility determination made by an asylum officer with the concurrence of a supervisor and a DHS manager cannot be reviewed by an Immigration Judge.[87] There may, however, be claimants who are placed by the DHS in regular removal proceedings (not the usual expedited removal proceedings), in which case their eligibility determination would have been made by an Immigration Judge.[88] In such cases, even though claimants who are caught by the safe third country measure would not by law be eligible for both asylum and withholding from removal, they could still apply for any other (discretionary) relief that they would be qualified for in the United States.[89]

Questioning the Agreement and Regimes

Interrogating the Canada-US "Safe Third Country" Designations
Viewed from the perspective of the US regime, it is interesting that very few, if any, significant concerns have ever been raised in that country about the safety of the Canadian regime for refugee claimants, either in absolute terms or vis-à-vis the US system. This may reflect an implicit general acceptance in both countries of the suggestion that the Canadian refugee determination regime tends to be significantly more generous than its US counterpart.[90]

As we have seen, an important effect of the *Agreement,* and a cardinal component of the regulations promulgated by both countries, is their mutual designation as safe third countries. Much, then, turns on this legal construction of Canada and the United States as "safe" in a virtually generic sense. Yet the issuance of such generic safety certification tags seems problematic in refugee law, policy, and practice – even at the conceptual level. For the most important question in refugee law, policy, and practice is not really the nature of a country's conditions as a whole but rather the nature of the claimant's personal circumstances: does the claimant face a serious risk on stated grounds in that country? While the nature of a country's conditions is, of course, a necessary chunk of the body of evidence that must be considered by the decision maker, viewed from the perspective of the "best practices" of refugee law and policy evidence as to the general state of affairs in a country is hardly a trump card. It would be unconvincing to suggest that any country in our world is safe all the time for *all* the people who find themselves within its territory – even in terms of respecting the obligation not to return people to places where they face a serious possibility of persecution or a substantial risk of torture. Alas, nowhere has the observance of human rights (or even of the non-*refoulement* principle) ever been "a mass cultural fact."[91]

From the perspective of the Canadian implementing regime, the designation of the United States as safe was done within the meaning of s 101(e) of the *IRPA* and in an attempt to comply with the preconditions for such designations stated in s 102(2) of the *IRPA*. As noted earlier, this provision stipulates that a country may be so designated if the Governor-in-Council determines that it, *inter alia*, respects its international obligations not to return persons to places where they are at risk of being persecuted, tortured, or subjected to certain forms of ill-treatment. While it is of course true that, even after 9/11, the United States remains safe for most of its citizens and residents (in the sense in which this term is being used here), the question remains: "For whom exactly is the United States either safe or unsafe?" Given developments in the post-Obama era, this question is even more pertinent.

Many critics of the *Agreement* and its implementing regime have argued that, for certain classes of refugee claimants who would be refused access to the Canadian system under the safe third country measure, the United States is either not safe or significantly less safe than Canada.[92] This is not surprising given that the main concern raised by critics of the pre-publication draft of the Canadian *Regulations* "centred on whether or not the United States is a safe country for refugees."[93] Such critics have tended to rely on a number of arguments to justify their conclusions. First, some have contended that although the United States is safe for many of the non-citizens who are resident there, it is certainly not as safe as it once was for all too many persons of either Muslim heritage or Arab descent.[94] These critics sometimes point to the high-profile case of Maher Arar's rendition to torture.[95] Most US residents of Muslim heritage or Arab descent also know all too well that, at least in the years immediately following 9/11, they faced a serious risk of suffering this kind of fate at the hands of US authorities. Many US government officials of that era spoke openly of justifications for torturing and meting out ill treatment to (largely Muslim/Arab) terrorist suspects.[96] Most observers would accept that a US law enforcement dragnet aimed directly at the Muslim and Arab communities was cast in those years.[97] It was therefore not surprising that during the early post-9/11 period, hundreds, if not thousands, of Muslims and Arabs (including many long-time US residents) thronged to Canadian border posts in the hope of gaining entry as refugee claimants and escaping the harsh treatment meted out to many of them in the United States.[98] Although the Obama Administration significantly improved the official legal and institutional climate for US-based Muslims and Arabs (e.g., torture, renditions, and deportations to torture may have occurred but were no longer official policy, and roundups decreased in frequency), they were still disproportionately targeted as security risks and many who were refugee claimants were still subject to targeted mandatory detention.[99] Moreover, the political and social climate has worsened for Muslims in America following Donald Trump's victory in the 2016 US presidential election and his calls for – and executive action authorizing – a ban on Muslims from certain countries entering the United States, which was supported by a significant proportion of the American public.[100] Although a number of US federal courts struck down both President Trump's initial executive order and the one that replaced it, the US Supreme Court upheld it.[101]

Second, some of these critics have argued that important aspects of US refugee law and practice do not meet either the equivalent Canadian or the relevant international standards, or fail to meet both. They often point to

- the routine detention of refugee claimants and other immigrants and their being held in prison-like and subpar conditions that characterizes the US system[102]
- the overbroad way in which the statutory bar from asylum and withholding from removal imposed on those who are determined to have provided material support to terrorist organizations is couched and interpreted in US refugee law[103]
- the fact that asylum claims must be made within one year of the claimant's arrival in the United States, which limits the ability of many persons to claim asylum in that country, contrary to Canadian practice and international law[104]
- the fact that the Canadian system offers a significantly broader range of protections for those whose claims are grounded in their gender,

implying that the United States would not be safe for many such claimants[105]
- the increased likelihood that genuine refugees may be denied protection in the United States because of provisions of the *REAL ID Act* requiring increased corroboration of an asylum or withholding of removal claim, demonstration that the "Convention ground" on which the claimant relies (race, religion, political opinion, etc.) was the "central motive" for the claimant's persecution or attempted persecution, and assessment of credibility[106]
- the fact that the frequency with which federal judges reverse the immigration courts and the vituperative tone in which such reversals are too often couched evokes serious concern about the fairness of the US system compared with its Canadian equivalent[107]
- the fact that, unlike in Canada, no publicly funded legal aid system exists in the United States and that this has unfairly disadvantaged refugee claimants in that country.[108]

In defence of the safety of the US refugee system for refugee claimants returned there by Canada, some have argued that

- although mandatory and routine detention is experienced by many refugee claimants, only a small overall percentage are actually detained in the end[109]
- the one-year rule for lodging asylum claims is not inconsistent with the principle of non-*refoulement* under international refugee law, and persons falling outside the one-year time limit may still be able to either take advantage of one of the exceptions to the rule or be eligible for withholding of removal and protection from *refoulement* under the 1951 *Refugee Convention* and the *Convention against Torture*[110]
- critics exaggerate the effect of the differences between the Canadian and US approaches to gender-based claims[111]
- Canada and the United States have broadly comparable overall refugee claim acceptance rates (at least for most of the post-9/11 period)[112]
- the frequent reversal of Immigration Judges by the federal courts is actually evidence that the US system is fair and safe for refugee claimants[113]

- all claimants have a right to counsel under US law and, although this right is exercised at no expense to the government, information is provided to claimants about organizations and lawyers who take cases *pro bono*[114]
- the United States has clear guidelines on immigration detention that meet international standards[115]
- exemptions have been put in place for those caught by the overbroad "material support to terrorists" bar[116]
- certain US court decisions as well as signals sent by the Obama Administration indicate that human rights will continue to be safeguarded in the United States[117]
- "the US remains a country that meets a high standard with respect to the protection of human rights"[118]
- the Office of the United Nations High Commissioner for Refugees (UNHCR) considers the United States a safe third country for refugee claimants.[119]

It should be noted, though, that more recent policy turns and events in the United States appear to call the last argument into question. For example, the Trump Administration has engaged in consistent anti-refugee rhetoric, banned refugees from certain Muslim-majority countries from entry into the United States, and expanded the mandatory detention of refugees.[120]

These important questions about the US qualification to be designated by Canada as a safe third country, the intimately related concern over whether the Canadian Cabinet acted reasonably in so designating the United States, and the actual operation of the regimes put in place to implement the *Agreement* have all been the subject of litigation in Canadian courts. In the first case, three related decisions are relevant. In the first, a preliminary matter referred to as *Canadian Council for Refugees et al v the Queen*[121] was brought by the Canadian Council for Refugees, the Canadian Council of Churches, Amnesty International, and an out-of-status Colombian national living in the United States (anonymously referred to as "John Doe" in order to protect him and his family from possible retaliation by Colombian rebels). The applicants asked the Federal Court of Canada (per Justice Roger Hughes) for a mandatory injunction restraining the Canadian government from denying John Doe and his wife entry into Canada from the United States under the authority of the *Agreement,* or alternatively, an Order directing the government to allow them to enter Canada from the United States.[122] The context for this particular matter was a broader matter (discussed below) in which the same applicants challenged the validity of Canada's designation of the United States as a safe third country and the regulatory provisions that implemented the *Agreement* in Canada.[123] They alleged that unless John Doe (whose asylum and withholding of removal claims had been denied and who was at the time on the verge of being removed from the United States) was allowed to enter Canada and claim refugee status here, something not permitted under the *Agreement,* he and his wife would be deported to Colombia, where they faced serious risks of persecution, torture, and ill-treatment, and a serious risk to their lives.[124]

In dismissing the application, the Federal Court of Canada held that, although the main application that the applicants had filed before the Court raised a serious issue to be tried (an important requirement for granting such injunctions), the applicants had failed to meet the burden on them to show that the injunction should be granted.[125] The Court offered two main reasons for this conclusion. The first was that they had not, as the law requires, shown that the applicant would suffer "irreparable harm" if the injunction were not granted. According to the Court, John Doe "had not exhausted the remedies that still remain open to him in the United States"; the applicants had not substantiated with clearer evidence their argument that Doe lacked the funds to continue pursuing these remedies; they did not also lead evidence to counter the suggestion of the respondents that Doe would be able to enter a number of other countries without a visa; the evidence of irreparable harm in an affidavit sworn by an assistant to the solicitor for Doe was hearsay and "unsatisfactory by way of evidence"; and the evidence from Doe himself as to irreparable harm was "not robust."[126] The second main reason offered by the Court was that the balance of convenience did not favour the applicants, since making the Order would render regulations duly enacted in the public interest essentially inoperative not just against Doe but possibly against many others, and the "private interests of those such as Doe must yield to the public interest unless and until the Regulations have been held to be invalid."[127]

In the main judicial review application brought by the same group of applicants against the same respondent, and involving basically the same facts,[128] the applicants challenged the validity of the *Agreement,* and asked the Federal Court of Canada (per Justice Michael Phelan) to declare invalid and unlawful the designation of the United States as a safe third country for refugee claimants and the resulting ineligibility for refugee protection in Canada of certain claimants.[129] After an extensive and detailed review of Canadian and US laws and practices and the relevant international legal norms (including some merely persuasive European legal positions), the Court basically made two main decisions that are relevant here. First, it held that since the Governor-in-Council (Cabinet) can enter into a Safe Third Country Agreement (STCA) with a country that meets the stated preconditions for designation as such,[130] and Canadian jurisprudence confirms that the Court can review whether a regulation complies in substance with the condition precedent to the power to enact it,[131] and US laws, policies, and practices do not allow that country to meet the stated preconditions,[132] the designation of the United States as a safe third country was unlawful and invalid.[133] In coming to this first conclusion, the Court held that

> the Court will only find that the GIC [Governor-in-Council] lacked jurisdiction to designate the US as a safe third country if the GIC erred in concluding that the preconditions existed, and that any reasonable inspection of the evidence of US law and practice would lead to the conclusion that the US is not in compliance with Article 33 of the Refugee Convention and Article 3 of the Convention against Torture.[134]

In the Court's view, although Cabinet was entitled to some deference in weighing the available evidence in relation to the conditions that must be met before a country could be designated as a safe third country, the appropriate standard of review was the "reasonableness" of the GIC's decision.[135] The Court found the applicant's expert witnesses more credible than those of the government.[136] It then applied this standard in reaching the conclusion that it was *not* reasonable for Cabinet to conclude that the United States was in compliance with the 1951 *Refugee Convention* (and others) and was a safe third country, because 1) its one-year bar to asylum was inconsistent with international law; 2) its "support for terrorism" bars to asylum and withholding of removal "puts genuine refugees in danger" and are "extremely harsh, and cast a wide net which will catch many who never posed a threat"; 3) women at risk of domestic violence faced a serious concern that US refugee law would not sufficiently protect them; and 4) the quite inconsistent application of the aspect of the US test for the existence of "persecution" that dealt with the central motive of the persecutor.[137] In addition, the Court found that since "the US takes a narrow interpretation of the prohibition of *refoulement* to torture," this reinforces the unreasonableness of Cabinet's designation of that country as a safe third country.[138]

The second of the two main relevant decisions was that the designation of the United States as a safe third country was also unlawful under the *Canadian Charter of Rights and Freedoms*.[139] The Court reasoned that the *Charter* was engaged by the *Canada-US Safe Third Country Agreement* since "the *Charter* would apply to a refugee claimant at the Canadian border and under the control of Canadian immigration officials."[140] The Court then found that the designation contravened ss 7 and 15 of the *Charter* because it discriminated against people who fell into the areas of the law where the United States was not compliant with international law, and also discriminated against this class of persons and exposed them to risk based solely on their method of arrival in Canada.[141] As such discrimination was not justifiable under s 1 of the *Charter*, it rendered the designation unlawful and invalid.[142]

Following the decision of Phelan J at the Federal Court to grant the Canadian government's application to certify three questions to the Federal Court of Appeal (FCA), the government successfully appealed his judgment to the latter court.[143] At the outset, it should be noted that prior to the hearing and determination of the main matter, the FCA stayed implementation of Phelan's decision pending determination of the government's appeal.[144] The government's main arguments were that Phelan J erred in law in treating and reviewing the relevant *Regulations* "as if they were administrative decisions"; erred in law and fact in concluding that there was a real risk of *refoulement* where a refugee was returned by Canada to the United States; erred in law in concluding that the *Regulations* violated the *Charter;* and erred by taking a "'perverse' approach to the evidence."[145] The FCA held as follows:

1. The standard of review of the *vires* of the relevant *Regulations* (i.e., whether they are *ultra vires* and of no effect) is "correctness," and not "reasonableness" as was held by Phelan J.[146]

2. Phelan J erred in reading the statutory (*IRPA*-based) scheme for the designation of certain countries as safe third countries. He "transformed" the statutory objective of designating countries that comply with relevant conventions into a condition precedent and concluded in error that what must be established is "actual" compliance or compliance "in absolute terms."[147] In the Court's view, once the Cabinet has duly considered the four factors that it must consider in reaching a decision to designate a country as a safe third country, and has formed the opinion that the candidate country is compliant, then "there is nothing left to be reviewed judicially," as long as the GIC has not acted "in bad faith or for an improper purpose."[148]

3. Even if actual compliance was a condition precedent to the designation of a country as a safe third country, the conclusion reached by Phelan J (that the United States was not in compliance with significant aspects of its obligations under international refugee and human rights law) could not stand since it was "largely based on evidence which postdates the time of the designation."[149]

4. As such, the designation of the United States as a safe third country and the regulations that implemented the *Agreement* were not *ultra vires* the Cabinet.[150]

5. In addition, the *Charter* challenge (by a John Doe who had never presented himself at the border and had never been denied entry) ran directly against the established principle that *Charter* challenges cannot be mounted on the basis of hypothetical situations, and should not have been entertained by Phelan J.[151]

With the greatest respect to the Court, its reasoning in 2) above is weak and rather unconvincing. Consider the established fact that Canada does in certain circumstances remove refugee claimants to places that its own border officers consider so unsafe that they would not accompany the deportee there (places like Somalia, for example).[152] Many reasonable observers would consider the decision to do so a perverse one.[153] Canada has also been known to remove refugee claimants to less troubled (but still quite unsafe) lands that do not respect human rights and their non-*refoulement* obligations.[154] In this context, what should a court be reasonably expected to do when reviewing a Cabinet decision to designate a given country as a safe third country? Clearly, to be meaningful, the role of the reviewing court must be substantive to some degree. Its review cannot be merely formalistic. To conclude otherwise, as the FCA has done, is to hollow out the relevant statutory scheme and transform it into a formalist shell. Thus, in my view, Phelan J was exactly right on the point that if the courts do not read the statutory scheme as requiring the government to designate as safe third countries only those countries that, more or less, "actually comply" with their non-*refoulement* and human rights obligations, the courts would in effect be creating a scheme in which the Cabinet would be free to designate – if it so wished or if it were (as is too often the case) politically expedient – countries that do not actually comply. Thus, contrary to the FCA's logic, it was not Phelan J who "transformed" the statutory scheme into something that it was not meant to be; rather, it was the FCA that did so. For of what use would a judicial review of such governmental action be (based, as the FCA itself held, on the relatively low standard of correctness) if, in effect, a reviewing court could not really assess the *correctness* of the government's decision? The point here has not been to equate the human rights conditions faced by refugee claimants in the United States with those they face in much more troubled lands. The point is to problematize the FCA's overly formalistic reasoning, which led it to conclude in error that once Cabinet has duly considered the four stipulated factors and labelled a country a safe third country, and has not acted in bad faith or for an improper purpose, then the only reviewing role that the Canadian courts can play – even when applying a (low) correctness standard of deference to the government – is basically a rubber stamp one.

Some of the other conclusions reached in the FCA decision can also be questioned. Its conclusion that part of the reason why the Phelan decision was problematic was that it was "largely" based on evidence that postdated the time of designation can be challenged on the grounds that while the FCA is partially correct here, there is much in the way of adequate evidence cited in the Phelan decision (relating, for example, to the one-year bar, the treatment of victims of domestic violence, and even the material support bar) that did not postdate the impugned designation as a safe third country, or at least the coming into force of that designation in December 2004, and Phelan J could still have reached the conclusion he reached based on such evidence. Thus, if, as I have argued, the FCA was wrong in holding that Phelan J erred in reviewing the "actual compliance" of the United States with its obligations, then the FCA could have struck down the portions of the evidence that postdated Cabinet's designation and/or the entry into force of the implementing *Regulations*, and still have sufficient evidence to support Justice Phelan's finding that the United States failed to "actually comply."

The FCA's argument and holding that Phelan J should not have entertained the *Charter* aspect of the judicial review application because it was based on a hypothetical situation is more difficult to dispute. Nevertheless, it can be argued that the circumstances warranted a departure from the established principle against hypothetical *Charter* challenges. In this case, it may be unreasonable to expect members of the class of persons affected by the *Regulations* to actually present themselves at a Canadian border post, where they would almost certainly have been rejected and sent back to the United States, especially when their refugee claims – like that of John Doe – had already been, or were almost certain to be, rejected, and they also faced a serious risk of death and/or *refoulement* to places like Colombia. Thus, since almost no claimants in their right mind would agree to present themselves at the Canadian side of the border to establish facts that would allow the constitutionality of the *Regulations* to be tested, disallowing a hypothetical *Charter* challenge from groups like the applicants in the matter before Phelan J would effectively insulate the *Regulations* from constitutional challenge – something clearly not in the public interest.

Thus, while the FCA decision is partly correct and does add much to our understanding of the issues at hand, it is, on balance, unsupportable in its core logic and broad conclusion. Warts and all, the Phelan decision articulates the better view. It is regrettable that the Supreme Court of Canada declined to hear the appeal filed by the Canadian Council for Refugees and others, but this may be rectified by an effort launched in 2018 to relitigate in the Canadian courts the validity of the US designation as a safe third country.[155]

Absence of General Fail-Safe Exceptions

As we have seen, the *Agreement* and the Canadian and US regulations provide, on compassionate or public interest grounds, a number of highly restrictive exceptions that could mitigate the hardships imposed by the safe third country regime on refugee claimants who come to Canada through the United States, but the vast majority of such claimants will not be able to benefit from them. Despite this, the Canadian *Regulations* do not provide a generic "fail-safe" exception to the general rule that these claimants must be returned to the United States.[156] The Canadian government, in fact, explicitly rejected the recommendation of the Parliamentary Standing Committee on Citizenship and Immigration to include such a provision in the *Regulations*.[157] Instead, a number of discrete and restrictive exceptions were explicated in the *Regulations* on public interest grounds.

This contrasts with the situation in the United States, where, as we have seen, a generic, broadly stated fail-safe exception is part of the law.[158] The downside with the US position, however, is that determinations as to who falls within the boundaries of the public interest exception are made in the total unreviewable discretion of the Director of the USCIS, an administrative official.[159]

The Possibility of Chain Refoulement

Despite the attempt in Article 3 of the *Agreement* to prevent the incidence of chain *refoulement*, the *Agreement* and the implementing domestic regimes in both countries have been criticized on the basis that, in some cases, they could have the effect of facilitating the chain *refoulement* of a refugee claimant to a place where he or she is at serious risk of persecution, torture, or even death.[160] This is not far-fetched. For one, Canada still reserves the right to deport a person to torture in exceptional circumstances, or when decision makers simply do not believe that the risk of torture is "substantial" enough. In addition, there is at times wide variance in the way Canadian and US courts interpret the relevant international instruments. As we have seen, more often than not Canada's interpretation of international refugee law is more liberal than that favoured in the United States. In the light of this risk, Article 3's provisions that either Canada or the United States must determine a refugee claim before the claimant's removal to a third country, and that a claimant returned by a party to the *Agreement* to the other party shall not be removed to any other country pursuant to any other safe third country agreement or regulation, are to be commended.[161]

Interrogating the Responsibility-Sharing Justification

As we have seen, the need for more "responsibility sharing" in taking in refugees is an important justification offered by the Canadian government for negotiating the agreement with the United States. It is also clear from the available evidence that Canada intended the implementation of the *Agreement* to help reduce the processing backlog in its refugee determination system.[162] It is questionable, however, whether this justification holds much water. While Canada does enjoy a well-deserved reputation as a comparatively generous refugee-receiving state, it is extremely important to keep things in perspective. For instance, the UNHCR has found that in 2010 the much poorer developing countries of our globe were host to four-fifths of the world's refugees.[163] According to the Canadian government itself, Canada received only about 13,500 refugees in 2014.[164] It did, however, receive many more in 2016, about 46,000 of them.[165] Given that Canada is one of the wealthiest countries in the world, it is unconvincing to base the signing of the *Agreement* on Canada's need to share its refugee protection responsibility.

This justification is also clearly untenable from a US perspective, as a much smaller number of refugee claimants move from Canada to the United States. Instead, since the vast majority of claimants move from the United States to Canada, the *Agreement* was expected by many to add significantly to the backlog of asylum cases in the United States.[166]

Promoting Clandestine/Irregular Crossings?

The *Agreement* and its implementing regimes may also be seen as questionable as a result of their stipulation that, in general, only those refugee claimants who arrive at a Canadian or US land border post designated as a "port of entry" may be refused access to the Canadian refugee determination system at the IRB.[167] On the face of it, the restricted nature of this provision appears to help rather than harm refugee claimants. By implication, claimants who arrive by air from one state party into the other will not be refused access, although this kind of ingress into either country is far more difficult to achieve these days because of interdiction measures put in place overseas by both countries.[168] Likewise, those who arrive by sea will not be excluded from having their refugee claims processed in Canada, although this is also very difficult to accomplish these days because of interdiction measures on the high seas and in territorial waters.[169] Most important is the fact that those who just show up and make a claim anywhere on Canadian or US territory are also exempt from the safe third country measures in both countries. This is the crux of the matter. The only ways for those without Canadian or US visas to enter Canada, or even get to Canada or the United States at all, are to be smuggled there or cross at an unofficial point along the border. In addition, the visa option is unrealistic for the vast majority of refugee claimants around the world. For both of these reasons, the regulations in effect send a signal to potential claimants that the easier or even the only way to access Canada's refugee determination processes is to be smuggled into Canada or the United States in one way or another. Indeed, the *Agreement* may arguably even provide an incentive and generate an even larger "market" for human smuggling operations and irregular crossers. In sum, "the irony is that ... the Agreement is more likely to produce illegality than reduce it."[170]

The Canadian government's official response to this concern is noteworthy. Its position is that while it is concerned about clandestine border crossings and people smuggling, the *Agreement* "cannot be viewed in isolation" as it is only "one component of the 30-Point Action Plan developed from the Smart Border Declaration signed by Canada and the United States in December 2001."[171] Although this is a plausible argument, it does not enlighten us as to why the two countries should in the first place seek to generate more of the very clandestine/irregular crossings that they spend even more taxpayer resources trying to curb or manage through other measures.

Recent clandestine crossings and crossings at unofficial points of entry into Canada from the United States bear eloquent testimony to this point.[172] Nearly 39,000 people, most of them attempting to avoid President Trump's harsh refugee/immigration policies, are estimated by the IRB to have crossed into Canada in an irregular manner between 2017 and December 2018.[173] This has led to strong pushback in some quarters, which appears to have forced the Trudeau government to move to renegotiate the *Agreement* with the United States.[174]

Issues Arising from the Practical Implementation of the Regimes

A full two years elapsed between the signing of the *Agreement* and its implementation, but once it was implemented, it began to have a number of practical impacts on the experience of refugee claimants in both countries.[175] Since the refugee claimant traffic largely flows from the United States toward Canada, the bulk of those feeling these impacts were those minded, or attempting, to make their refugee claims in Canada.

Processing Backlogs

Has the implementation of the *Agreement* contributed to the accentuated or diminished processing backlogs in either country? The available specific evidence as of 2005 indicates that it had relatively little immediate impact at US land border posts, where the number of refugee claims merely rose from an average of fifty-eight per annum in 2000–04 to sixty-six in 2005.[176] This, however, does not tell us all that much about the *Agreement*'s contribution to a greater or smaller number of claims processed within the United States. For example, the *Agreement* has clearly deterred a large number of claimants from heading to the Canadian border from the United States.[177] These potential claimants would have had to either go underground in the United States or file a claim there.

In any case, many such claimants later tend to become implicated in the US refugee/removal system and add to the backlog in the workload of the relevant immigration processing officials. One thing is certain from an analysis of data up to the year 2010: the processing backlog in the US Immigration Courts has continued to grow.[178] It actually rose sharply in 2005 (the year after the *Agreement* was implemented), fell in 2006, and then continued to rise since then.[179] While this does not constitute conclusive evidence of the impact of the *Agreement* and the extant data refer to more "files" than just those concerning refugee claims, it offers some insight into the post-*Agreement* situation in the United States with regard to backlogs.

The total number of claims made in Canada rebounded after a dramatic dip in 2007, and has been undulating since then.[180] Thus, although the *Agreement* did initially help reduce the refugee claim processing backlog in Canada, its current impact is less clear. The backlog might have been larger if the *Agreement* had not been implemented, but it could also be that the *Agreement* has encouraged more clandestine crossings, and thus largely redirected claims from the land border to inland offices. If the latter were the case, the *Agreement*'s impact on the Canadian processing backlog would be less remarkable. What is more, the backlog has also been caused in part by other actions or lack of action on the part of the Canadian government.[181] Since 2017 at least, this backlog has been significantly augmented by claims filed by irregular crossers from the United States.

Drops in the Numbers of Claimants

In the immediate aftermath of the implementation of the *Agreement*, the safe third country measure that it introduced helped lead to a rather sharp drop in the number of claimants requesting refugee status at Canadian land border ports of entry, as well as a similar drop in the overall numbers of refugee claimants dealt with by the Canadian refugee determination system. For example, between December 29, 2004, and December 28, 2005, the average total number of claimants processed at Canada-US land border posts fell by about 50 percent.[182] This trend continued in 2005–06.[183] The number of legal border crossings by refugee claimants fell as sharply between 2004 and 2007.[184] One commentator has even described this as a "staggering decline."[185] It should be noted that though the *Agreement* was clearly not the only factor, it was a significant one.[186] However, despite a continued drop in the numbers of claims processed in terms of those presenting themselves at a land border post, the overall numbers of claimants processed by Canada (at land, sea, air, and inland offices) has rebounded and continues to show an upward, if undulating, swing.

The implementation of the *Agreement* obviously increased the number of claimants processed by the United States. This is because, as we have seen, the bulk of the Canada-US refugee claimant movement has always been from the United States to Canada and not the other way around. Thus, the reduction in the number of those claiming refugee status at Canadian land border posts means that more persons were forced to lodge their claims in the United States.

The Actual Incidence of Exclusion at the Border

There is no doubt whatsoever that the *Agreement* has contributed considerably (though not as much as first imagined) to the exclusion of a large number of refugee claimants from access to the Canadian refugee determination system. For example, in 2006, 71 percent of the claims declared ineligible suffered this fate on the basis of their being caught by the *Agreement*.[187] That same year, only 20 percent of claims made in Canada were made at the border, as opposed to 35 percent in 2004, the year the *Agreement* entered into force.[188]

Here it is important to note that despite access to the Canadian refugee determination system having been "a critical safety valve" for them due to their much lower claim success rates in the US system, claimants from Central America, especially Colombia, have been among the most badly affected by the exclusionary effects of the implementation of the *Agreement*.[189] For example, after the *Agreement* went into effect, the number of Colombian claimants who entered Canada from the United States declined by approximately 82 percent, a very dramatic number that provides insight into the great degree to which such claimants have been excluded or deterred from seeking refugee protection in Canada.[190]

With respect to the US regime, the fact that relatively few claimants enter from Canada has obviously meant that the United States has not had to exclude all that many claimants from access to its system because of the *Agreement*.

Direct-Backs

As the direct-back policy does not have nearly as much significance in terms of direct-backs from the United States to Canada, this analysis will focus mostly on the Canadian position.[191] It should be noted, however, that the United States has declined to end its own policy of direct-backs, arguing that this power is "not exercised often" by its officers.[192] In any case, it has directed back only a very small number of claimants arriving from Canada, either because there was insufficient detention space or as a courtesy to the claimant.[193]

The direct-back policy was established by Canada in 2003, after the *Agreement* was signed but before it was implemented.[194] The rationale offered was that there were insufficient resources at Canadian land border posts to deal with the large and sudden influx of persons arriving from the United States who wanted to lodge their claims in Canada before the entry into force of the *Agreement*.[195] Many such claimants who could not be attended to immediately or on the same day due to the backlog at the border were directed back to the United States and asked to return to the Canadian border post another day.[196] This policy resulted in many of these claimants being detained in the United States and possibly removed from that country, as a result of which they were unable to return to the Canadian border post.[197] The treatment of Benamar Benatta, an Algerian national who was directed back to the United States by Canadian immigration officers in the days immediately following 9/11 (in his case for investigatory purposes), and who was then detained for several years in harsh conditions, is illustrative.[198] By February 2007, the direct-back policy had been ended by Canada and will, going forward, be used only in exceptional cases.[199]

Clandestine and Irregular Crossings

As most of the relevant refugee claimant traffic between the two countries is oriented toward Canada, and as the relevant US evidence is not readily available, the Canadian evidence will suffice to illustrate the argument made here. The situation in both countries, especially Canada, with regard to clandestine crossings into either country by refugee claimants is aptly captured in Professor Deborah Anker's 2007 testimony to the House of Commons Standing Committee on Citizenship and Immigration that "15 months after implementation, the STCA [the *Agreement*] not only failed to accomplish its stated goal of securing the border, but indeed made the border less secure, endangering the lives of refugee claimants."[200] While Professor Anker did not offer any exact statistics to support this conclusion, it should be noted that she has offered some credible qualitative evidence that grounds her analysis. For example, as a Harvard Law School study conducted by her and others has found, "information collected from NGOs along [the] United States–Canada border indicates that the STCA has already led refugee claimants to enter Canada illegally, in marked contrast to the pre-STCA regularized movement of claimants."[201] Again, from the point of view of many refugee advocates, logic and the available qualitative indicators suggest that some of the increase in inland refugee claims made within Canada since the *Agreement*'s implementation can be attributed to a significant extent (though not entirely) to clandestine and other irregular crossings into that country.[202] It does not necessarily follow, however, that a rise in inland claims must have resulted from a rise in clandestine crossings. Other factors could have produced this.

The Canadian government has argued that the implementation of the *Agreement* has not led to a rise in clandestine crossings. The evidence it relies on includes its contentious point that the apprehension of people trying to cross clandestinely into Canada had decreased and did not increase between 2004 (when the *Agreement* was implemented) and 2006.[203] It has also contended that, although the proportion of the overall number of refugee claims that were made inland did rise because of the decline in claims made at land borders, there has been no appreciable increase in inland claims per se (i.e., in absolute terms) since the *Agreement* came into force. While the government did at some point make a plausible case for its view, the fact that it apprehended a smaller number of would-be clandestine crossers does not necessarily mean there has not been a rise in such crossings. For example, clandestine crossers could have become more successful since the implementation of the *Agreement* by turning to the comparatively more experienced human smugglers to get them into Canada. There is some evidence that this might have been the case.[204] And the stability in the absolute number of inland claims could have resulted from an overall decline in the numbers of those entering Canada through air and sea ports at the same time that more claimants were being smuggled into Canada.

It is not surprising that both the government and refugee advocates tend to agree that, as most observers would acknowledge, it is extremely difficult to count the number of clandestine crossings into a country. This is principally because these crossings are, well, clandestine! Nevertheless, the evidence that front-line refugee workers on the US side of the border are noticing a significant rise in clients telling them about clandestine crossings is powerful.[205] This argument appears even more convincing when one considers the conclusion of the US Government Accountability Office that US and Canadian agencies lack the ability to detect clandestine crossings of drugs, weapons, and people along the vast majority of the Canada-US border. According to this 2011 report, only 50 kilometres out of over 6,400 kilometres of the border had attained an acceptable level of security.[206]

In any case, the evidence of irregular crossers arriving in Canada since at least 2017 (especially in Manitoba and Quebec) via locations that are not designated ports of entry further weakens the government's argument.[207] These refugees have been fleeing the United States after President Trump's inauguration and his implementation of a harsh raft of measures viewed by many as anti-refugee.[208]

Detention of Claimants Affected by the Agreement

The United States detains refugee claimants whose inadmissibility into that country is being considered, and this would usually include most claimants arriving from Canada (whose eligibility to make a claim in the United States is also under consideration).[209] The United States also detains those directed back from Canada, and has explicitly declined to end this practice.[210] By contrast, there have been relatively few instances in Canada of the detention of refugee claimants subject to the *Agreement*.[211] As the UNHCR has noted, however, this has not reduced the significant risk of detention in Canada and deportation therefrom for persons directed back to that country from the United States.[212]

Chain Refoulement

It is a fact that chain *refoulements* to torture occurred in the United States before and after the adoption of the *Agreement* (sometimes as part of the "extraordinary rendition program").[213] Although the possibility of chain *refoulement* remains a concern, there is little, if any, evidence that similar tragedies have occurred in either Canada or the United States specifically as a result of the application of the *Agreement*. However, given that there is no doubt that "the application of the safe country notion" in some other lands "has already resulted in cases of *refoulement* [including of the chain type]," this worry must be taken seriously.[214] In this context, the provisions of the *Agreement* that aim to prevent *refoulement* and the practical measure put in place by the United States (requiring its Immigration and Customs Enforcement [ICE] agents to contact Canadian officials prior to the removal from the United States of a claimant directed back from Canada) are as inadequate to totally guarantee against *refoulement* as they are very welcome developments.[215]

The Conformity of the Regimes with International
Legal Standards

Advocates of safe third country agreements tend to "assert that the concept is implicit in the [1951] Refugee Convention" and "point to Article 31 [of the *Convention*], which forbids countries from punishing refugees who, 'coming directly from a territory where their life or freedom was threatened,' enter a country without authorization."[216] The idea here is that the phrase "coming directly from a territory" implies that claimants passing through a third country (not the one where they are threatened) can be refused refugee protection if that third country is a "safe" one.[217] However, UNHCR, which is the principal international guardian of the *Refugee Convention,* has directly rejected this interpretation of Article 31.[218] Its argument is that the language in Article 31 was merely intended to exclude those claimants who had settled temporarily in a third country, and not those merely passing through such countries.[219] This interpretation is supported by many scholars.[220]

The UNHCR's interpretive opposition to the rationalization of safe third country measures as permissible under international law has, however, not stopped it from mostly standing aside while safe third country agreements gained ground, first across Europe and now between Canada and the United States.[221] By neither accepting nor condemning these agreements directly and focusing on what Andrew Moore sees as a "safeguard" role, the UNHCR basically facilitates their implementation.[222] It is no wonder, then, that two respected scholars of safe third country measures have concluded that the UNHCR accepted the notion of safe third countries in 1989, albeit with safeguards attached.[223] One broad safeguard is the UNHCR-enunciated principle that in framing their refugee laws, states should as far as possible take into account the preferred destination of refugee claimants.[224] Even this principle, however, has now been diluted by the UNHCR's effective co-optation in facilitating the safe third country practices of many, mostly Western, countries.[225] And, as Audrey Macklin has correctly noted, the UNHCR now appears to have gone as far as expressing support for measures to ensure an appropriate allocation of state responsibility for determining refugee status (otherwise referred to as "burden sharing"), including safe third country regimes.[226]

Yet, many knowledgeable scholars have expressed strong doubts regarding the compatibility with international standards of safe third country agreements such as the one between Canada and the United States. Some have gone as far as to question whether such agreements are known at all to the 1951 *Refugee Convention*, especially Articles 31 and 33.[227] One has even argued that such agreements have "scant foundation in international law."[228] What is clear is that although hard and soft international refugee law does not explicitly condemn safe third country measures, it does not explicitly authorize them either, and may, in effect, even discourage them. The latter view is supported by hard and soft international refugee law's insistence that the designated third country must be a "safe" one, and its condemnation of the direct-backs, chain *refoulements*, and other problematic actions and effects that are too often triggered by the implementation of such measures.[229]

In the context of the compatibility of the *Agreement* and its implementation with international standards, it is worth noting that the UNHCR has testified to a House of Commons committee that "they considered the United States to be a safe country, otherwise they would not have agreed to do the monitoring [of the implementation of the *Agreement*], and they would have said so at the very outset."[230] The UNHCR reached this conclusion despite having expressed concerns about aspects of the US refugee determination regime.[231] As noted earlier in this chapter, the safety or otherwise of the Canadian refugee system has never been a significant issue in the present connection.

The UNHCR has also noted the risk of chain *refoulement* occurring as a result of the implementation of the *Agreement*. There is no doubt that this agency would regard and condemn the incidence of chain *refoulement* as a violation of international law, but thus far it has not, to our knowledge, reported any such occurrence.[232] Commendably, its recommendation (designed to prevent chain *refoulement*) that the *Agreement* should be worded so as to ensure that no refugee claimant could be removed before his or her claim had been determined by one of the two countries was accepted and implemented.[233]

Regarding direct-backs, the UNHCR has strongly condemned it, stating that it is "deeply concerned" by its continued practice and requires its abolition.[234] To the extent that it has now been abolished on the Canadian side of the border, Canada is no longer in violation of the hard and soft international law against this practice.[235] As the UNHCR has said, such direct-backs risk triggering the *refoulement* of the affected claimants.[236] This would be an explicit violation of the hard international law prohibition of non-*refoulement*.[237] Similarly, the UNHCR Monitoring Report on the *Agreement* makes it clear that the continued practice of direct-backs by the United States is highly problematic and ought to be ended.[238]

The UNHCR has also found that the *Agreement* would "run counter to the interests of all parties, including individuals in need of protection" were it to be shown to promote clandestine border crossings.[239] As we have seen, although more evidence is needed to come to a definite conclusion, it may already be the case that clandestine crossings have increased in frequency along most of the Canada-US border, in part as a result of the implementation of the *Agreement*. The UNHCR's condemnation of agreements that would promote clandestine crossings is a soft international standard that sheds some light on how that agency would react were the feared harm to be proven. What is crystal-clear, though, is that the *Agreement* has promoted irregular crossings into Canada.

The UNHCR has also concluded that the specific nature of the US practice of detaining refugee claimants almost routinely (including those subject to the *Agreement*) tends to violate international refugee and human rights law.[240] In line with this conclusion, the Inter-American Commission on Human Rights has found that "immigration enforcement in the United States is plagued [*inter alia*] by unjust treatment of detainees [many of them refugee claimants] ... and the excessive use of prison-style detention."[241] Importantly, the Commission stated that it was "deeply troubled by the continual and widespread use of detention in immigration [including refugee] cases."[242] This is a very strong indictment, and underlines the great extent to which the detention of claimants subject to the *Agreement* (sometimes as part of the direct-back process) is considered unlawful and inappropriate by bodies charged with interpreting and monitoring the observance by states of the relevant international standards. While the detention of refugee claimants is not as widespread in Canada, the international standards and analysis discussed above do apply to that country as well.[243]

It should also be noted that while the UNHCR has expressed disappointment with the "significantly prolonged" processing times in the determination of whether a refugee claimant was excluded from filing a claim in the United States,[244] it has not found much blame with the relevant safe third country measure–related practices in both jurisdictions.[245] It has even commended Canadian Border Services Agency (CBSA) officers for making "an exemplary effort to determine whether an applicant qualifies for an exception under the Agreement."[246] In the UNHCR's view, most interviews conducted by these officers complied with international standards.[247]

Even more favourable to both governments is the UNHCR's conclusion that "the Agreement has generally been implemented by the parties according to its terms and, with regard to those terms, international refugee law."[248] This is a surprising conclusion, given the fact that the main European precursor of the *Canada-US Safe Third Country Agreement* has been strongly criticized (including by the UNHCR itself) as riddled with a long list of problems and as simply not working.[249] In any case, in my view, the wave of would-be clandestine crossings into Canada in 2017 illustrates the serious limitations of such agreements. It is doubtful that the UNHCR will reach the same conclusions in 2019, in an era of a large number of irregular crossings into Canada produced in part by the *Agreement*.

Analytical Insights from the Comparison of the Regimes

It seems remarkable that, in eleven of nineteen identified ways, the safe third country regime in Canada, a country not attacked on 9/11, has been more or less similar to its counterpart in the United States, the country that was actually attacked. Both domestic refugee law regimes

- share a similar understanding of what it means to be a safe third country
- have designated each other as safe
- have similar general rules regarding the safe third country measure
- do not apply this rule to each other's citizens
- have similar exceptions for unaccompanied minors
- couch and treat family member–based exceptions similarly
- provide the same kinds of visa-based exceptions
- exempt returning permanent residents from the general rule, even if they have been ordered to leave by another country (this is implied in the US exemption for claimants who arrive in that country with a valid US admission document)
- exempt stateless persons
- share similar rules regarding the burden and standard of proof
- have similar processes for review, by one or more supervisors, of eligibility decisions made by an officer.

The Canadian regime is worse, however, in two main respects: the much larger scale of implementation of the safe third country measure in Canada, and the lack of a general fail-safe exception in Canada. On the other hand, it is better than the US equivalent in six main ways:

- provide an exception for those facing the death penalty
- exempting those who have a family member who has made an application for permanent residence on humanitarian and compassionate

ground (under s 25 of the *IRPA*) and who have passed stage one of the assessment but have no lawful status in Canada

- making an exception for certain previously resident foreign nationals seeking re-entry into Canada even when they lack lawful status in Canada
- providing for the ability to seek review in Federal Court of negative eligibility decisions made by an officer
- making less use of detention in dealing with claimants affected by the safe third country measure
- no longer carrying out direct-backs.

All in all, it should be noted that the key difference in practice between the two safe third country regimes after 9/11 has been the much larger *scale* of its actual implementation in Canada. This is mainly because the refugee claimant traffic is mostly oriented toward the Canadian side of the border, and so a vastly disproportionate number of people have been sent back to the United States from Canada than vice versa.

However, unlike the position with regard to deportations to torture, detention, and terrorism-related inadmissibility, where, after 9/11, neither country changed its relevant texts and practices as much as might have been expected or as radically as suggested in some quarters, the safe third country regimes in both countries did undergo considerable transformation in the years after 9/11. Whereas no such regime had previously connected or divided the two countries, the situation with regard to safe third country regimes changed considerably soon after 9/11. Less clear is the precise extent to which the change in each country was caused by or was attributable to the events of 9/11. What does 9/11 have to do with it? First, it can of course be argued with confidence that 9/11 was a hugely important factor in the US decision to finally succumb to Canadian pressure to negotiate and conclude a safe third country agreement. Although the presumed benefits to Canada of such an agreement are fairly clear (since the cross-border refugee traffic flows mainly toward the Canadian side of the border), it is not as clear what the United States stood to gain in terms of a reduction in refugee flows to its territory from Canada: there is simply very little traffic in that direction.[250] It is therefore not surprising that the United States had, for some decades, resisted Canadian pressure for precisely this kind of agreement.[251] The fact that it finally yielded almost immediately after 9/11, and in the context of "border/ national security" negotiations with Canada, strongly indicates that its need to secure Canadian cooperation in its post-9/11 national security efforts must have been a highly important motivating factor. Another factor that could have influenced US leaders/technocrats in this area was the potential for such an agreement to dramatically reduce the number of refugee claimants entering the United States at its southern border en route to Canada, thereby serving the general tendency of the United States, especially after 9/11, to tighten its borders and curtail migration inflows. For if admission to Canada was no longer a real possibility for the thousands of refugee claimants who appeared at the Canadian border each year seeking entry from the US side, then significantly fewer Canada-bound claimants might seek to enter the United States in the first place. For these reasons, it appears incontrovertible that 9/11 may have had much (though not everything) to do with the US decision to participate in the safe third country regime with Canada.

For Canada's part, there may also be a link between 9/11 and US border-tightening tendencies on the one hand and Canada's successful negotiation and conclusion of the *Safe Third Country Agreement* with the US on the other. In the aftermath of 9/11, Canada was under a fair amount of pressure to help its main trading partner and closest neighbour to indirectly stem its migration inflows and secure its northern border, and to help the United States in more robust ways as part of the "war on terror."[252] It is doubtful (though not cut-and-dried) that the Canadian government would have mustered enough domestic political will and support to conclude the *Agreement,* especially in such a short period, if not for 9/11 and the ensuing mass hysteria over what many Canadian and American citizens continue to perceive as the immigrant/refugee threat.

Given the strong historical evidence that Canada had been seeking, unsuccessfully, to sign such an agreement with the United States in the decades before 9/11, it is difficult to conclude that the social, political, and economic climate precipitated by the 9/11 attacks directly caused Canada to negotiate and conclude the *Agreement.*[253] It is also clear that the United States did not pressure Canada to conclude the *Agreement;* rather, it was the other way around.[254] Furthermore, according to Canadian immigration officials, the *Agreement* is aimed squarely at reducing the number of claims made by persons arriving from the United States.[255] It would appear, therefore, that the events of 9/11 do not entirely explain Canada's desire for such a measure and its actual participation in establishing the post-9/11 safe third country regime with the United States.

The foregoing discussion also suggests that a multi-factorial explanation of the relationship between 9/11 and the establishment and implementation of the Canada-US safe third country regimes is to be preferred. To illustrate with the Canadian example, and to adapt from a model already applied in other chapters of this book, it is plausible to argue that several things combined to drive post-9/11 Canadian refugee law and practice in the safe third country area: the sympathy/empathy felt by many Canadians for their American cousins; Canada's deep economic dependence on its southern neighbour; Canada's own long-standing internal security anxieties; some US socio-political pressure on Canada; and a long-standing pro–immigration control element in Canadian society. By contrast, other factors helped push Canada in the other direction: the humanitarian instinct in much of Canadian society, some UNHCR oversight, and the historical reluctance of the United States to participate in a safe third country regime with Canada that did not seem to promise much benefit to it. The Canadian regime that emerged is a product of this constant and complex push-and-pull, as is the very fact that the regime exists at all, contains a general exclusionary rule, and includes a number of significant exceptions.

To illustrate further with the US example, it appears that several things combined to pull that country toward the establishment of the current Canada-US safe third country regime: the fact that the US was directly attacked on 9/11; has endured long-standing security anxieties dating to the mid-1990s; has had a long-standing, highly vocal pro–immigration control element in US society; felt a strong need for Canadian cooperation in the US war on terrorism; and felt some pressure from Canada to enter into such an agreement, both before and after 9/11. Other factors, however, tended to push it away from participating in a safe third country regime with Canada, such as the presence of a significant, numerous liberal element in the United States, and the apparent lack of a clear benefit to the United States from such participation.

In the final chapter, all the findings discussed so far in the book will be analyzed with a view to understanding what they and the relevant literature tell us both about the relationship between refugee law, 9/11, and national self-image in both countries, and the relationship between refugee law, 9/11, and "security relativism."

Conclusion: Refugee Law, Security Relativism, and National Self-Image in Canada and the United States after 9/11

This chapter has three principal objectives. The first is to provide bird's-eye-view explanations for the general character and orientation of the developments in the Canadian and US post-9/11 refugee law regimes. Why did each of these regimes assume the particular tenor that it did after 9/11? Why was each of these post-9/11 regimes characterized by the particular admixture of stability and instability, constancy and change, and continuity and discontinuity discussed in the preceding chapters? And what explains the differences between Canada and the United States regarding their respective post-9/11 refugee law regimes? The second objective is to tease out what, if anything, the post-9/11 character and orientation of the Canadian and US refugee law regimes, and the reasons behind them, tell us about the ways in which a mentality referred to in this book as "security relativism" has been expressed in, and exerted influence on, these regimes. The third is to analyze and outline what the post-9/11 treatment of refugee laws in Canada and the United States tells us about the dominant national self-image of each country. Consideration of these questions is important given the deep connections in both countries between their refugee laws, policies, and practices and their (partial) national self-identities as "nations of immigrants."[1]

To achieve these three objectives, the chapter has been organized into four main sections, including this introduction. In the next section, the focus is on offering general explanations for the character assumed post-9/11 by each of the two refugee law regimes under study, and the differences post-9/11 in the reactions of these regimes to the heightened security vigil triggered by the attacks of that day. Thereafter, the expression and impact of security relativism in the Canadian and US post-9/11 refugee law regimes are analyzed. The discussion in the section that follows is devoted to the analysis of what, if anything, the tenor of the developments in the Canadian and US refugee law regimes tell us about the cogency of the dominant national self-image of each country. The chapter ends in the next section with some brief concluding remarks.

General Explanations for Post-9/11 Developments and Differences

The Post-9/11 Character of Each Country's Refugee Regime

What explains the particular shapes and forms that the refugee law regimes in Canada and the United States each assumed following the events of 9/11, the specific reactions of each regime to the heightened security vigil triggered by those attacks? Why did the heightened post-9/11 security vigil in each country produce the particular kinds of reactions that it did, the specific mix of constancy and change that has been observed? Why was there less change overall in both countries than many had expected? Why did more change occur to some aspects of these regimes than to others? Regardless of the country concerned, the evidence discussed in Chapters 1 to 4 suggests multi-factorial (rather than unitary or purely 9/11-focused) explanations for these developments. As a result of the push and pull of these factors, their particular chemistry, each regime had a specific reaction to the post-9/11 heightened security vigil. Some of these factors have had a negative impact on refugee law in both countries, others a more positive impact. Note that in some cases it will be necesary to point to differences between the US and Canada in order to help explain the specific character assumed by their refugee law regimes after 9/11.

The Canadian Position

A number of factors coalesced to produce the observed outcomes – both negative and positive – in Canadian refugee law and practice. 9/11 itself aside, six factors pushed the regime toward the negative end of the spectrum of respect for refugee rights.

First, despite the fact that the relationship between Canada and the United States "has never been easy," Canada was at the time, and is still, the United States' closest neighbour. There was thus great empathy within state and society for the large-scale suffering and anxiety in the United States caused by the 9/11 attacks.[2] As Kent Roach has noted, Canada declared a national day of mourning after September 11, and then Prime Minister Jean Chrétien assured the US Ambassador that Canada "will be with the US every step of the way" and would stand with them "as friends, as neighbours, as family."[3] It was also significant that many Canadians were killed in New York in the 9/11 attacks.[4] Given this deep Canadian empathy, it is only reasonable to suggest that some of the changes made to the Canadian refugee regime after 9/11 (such as the increased use of preventive and identity-based detention measures, Canada's active facilitation of some US secret detention measures, and the increased removal of persons from Canada for terrorism-related inadmissibility) were motivated in part by a Canadian sense of solidarity with Americans – the sense that Canada had to react not simply to protect itself from terrorists but also to help its close friend, neighbour, and family protect itself from any further attacks on its homeland.

Second, this neighbourly empathy may have predisposed the Canadian security and civilian bureaucracy to look favourably on certain immigration and refugee control policies that aligned Canada with the harsher US reaction to 9/11. That this kind of bureaucratic empathy existed and to some extent shaped post-9/11 decision making and action in Canada is indisputable. For example, Prime Minister Chrétien was not even consulted before bureaucrats allowed stranded aircraft destined for the United States to land instead in Canada.[5] What is not all that clear, however, is precisely how much such empathy was responsible for rendering the Canadian security and civilian bureaucracy more amenable to making the specific changes to the Canadian refugee law regime observed after 9/11. For example, this factor certainly played a part in Canada's enthusiastic cooperation with the United States' post-9/11 practices of extraordinary rendition to torture and secret detention.

A third factor was Canada's well-known economic and security interdependence with its southern neighbour. As Roach has pointed out, "the United States and Canada are dependent on each other in security matters by virtue of their shared border."[6] He also recognizes the economic interdependence of the two countries.[7] However, given the obvious fact that Canada is far less powerful than the United States economically and militarily, it is perhaps more accurate to speak of Canada's economic and security vulnerability to the United States. This suggests that two interrelated subfactors were separately and jointly at play: 1) the need to act in ways that ensured that Canada's security and economic vulnerability to the United States did not open it up to harm in these and other aspects; and 2) the need to "keep up with the neighbours."[8] Against this background, it is only logical to argue that some of the changes to Canada's refugee law regime (such as its active support at times of US extraordinary renditions and secret detentions) stemmed in part from Canadian sensitivity to this vulnerability.

A fourth factor was pressure (whether overt or subtle) exerted on Canada by the United States to act in certain ways. We know for sure of pressure on Canada to keep up with US policies and actions, to take more measures to secure the United States' northern border, and to modify its refugee law regime to the extent necessary to achieve these objectives. For example, an official publication issued by the Library of Congress referred to Canada as "a favoured destination for terrorists"[9] and contended that Canada was a significant base for terrorist activity because of its lax immigration controls.[10] False suspicions even circulated in influential US circles that the 9/11 hijackers entered that country through Canada.[11] The fact that the "would be millennium bomber Ahmed Ressam was apprehended by an alert American Customs official [while attempting to enter] the United States from Canada" two years or so before 9/11 lent credence to these claims. Such chatter put palpable pressure on Canada to get tough on refugees in order to more firmly secure the common border. It must be emphasized that while there was no clear-cut evidence of overt US economic pressure on Canada, there was certainly some implicit pressure. The spectre of a closed border posed a real threat to the Canadian economy, and thus to the political future of the governing party. To avoid a closed border and consequent economic disaster, Canada had to follow the American lead on their common border, migration control, refugee law, and so on.[12] There was thus "enormous pressure" on the Canadian government to cooperate with the Americans in the aftermath of 9/11.[13]

A fifth factor was Canada's own long-standing internal security anxieties. As Roach has put it, Canada had experienced terrorism well before 9/11, for example, the FLQ crisis in 1970, aircraft hijackings to Cuba in 1971, and the Air India bombing in 1985.[14] Although, none of these terrorist attacks was on the scale of 9/11, they did markedly sensitize state and society in Canada to the menace of terrorism and the country's vulnerability to it.[15] In addition, the Canadian government had long been aware of, and taken active steps to curtail, the activities of certain foreign organizations on Canadian soil in support of actions abroad that Canada had classified as terrorism.[16] This marked sensitization to the threat that terrorism poses to Canada and its allies helped shape Canada's post-9/11 refugee law regime. For example, the concept of "security interdependence" helped make Canada more willing to actively support the secret detentions and extraordinary renditions program of the US government.

A sixth factor was Canada's homegrown (and equally long-standing) immigration/refugee control impulse, driven largely by internal socio-political pressure exerted on refugee policy makers and implementers by Canada's own "right wing."[17] Canadian society has always had an immigration control and anti-refugee strain.[18] Although it has become more salient more recently, in the age of Trump, this strain has tended to largely overlap with sections of the social conservative political elements who have, in general, found a political home in the most conservative parties of the given era, from the Reform Party of the 1990s to the current, unified Conservative Party of Canada.[19] This strain has not been a very significant one in more recent times, and certainly not in the last two decades or so. For example, even the Conservative Party led by Stephen Harper, which governed Canada for about a decade between 2006 and 2015, never received as much as 40 percent of the popular vote, despite its not being an exclusively social conservative party.[20] The other 60 percent of the vote tended to go to a number of left-leaning and centrist political parties.[21] In other words, at least six in ten Canadians consistently rejected the generally right-leaning immigration ideology of the Harper Conservatives. However, even the more centrist and leftist parties (aside from having to deal with their own much "softer" immigration control wings) have had to carefully manage and attempt to neutralize the political risk posed by these right-wing immigration control elements by adopting certain tougher refugee/immigration policies. For example, most of the erosions of refugee law witnessed in Canada after 9/11 (from the increased use of refugee detention and terrorism-related inadmissibility provisions to the introduction of the safe third country regime), were authored by a left-of-centre to centrist Liberal government.[22]

In contrast to the foregoing factors, others have pulled that regime toward the positive end of the refugee rights protection spectrum. The first such factor is Canada's eternal (if difficult) struggle, driven by its "sovereign nationalism," to carve out policy directions that are independent of its far more powerful southern neighbour.[23] This perennial concern to demonstrate that Canada is substantially independent of the United States and makes its own policies without undue interference from that country has been so strong that even years after 9/11, then Deputy Prime Minister Anne McLellan made sure to point out during the parliamentary review of Canada's *Anti-terrorism Act* that "the Act represents a made-in-Canada response."[24] There is, of course, some truth to this claim. For one, there was more vigorous and formative debate in Canada than in the United States over the appropriate policy responses to the 9/11 attacks.[25] The fact that the relevant policies and actions did differ positively in some important respects from their US counterparts strengthens this argument. For example, there were no large-scale roundups in Canada of Arab/Muslim refugees and other non-citizens.

Second, although many Canadians lost their lives as a result of the 9/11 attacks, those attacks did not occur on Canadian soil. It was perhaps relatively easier, therefore, for state and society in Canada to rein in their immigration control right wings. Had the attacks occurred in Canada, the story might have been different. Canada's very harsh reaction to the Front de libération du Québec (FLQ) crisis of 1970, which unfolded on a much smaller scale than the 9/11 crisis, suggests that this would have been the case.[26] At the very least, the Canadian state would have reacted in a fashion quite similar to the US reaction to 9/11, and the reaction of the Canadian public would not have been far behind.

A third positive factor was Canada's dominant socio-political character and ethos as a liberal democratic state/society that tends to adhere to the supremacy of its *Charter of Rights and Freedoms*. To their credit, since the entry into force of this Constitutional bill of rights in 1982, Canadian governments have generally felt constrained to at least attempt to demonstrate the adherence of their policies and actions to its dictates. For instance, soon after 9/11, then Deputy Prime Minister Anne McLellan took pains to point out that the government's *Anti-terrorism Act* was drafted in a way that was "consistent with Canadian law and the Charter of Rights and Freedoms."[27] This factor helped prevent even harsher policy proposals or actions from gaining traction and further weakening the legal protections afforded to refugees in Canada. For instance, the Supreme Court of Canada's decision soon after 9/11 that deportations to torture of refugees and other non-citizens would be illegal in almost every case was heavily grounded in the provisions of the *Charter*.[28]

Fourth, the left-of-centre to centrist political ethos of the Liberal Party of Canada, the party in power at the time of the 9/11 attacks and for several years thereafter, also played an important role in orienting the changes to Canada's post-9/11 refugee law regime in a positive direction in many cases. This factor, together with the fact that centrist to leftist elements within the Canadian electorate have tended over the last two decades to enjoy a majority of over 60 percent, and that the Liberal Party's electoral success is, of course, dependent on the votes of many within this large swath of the Canadian population, ensured that the Canadian refugee regime's response to 9/11 was, on the whole, somewhat less harsh than that of the US regime. Had Canada had a more conservative party in office on 9/11 and in the years immediately following, the situation in Canada might have been different. Political ideology does matter.[29]

Just as importantly, despite the existence of a much marginalized and oppressed Indigenous population, Canada has for some time now been an increasingly diverse immigrant society, with a significant proportion of immigrants from the Global South and their offspring.[30] Although not a monolith, of course, most of these immigrants and their descendants enjoy the right to vote and indeed do vote in Canadian elections, often with a pronounced impact on electoral outcomes in certain vote-rich parts of the country.[31] Thus, any serious threat (real or perceived) to the rights or dignity of this broad group, many of whom came to Canada as refugees themselves, or of those who look like them (i.e., refugees from the Global South), almost always carries political risk for the government of the day. The Harper Conservatives learned this the hard way in 2015, when they were punished severely at the polls by most in the immigrant community for, *inter alia*, enacting a statute that authorized the removal from Canada of dual Canadian citizens (read, immigrants and their offspring) who have been convicted of terrorism-related offences, and establishing a "barbaric cultural practices hotline" (to enable Canadians to report on the cultural practices of their immigrant neighbours).[32] It is thus only reasonable to suppose that, in the liberal democratic political system in which the governing Liberal party operated before and after 9/11, the government must have had its political survival and future in mind while crafting its post-9/11 refugee law–related policies.[33]

The US Position

Many of the factors discussed above that combined to shape the character of Canada's post-9/11 refugee law regime were also at play in the US context, if sometimes in different ways. A number of them had a negative impact on the US refugee law regime. For example, the United States' economic and security interdependence with Canada helped shape the US modification or otherwise of refugee law after 9/11. This is best illustrated by the US decision to yield to Canada's desire for a safe third country regime between the two countries. Prior to 9/11, the United States had successfully resisted Canadian pressure; after 9/11, the safe third country agreement became a quid pro quo for Canadian security cooperation.

A second factor was the United States' well-known and long-standing security anxieties. Well before 9/11, the United States had been the target of a number of terrorist attacks, both on its home soil and against its assets abroad.[34] The 9/11 attacks exacerbated an existing atmosphere of substantial anxiety over terrorism within the American state and society.

This is a major reason why, as we have seen in the preceding chapters, the state of US refugee law was already quite troubling long before 9/11. It is also the major reason why so many of the changes made to the US refugee law regime after 9/11 accentuated an existing trend much more than they created departures from an unproblematic status quo ante.

A third factor was a greater predisposition within the US immigration processing/enforcement bureaucracy to keeping terrorists away from the US homeland. As we have seen, this gatekeeping culture was instrumental in producing important negative impacts on US refugee law.[35] The importance of this factor is underscored by the fact that it is the immigration enforcement bureaucracy that implements in detail, and thus exercises in a quotidian way, the most concrete, if interstitial, discretion involved in these processes.

A fourth factor was the well-developed and long-standing immigration control impulse within a section of the US population that would keep immigration and the entry of refugees to, at the very least, a bare minimum.[36] This impulse has, over the last several decades, tended to find strong expression within the Republican Party.[37] Given, for example, the results of the 2016 US presidential elections, in which close to half of Americans voted for a candidate who openly and consistently attacked vast groups of immigrants (Latinos and Muslims), and who promised to halt Muslim immigration to and asylum in the United States (however temporarily), it is only logical to suppose that this kind of harsher anti-immigrant sentiment is widespread within state and society in the United States.[38] This tendency appears to be more pervasive in the United States than in Canada, and may explain in part the tendency of the US refugee law regime to conceive of terrorism in over-broad terms, even to the point of including within that concept many refugees who have themselves been victimized by terrorism. It may also explain in part the mass post-9/11 roundups of Arab/Muslim refugees and other non-citizens in the United States.

A fifth factor was the ideology and ethos of the ruling party at the relevant times. On 9/11 and for many years after, the United States was governed by right-wing Republicans in the Bush Administration. While President George W. Bush himself was not necessarily anti-immigrant, his party and administration comprised many who were. The Bush

Administration was in office until January 2009. This was an important factor that shaped the US refugee law regime in the years after 9/11, as Republicans tend to be the tougher of the two main US political parties when it comes to immigration and refugees. This right-wing ethos therefore provides a partial explanation for many of the kinds of changes made to the US refugee law regime in the months and years following 9/11, including the sheer scale of the mass roundups of Arab/Muslim refugees. While the Obama Administration (which governed between January 2009 and January 2017) was quite tough in deporting recently arrived unauthorized border-crossers, and immigrants and refugees who had committed crimes, it was quite liberal overall on immigration/refugee issues.[39] It is therefore unsurprising that not only did the Obama Administration not worsen US refugee law significantly but it actually improved it in a number of important respects.[40] By contrast, the Trump Administration, which took office in January 2017, has been even more hard-line on immigration/refugee issues than the Bush Administration, and has worsened the status of refugees in the United States.[41]

One of the most important factors was the simple fact that it was the United States that was hit directly by terrorism on 9/11. The damage done was closer to home, and the fear was much more proximate and visceral. This also heightened the emotional reaction to the attacks and the sense among many Americans that a very tough reaction was justified. This may partially explain (though not excuse) the sharp and sometimes shocking US reaction to the attacks.

Other factors functioned to ameliorate the negative impact of those discussed so far. One is the predominantly liberal democratic character of state and society in the United States, a country whose Constitution (which contains a Bill of Rights) is the supreme law, and in which governments (of whatever political stripe) tend to adhere to the rule of law. A second positive factor is the fact that, in part because of its historically gross maltreatment of its Indigenous population and its acceptance over the years of substantial inflows of immigrants and refugees, the United States is an increasingly diverse immigrant society, and has been so for a long time. Here, the argument is similar to that made with respect to Canadian society and need not detain us here, except to note that, while President Trump's triumph tends to confirm the point made earlier that US anti-immigrant elements are more influential than their Canadian counterparts, it does not obviate the fact that the vast majority of immigrants and their offspring voted against him in the 2016 presidential election.[42]

General Explanations for the Differences and Similarities in the Post-9/11 Characters of the Two Regimes

Factors that Contributed to the Harsher US Reaction in Some Respects

The simple fact that it was the United States that had been directly attacked on 9/11 is one of the key factors that explain (albeit without necessarily justifying) the overly harsh reaction of its refugee law regime to the heightened security vigil triggered by the attacks. Clearly, empathy is one thing, direct victimhood another.

Another factor that contributed to the harsher reaction in the United States than in Canada was that it had a more right-wing party in power on 9/11 and for some years thereafter than Canada did, a party with an influential anti-immigrant base. Once that party lost power in early 2009 to a more liberal one, the harshness of the post-9/11 US refugee law regime became tempered in important respects.

Third, the fact that, based on the approximate proxy of voting patterns, a significantly larger percentage of the US population has had a generally nativist (anti-immigrant/anti-Muslim) ideological mindset than in Canada also helped produce this comparatively harsher post-9/11 refugee law regime in that country.

Fourth, the United States is much more powerful than Canada and is also by far the most powerful and influential country in the world. As such, it can get away with much more internationally than Canada can. With a right-wing government in place on 9/11 and for many years after, which famously declared that it did not need a "permission slip" from the United Nations or any other entity before invading another country, it was no wonder it felt freer than Canada ever would to violate international human rights and refugee laws by, for example, deporting many refugees and other non-citizens to torture.[43]

Factors that Contributed to the Comparatively Milder US Reaction in Two Main Respects

As we have seen, the reaction of the US refugee law regime to the heightened security vigil that has characterized the post-9/11 era has been comparatively milder than Canada's in only very few respects. These relate to aspects of the Canada-US safe third country measure discussed in Chapter 4, namely, the much larger scale of its implementation in Canada, and the lack in Canada of the kind of general fail-safe exception that the United States has instituted. The key reason for this is that the United States did not see much to gain from a robust implementation of the safe third country regime, as almost all refugees directed away from the second of two countries that they entered would be directed toward the United States for processing, putting additional pressure on American resources.

Factors that Contributed to the Observed Similarities between the Two Regimes

A number of factors contributed to the remarkable similarities (at least in terms of the relevant textual provisions) between the post-9/11 Canadian and US refugee law regimes. First, state and society in both countries have had very similar (albeit not exactly co-extensive) security/ anti-terrorism anxieties (e.g., scars from past attacks within their territories; concerns about impending attacks, "sleeper cells," and not becoming safe havens for terrorists; and the notion that their democratic character was supposedly making them more vulnerable to terrorist attacks). Second, both countries adhere to high standards of constitutionalism and liberal democracy. Third, both countries had to respond at once to an influential nativist wing and a strong liberal strain within their borders. The nativist wing in the United States is proportionately higher and more influential, but Canada's is still of significant size and influence. Fourth, both countries have a significant population of immigrants and their offspring who tend to react unfavourably (though not monolithically) to policies they perceive as unfair to them or persons in their communities. Fifth, the interdependence of the two countries was also a factor that led their refugee law regimes to react similarly to the post-9/11 heightened security vigil.

Refugee Law and Security Relativism in Canada and the United States after 9/11

This section focuses on analyzing what the reorientation of each of the refugee law regimes after 9/11, including the extent to which they were shaped by adherence to "security relativism," tells us about the cogency, coherence, and integrity of the national self-images of both countries. At the outset, it is important to explain the sense in which the expression "security relativism" is used here.[44]

The Concept of Security Relativism

The term "relativism" has a special meaning in the context of human rights discourse and praxis. As Jack Donnelly has noted, the *Oxford English Dictionary* defines the term "relative" as "arising from, depending on, or determined by, relation to something else or to each other," and "constituted, or existing, only by relation to something else; not absolute or independent."[45] Thus, for instance, "human rights are culturally relative to the extent that they arise from, are determined by, or are in some other sense depend[ent] on culture."[46] The expression "security relativism" is grounded in this same logic. And so, human rights, including those of refugees, would be "national-security-relative" to the extent that they are held to arise from, or to be determined by, or in some other sense to be dependent on, national security.[47]

As important, however, as Upendra Baxi has shown in the general human rights context, relativism itself is "a coat of many colours."[48] Accordingly, as Donnelly's work suggests, there are different types of relativism: radical relativism (the view that something else is the sole source of the validity of rights), strong relativism (the view that something else is the principal source of the validity of rights), and weak relativism (the view that something else can be a secondary source of the validity of rights).[49] Elsewhere, Donnelly also refers to radical relativism as "absolutist relativism."[50] It is also worth noting that, for Donnelly, the difference between "strong" and "weak" relativism is the extent of variation in the conception of human rights that is required by the supposed external referent, be it culture, security, religion, or something else.[51] Departing somewhat from Donnelly's verbal schematic, the distinction that we make here is between strong and weak security relativism.

In this context, "strong security relativism" represents the notion that national security considerations should trump, or at least abridge almost entirely, the enjoyment of any right; and that even core rights protections (such as the bans on torture and deportations to torture) should give way totally or almost entirely in the face of a threat to national security.[52] Examples of such strong security relativism include Richard Posner's argument that all human rights, including the prohibition against torture, "should wax and wane with changes in the [security] danger level" faced by a given country.[53] Alan Dershowitz's controversial proposal for judicially sanctioned torture of alleged terrorists who are reasonably supposed to possess information about the locations of ticking bombs is another good example.[54]

The expression "weak security relativism" is used here to stand for the notions that national security considerations ought to enjoy some priority over the enjoyment of *most* human rights (not including those treated as core in international human rights law), and/or that the protection of these non-core rights should somehow be balanced against such security considerations. A good example of weak security relativism is Michael Ignatieff's argument that while "defeating terrorism may sometimes require the violation of rights," it ought to be firmly understood that "actions which violate foundational commitments to justice and dignity – torture, illegal detention, unlawful assassination – should be beyond the pale."[55] The fact that such views are widely held, even among the fiercest defenders of human rights, is exemplified by the argument made by Arthur Helton and Dessie Zagorcheva that "measures taken in order to increase the security of citizens and to bring to justice the perpetrators of the horrific attacks on September 11 should not infringe unnecessarily on the civil liberties and human rights of migrants, asylum seekers, and refugees."[56] It bears highlighting here that while most commentators would agree that a balance ought to be maintained between non-core rights and national security considerations, an approach that has been entrenched in international human rights law for a very long time, it is their rejection of any attempt to "balance away" or "trade off" *core* human rights protections (such as the anti-torture prohibition) that principally distinguishes weak relativists from the adherents of strong relativism.[57]

Given these understandings of security relativism (strong and weak), how has the mentality it denotes been expressed in the post-911 Canadian and US refugee law regimes, and with what impact? Did this mentality express itself in the same ways and/or have the same impacts on both regimes?

The Canadian Position

Although when viewed in its broad terms, Canada's post-9/11 regime strikingly resembled its pre-9/11 self, the fact remains that certain significant abridgements of refugee rights still occurred in Canada after 9/11, violations that, when examined together, may paint a picture of the ways in which security relativism (strong or weak) was expressed in the Canadian refugee law regime.

What precisely do the changes made after 9/11 to the legal texts and actual operations that constitute the Canadian refugee law regime tell us about the operation and influence of the mentality of strong security relativism? Given space constraints, this question will be answered through the discussion of a very small representative sample of the material examined earlier in this book. First, in the *Suresh* case, the Supreme Court of Canada left open the possibility that Canada could one day lawfully deport a refugee to torture as a result of a national security or other such grave threat.[58] Yet, the prohibitions of torture and deportations to torture are core human rights protections that, according to international law, ought to be available, with no exceptions, to each and every refugee in Canada. Given the gravity of torture, this is a strong security relativist position. What is more, the fact that Canada did significantly help the United States render at least one Canadian who was suspected of terrorism to torture in another country also exemplifies the significant influence that strong security relativism has had, and can have, within Canada's refugee law regime. Additionally, the increased racial profiling of Arab/Muslim refugees and other non-citizens by Canadian authorities after 9/11 was publicly justified on national security grounds. These examples suffice to illustrate the point that strong security relativism has operated quite influentially within Canada's refugee law regime and, as a result, has played an important, not necessarily positive role in moulding that regime into the form, substance, and orientation it assumed after 9/11.

It is also crucial to consider, based on the examination of a few representative samples, what exactly the changes made to the Canadian refugee law regime after 9/11 tell us about the operation and impact of the mentality of weak security relativism on the system. It should be stated upfront that, as many students of refugee law and national security know, weak security relativism has exerted a strong influence on Canada's refugee law regime. It is in fact the very reason that a great deal of the restrictions on refugee law that characterize this regime exist in the first place. For, were the Canadian government and most Canadians to have rejected that notion and held that the human rights of refugees should never be abridged even in the face of a national security threat, most of the restrictions on the rights of refugees that have been discussed in this book would have been untenable. Thus, the embrace of weak security relativism by the government and a great number of Canadians is a key reason that certain measures have been legal in Canada at least since 9/11, for example, mandatory/automatic detentions of refugees suspected reasonably of terrorism (until 2008), and the indefinite/prolonged detention of this same class of persons (at least up to a point).

It should be remembered, however, that the foregoing arguments do not suggest that security relativism, weak or strong, has had a stranglehold on the post-9/11 Canadian refugee law regime. If it had, that regime would not have any positive aspects whatsoever, which is certainly not the case.

The US Position

No matter how major or minor the post-9/11 textual and operational changes to the US refugee law regime were, a range of refugee rights violations did occur in that country after 9/11. Examined as a whole, these rights abridgements may provide us with some insight into the ways in which security relativism (strong or weak) may have been expressed in the US refugee law regime, and its impact on that system.

What precisely do the post-9/11 changes tell us about the influence of the mentality of strong security relativism? Here again, examination of a small representative sample of material will suffice to answer this question. First, the existence of many loopholes that allow for the deportation to torture of certain refugees considered national security risks (a position that contravenes international law) exemplifies the significant influence of strong security relativism on the post-9/11 US refugee law regime. And second, the many frontal assaults, especially since 9/11, on the general bar against deportations to torture, almost all of which have been framed in terms of the need to protect national security by removing from the United States those who are considered to pose a threat to that country, even if this means their deportation to places where they face a substantial risk of torture, indicate the ascendancy – at least for a time – of the pro-torture view within US governmental institutions, including those charged with designing and implementing the refugee law regime. More importantly, these two examples exemplify the ways in which strong security relativism has been at work in the US refugee law regime, for the mentality of both those who deport refugees to torture and those who challenge the general bar against such a practice is that the enjoyment by certain refugees of the core human right to be free from torture should be trumped by national security reasons, or almost entirely abridged on those grounds.

Perhaps even more importantly, what exactly do the post-9/11 changes tell us about the impact of weak security relativism within the US refugee law regime? Given the discussion in this book, the reader should not be surprised to learn that, both before and after 9/11, weak security relativism has played a key role in shaping almost all aspects of the US refugee law regime. For example, it is largely because of an overt and internalized mentality of weak security relativism that this regime permits the harsh system of mandatory/automatic detention of most refugees on arrival in the United States, and the inclusion of all too many victims of terrorism within its definition of terrorism-related inadmissibility (regardless of actual practice).

Again, this discussion is not meant to suggest that security relativism has enjoyed complete sway over the post-9/11 US refugee law regime. Weak security relativism did not have a totalizing effect on this regime, in part because the countervailing forces examined earlier in this chapter sometimes limited its impact on refugee law in the United States.

A Brief Comparison

As the foregoing discussion shows, strong and weak security relativism were each expressed in both the Canadian and US refugee law regimes, with weak security relativism being more evenly expressed in both regimes. This is not surprising, given that both countries have had long-standing security anxieties related to previous terrorist attacks, and each was under some pressure from supporters of immigration control within their populations. Strong security relativism was more pronounced in the US refugee law regime than in its Canadian counterpart.

Refugee Law and National Self-Image in Canada and the United States after 9/11

What can we learn about the cogency, coherence, and integrity of the national self-images of Canada and the United States from an understanding of the extent to which their refugee law regimes were reshaped after 9/11?

The Concept of National Self-Image

By the expression "national self-image" is meant the image that a people (a "nation," if you will) have of themselves – their self-identity. A skeptic may view this expression as problematic given the "fabricated," "imagined," "conjured and connected," and even contingent nature of all nationhood, and doubts as to whether such a thing as a coherent, integral nation can ever exist.[59] Yet, as Catherine Dauvergne and Wesley Pue tell us, nation persists, and has done so "despite the poignancy of [such] academic critique."[60] In John Morss's similar words, "the spectre [of nation] lingers."[61] Nation is imagined enough that it is all but real in the minds of those imagining it – warts, contingencies, and all – and thus tends to display certain properties. Other critics of this expression may charge that even if nations do exist, they can never possess one unified, monolithic self-image or self-identity. This is true, of course. However, our usage here of the expression "national self-image" recognizes the fact that different, and even competing, national self-images do usually exist among one and the same "people," in one and the same country.[62] And so although the concern here is basically with the dominant national self-image in the country at issue, attention is also paid to the relevant alternative national self-imaginary.

That said, it should also be pointed out that a country's national self-image (dominant or alternative) is usually a complex composite of its self-images in relation to a number of different things. For example, the people of most countries tend to share a dominant self-image regarding that country's relationship to the rule of law, human rights, immigration, diversity, democracy, independence from external powers, respect for international law, and humanitarianism. All of these separate national self-images may or may not be aggregated under one moniker, and may or may not be merged into one umbrella conception of that country as "good" or "evil," democratic or dictatorial, pro-immigration or xeno-phobic. There can of course be shades in between.

It should also be noted that while there can be, and there usually is, a gap between how a given people or nation view themselves (their national self-image) and how they are viewed by outsiders, this question does not concern us here.[63] Neither are we concerned with how and why the people of a particular country came to acquire the particular kind of dominant national self-image that they possess. Our focus is rather on analyzing the dominant national self-image that the relevant people do in fact possess.

In what follows, the relationship between the state of refugee law after 9/11 in each country under study, and the dominant/alternative national self-images of the people that constitute the given country will be considered. This will be followed by a brief discussion of the extent to which the dominant national self-image of each country was more troubled (compared with that of the other country) by the response of its refugee law regime to the heightened security vigil triggered by the 9/11 attacks.

The Canadian Position

Canada's dominant national self-image is that of a remarkably (even unusually) humane and inclusive country that enjoys a very positive relationship to human rights, humanitarianism, immigration, multicul-turalism/diversity, democracy, the rule of law, independence from the sometimes negative influence of more powerful external powers, and respect for international law. In 2004, a national policy paper issued by the Canadian government articulated this well, noting that

> Canadians have built a remarkable country shaped by a deep attachment to democracy, the rule of law, respect for human rights and pluralism. Our way of life is based on an openness to ideas and innovations, and to people from every part of the world – a commitment to include every individual and every community in the ongoing project that is Canada – and a steadfast rejection of intolerance, extremism and violence.[64]

In 2012, David MacKenzie, then Parliamentary Secretary to the Minister of Public Safety, reinforced this self-image when he declared in Parliament that "Canada is known internationally as a welcoming and compassionate country."[65] And there is no doubt whatsoever that this dominant national self-image persists to this day. For instance, in late 2015, Prime Minister Justin Trudeau spoke of "compassion ... diversity and inclusion" as the things "that have made Canada strong and free" and "not just in principle, but in practice."[66] This official view is widely shared within Canadian society itself. For example, James Cameron and John Berry have correctly noted that Canadians derive great pride from the national institutions and policies such as humanitarianism, multiculturalism (implying a positive relationship to immigration and pluralism), and the human rights/democratic protections offered by the *Canadian Charter of Rights and Freedoms*.[67] This point is at least implied in the separate writings of David Hornsby and Bernard Duhaime.[68]

There is also much support in the literature for each of the constituent elements of this dominant national self-image. A few examples will suffice to illustrate. Kent Roach has flagged the perception (even stereotype) that Canada is so concerned with human rights that it is unable to respond to perceived security threats.[69] He has also correctly noted that Canada is a nation that prides itself on its role in developing and adhering to international law.[70] The Canadian government itself speaks regularly about Canada's "humanitarian tradition."[71] Will Kymlicka has reported (albeit somewhat critically) about the widely held belief in Canada that multiculturalism and diversity are Canadian values.[72] And as the book edited by Shibao Guo and Lloyd Wong suggests, public opinion indicates that a growing majority of Canadians identify multiculturalism as one of the most important symbols of Canada's national identity.[73] Others, both in and outside the government, have commented on Canada's national self-image as a firmly pro-immigration and refugee country, and its "openness" to its "others."[74] In relation to Canada's self-image as a country that is, or strives to be, independent from the sometimes negative influence of stronger external powers (such as the United States), Reg Whitaker has correctly noted that "Canadian public opinion [often] demands some distance from the appearance that Canadian policy is being dictated from Washington.[75] And Roach has noted the widespread sense among Canadians that Canada is, or at least ought to be, committed to the rule of (international) law.[76] He also remarked on what he sees as "the Canadian penchant for being even handed."[77]

Importantly, it should be kept in mind that there is much justification for the existence of Canada's dominant national self-image of a humane and inclusive country. The following examples suffice to illustrate this point. In 2007, 84 percent of a sample of immigrants who were surveyed four years after their arrival in Canada expressed positive views about their decision to come to Canada.[78] That same year, 90 percent of Canadians disagreed with the view expressed by some within the anti-immigration wing of Canadian society that immigrants to Canada should "go back to where they came from."[79] Canada's self-image as a model in the protection of refugees is widely shared by knowledgeable outsiders around the world.[80] As remarkably, the national self-image of Canada as a diverse society is justified by the 2006 census figures, and supported by the comparable statistics.[81] The census found that roughly 20 percent of Canadians were foreign-born (one of the highest percentages in the Global North), and that this percentage was growing.[82] Furthermore, Canadian democracy is well established and vibrant, and so is obedience to the rule of law by Canada's government. It is also widely accepted that the *Charter of Rights and Freedoms* works in practice to significantly limit state action in Canada. This much is evident from the analyses in the Introduction up to and including Chapter 4, for instance, from the discussion of the *Suresh* case. These same chapters also show that while Canada is often influenced by its much more powerful neighbour to the south, it does not always pursue the course of action that would have pleased that country. What is more, Canada does possess a long history of humanitarian action around the world (or at least action that has been framed in such terms).[83] Finally, Canada has tended to comply with international law to the point that even its courts, especially the Supreme Court of Canada, have at times oriented their decisions toward correspondence with even formally non-binding international law norms. The decision in the case of *Baker v Canada* is a good example of this.[84] It should be noted, however, that, robust as it has often been, this Canadian tendency to comply with international law has never been optimal. For instance, as we saw in the Introduction, Canada's failure to totally outlaw deportations to torture is a serious violation of the absolute bar against that practice in international human rights law.

It must also be stressed that despite the fact that Canada's dominant national self-image is to a high degree rooted in reality, other non-dominant and competing national self-images do exist, and these are also grounded in facts. These other self-images may be seen as alternative or counter national self-images. The most important of these, for our purposes in this book, portrays Canada as a country that is not as humane and inclusive as Canadians and outsiders tend to imagine. For example, even while constructing the self-image of Canada as a pro-immigrant/refugee country, government officials have themselves often taken almost as much care to offer an alternative self-image of Canada as a country that is also (justifiably) tough on, and unwelcoming to, "undesirables who pose a danger" to Canada.[85] The idea here is that there are justifiable limits to Canada's welcoming nature and image. For its part, the Canadian Council for Refugees (CCR) often emphasizes its view that Canada still has a long way to go before it can rid itself of racial and other forms of discrimination, especially within the immigration and refugee system, and highlights the fact that Canadian society has long had an influential anti-immigrant current.[86] The CCR's alternative self-image of Canada is to a degree also rooted in reality. For example, within weeks of the 9/11 attacks, 48 percent of Canadians reported that they approved of racial profiling, a highly discriminatory measure that violates international human rights law.[87] What is more, in 2007, 47 percent of Canadians were willing to admit to a pollster that they were a bit racist.[88] In response to this poll, the Secretary of State for Multiculturalism warned that "Canadians should never be lulled into believing that this country is an inclusive utopia."[89] The statistics that he was reacting to when he issued this warning have not changed significantly since then.[90] Since, as Reem Bahdi has correctly noted, racial profiling (and by implication, racism) excludes those who are targeted from the ranks of those imagined as belonging to the Canadian community, it is difficult to suppose that the host of persons who have been profiled (and thereby excluded) would imagine that Canada is as inclusive as most Canadians tend to think it is.[91]

In light of the foregoing analysis, what does the nature of the post-9/11 changes to the texts and operations constituting Canada's refugee law regime tell us about Canada's national self-image? A brief consideration of a couple of examples will suffice to answer this. Regarding the deportation of refugees to torture, the fact that this practice is, in partial compliance with international human rights law, generally outlawed in Canada tends to reinforce many aspects of Canada's dominant national self-image. However, the fact that Canadian law does allow this practice under some exceptional circumstances does significant damage to the coherence of that dominant self-image, and bolsters the credibility of the alternative self-image of Canada as a country that is not really as humane or obedient to international law as many Canadians imagine it to be. Also, the fact that, despite a number of important differences, the Canadian and US refugee law regimes still looked strikingly similar in most respects in the years immediately after 9/11 troubles Canada's dominant national self-image to some degree. Given that the 9/11 attacks occurred in the United States and that Canada was not directly attacked, the Canadian refugee law regime's harsh reaction in important respects undermines to some degree the integrity of the national self-image of Canada as a remarkably humane country. Thus, the story of the relationship between Canada's refugee law regime and its national self-image is a rather complicated one.

The US Position

Put simply, the United States' dominant national self-image is of a "shining city on a hill,"[92] of a country that is deeply and positively attached to democracy, the protection of human rights, the rule of law, the acceptance of immigrants, the protection of refugees, inclusion, and humanitarianism, and of a state/society that should be an example to others. And while many Americans (especially Native Americans, African Americans, and others who have been grossly dispossessed and oppressed over centuries) may question whether the United States has ever lived up to these values, many Americans tend to see their country in these terms, and would likely speak proudly of "the American tradition of humanitarian concern and conduct."[93]

A key aspect of this dominant national self-image is the American self-image as pro-immigrant/refugee, and therefore as an inclusive society. At least until the Trump era, immigration (including the acceptance of refugees) was often viewed as being at the core of US identity.[94] As Krissy Katzenstein has pointed out: "Since elementary school, many US students have learned that 'America' has welcomed immigrants from around the world and that the success of this country has been built on the hard work of all Americans, including immigrants."[95] As a partial result, it is common for Americans to describe themselves as "a nation of immigrants."[96] Thus, most Americans would tend to agree that "America has been a sanctuary for immigrants, both historically and fundamentally."[97]

As significantly rooted in reality as this dominant US self-image is, it is still a much contested one. As one commentator has noted, "Americans have always been ambivalent about immigration."[98] Against this background, it is no wonder that at least one alternative US national self-images does exist – of a country that is not as much of a shining city on a hill as many Americans imagine, and not as pro-immigration, pro-refugee, pro-inclusion, pro-humanitarianism, pro–human rights, and pro–international law as many of them think. Those who share this alternative national self-image note, quite correctly, that the United States has over the years intentionally closed its borders to those it has deemed "undesirable," sometimes without just cause, including many among the so-called huddled masses and the homeless. Others have noted the strong (albeit not always dominant) anti-immigrant current in US society.[99]

With this analysis in mind, what does the post-9/11 behaviour of the US refugee law regime tell us about that country's national self-image? To what extent is it exemplified or troubled by the post-9/11 developments within this regime? A brief consideration of a couple of examples will suffice to shed light on these pertinent issues. The credibility of the dominant US national self-image is reinforced by the fact that there is an absolute general bar in that country against the deportation of refugees (and other non-citizens) to torture. However, the fact that the United States did deport a fairly large number of refugees and other non-citizens to torture after 9/11 does significantly trouble the cogency of this dominant self-image. This ill-treatment of many refugees and other non-citizens thus reinforces the alternative national self-identity. The fact that even the generally liberal Obama Administration appeared to back away after some time from its initially absolute opposition to such deportations to torture is highly instructive in this regard.

Thus, the story of the relationship between the US refugee law regime and its national self-image is hardly a simple and straightforward one. That country's dominant national self-image as a shining city on the hill is at once exemplified and troubled by certain post-9/11 developments in its domestic refugee law regime.

A Brief Comparison

Which country's dominant national self-image was more troubled by post-9/11 developments in its refugee law regime – Canada or the United States? Perhaps not surprisingly, the answers to these questions are more complicated than some might have expected. These answers tend to challenge to some extent the familiar stereotypes about Canada's being significantly better at the protection of human rights, immigrants, and refugees than the United States.[100] When examined against the Canadian post-9/11 refugee protection record, and the 9/11-related evidence discussed in this book, the United States' dominant national self-image as "a shining city on a hill" appears to be less coherent than Canada's. At the same time, however, the fact that Canada was not the country attacked on 9/11, and was therefore not nearly as enveloped and consumed by the fear and emotion that those attacks precipitated, gives much cause for pause here. Had Canada been attacked the way the United States was on 9/11, how would it have reacted? Without a crystal ball, these questions are difficult to answer. We do know this, however: Canada's reaction on the one occasion that it felt under a very serious and sustained direct threat to its homeland from terrorism, namely, during the FLQ crisis in 1970, was hardly brilliant from a human rights perspective.

Notes

Introduction: Refugee Law after 9/11

1 See Reg Whitaker, "Refugee Policy after September 11: Not Much New" (2002) 20:4 Refuge 29 at 29 ["September 11"]. See also Kent W. Roach, "Did September 11 Change Everything? Struggling to Preserve Canadian Values in the Face of Terrorism" (2002) 47:4 McGill LJ 893 at 894; and Larry Minear, "Humanitarian Action in an Age of Terrorism," Working Paper No. 63 (Medford, MA: Fletcher School of Law and Diplomacy, Tufts University, 2002) at 2.

2 See Whitaker, *ibid;* Roach, *ibid;* and Reem Bahdi et al, "Racial Profiling" in Richard Marcuse, ed, *Racial Profiling: A Special BCCLA Report on Racial Profiling in Canada* (Vancouver: BC Civil Liberties Association, 2010) 31 at 35–36.

3 Whitaker, *ibid* at 31–32.

4 *Ibid* at 29.

5 See James Fallows, "The Right and Wrong Questions about the Iraq War," *The Atlantic* (May 19, 2015), online: <https://www.theatlantic.com/politics/archive/2015/05/the-right-and-wrong-questions-about-the-iraq-war/393497/>.

6 See Donald Kerwin, "US-Canada Study and Report" (2002) 3; ABA Immigration and Nationality Committee Newsletter 1 at 1–2; and Doris Meissner, "Immigration in the Post 9-11 Era" (2002) 40 Brandeis LJ 851 at 851–52.

7 Whitaker, "September 11," *supra* note 1 at 29.

8 Reg Whitaker, "Keeping Up with the Neighbours? Canadian Responses to 9/11 in Historical and Comparative Context" (2003) 41:2 Osgoode Hall LJ 241 ["Neighbours"].

9 Whitaker, "September 11," *supra* note 1 at 31.

10 See Andrew I. Shoenholtz, "Refugee Protection in the United States Post–September 11" (2005) 36 Colum HRL Rev 323 at 324.

11 *Ibid* at 326.

12 Stephen D. Krasner, "Structural Causes and Regime Consequences: Regimes as Intervening Variables" (1982) 36 International Organization 185 at 185.

13 See Joanne J. Meyerowitz, "Introduction" in J. Meyerowitz, ed, *History and September 11th* (Philadelphia: Temple University Press, 2003) 1 at 1; and Obiora C. Okafor, "Newness, Imperialism and International Legal Reform in Our Time: A TWAIL Perspective" (2005) 43 Osgoode Hall LJ 171 at 181.

14 For example, the Canadian government has defined "national security" in the following way: "National Security deals with threats that have the potential to undermine the security of the state or society." See *Securing an Open Society: Canada's National Security Policy* (Ottawa: Privy Council Office, April 2004) at 7, online: <http://publications.gc.ca/collections/Collection/CP22–77–2004E.pdf>.

15 This is an adaptation of Jack Donnelly's definition of "cultural relativism" in human rights theory. See Jack Donnelly, "Human Rights: Both Universal and Relative (A Reply to Michael Goodhart)" (2008) 30:1 Hum Rts Q 194 at 195.

16 This distinction is also adapted from Jack Donnelly's work on "cultural relativism," albeit more slightly in this case. See J. Donnelly, *Universal Human Rights in Theory and Practice* (Ithaca, NY: Cornell University Press, 2003) at 89–90; and J. Donnelly, "Cultural Relativism and Universal Human Rights" (1984) 6:4 Hum Rts Q 400 at 401.

17 See University of California at Berkeley School of Law, "The Common Law and Civil Law Traditions," online: <https://www.law.berkeley.edu/library/robbins/CommonLawCivilLawTraditions.html> (accessed March 17, 2018) and @ WashULaw, "Major Differences between the Mexican and the US Legal Systems" (July 15, 2014), online: Washington University in St. Louis School of Law <https://onlinelaw.wustl.edu/blog/major-differences-mexican-u-s-legal-systems/>.

18 See Kent Roach, "Uneasy Neighbours: Comparative American and Canadian Counter-Terrorism" (2012) 38:5 Wm Mitchell L Rev 1701 at 1708 ["Uneasy Neighbours"].

19 For example, *ibid;* and Craig Forcese and François Crépeau, eds, *Terrorism, Law and Democracy: 10 Years after 9/11* (Montreal: Canadian Institute for the Administration of Justice, 2012). See also Ronald Daniels et al, eds, *The Security of Freedom: Essays on Canada's Anti-Terrorism Bill* (Toronto: University of Toronto Press, 2001); Niklaus Steiner et al, eds, *Problems of Protection: The UNHCR, Refugees and Human Rights* (New York: Routledge, 2003).

20 For example, see Roach, "Uneasy Neighbours," *supra* note 18.

21 For example, see Howard Adelman, "Refugees and Border Security Post–September 11" (2002) 20:4 *Refuge* 5 at 6–8; Sharryn J. Aiken, "Of Gods and Monsters: National Security and Canadian Refugee Policy" (2001) 14:2 RQDI 1; Sharryn J. Aiken, "National Security and Canadian Immigration: Deconstructing the Discourse of Trade-Offs" in François Crépeau, ed, *Les migrations internationals contemporaines: une dynamique complexe au coeur de la globalization* (Montreal: Presses de

l'Université de Montréal, 2009) 172 at 175 ["National Security"]; Reem Bahdi et al, *supra* note 2; Muzaffar A. Chishti et al, *America's Challenge: Domestic Security, Civil Liberties, and National Unity after September 11* (Washington, DC: Migration Policy Institute, 2003); David Cole, "In Aid of Removal: Due Process Limits on Immigration Detention" (2002) 51 Emory LJ 1003; François Crépeau, "Anti-Terrorism Measures and Refugee Law Challenges in Canada" (2011) 29:4 Refugee Survey Quarterly 31; Catherine Dauvergne, "Security and Migration Law in the Less Brave New World" (2007) 16:4 Soc & Leg Stud 533 ["Security"]; Joan Fitz-patrick, "Rendition and Transfer in the War against Terrorism: Guantanamo and Beyond" (2003) 25 Loy LA Int'l & Comp LJ 457; Regina Germain, "Rushing to Judgment: The Unintended Consequences of the USA PATRIOT Act for Bona Fide Refugees" (2002) 16 Geo Immig LJ 505; Lawrence M. Lebowitz & Ira L. Podheiser, "A Summary of the Changes in Immigration Policies and Practices after the Terrorist Attacks of September 11, 2001: The USA PATRIOT Act and Other Measures" (2002) 63 U Pitt L Rev 873; Audrey Macklin, "Borderline Secur-ity" in R. Daniels et al, *supra* note 19 at 384; Whitaker, "September 11," *supra* note 1; and Volker Turk, "Opinion: Forced Migration and Security" (2003) 15:1 Int'l J Refugee L 113 at 114.

22 See Whitaker, *ibid;* and Whitaker, "Neighbours," *supra* note 8.

23 See Dauvergne, "Security," *supra* note 21.

24 See Monica K. Juma and Peter M. Kagwanja, "Securing Refuge from Terror: Refugee Protection in East Africa after September 11" in Steiner et al, *supra* note 19 at 233.

25 See Catherine Dauvergne, "Sovereignty, Migration and the Rule of Law in Global Times" (2004) 67:4 Mod L Rev 588 at 589.

26 I borrow this expression from Reg Whitaker's work. See Whitaker, "September 11," *supra* note 1. For another early recognition of this reality, see Catherine Dau-vergne, "Evaluating Canada's New Immigration and Refugee Protection Act in Its Global Context" (2003) 41 Alta L Rev 725.

27 For example, see Macklin, *supra* note 21 at 384; Aiken, "National Security," *supra* note 21 at 175; Adelman, *supra* note 21 at 6–8; Turk, *supra* note 21 at 114; and Juma and Kagwanja, *supra* note 24 at 227–29.

Chapter 1: Deportations to Torture

Acknowledgment: Minor portions of this chapter have been culled from Obiora Okafor & Pius Okoronkwo, "Reconfiguring Non-Refoulement? The Suresh Deci-sion, Security Relativism and the International Human Rights Imperative" (2003) 15 Int'l J Refugee L 30.

1 For a critique of this position, see Reg Whitaker, "Refugee Policy after September 11: Not Much New" (2002) 20:4 Refuge 29 at 29–30 ["Refugee Policy"].

2 *Ibid.*

3   *Ibid.*
4   *Convention against Torture and Other Cruel, Inhuman or Degrading Treatment or Punishment,* December 10, 1984, 465 UNTS 85 (entered into force June 26, 1987).
5   *International Covenant on Civil and Political Rights,* December 19, 1966, 999 UNTS 171 (entered into force March 23, 1976) [*ICCPR*].
6   See UN Human Rights Committee, "General Comment No. 20, Article 7" (44th Sess, 1992), reproduced in the Compilation of General Comments and General Recommendations Adopted by Human Rights Treaty Bodies, UN Doc HRI\ GEN\1\Rev.1 at 30 (1994) [noting in para 7 that, in the view of the Committee, States parties must not expose individuals to the danger of torture or cruel, inhuman, or degrading treatment or punishment on return to another country by way of their extradition, expulsion, or *refoulement*].
7   *Ahani v Canada,* Communication No 1051/2002, UN Doc CCPR/C/80/D/1051/2002 (2004) [*Ahani* HRC].
8   See paras 3.5, 8.1, 8.2, and 10.10. These paragraphs must be read together to suggest this conclusion.
9   See *Khan v Canada,* Communication No 15/1994, (1994) IIHRL 97 (Committee against Torture); and *Chahal v United Kingdom,* [1996] ECHR 54, (1996) 23 EHRR 413 (European Court of Human Rights).
10   See Dawn J. Miller, "Holding States to Their Convention Obligations: The United Nations Convention against Torture and the Need for a Broad Interpretation of State Action" (2003) 17:2 Geo Immig LJ 299 at 299–300.
11   See Deborah E. Anker, *The Law of Asylum in the United States* (Boston: Refugee Law Center, 1994) at 466–67.
12   Pub L No 105-277, s 2242, 112 Stat 2681-822 (21 October 1998); 64 Fed Reg 8478 (1999) [as corrected by 64 Fed Reg 13881 (1999)], respectively.
13   Although this point is not controversial at all, see Anker, *supra* note 11 at 466–67; Barbara Hines, "Asylum and Withholding of Removal" in R. Patrick Murphy et al, eds, *Practice under IIRAIRA: One Year Later* (Washington, DC: American Immigration Lawyers Association, 1997) at 148; Miller, *supra* note 10 at 303.
14   Formerly styled the US Immigration and Naturalization Service (INS), this bureaucracy has now been abolished and split into at least two units within the US Department of Homeland Security. See US, Bill HR 5005, *Homeland Security Act of 2002,* 107th Cong, 2002, s 471 (enacted) [*Homeland Security Act*].
15   See 64 Fed Reg 8489 (1999) [as corrected by 64 Fed Reg 13881 (1999)].
16   See US, Office of Chief Immigration Judge, Executive Office of Immigration Review, US Department of Justice, *Operating Policies and Procedures Memorandum No 99-5: Implementation of Article 3 of the UN Convention against Torture* (May 14, 1999) at 4.
17   *Cheema v Ashcroft,* 383 F.3d 848 (9th Cir 2004) [*Cheema*].
18   See US, *Asylum,* 8 USC, ss 1158(b)(2)(A)(iv)–(v) (2011).
19   *Bellout v Ashcroft,* 363 F.3d 975 at 979 (9th Cir 2004).

20 *Ibid*.

21 See *Charlotte Observer* (May 9, 2004), online: <http://www.charlotte.com/> (quoting an expert who argues that very few people defended torture before 9/11, and that at that time pollsters did not even ask the question).

22 For example, see s 1(c) of US, Department of State, *Country Reports on Human Rights Practices for 2003: Egypt* (February 25, 2004), online: Department of State <http://www.state.gov/g/drl/rls/hrrpt/2003/27926.htm> (accessed December 14, 2004).

23 For example, see US, Bill HR 4309, *Torture Victims Relief Act of 1998*, 105th Cong, 1998; and HR 2367, *Torture Victims Relief Reauthorization Act of 1999*, 106th Cong, 1999.

24 See Manfred Nowak, Mortiz Birk, & Tiphanie Crittin, "The Obama Administration and Obligations under the Convention against Torture" (2012) 20 Transnat'l L & Contemp Probs 33 at 64.

25 See Matthew Weaver & Spencer Ackerman, "Trump Claims Torture Works but Experts Warn of Its 'Potentially Existential' Costs," *The Guardian* (January 26, 2017), online: <https://www.theguardian.com/us-news/2017/jan/26/donald-trump-torture-absolutely-works-says-us-president-in-first-television-interview>; Adam Serwer, "Can Trump Bring Back Torture?" *The Atlantic* (January 26, 2017), online: <https://www.theatlantic.com/politics/archive/2017/01/trump-torture/514463/>.

26 See *Suresh v Canada*, 2002 SCC 1, [2002] 1 SCR 3 [*Suresh* SCC]; *Ahani v Canada*, 2002 SCC 2, [2002] 1 SCR 72 [*Ahani*].

27 *Suresh* SCC, *ibid*.

28 *Ibid* at para 129 [emphasis added]. The italicization of the word "Charter" is reproduced from the decision.

29 *Ibid* at paras 78 and 130, respectively.

30 SC 2001, c 27. Although passed by Parliament in 2001, the *IRPA* did not enter into force until 2002.

31 For more on the import of s 113, see Lorne Waldman, *Canadian Immigration and Refugee Practice* (Markham, ON: LexisNexis Butterworths, 2003) at 17.

32 See *Suresh* SCC, *supra* note 26 at para 51.

33 Notice how in the international litigation version of the *Ahani* case, the UN Human Rights Committee noted its displeasure at the gap between the Canadian position and the international norm in this respect, and declared that "the prohibition on torture ... is an absolute one that is not subject to countervailing considerations." See *Ahani* HRC decision, *supra* note 7 at para 10. See also Gib van Ert, "Torture and the Supreme Court of Canada" (2014) 65 UNBLJ 21 at 24–25. The point that the Canadian position on this question is basically similar to the US one is not effectively countered by arguing, as some may, that customary international law is a part of Canadian law. Yes, it is, but it is still international law. More importantly, the Supreme Court of Canada was aware of this position when it reached its decision.

34 Ellen Chung, "A Double-Edged Sword: Reconciling the United States' International Obligations under the Convention against Torture" (2002) 51 Emory LJ 355 at 360.

35 See US, Bill HR 3058, *Anti-Atrocity Act of 1999*, 106th Cong, 1999; HR 2642, 106th Cong, 1999; and S 1375, 106th Cong, 1999, which all failed to pass. See also HR 1449, 107th Cong, 2001; and S 864, 107th Cong, 2001 – both bills were reintroduced versions of the earlier bills and also failed to pass.

36 See US, Bill S 1754, *Denying Safe Haven to International and War Criminals Act of 2000*, 106th Cong, 1999, which also failed to pass.

37 See Chung, *supra* note 34 at 371.

38 See US, Bill HR 5285, *Serious Human Rights Abusers Accountability Act of 2000*, 106th Cong, 2000.

39 This bill lapsed in the Senate Judiciary Committee and did not pass Congress as such.

40 See James T. Gathii, "Torture, Extraterritoriality, Terrorism, and International Law" (2003) 67 Alb L Rev 335.

41 For example, see Jonathan Alter, "Time to Think about Torture," *Newsweek* (November 4, 2001), online: <http://www.newsweek.com/time-think-about-torture-149445> (arguing in favour of some forms of torture); and Richard H. Weisberg, "Response to Sanford Levinson," *Dissent* (Summer 2003) (arguing against the emboldened pro-torture movement).

42 For an overview and human rights analysis of this scandal, see Human Rights Watch, *The Road to Abu Ghraib* (New York: Human Rights Watch, 2004) [*Abu Ghraib*].

43 *Ibid* at 1, 3, 4, 10, and 27–30.

44 *Ibid.*

45 *Ibid* at 1, 2, 3, 7–9, 10, 17, 21, and 30–32.

46 See Letter from Deputy US Assistant Attorney General John C. Yoo to White House Counsel the Hon. Alberto Gonzales (August 1, 2002) at 3–4 (on file with the author). See also Memorandum opinion from Jay Bybee, US Assistant Attorney General to White House Counsel the Hon. Alberto Gonzales (August 1, 2002) at 39–46 (on file with the author).

47 *Ibid.*

48 See US, *Cong Rec*, vol. 150, at 1291 (June 25, 2004) (Hon. Edward J. Markey, "Extension of Remarks on the 2004 International Day in Support of Victims of Torture").

49 One such saga is illustrative. It took nearly a year of very public struggle, including a freedom of information request and a lawsuit, for the American Civil Liberties Union to obtain the memo from the Department of Justice and other key records relating to the government's practice and support of torture. See <https://www.aclu.org/press-releases/defense-department-files-secret-arguments-further-attempt-suppress-abu-ghraib-photos>. See also *American Civil Liberties Union and Others v Department of Defense and Others*, 389 F. Supp. 2d 547(S.D.N.Y 2005), September 29, 2005.

50 Joan Fitzpatrick, "Rendition and Transfer in the War against Terrorism: Guant-anamo and Beyond" (2003) 25:3 Loy LA Int'l & Comp LJ 457.
51 *Ibid.*
52 See CBC News, "The Maher Arar Inquiry: Frequently Asked Questions" (September 18, 2006) online: CBC News <http://www.cbc.ca/news2/background/arar/arar_faq.html>. For more on the Arar rendition saga, see US, *America after 9/11: Freedom Preserved or Freedom Lost? Hearing before the Senate Committee on the Judiciary,* 108th Cong, 1st Sess (November 18, 2003) at 6, 19, 29, and 31 [*America after 9/11*].
53 *Ibid.*
54 *Ibid.*
55 *Ibid.*
56 See the *Report of the Events relating to Maher Arar: Analysis and Recommnedations,* Dennis R. O'Connor, 2006, online: Library and Archives Canada <http://publications.gc.ca/collections/Collection/CP32-88-1-2006E-AR.pdf> at 9.
57 See US, Department of State, *Country Reports on Human Rights Practices for 2002: Syria* (March 31, 2003), online: Department of State <https://www.state.gov/j/drl/rls/hrrpt/2002/>.
58 *Arar v Ashcroft,* Suit No CV-00249-DGT (EDNY) (filed on January 22, 2004). See the *Complaint and Request for Jury Trial, supra* note 56 at 16.
59 Commission of Inquiry into the Actions of Canadian Officials in Relation to Maher Arar, Dennis R. O'Connor, *Report on the Events Relating to Maher Arar, Factual Background,* vol 1 (2006), online: Library and Archives Canada <http://epe.lac-bac.gc.ca/100/206/301/pco-bcp/commissions/maher_arar/07–09–13/www.ararcommission.ca/default.htm> [*Arar Report*].
60 See Human Rights Watch, *Abu Ghraib, supra* note 42 at 10–11 (reporting four cases); Morton Sklar, "The Blood Doesn't Wash Off," *Globe and Mail* (November 10, 2003), online: <https://www.theglobeandmail.com/opinion/the-blood-doesnt-wash-off/article773692/> (reporting suggestions that over 100 non-citizens had suffered such renditions since 9/11).
61 Fitzpatrick, *supra* note 50 at 479.
62 US, Bill HR 3522, *Securing America's Future through Enforcement Reform Act of 2003,* 108th Cong, 2003. This bill lapsed in committee and so was not passed into law.
63 US, Bill HR10, *9/11 Recommendations Implementation Act of 2004,* 108th Cong, 2004. This bill passed the House on October 8, 2004, in a 282–134 voted (Roll No 523). Due to its differences with the Senate version, a conference committee was set up to reconcile both versions. A new version of the bill was engrossed on October 16, 2004, but was not passed in that form.
64 See US, Bill S 2845, *Intelligence Reform and Terrorism Prevention Act of 2004,* 108th Cong, 2004, online: Congress.gov <https://www.congress.gov/bill/108th-congress/senate-bill/2845/text>.
65 See CQ Press, online: <https://library.cqpress.com/cqalmanac/document.php?id=cqal04-836-24351-1084572>.

66 Memo from the FBI General Counsel to All Divisions (May 19, 2004) at 1 (on file with the author). See also Shadi Mokhtari, *After Abu Ghraib: Exploring Human Rights in America and the Middle East* (New York: Cambridge University Press, 2009) at 63–112.

67 *Ibid.*

68 See US, Office of Management and Budget, Executive Office of the President, *Statement of Administration Policy: H.R. 10 – 9/11 Recommendations Implementation Act* (October 7, 2004), online: American Presidency Project <http://www.presidency. ucsb.edu/ws/index.php?pid=24761>.

69 US, Bill HR 4674, *To Prohibit the Return of Persons by the United States, for Purposes of Detention, Interrogation, or Trial, to Countries Engaging in Torture or Other Inhuman Treatment of Persons,* 108th Cong, 2004. This bill was referred to the House Committee on International Relations on June 23, 2004, but was not passed by the 108th Congress.

70 See US, *Cong Rec,* E.1291, Vol. 150 No. 90, 108th Congress, 2nd Session (25 June 2004) "The 2004 International Day in Support of Victims of Torture"), per Hon. Edward Markey.

71 *Ibid.*

72 Pakistan is now a key US ally in the war on terrorism, and support for Pakistan has now been elevated as a key objective of US foreign and security policy. For instance, see s 7103 of the *Intelligence Reform and Terrorism Prevention Act of 2004* (which commits the US to continuing assistance to Pakistan on the basis of its strategic importance to the war on terrorism), *supra* note 64.

73 The latest State Department Human Rights Report on Pakistan states explicitly that in 2003 Pakistani "security force personnel continued to torture persons in custody throughout the country. For example, according to Human Rights Watch (HRW), Rasheed Azam was beaten and tortured at Khuzdar military cantonment. In September, two prison officials allegedly beat and killed 18-year-old Sunil Samuel at Camp Jail in Lahore after he was sexually assaulted by inmates. Over the years, there have been allegations that common torture methods included: Beating; burning with cigarettes; whipping the soles of the feet; sexual assault; prolonged isolation; electric shock; denial of food or sleep; hanging upside down; forced spreading of the legs with bar fetters; and public humiliation. Human rights organizations and the press have criticized the provision of the Anti-Terrorist Act that allows confessions obtained in police custody to be used in 'special courts,' because police torture of suspects is common. Police generally did not attempt to use confessions to secure convictions under this law." See US, Department of State, *Country Reports on Human Rights Practices for 2003: Pakistan* (February 25, 2004), online: Department of State <http://www.state.gov/g/drl/rls/hrrpt/2003/27950. htm> (accessed 10 December 2004).

74 US, Executive Order No 13491, *Ensuring Lawful Interrogations,* 74 Fed Reg 164893 (2009), online: <http://www.presidency.ucsb.edu/ws/?pid=85669> (accessed

December 10, 2004); and *Joint Study on Global Practices in Relation to Secret Deten-tion in the Context of Countering Terrorism*, UNHRC, UN Doc A/HRC/13/42 (2010) at 150–52.

75 Nowak, Birk, & Crittin, *supra* note 24 at 64.

76 *Ibid*.

77 Canadian Heritage/Human Rights Directorate, *International Covenant on Economic, Social and Cultural Rights: Canada's Fifth Report under the United Nations Convention against Torture and Other Cruel, Inhuman or Degrading Treatment or Punishment* (2005), online: Government of Canada <http://publications.gc.ca/site/eng/279049/publication.html> [*Canada's Fifth Report*].

78 Section 53(1)(b) of the old act provides that "the person is a member of an inadmis-sible class described in paragraph 19(1) (e), (f), (g), (j), (k), or (l) and the minister is of the opinion that the person constitutes a danger to the security of Canada." *Canada: Immigration Act*, SC 1976–77, c 52.

79 *Almrei v Canada*, 2005 FCA 54; [2005] 3 FCR 142 at paras 120–26.

80 *Suresh Re* (1997), 40 Immigration Law Reporter (2d) 247 at 260–62 (FCTD) [*Suresh* FCTD].

81 *Suresh v Canada (Minister of Citizenship and Immigration)*, [2000] 2 FCR 592, 2000 CanLII 17101 (FCA) [*Suresh* FCA].

82 *Suresh* SCC, *supra* note 26 at para 78. See also Obiora C. Okafor & Pius L. Oko-ronkwo, "Reconfiguring Non-Refoulement? The *Suresh* Decision, Security Relativ-ism and the International Human Rights Imperative" (2003) 15 Int'l J Refugee L 30 at 65–66.

83 See *Ahani* HRC, *supra* note 7 at para 10.

84 *Consideration of Reports Submitted by States Parties under Article 19 of the Convention: Concluding Observations of the Committee against Torture*, UNCATOR, 48th Sess, UN Doc CAT/C/CAN/CO/6 (2012) at para 9.

85 For example, see Canadian Council for Refugees, "Bill C-11 Brief" (March 25, 2001) at 11–12, online: Canadian Council for Refugees <http://ccrweb.ca/en/c-11-brief>.

86 The inquiry that established this was constituted on February 5, 2004, under Part I of the Inquiries Act, on the recommendation of the Deputy Prime Minister and the Minister of Public Safety and Emergency Preparedness to investigate and report on the actions of Canadian officials in relation to Maher Arar. The Honourable Dennis R. O'Connor, Associate Chief Justice of Ontario, was appointed Commis-sioner of the Inquiry. See *Arar Report*, *supra* note 59.

87 *Ibid* at 93–94.

88 See *Internal Inquiry into the Actions of Canadian Officials in Relation to Abdullah Almalki, Ahmad Abou-Elmaati, and Muayyed Nureddin* (October 2008), online: Amnesty International <https://www.amnesty.ca/sites/amnesty/files/imce/images/Iacobucci%20Inquiry%20Report.pdf> [Iacobucci Report]; and CBC News, "Federal Officials Contributed Indirectly to Torture of Canadians: Report" (October 21, 2008),

online: CBC News <https://www.cbc.ca/news/canada/federal-officials-contributed
-indirectly-to-torture-of-canadians-report-1.740659>. See also Reem Bahdi, "Torture,
Tort and Terror: The Non-Delegable Duty to Protect Citizens from Terror Abroad"
(2009) 44 SCLR 232.

89 *Suresh* SCC, *supra* note 26 at para 88.

90 Human Rights Watch, *Abu Ghraib, supra* note 42 at 14.

91 Miller, *supra* note 10 at 302.

92 US Senate Foreign Relations Committee, *Executive Report 101-30 on the Convention
against Torture and other Cruel, Inhuman and Degrading Treatment or Punishment,*
101st Cong, 2d Sess, August 30, 1990, at 30 [Text of US Resolution of Ratification;
emphasis added]. The US government took this approach in part as a result of a
desire to shield its officials from possible prosecution for torture. See Irene Scharf,
"Un-Torturing the Definition of Torture and Employing the Rule of Immigration
Lenity" (2013) 66:1 Rutgers L Rev 1 at 2.

93 *Implementation of the Convention against Torture,* 8 CFR s 208.18(a)(4) (2002) [empha-
sis added].

94 Although Samuel David is correct in concluding that the jurisprudence of the UN
Committee against Torture can be read as unsettled in this respect, it seems that the
law of that committee is that where it can be shown that the non-state actor is acting
in place of the state, such as where a failed state without a central government exists,
then torture by the non-state actor will equate to torture by a "public official." See
Elmi v Australia, UNCATOR, UN Doc CAT/C/22/D/120/1998 (1999). See also Samuel
David, "A Foul Immigration Policy: US Misinterpretation of the Non-Refoulement
Obligation under the Convention against Torture" (2003) 19 NYL Sch L Rev 769 at
774–77. However, in cases where a central government exists and is locked in a military
struggle with rebels, then the claimant must show acquiescence by officials acting on
behalf of the state itself, even when the rebels are in effective control of a portion of
the territory of that state. See *SV v Canada,* UNCATOR, UN Doc CAT/C/26/D/49/1996
(2001). Although this position still falls short of the requirements of the general
international law on statehood, it is better than the current US position.

95 See David, *ibid* at 770–71.

96 *Ibid* at 778–82.

97 *Re S-V,* Interim Decision #3430, 2000 WL 562836 (BIA 2000) at 9; *Re Y-L, A-G, and
R-S-R,* 23 I&N Dec 270 at 280 (AG 2002).

98 *Khouzam v Ashcroft,* 361 F.3d 161 (2d Cir 2004) [*Khouzam*].

99 *Ibid* at 3.

100 *Ibid* at 22.

101 *Ibid.*

102 *Implementation of the Convention against Torture,* 8 CFR s 208.18(a)(7) (2002).

103 *Khouzam, supra* note 98.

104 *Zheng v Ashcroft,* 332 F.3d 1186 (9th Cir 2003); *Silva-Rengifo v Attorney General of
US,* 473 F.3d 58 (3d Cir 2007).

105 Miller, *supra* note 10 at 304.

106 See US, *Cong Rec,* daily ed, vol 136, at S19491–92 (October 27, 1990) ("US Reservations, Declarations, and Understandings, Convention against Torture and Other
Cruel, Inhuman or Degrading Treatment or Punishment") (resolution stating the
Senate's advice and consent that the *Convention* be ratified subject to the understanding "that, in order to constitute torture, an act must be specifically intended
to inflict severe physical or mental pain or suffering"; Scharf, *supra* note 92 at 3–14.

107 See *Dalegrand v Attorney General,* 288 F App'x 838 (3d Cir 2008). See also Scharf,
ibid at 3.

108 See *Dalegrand v Attorney General,* 288 F App'x 838 (3d Cir 2008).

109 *Ibid.*

110 *Ibid.*

111 Scharf, *supra* note 92 at 3.

112 *Ibid* at 13.

113 See the opinion of US District Court Judge Marsha Pechman in *Ali Ali v Ashcroft,*
213 FRD 390 (9th Cir 2003) at 411.

114 *Ibid.*

115 See US, Bureau of Citizenship and Immigration Services, Department of Homeland
Security, *Extension of the Designation of Temporary Protected Status for Somalia,*
69 Fed Reg 47937 (August 6, 2004) [emphasis added].

116 See the opinion of US District Court Judge Arthur Boylan in *Jama v INS,* US Dist
LEXIS 8255 (2002) at 7–8.

117 *Jama v INS,* 329 F.3d 630 at 633–35 (8th Cir 2003) [*Jama v INS*].

118 *Jama v Immigration and Customs Enforcement,* 125 S Ct 684 (2005).

119 *Ali Ali v Ashcroft,* 346 F.3d 873 (9th Cir 2003). A similar decision was also reached
in the US District Court for the District of Minnesota in *Omar v INS,* US Dist
LEXIS 6327 (2003).

120 US, Department of Homeland Security, *Execution of Removal Orders; Countries to
Which Aliens May Be Removed,* 69 FR, No 137, 42901 at 42903 (2004).

121 *Jama v INS, supra* note 116.

122 See *Implementation of the Convention against Torture,* 8 CFR s 208.18(c) (2002).

123 See 64 Fed Reg 8478 at 8484 (1999).

124 See *Attia v Sweden,* Communication No199/2002, UNCATOR, UN Doc CAT/
C/31/D/199/2002 (2003).

125 See Human Rights Watch, *"Empty Promises": Diplomatic Assurances No Safeguard
against Torture* (New York: Human Rights Watch, 2004) at 13–14 [*Empty Promises*].
See also Human Rights Watch, *Still at Risk: Diplomatic Assurances No Safeguard
against Torture* (New York: Human Rights Watch, 2005); and Human Rights Watch,
Cases Involving Diplomatic Assurances against Torture (New York: Human Rights
Watch, 2007).

126 See *Concluding Observations on the Fourth Periodic Report of New Zealand,* UNHRC,
CCPR/CO/75/NZ (August 7, 2002) at para 11; *Report of the Special Rapporteur on*

Torture to the UN Commission on Human Rights, UNCHR, 58th Sess, E/CN.4/2002/137 (2002) at para 15.

127   See *Suresh* SCC, *supra* note 26 at para 124.

128   See *Chahal v United Kingdom, supra* note 9 at para 105.

129   Human Rights Watch, *Empty Promises, supra* note 125 at 4.

130   See *Coalition Sign-on Letter* (July 16, 2004) at 2 (on file with the author).

131   *Convention Relating to the Status of Refugees,* July 28, 1951, 189 UNTS 150, CTS 1969/6 (entered into force April 22, 1954); see *INS v Cardoza-Fonseca,* 480 US 421 (9th Cir 1987); see also *Al-Harbi v INS,* 242 F.3d 882 at 888 (9th Cir 2001) (holding that the clear probability standard for both withholding of removal – same as for *Convention against Torture* relief – is more stringent than the standard of proof required for asylum claims to succeed).

132   See Text of US Resolution of Ratification, *supra* note 92 at 30.

133   *Kamalthas v INS,* 251 F.3d 1279 at 1284 (9th Cir 2001). See *Garcia v Holder,* 748 F.3d 785 at paras 7–9 (9th Cir 2014); *Shen v INS,* Suit No 02-4100 (2d Cir 2004); *Wang v Ashcroft,* 320 F.3d 130 at 143–44 (2d Cir 2003); *Mohammad v Ashcroft,* 90 F App'x 746 at 753 (5th Cir 2004); *Shah v Ashcroft,* 72 F App'x 875 at 881 (3d Cir 2003).

134   *In Re J-E,* Interim Decision #3466, 23 I&N Dec 291 at 303–4 (BIA 2002).

135   *Ibid* at 307.

136   *Ibid.*

137   *Ibid* at 308.

138   *In Re M-B-A-,* Interim Decision #3480, 23 I&N Dec 474 (BIA 2002).

139   *Ibid* at 475.

140   *Ibid* at 475–76.

141   *Ibid* at 478–79.

142   *Ibid* at 480–90.

143   *Antoine v US,* 204 FSupp 2d 115 at 6–8 (D Mass 2002).

144   *Camara v Ashcroft,* 725 F.3d 11 at 16 (4th Cir 2004).

145   *Cole v Holder,* 659 F.3d 762 (9th Cir 2011).

146   *Ibid* at 780–81.

147   *Vinh Tan Nguyen v Holder,* 763 F.3d 1022 (9th Cir 2014).

148   *Ibid.*

149   *Ibid.*

150   "Substantial evidence": see *Andriasian v INS,* 180 F.3d 1033 at 1040 (9th Cir 1999); *Melkonian v Ashcroft,* 320 F.3d 1061 at 1065 (9th Cir 2003). "Compelling evidence": see *Yu v Ashcroft,* Suit No 03-3137 at 3–4 (6th Cir 2003).

151   See *Shah v Ashcroft,* 72 F App'x. 875 at 894 (US Court of Appeals, 3rd Circuit, 2003); *Mohammad v Ashcroft, supra* note 133 at 748.

152   See *Himri v Ashcroft,* 378 F.3d 932 at 940 (9th Cir 2004).

153   See *Abdulrahman v Ashcroft,* 330 F.3d 587 at 617 (3rd Cir 2003) [emphasis added].

154   See *Laoye v Attorney General US,* 624 F App'x 791 at 793 (2015).

155   See *Nigussie v Ashcroft,* 383 F.3d 531 at 1874–75 (7th Cir 2004).

156 *Cheema v Ashcroft, supra* note 17.

157 *Ibid* at 12982.

158 The term "immigration bureaucrats" will be used here to refer to both the immigration units that have been moved to the US Department of Homeland Security (the Bureau of Citizenship and Immigration Services or CIS, and the Bureau of Immigration and Customs Enforcement or ICE) and the administrative tribunals that have remained under the authority of the US Attorney General (the BIA and immigration judges). "Gatekeeping" stems from the adoption by the relevant bureaucrats of a somewhat inhospitable image of non-citizens subject to removal as persons who have no business being in the United States and yet are trying desperately to stay there. See Michael G. Heyman, "Immigration Law in the Supreme Court: The Flagging Spirit of the Law" (2003) 28:1 J Legis 113 at 114 (arguing that such gatekeeping has also affected the reasoning of the US Supreme Court in immigration cases).

159 For example, Mr. Ashcroft stated that "[f]orty years ago, the Department of Justice, under Attorney General Robert Kennedy, undertook an extraordinary law enforcement campaign to root out and to dismantle organized crime. *The Kennedy Justice Department, it is said, would arrest a mobster for spitting on the sidewalk, if it would aid in the war against organized crime. In the war on terror, it is policy of this Justice Department to be equally aggressive.*" See "Attorney General Ashcroft's Briefing on New Anti-Terrorism Immigration Policies" (on file with the author).

160 On the transfer of INS functions to CIS and ICE, see *Homeland Security Act, supra* note 14 at s 471.

161 Regina Germain, "Rushing to Judgement: The Unintended Consequences of the USA PATRIOT Act for Bona Fide Refugees" (2002) 16 Geo Immig LJ 505 at 528 [emphasis added].

162 Heather Jacobson, "Refugees and Humanitarian Emergencies" (2003) 17 Geo Immig LJ 667 at 672–73. The Department of Homeland Security was created after 9/11 in order to better secure the US "homeland." Of its seven stated primary missions, five are squarely focused on national security. The preservation of human rights is not explicitly stated as a primary mission of this department. See *Homeland Security Act, supra* note 14 at s 101.

163 See Gathii, *supra* note 40 at 369. See also Susan M. Akram & Kevin R. Johnson, "Race, Civil Rights and Immigration Law after September 11, 2001: The Targeting of Arabs and Muslims" (2002) 58:3 NYU Annual Survey of American Law 295 at 295–96, 301–16; and Khaled Beydoun, *American Islamophobia* (Oakland, CA: University of California Press, 2008) (on the orientalist roots of the fear of Arabs and Muslims in the United States).

164 For a discussion of aspects of the nature of expedited removal procedures, see Michele R. Pistone, "Assessing the Proposed Refugee Protection Act: One Step in the Right Direction" (2000) 14:3 Geo Immig LJ 815 at 815–27. For a discussion of the nature of such interdictions, see Lory D. Rosenberg, "The United States'

Interdiction Experience and Its Impact on Refugees and Asylum Seekers" (2003) 17 Geo Immig LJ 199 at 200–3, 206–18.

165 Pistone, *ibid* at 815.

166 See US, *Inspection by Immigration Officers; Expedited Removal of Inadmissible Arriving Aliens; Referral for Hearing*, 8 USC, s 1225 (2011).

167 See US, Executive Order No 13767, *Border Security and Immigration Enforcement Improvements*, 82 Fed Reg 8793 (2017), online: The White House <http://www. whitehouse.gov/the-press-office/2017/01/25/executive-order-border-security-and -immigration-enforcement-improvements>. See also Michael D. Shear & Ron Nixon, "New Trump Deportation Rules Allow Far More Expulsions," *New York Times* (February 21, 2017), online: <https://www.nytimes.com/2017/02/21/us/politics/ dhs-immigration-trump.html?_r=0>.

168 *Criminal Code*, RSC 1985, c C-46, s 269.1.

169 *Ibid*.

170 See *Suresh* cases, *supra* notes 26, 80, and 81. See also *Canada's Fifth Report*, *supra* note 77 at para 16.

171 *Criminal Code*, *supra* note 168 at s 269.1; see also *Suresh* SCC, *supra* note 26 at para 68; *Yi Mei Li v Canada (Minister of Citizenship and Immigration)*, [2003] FCJ No 1934; 2003 FC 1514; *Bouaouni v Canada (Minister of Citizenship and Immigration)*, 2003 FC 1211; and *Bhatti v Canada* (1996), FCAD 1660.

172 *Ibid*.

173 *Ibid*.

174 See Canadian Council for Refugees, "Somalis and Canadian Immigration Policy" (February 2015), online: Canadian Council for Refugees <http://ccrweb.ca/sites/ ccrweb.ca/files/somali_issues_in_canadian_immigration-2016.pdf>.

175 *Ibid*.

176 *Suresh* SCC, *supra* note 26 at para 124.

177 See Human Rights Watch, *Empty Promises*, *supra* note 125 at 16.

178 *Suresh SCC*, *supra* note 26, at para 123.

179 *Suresh* SCC, *supra* note 26 at para 77 (using the term "substantial risk of torture" to describe the standard set out in the *Convention against Torture*). See also *Jaballah, Re*, 2006 FC 1230 at para 81.

180 *Ibid*.

181 *Ibid*.

182 See Waldman, *supra* note 31 at 17.

183 *Suresh* SCC, *supra* note 26 at para 39.

184 *Ibid* at para 38.

185 *Ibid* at para 39.

186 Okafor & Okoronkwo, *supra* note 82 at 56–61.

187 *Ibid* at 59.

188 For more on this point, see *ibid* at 56–59.

189 These points are explained more fully in the previous section's discussion of the US position.

190 James C. Hathaway & Alexander Neve, "Fundamental Justice and the Deflection of Refugees from Canada" (1996) 34:2 Osgoode Hall LJ 214 at 223–24.

191 *Ibid* at 23–24.

192 See *Vancouver Sun* (February 18, 1997) as quoted in Canadian Council for Refugees, "Interdicting Refugees" (May 1998) at 3. See also Andrew Brouwer, "Attack of the Migration Integrity Specialists! Interdiction and the Threat to Asylum" (2003), online: Canadian Council for Refugees <http://www.ccrweb.ca/sites/ccrweb.ca/files/static-files/interdictionab.htm>.

193 Hathaway & Neve, *supra* note 190 at 219.

194 Emphasis added.

195 See 8 CFR ss 208.16–208.18.

196 *Ibid*, s 208.16(c)(4).

197 Chung, *supra* note 34 at 358.

198 *Suresh* SCC, *supra* note 26 at paras 87–90.

199 See US, *Immigration Relief under the Convention against Torture for Serious Criminals and Human Rights Violators: Hearing before the Sub-Committee on Immigration, Border Security and Claims of the US House of Representatives*, 108th Cong, 1st Sess (July 11, 2003) at 1, 2, 3, and 6 [*Immigration Relief*]. During these hearings, Congressman Steve King even declared [at 6]: "You know, the concept that we cannot return a person who is guilty of torture to those whom he has tortured is something that baffles me." For countervailing pro-*Convention* sentiments, see 2–3, 4, 14, and 24.

200 See *Zadvydas v Davis*, 53 US 1 (2001) [*Zadvydas*] (generally outlawing such detentions in the United States); and *Canada v Kamail*, 2002 FCT 381, [2002] FCJ No 490 (QL) at paras 37–38 (suggesting that the indefinite detention of a deportable non-citizen who was being held for an immigration violation would have been illegal had it not resulted from his own refusal to sign an application for his travel document).

201 US, Committee of the Judiciary, House of Representatives, News Advisory, "House Approves 9/11 Recommendations Implementation Act" (October 8, 2004) [emphasis added].

202 *Zadvydas, supra* note 200.

203 *Charkaoui v Canada*, 2007 SCC 9, [2007] 1 SCR 350.

204 *Zadvydas, supra* note 200 at 11.

205 See 8 CFR s 241.14 (2001).

206 See Department of Homeland Security testimony in *Immigration Relief, supra* note 199 at 13.

207 *Nielsen v Preap*, No. 16-1363, 586 US xxx (March 19, 2019). The case interpreted 8 USC, s 1226(c)(2).

208 Chung, *supra* note 34 at 371.

209 US, Executive Office of Immigration Review, Department of Justice, *Statistical Yearbook 2016* (April 2016) at M1, online: Department of Justice <https://www.justice.gov/sites/default/files/pages/attachments/2016/04/08/fy15syb.pdf> (accessed November 19, 2016).

210 Chung, *supra* note 34 at 366. This is supported by the statistics offered by Samuel David, *supra* note 94 at 770.

211 See Congressional Research Service, "Immigration: Terrorist Grounds for Exclusion of Aliens" (March 2005) at 8 (on file with the author).

212 *Zadvydas, supra* note 201 at 2 and 12.

213 *Clark v Martinez,* 543 US 371 (2005).

214 *Zadvydas, supra* note 201 at 16.

215 *Ibid.*

216 On prosecuting and convicting, see *Immigration Relief, supra* note 200 at 5. On deporting to another country, see *Zadvydas, supra* note 201 at 4.

217 For more on this argument, see Okafor & Okoronkwo, *supra* note 82 at 42.

218 *Ibid* at 43–49.

219 *Ibid* at 49–55.

220 See US, *America after 9/11, supra* note 52 at 29–30.

221 Whitaker, "Refugee Policy," *supra* note 1 at 32.

222 Joanne Van Selm, "Refugee Protection in Europe and the US after 9/11" in Niklaus Steiner, Mark Gibney, & Gil Loescher, eds, *Problems of Protection: The UNHCR, Refugees and Human Rights* (New York: Routledge, 2003) 237 at 255.

223 Reg Whitaker, "Keeping Up with the Neighbours? Canadian Responses to 9/11 in Historical and Comparative Context" (2003) 41 Osgoode Hall LJ 241 at 252 ["Neighbours"].

224 *Ibid* at 253–59.

225 *Ibid* at 253.

226 See Gregory Krieg, "It's Official: Clinton Swamps Trump in Popular Vote," *CNN* (December 22, 2016), online: <http://www.cnn.com/2016/12/21/politics/donald-trump-hillary-clinton-popular-vote-final-count/>.

227 See Howard Adelman, "Refugees and Border Security Post-9/11" (2002) 20:4 Refuge 5 at 7–8; and Kent Roach, "Uneasy Neighbours: Comparative American and Canadian Counter-Terrorism" (2012) 38 Wm Mitchell L Rev 1701 at 1702.

228 Whitaker, "Neighbours," *supra* note 223 at 254.

229 *Ibid.*

230 *Ibid* at 265. See also Whitaker, "Refugee Policy," *supra* note 1 at 32.

231 See *The 9/11 Commission Report* at 81 and 176–79 (on file with the author).

232 Doris Meissner, "Immigration in the Post 9-11 Era" (2002) 40 Brandeis LJ 851 at 858.

233 See US, Bill HR 3162, *Uniting and Strengthening America by Providing Appropriate Tools Required to Intercept and Obstruct Terrorism (USA PATRIOT ACT) Act of 2001,* 107th Cong, 2001 at ss 401–5; and the defunct US, Bill HR 5904, *Justice against Sponsors of Terrorism Act (9/11 Bill),* 112th Cong, 2012 at ss 901–4.

234 Adelman, *supra* note 227 at 6.

235 This much was implicitly acknowledged by Judy Sgro, Canada's Minister for Citizenship and Immigration. See "Canada's Refugee Program: Upholding Our Humanitarian Tradition into the 21st Century at the Consultative Committee on

Practices and Procedures of the Immigration and Refugee Board" (Ottawa, May 11, 2004) (on file with the author).

236 See Kent Roach, *September 11: Consequences for Canada* (Montreal and Kingston: McGill-Queen's University Press, 2003) at 5.

237 John Fredriksson, "Bridging the Gap between Rights and Responsibilities: Policy Changes Affecting Refugees and Immigrants in the United States since 1996" (2000) 14 Geo Immig LJ 757 at 758–60; and Marc L. Miller, "Immigration Law: Assessing New Immigration Enforcement Strategies and the Criminalization of Migration" (2002) 51 Emory LJ 963 at 967.

238 Whitaker, "Refugee Policy," *supra* note 1 at 30 [emphasis added].

239 Michele Pistone & Philip G. Schrag, "The New Asylum Rule: Improved but Still Unfair" (2001) 16:1 Geo Immig LJ 1.

240 The *Illegal Immigration Reform and Immigrant Responsibility Act*, Pub L 104–208, Division C (2006); and the *Anti-Terrorism and Effective Death Penalty Act*, Pub L No. 104-32. See also Jacobson, *supra* note 162 at 671–72.

241 The debates and consultations grounding the legal reforms that eventually led to the enshrinement of Canada's current immigration and refugee law regime date back to the 1990s.

Chapter 2: The Detention of Asylum Seekers and Refugees

Note: In this chapter, the term "refugee(s)" will, with a few exceptions, be used to refer to both refugees and asylum seekers. Similarly, as used here, the expression "refugee law" includes "asylum law."

Epigraphs: "Statement of Senator Patrick Leahy," in US, America after 9/11: Freedom Preserved or Freedom Lost? *Hearing before the Senate Committee on the Judiciary,* 108th Cong, 1st Sess (2003) at 313 [*America after 9/11*]; "Statement of Viet Dinh" in *ibid* at 53.

1 Leslie Castro et al, "Perversities and Prospects: Whither Immigration Enforcement and Detention in the After-Terrorism Aftermath? Panel Discussion, 25 October 2001" (2002) 9:1 Geo J on Poverty L & Pol'y 1 at 10.

2 See the *Intelligence Reform and Terrorism Prevention Act,* 50 USC c 15, s 401 *et seq* (2004). See also Bill Frelick, "US Detention of Asylum Seekers and Human Rights," *Migration Information Source* (March 1, 2005), online: Migration Policy Institute <https://www.migrationpolicy.org/article/us-detention-asylum-seekers-and -human-rights>.

3 See US, Department of Homeland Security, *Budget of the United States Government, Fiscal Year 2006* (PR Ex 2.8:2006) (2006), online: The White House <http://www. whitehouse.gov/omb/budget/fy2006/dhs.html> (accessed August 19, 2017) [2006 Budget]. See also Frelick, *ibid.*

4 See Department of Homeland Security, *ibid;* and Frelick, *ibid.*

5 US, Executive Order No 13767, *Border Security and Immigration Enforcement Improvements,* 82 Fed Reg 8793 (2017), online: The White House <http://www.whitehouse.

gov/the-press-office/2017/01/25/executive-order-border-security-and-immigration-
enforcement-improvements>; Center for Migration Studies, "President Trump's
Executive Orders on Immigration and Refugees," online: Center for Migration
Studies <http://cmsny.org/trumps-executive-orders-immigration-refugees/>.

6 US, Department of Homeland Security, *Budget-in-Brief: Fiscal Year 2016* (PR Ex
2.8:2016) (2016), online: DHS <http://www.dhs.gov/sites/default/files/publications/
FY_2016_DHS_Budget_in_Brief.pdf>.

7 US, Department of Homeland Security, *Budget-in-Brief: Fiscal Year 2015* (PR Ex
2.8:2015) (2015), online: DHS <http://www.dhs.gov/sites/default/files/publications/
FY15BIB.pdf>.

8 D. Lind, "Congress's Deal on Immigration Detention, Explained," Vox.com,
February 12, 2019, online: <https://www.vox.com/2019/2/12/18220323/immigra-
tion-detention-beds-congress-cap>. See also Center for Migration Studies,
supra note 5.

9 Anna Pratt, *Securing Borders: Detention and Deportation in Canada* (Vancouver:
UBC Press, 2005) at 43.

10 See Department of Finance Canada, *The Budget Plan 2003* (Ottawa: Department
of Finance Canada, 2003) at 164–65, online: <https://fin.gc.ca/budget03/pdf/
bp2003e.pdf>. See also Canadian Council for Refugees (CCR), "Anti-Terrorism
and the Security Agenda: Consequences on Citizenship, Immigration and Refugee
Policies in Canada" (February 17, 2004), online: CCR <http://ccrweb.ca/en/anti
-terrorism-and-security-agenda-consequences-citizenship-immigration-and-refugee
-policies-canada>.

11 See Office of the Auditor General of Canada (OAG), *Report of the Auditor General
of Canada to the House of Commons*, c 5, "Citizenship and Immigration Canada:
Control and Enforcement" (April 2003) at ss 5.18–5.19, online: OAG <http://www.
oag-bvg.gc.ca/internet/docs/20030405ce.pdf>.

12 See Office of the Auditor General of Canada, *Report of the Auditor General of Canada
to the House of Commons*, c 7, "Detention and Removal of Individuals – Canada
Border Services Agency" (May 2008) at 14–16, online: OAG <http://www.oag-bvg.
gc.ca/internet/docs/aud_ch_oag_200805_07_e.pdf>.

13 Delphine Nakache, *The Human and Financial Cost of the Detention of Asylum-Seekers
in Canada* (Study written for the Office of the UN High Commissioner for Refugees, December 2011) at 40–41.

14 For example, see Canadian Council for Refugees (CCR), "Immigration Detention
Statistics 2015" (March 2016), online: CCR <http://www.ccrweb.ca/sites/ccrweb.
ca/files/immigration-detention-statistics-2015.pdf> ["Immigration Detention Statistics 2015"].

15 Pratt, *supra* note 9 at 23.

16 *Ibid* at 44.

17 Castro et al, *supra* note 1 at 4 [emphasis added].

18 *Ibid*.

19 *Ibid*. In fiscal year 2003, the average length of detention of refugees in the United States reported by Immigration and Customs Enforcement (ICE) was sixty-four days (well over two months). Physicians for Human Rights reported a much longer average period (ten months) for those included in their study of persons held in three states. For both points, see Frelick, *supra* note 2 at 4.

20 Frelick, *ibid* at 6; US, Department of Homeland Security, *Budget of the United States Government for the Department of Homeland Security, Fiscal Year 2003*, in United States Government, *Securing the Homeland, Strengthening the Nation*, online: DHS <http://www.dhs.gov/sites/default/files/publications/homeland_security_book.pdf>; US, Department of Homeland Security, *Performance Budget Overview, Fiscal Year 2007* (PR Ex 2.8:2007) (2007) at 8, online: DHS <http://www.dhs.gov/sites/default/files/publications/Budget_PBO_FY2007_0.pdf>; US, Department of Homeland Security, *Budget of the United States Government for the Department of Homeland Security, Fiscal Year 2009* (PR Ex 2.8:2009) (2009), online: DHS <http://www.dhs.gov/sites/default/files/publications/budget_fy2009.pdf>; US, Department of Homeland Security, *FY 2011: Budget in Brief* (PR Ex 2.8:2011) (2011), online: DHS <https://www.dhs.gov/sites/default/files/publications/budget_bib_fy2011.pdf> [2011 Budget]; Elizabeth Aguilera, "ICE Budget Cut 4% in 2013 DHS Budget," *San Diego Union-Tribune* (February 15, 2012), online: <http://www.sandiegouniontribune.com/sdut-ice-budget-down-4-in-2013-dhs-budget-2012feb15-story.html> (indicating that somewhat decreased funding for immigration detention was proposed for the 2013 fiscal year); and Human Rights First, Fact Sheet, "Immigration Detention: How Can the Government Cut Costs?" (March 31, 2013), online: <http://www.humanrightsfirst.org/uploads/pdfs/immigration-detention-fact-sheet-jan-2013.pdf>.

21 Department of Homeland Security, 2011 Budget, *supra* note 20 at 25.

22 Philip L. Torrey, "Rethinking Immigration's Mandatory Detention Regime: Politics, Profit, and the Meaning of 'Custody'" (2015) 48:4 U Mich JL Ref 879 at 879.

23 John F. Simanski & Lesley M. Sapp, "Immigration Enforcement Actions: 2012" (Department of Homeland Security, Office of Immigration Statistics, December 2013), online: DHS <http://www.dhs.gov/sites/default/files/publications/ois_enforcement_ar_2012_1.pdf>.

24 Frelick, *supra* note 2 at 4.

25 On the "Central American refugee crisis," see Castro et al, *supra* note 1 at 4.

26 *Ibid*.

27 US, *The Detention and Treatment of Haitian Asylum Seekers: Hearing before the Subcommittee on Immigration of the Senate Committee on the Judiciary*, 107th Cong, 2d Sess, S Hrg107–973 (October 1, 2002) at 5 (T.G. Wenski).

28 CRS (Congressional Research Service), "Report to Congress: US Immigration Policy on Haitian Immigrants" (January 21, 2005), Order Code RS21349 at 1 (on file with the author).

29 The facts of this saga are recorded in a suit brought by advocates and representatives of many of these Cuban and Haitian refugees seeking to bar the US from

repatriating them to their respective countries and to grant them refugee status. For example, see *Cuban American Bar Association, Inc. v Christopher*, 43 F.3d 1412 at 2–4 (11th Cir 1995).

30 *Ibid* at 2.

31 CRS, *supra* note 28 at 1.

32 Olga Velez, "Liberty and Justice for All: The Violations of Basic Human Rights in Detention Centers across the United States" (2014) 25:2 U Fla JL & Pub Pol'y 187 at 192; *Clark v Martinez*, 543 US 371 (2005), 125 S Ct 716.

33 *Ibid* at 4.

34 *Ibid* at 1.

35 Velez, *ibid*. See also US, Department of Homeland Security, *Notice Designating Aliens Subject to Expedited Removal Under Section 235(B)(1)(a)(iii) of the Immigration and Nationality Act*, 67 Fed Reg 68923 (2002) [*Notice Designating Aliens*].

36 US, *ICE Response to the US Commission on International Religious Freedom's Report on Asylum Seekers in Expedited Removal* (Washington, DC: USICE, February 8, 2005) (on file with the author). See also Frelick, *supra* note 2 at 6 [emphasis added].

37 See Letter from Daniel J. Bryant, US Assistant Attorney General, to Senators Edward Kennedy and Sam Brownback (September 25, 2002), reproduced in US, *The Detention and Treatment of Haitian Asylum Seekers, supra* note 27 at 30–32.

38 See *In Re D-J*, Interim Decision #3488, 23 I&N Dec.572 (AG 2003). For a commentary on this case and interview with the young refugee involved, see Susan Benesch, "Haitians Trapped by 'War on Terrorism'" (2003) 29:3 Amnesty Now 13.

39 *Ibid* at 572.

40 David Cole, "In Aid of Removal: Due Process Limits on Immigration Detention" (2002) 51 Emory LJ 1003 at 1006.

41 CRS, *supra* note 28 at 5.

42 The fact that this treatment equates to punishment is underlined by the conditions in which these Haitian refugees have been detained. As Cheryl Little has noted, the facilities in which they are detained are in general terribly overcrowded, mostly unsanitary, and definitely traumatizing for many of them. One of them, detained at the Krome facility, committed suicide. See "Statement of Cheryl Little" in US, *The Detention and Treatment of Haitian Asylum Seekers, supra* note 27 at 11.

43 "Statement of Senator Edward Kennedy" in US, *The Detention and Treatment of Haitian Asylum Seekers, ibid* at 2.

44 CRS, *supra* note 28 at 6.

45 "Statement of Senator Edward Kennedy," *supra* note 43 at 1.

46 See "Statement of Representative John Conyers" in US, *The Detention and Treatment of Haitian Asylum Seekers, supra* note 27 at 27.

47 Cole, *supra* note 40.

48 See UN High Commissioner for Refugees (UNHCR), *UNHCR's Revised Guidelines on Applicable Criteria and Standards Relating to the Detention of Asylum-Seekers* (February 26, 1999), online: Refworld <http://www.unhcr.org/refworld/docid/3c2b3f844.html>; "UNHCR Advisory Opinion on the Detention of Haitian Asylum Seekers in the US, 15 April 2002," reproduced in US, *The Detention and Treatment of Haitian Asylum Seekers, supra* note 27 at 108–10.

49 Frelick, *supra* note 2 at 4.

50 *Ibid.*

51 Harvard Immigration and Refugee Clinical Program, *The Impact of President Trump's Executive Orders on Asylum Seekers* (Cambridge, MA: Harvard Law School, February 8, 2017) at 5–6.

52 Pratt, *supra* note 9 at 46–51.

53 Alex Neve and Tiisetso Russell, "Hysteria and Discrimination: Canada's Harsh Response to Refugees and Migrants Who Arrive by Sea" (2011) 62 UNBLJ 37 at 42–43.

54 CCR (Canadian Council for Refugees), "Refugees and Non-Refugees in Canada: Key Concerns Regarding Canada's Compliance with the Covenant on Civil and Political Rights (CCPR). Submission to the Human Rights Committee of the United Nations" (September 16, 2005) at 7, online: CCR <http://www.ccrweb.ca/CCPR2005.pdf>.

55 Canada, *Government Response to the Report of the Standing Committee on Citizenship and Immigration, "Immigration Detention and Removal"* (October 23, 1998) [*Government Response* 1998].

56 Nakache, *supra* note 13 at 57.

57 *Ibid.*

58 *Ibid.*

59 *Ibid* at 57–62; Neve and Russell, *supra* note 64 at 42–43.

60 Nakache, *supra* note 13 at 59–60.

61 Neve and Russell, *supra* note 53 at 42–43.

62 *Ibid.*

63 *Ibid.*

64 *Ibid.*

65 *Ibid.*

66 See Andrew Brouwer, "Attack of the Migration Integrity Specialists! Interdiction and the Threat to Asylum," (2003), online: CCR <http://www.ccrweb.ca/sites/ccrweb.ca/files/static-files/interdictionab.htm>; and Nicholas Keung, "Roma Say They're Being Barred from Flights to Canada," *Toronto Star* (May 6, 2017), online: <http://www.thestar.com/news/immigration/2017/05/06/roma-say-theyre-being-barred-from-flights-to-canada.html>.

67 See USCIRF (United States Commission on International Religious Freedom), *Report on Asylum Seekers in Expedited Removal* (Washington, DC: USCIRF, 2005) at 4 [*Asylum Report*]. See also William A. Stock, "Mandatory Detention and Bond

Eligibility" in R. Patrick Murphy et al, eds, *Practice under IIRAIRA: One Year Later* (Washington DC: American Immigration Lawyers Association, 1997) at 99.

68 See USCIRF, *ibid* at 71.

69 See US, Bill HR 3610, *Illegal Immigration Reform & Immigration Responsibility Act of 1996 (IIRIRA)*, 104th Cong, 1996, s 235(b)(1). See also USCIRF, *ibid*.

70 USCIRF, *ibid*.

71 *Ibid* at 72.

72 Stock, *supra* note 67 at 100–2.

73 See USCIRF, Special Report, *Assessing the US Government's Detention of Asylum Seekers: Further Action Needed to Fully Implement Reforms* (April 2013) at 9, online: USCIRF <http://www.uscirf.gov/sites/default/files/resources/ERS-detention%20 reforms%20report%20April%202013.pdf> [Special Report].

74 *Ibid*.

75 *Ibid* at 8.

76 *Ibid* at 9.

77 Stock, *supra* note 67 at 80.

78 See American Immigration Council, "Removal without Recourse: The Growth of Summary Deportations from the United States" (April 28, 2014), online: <http:// www.americanimmigrationcouncil.org/sites/default/files/research/removal_ without_recourse.pdf>.

79 *Ibid* at 81.

80 *Ibid*.

81 American Immigration Lawyers Association, Issue Paper, "Restore Fairness and Due Process: 1996 Immigration Laws Go Too Far" Undated at 1, online: Law Offices of Carl Shusterman <https://shusterman.com/pdf/aila-issues304.pdf>.

82 *Ibid*. In the 107th Congress, the bipartisan *Immigrant Fairness Restoration Act* (S 955) and *Restoration of Fairness in Immigration Act* (HR 3894) were introduced but not passed. In the 108th Congress, HR 47, the *Keeping Families Together Act* (HR 3309), and the *Restoration of Pre-IIRAIRA Avenues of Relief Act* (HR 836) were introduced but not passed.

83 See USCIRF, *Asylum Report, supra* note 67 at 332.

84 USCIRF, "Expedited Removal Study Report Card: 2 Years Later" (February 8, 2007) at 5, online: USCIRF <http://www.uscirf.gov/sites/default/files/Reportcard%20 Scorecard_0.pdf> ["Report Card"].

85 See Department of Homeland Security, *Notice Designating Aliens, supra* note 35. See also USCIRF, *Executive Summary: Asylum Seekers in Expedited Removal* (Washington, DC: USCIRF, 2005) at 2 [*Executive Summary*].

86 See US, Department of Homeland Security, *Designating Aliens for Expedited Removal*, 69 Fed Reg 48877 (2004). See also USCIRF, *ibid*.

87 US, Bill HR 10, *9/11 Recommendations Implementation Act*, 108th Cong 2004 (not passed), online: GovTrack.us <http://www.govtrack.us/congress/bills/108/hr10>.

88 US, Bill S 2845, *Intelligence Reform and Terrorism Prevention Act of 2004*, 108th Cong, 2004 (enacted), online: <http://www.dni.gov/index.php/about/organization/ic-legal-reference-book-2012/ref-book-irtpa> (accessed August 12, 2012).

89 *Intelligence Reform and Terrorism Prevention Act of 2004*, Pub L No 108-458, 118 Stat 3638, online: govinfo <http://www.gpo.gov/fdsys/pkg/PLAW-108publ458/content-detail.html>.

90 USCIRF, *Asylum Report, supra* note 67 at 4.

91 See *Immigration Act*, SC 1976–77, *c 52*, s 103.1(1)(a).

92 See Library of Parliament, *Bill C-11 – The Immigration and Refugee Protection Act, Legislative History of Bill C-11* (January 31, 2002), online: Library of Parliament <http://www.lop.parl.gc.ca/About/Parliament/LegislativeSummaries/bills_ls.asp?ls=c11&Parl=37&Ses=1> (accessed 5 March 2003).

93 See *Immigration and Refugee Protection Act (IRPA)*, SC 2001, c 27, s 55(2)(b) [*IRPA*]. See also *Immigration and Refugee Protection Regulations*, s 247.

94 For example, see CCR, "Immigration Detention Statistics 2015," *supra* note 14 at 2.

95 See Standing Committee on Citizenship and Immigration, News Release, "Committee Tables Report on Immigration Detention and Removals" (June 11, 1998) at 30, online: Parliament of Canada <http://www.parl.gc.ca/HousePublications/Publication.aspx?DocId=1031290&Language=E&Mode=2&Parl=36&Ses=1>.

96 Canada, *Government Response 1998, supra* note 55.

97 Pratt, *supra* note 9 at 51.

98 *Ibid*.

99 *Ibid*.

100 Department of Justice, "Immigration and Refugee Legal Aid Cost Drivers" (2002) at 3.10, online: Department of Justice Canada <http://www.justice.gc.ca/eng/rp-pr/other-autre/ir/rr03_la17-rr03_aj17/p37.html>.

101 See CCR, *Submission of the Canadian Council for Refugees on the Occasion of the Visit to Canada of the UN Working Group on Arbitrary Detention* (June 8, 2005), online: CCR <http://www.ccrweb.ca/WGAD.HTM>.

102 *Ibid*.

103 Nakache, *supra* note 13 at 40–41.

104 CCR, "Immigration Detention Statistics 2015," *supra* note 14 at 2.

105 ABA-CI & LCCR, *American Justice through Immigrants' Eyes* (Washington, DC: ABA-CI & LCCR, 2004) at 103.

106 *Ibid* at 59–72. On orientalism as being at the root of this treatment of Arabs and Muslims, see Khaled Beydoun, *American Islamophobia* (Oakland, CA: University of California Press, 2008).

107 David A. Martin, "Testimony before the National Commission on Terrorist Attacks on the United States, December 8, 2003" (2004) 18 Geo Immig LJ 305 at 316.

108 See Edward Alden, *The Closing of the American Border* (New York: HarperCollins, 2008); ACLU (American Civil Liberties Union), *America's Disappeared: Seeking*

International Justice for Immigrants Detained after September 11 (New York: ACLU, 2004). See also "Statement of James Zogby" in US, *America after 9/11: Freedom Preserved or Freedom Lost? Hearing before the Senate Committee on the Judiciary,* 108th Cong, 1st Sess (November 18, 2003) at 16.

109 ACLU, *Sanctioned Bias: Racial Profiling since 9/11* (New York: ACLU, 2004) at 4 [*Sanctioned Bias*].

110 See Mary Beth Sheridan, "Immigration Law as Anti-Terrorism Tool," *Washington Post* (June 13, 2005) at 1, online: <http://www.washingtonpost.com/wp-dyn/content/article/2005/06/12/AR2005061201441.html>.

111 *Ibid.*

112 *Ibid.*

113 "Press Releases: Operation Liberty Shield" at 2, online: DHS <http://www.dhs.gov/dhspublic/interapp/press_release/press_release_0115.xml> (accessed March 17, 2003). See also Siobhan Roth, "Immigration Vise Tightened – Again," *Legal Times* (March 24, 2003) at 1 (of LexisNexis copy).

114 *Yusuf Ali Ali v John Ashcroft,* 213 FRD 390 at 396 (9th Cir 2003) [emphasis added].

115 Sheridan, *supra* note 110 at 1.

116 See US, *Registration and Monitoring of Certain Nonimmigrants,* 67 Fed Reg 52584 (2002). This regulation amended the existing regulation in 8 CFR s 214.1[f]. See also 67 Fed Reg 57032 (2002); 67 Fed Reg 67577 (2002); 67 Fed Reg 67765 (2002); 67 Fed Reg 70526 (2002); *ABA Immigration and Nationality Committee Newsletter,* vol. 6, issue 1 (Winter 2003) at 5 [*ABA Newsletter*]; and Stanley Mailman and Stephen Yale-Loehr, "The New Rule on Alien Registration," *New York Law Journal* (October 28, 2002).

117 Mailman and Yale-Loehr, *ibid* at 1 (of LexisNexis copy).

118 *Ibid* at 2.

119 *Ibid.*

120 *Ibid.* See also *ABA Newsletter, supra* note 116 at 5.

121 Mailman and Yale-Loehr, *supra* note 116.

122 *Ibid.*

123 See American Immigration Lawyers Association, *supra* note 81 at 44. See also "Statement of James Zogby" in US, *America after 9/11, supra* note 108 at 17; and "Statement of Senator Richard Durbin," in US, *America after 9/11, ibid* at 53.

124 US, Department of Homeland Security, "DHS Removes Designated Countries from NSEERS Registration (May 2011)" (September 29, 2015), online: DHS <http://www.dhs.gov/dhs-removes-designated-countries-nseers-registration-may-2011>.

125 AILF (American Immigration Law Foundation), *Targets of Suspicion: The Impact of Post-9/11 Policies on Muslims, Arabs, and South Asians in the United States* (Washington, DC: AILF, 2004) at 3.

126 *Ibid.*

127 *Ibid.*

128 See US, Executive Order No 13768, *Enhancing Public Safety in the Interior of the US,* 82 Fed Reg 8799 (2017), online: The White House <http://www.whitehouse.gov/

the-press-office/2017/01/25/presidential-executive-order-enhancing-public-safety-interior-united>.

129 In the current context, racial profiling can be defined as referring to "the law enforcement technique of singling out a person for a stop, interrogation, arrest, or other investigation because of race or ethnic appearance." See Carrie L. Arnold, "Racial Profiling in Immigration Enforcement: State and Local Agreements to Enforce Federal Immigration Law" (2007) 49 Ariz L Rev 113 at 114.

130 Nancy Murray, "Profiled: Arabs, Muslims, and the Post-9/11 Hunt for the 'Enemy Within'" in Elaine Hagopian, ed, *Civil Rights in Peril: The Targeting of Arabs and Muslims* (Chicago: Haymarket Books, 2004) at 27. The widely shared view that some countries (especially the Arab or majority Muslim ones) and their natives tend to pose the greater risk to US national security than others is reflected in a 2003 US Library of Congress Research Report. See Library of Congress, *Nations Hospitable to Organized Crime and Terrorism: A Report Prepared by the Federal Research Division, Library of Congress* (October 2003), online: Library of Congress <https://www.loc.gov/rr/frd/pdf-files/Nats_Hospitable.pdf>; Maureen A. Sweeney, "Shadow Immigration Enforcement and Its Constitutional Dangers" (2014) 104 J Crim L & Criminology 227.

131 See US, Department of Justice, "Guidance on the Use of Race by Federal Law Enforcement Agencies" (June 2003), online: Department of Justice <https://www.justice.gov/sites/default/files/crt/legacy/2010/12/15/guidance_on_race.pdf>.

132 Arnold, *supra* note 129 at 130.

133 Muzaffar A. Chishti et al, *America's Challenge: Domestic Security, Civil Liberties, and National Unity after September 11* (Washington, DC: Migration Policy Institute, 2003) at 12–13 (Executive Summary) and 39–52 (Main Report).

134 See "Statement of Senator Richard Durbin," in US, *America after 9/11, supra* note 108 at 54. See also Robert C. Hill & Donald Kerwin, "International Legal Developments in Review: 2001" (2002) 36 Int'l Law 527 at 535–36.

135 Human Rights Watch, *Presumption of Guilt: Human Rights Abuses of Post-September 11 Detainees* (New York: Human Rights Watch, 2002) at 9.

136 *Ibid* at 12–16.

137 See "INS Custody List" (on file with the author). See also Whitney D. Frazier, "The Constitutionality of Detainment in the Wake of September 11th" (2001/02) 90 Ky LJ 1089 at 1092; and "Petition to the United Nations Working Group on Arbitrary Detention, Submitted on Behalf of Certain Immigrants Detained by the United States in Connection with Its Investigation into the Events of September 11, 2001" (January 27, 2004) (on file with the author).

138 Human Rights Watch, *supra* note 135 at 10.

139 See US, Office of the Inspector General of the US Department of Justice (OIG-DOJ), *The September 11 Detainees: A Review of the Treatment of Aliens Held on Immigration Charges in Connection with the Investigation of the September 11 Attacks* (Washington, DC: Department of Justice, 2003) at 20–21 [OIG Report].

140 See Mike Fox, "Pakistanis Flee US for Canada," *BBC News* (March 4, 2003), online: <http://news.bbc.co.uk/2/hi/south_asia/2804235.stm>.

141 Sameer M. Ashar, "Immigration Enforcement and Subordination: The Conse-quences of Racial Profiling" (2002) 34 Conn L Rev 1185 at 1192–96; Marie A. Taylor, "Immigration Enforcement Post-September 11: Safeguarding the Civil Rights of Middle Eastern and Immigrant Communities" (2002) 17 Geo Immig LJ 63 at 112; and Mariano-Florentino Cuellar, "Choosing Anti-Terror Targets by National Ori-gin" (2003) 6 Harv Latino L Rev 9.

142 See Letter to John Ashcroft, Attorney General of the United States (December 23, 2003), online: <http://shusterman.com/spreg-122302.html> (accessed June 19, 2004); "Statement of Senator Richard Durbin," in US, *America after 9/11, supra* note 108.

143 ACLU, *Sanctioned Bias, supra* note 109 at 6.

144 D. Martin, *supra* note 107 at 308.

145 See *American-Arab Anti-Discrimination Committee v Ashcroft*, 241 FSupp 2d 1111 (CD Cal 2003).

146 See Center for Migration Studies, *supra* note 5.

147 Susan M. Akram & Kevin R. Johnson, "Race and Civil Rights Pre-September 11, 2001: The Targeting of Arabs and Muslims" in Hagopian, *supra* note 130 at 10–17. The authors point to the production and dissemination of negative images of Arabs and Muslims in US popular culture and the excessive targeting of such persons by US law enforcement as key reasons for the existence even before 9/11 of a strong anti-Muslim current in US public opinion.

148 *Ibid* at 9–10.

149 Elaine Hagopian, "Preface" in Hagopian, *supra* note 130 at x.

150 Pratt, *supra* note 9 at 51.

151 See Anne McLellan, "Speaking Notes for an Address to the Sub-Committee on Public Safety and National Security Reviewing the Anti-Terrorism Act" (March 22, 2005) at 4–5.

152 Reem Bahdi, "No Exit: Racial Profiling and Canada's War against Terrorism" (2003) 41 Osgoode Hall LJ 293 at 294.

153 *Ibid* at 296.

154 See Kathleen Harris, "Canadians Admit Racist Tendencies," *Toronto Sun* (January 15, 2007) at 7.

155 See Tasha Kheiriddin, "Guess What Canada: We're Kinda Racists, Too," *iPolitics Insights* (March 13, 2017), online: iPolitics <http://www.ipolitics.ca/2017/03/13/guess-what-canada-were-racists/> (citing a poll on the topic).

156 Bahdi, *supra* note 152 at 297.

157 *Ibid* at 295, fn 4.

158 *Ibid* at 295.

159 *Ibid* at 296.

160 *Ibid*.

161 *Ibid* at 298, fn 19.

162 *Ibid* at 299–300.

163 Pratt, *supra* note 9 at 208.

164 *Ibid.*

165 CCR, "Brief to the House of Commons Subcommittee on Public Safety and National Security of the Standing Committee on Justice, Human Rights, Public Safety and Emergency Preparedness: Anti-Terrorism Act Review" (September 8, 2005) at 2, online: CCR <http://www.ccrweb.ca/ATAcomments.pdf> ["Brief"].

166 *Ibid.*

167 See Michelle Shephard, "RCMP Clears Itself in 'Terror Cell' Sweep," *Toronto Star* (October 6, 2004) at A01.

168 See Commission of Inquiry into the Actions of Canadian Officials in Relation to Maher Arar, Dennis R. O'Connor, *Report on the Events Relating to Maher Arar, Factual Background*, vol 1 (2006), online: Library and Archives Canada <http://epe. lac-bac.gc.ca/100/206/301/pco-bcp/commissions/maher_arar/07–09–13/www. ararcommission.ca/default.htm> [*Arar Report*].

169 Bahdi, *supra* note 152 at 294.

170 *Ibid.*

171 Pratt, *supra* note 9 at 45.

172 See the then provisions of 8 CFR s 236.1(c). See also Stock, *supra* note 67 at 99.

173 Cole, *supra* note 40 at 1006–7, 1029.

174 Human Rights Watch, *supra* note 135 at 9.

175 Kate Martin, "Preventive Detention of Immigrants and Non-Citizens in the United States since September 11th" (2002) 20 Refuge 4 at 24.

176 Stock, *supra* note 67 at 107–8. The term "security-related" shall include terrorism-based and other such suspicions or charges.

177 *Ibid* at 108–9.

178 Cole, *supra* note 40 at 1010.

179 OIG-DOJ, OIG Report, *supra* note 139 at 74–75.

180 See Memorandum from Asa Hutchinson, Under Secretary for Border and Transportation Security, to Clark Kent Ervin, Acting Inspector General, "Analysis of the Second Response by the Department of Justice to Recommendations in the Office of the Inspector General's June 2003 Report on the Treatment of September 11 Detainees" (November 21, 2003) at 4, online: Department of Justice <http://www.usdoj.gov/oig/special/0401/appb.htm>.

181 US, Bill HR 3162, *Uniting and Strengthening America by Providing Appropriate Tools Required to Intercept and Obstruct Terrorism (USA PATRIOT) Act of 2001*, 107th Cong, 2001.

182 K. Martin, *supra* note 175 at 24; Lawrence M. Lebowitz & Ira L. Podheiser, "A Summary of the Changes in Immigration Policies and Practices after the Terrorist Attacks of September 11, 2001: The USA PATRIOT Act and Other Measures" (2002) 63 U Pitt L Rev 873 at 876.

183 See US, *Immigration and Nationality Act (INA)*, 8 U.S.C. 1101. See also Catalina J. Vergara, "Trading Liberty for Security in the Wake of September Eleventh:

Congress' Expansion of Preventive Detention of Non-Citizens" (2002) 17 Geo Immig LJ 115.

184   K. Martin, *supra* note 175 at 24.

185   See *Disposition of Cases of Aliens Arrested without Warrant*, 8 CFR s 287.3(d) (2001).

186   D. Martin, *supra* note 107 at 314; Margaret H. Taylor, "Dangerous by Decree: Detention without Bond in Immigration Procedures" (2004) 50 Loy L Rev 149 at 153–54; Yogev Tuval, "Anti-Terrorism Legislation in Britain and the US after 9/11" (September 10, 2008), online: Israel Democracy Institute <https://en.idi.org.il/articles/6936>.

187   See 8 CFR s 287.3(d) (2001). See also Regina Germain, "Rushing to Judgment: The Unintended Consequences of the USA PATRIOT Act for Bona Fide Refugees" (2002) 16 Geo Immig LJ 505 at 516; D. Martin, *supra* note 107 at 314; Raquel Aldana-Pindell, "The 9/11 'National Security' Cases: Three Principles Guiding Judges' Decision-Making" (2002) 81 Or L Rev 985 at 989.

188   D. Martin, *supra* note 107 at 311.

189   See 8 CFR s 3.19(i)(2) (2001) or 66 Fed Reg 54 at 909–12 (2001). See also Taylor, *supra* note 186 at 158–59; Lori Adams, "Refugee Law in the US Scaled Back by Recent Anti-Terrorism Legislation: Are We Violating the United Nations Refugee Convention?" (2003) 19 NYL Sch Journal of Human Rights 807 at 811.

190   D. Martin, *supra* note 107 at 312–13.

191   *Ibid* at 313.

192   *Zavala v Ridge*, 310 FSupp 2d 1071 (ND Cal 2004). The regulation was upheld in *Gonzales v O'Connell*, 355 F.3d 1010 (7th Cir 2004); *Pisciotta v Ashcroft*, 311 FSupp 2d 445 (DNJ 2004); *Ali v Achim*, 342 FSupp 3d 769 (ND III 2004).

193   OIG-DOJ, OIG Report, *supra* note 139 at 37–40.

194   Taylor, *supra* note 186 at 153–55.

195   *Ibid* at 155–58.

196   OIG-DOJ, OIG Report, *supra* note 139 at 76–80.

197   Taylor, *supra* note 186 at 157–58.

198   OIG-DOJ, OIG Report, *supra* note 139 at 76–80.

199   *Ibid* at 15.

200   *Ibid* at 109.

201   See the Constitution Society, *Domestic Security Enhancement Act of 2003: Section by Section Analysis* (January 9, 2003), online: <https://www.constitution.org/abus/terror/dsea2003.htm>, at 23 [*PATRIOT II: Analysis*].

202   See US, Department of Homeland Security, Bureau of Immigration and Customs Enforcement, *Endgame: Office of Detention and Removal Strategic Plan, 2003–2012. Detention and Removal Strategy for a Secure Homeland* (August 15, 2003) at 2–5, online: DHS <http://www.hsdl.org/?view&did=470051> [*Endgame*].

203   Cole, *supra* note 40 at 1009.

204   *Ibid* at 1005.

205   D. Martin, *supra* note 107 at 310.

206 CCR, "Brief," *supra* note 165 at 1.

207 See *Immigration Act*, RSC 1985, c I-2 (repealed).

208 Davies Bagambiire, *Canadian Immigration and Refugee Law* (Aurora, ON: Canada Law Books, 1996) at 106; Donald Galloway, *Immigration Law* (Concord, ON: Irwin Law, 1997) at 222.

209 Galloway, *ibid* at 224.

210 Bagambiire, *supra* note 208.

211 Galloway, *supra* note 208 at 222.

212 See *Immigration Act*, *supra* note 207, s 103(1).

213 Kent Roach, *Criminal Law*, 6th ed (Toronto: Irwin Law, 2015).

214 Pratt, *supra* note 9 at 43–45.

215 *Ibid* at 45. See McLellan, *supra* note 162 at 2.

216 McLellan, *supra* note 151 at 3.

217 See *IRPA*, *supra* note 93, s 77.

218 See *ibid*, s 78.

219 *Ibid*.

220 See Bill C-3, *An Act to Amend the Immigration and Refugee Protection Act (Certificate and Special Advocate) and to Make Consequential Amendments to Another Act*, 2nd Sess, 39th Parl, 2007, online: Justice Law Website <http://laws-lois.justice. gc.ca/eng/AnnualStatutes/2008_3/page-1.html>. This *Act* was prepared and passed in response to the Supreme Court of Canada's decision in *Charkaoui v Canada (Citizenship and Immigration)*, 2007 SCC 9, [2007] 1 SCR 350 [*Charkaoui*].

221 See the old s 84(2) of the *IRPA*, *supra* note 93.

222 See *Almrei v Canada (Minister of Citizenship and Immigration)*, 2005 FC 355.

223 See the old s 83 of the *IRPA*, *supra* note 93.

224 See s 82(1) of the *IRPA*, *ibid*.

225 See *Mugesera v Canada (Minister of Citizenship and Immigration)*, 2005 SCC 40, [2005] 2 SCR 100. See also Emily Carasco et al, eds, *Immigration and Refugee Law* (Toronto: Emond Montgomery, 2007).

226 CBSA officers currently perform most of the enforcement responsibilities mandated by the *IRPA*.

227 *Anti-terrorism Act*, SC 2001, c 41.

228 Sharryn J. Aiken, "National Security and Canadian Immigration: Deconstructing the Discourse of Trade-Offs" in François Crépeau, ed, *Les migrations internationals contemporaines: une dynamique complexe au coeur de la globalization* (Montreal: Presses de l'Université de Montréal, 2009) 172 at 175.

229 Public Safety and Emergency Preparedness Canada, *Annual Report on the Use of Arrest without Warrant Pursuant to the Anti-Terrorism Act, Subsection 83.31(3) of the Criminal Code* (2002–04), online: Public Safety Canada <http://www.publicsafety. gc.ca/cnt/rsrcs/pblctns/rrsts-wtht-wrrnt-2003-en.aspx>.

230 *Ibid*.

231 The only known case in which it was utilized is the so-called Air India Case. See McLellan, *supra* note 151 at 5.

232 Public Safety and Emergency Preparedness Canada, *Annual Report Concerning Recognizance with Conditions: Arrests without Warrants* (2006–07), online: Public Safety Canada <http://www.publicsafety.gc.ca/cnt/rsrcs/pblctns/rrsts-wtht-wrrnt -2007-en.aspx#a04> [*Arrests without Warrants*].

233 For example, see Allison Jones, "Suspects Arrested in VIA Train Terror Plot Linked to Al-Qaida in Iran: RCMP," *News 1130* (August 22, 2013), online: <http://www. news1130.com/2013/04/22/arrests-made-in-ontario-quebec-in-alleged-terror-plot -cbc-news/>.

234 See Tonda MacCharles & Alex Ballingall, "RCMP, FBI Combine to Stop Terror Attack in Ontario," *Toronto Star* (August 11, 2016), online: <http://www.thestar. com/news/canada/2016/08/11/rcmp-fbi-combine-to-stop-terror-attack-in-ontario. html>.

235 There was at least one significant utilization of this power in 2004. See *In the Matter of an Application under Section 83.28 of the Criminal Code*, 2004 SCC 42, [2004] 2 SCR 248.

236 Audrey Macklin, "Borderline Security" in Ronald Daniels et al, eds, *The Security of Freedom: Essays on Canada's Terrorism Bill* (Toronto: University of Toronto Press, 2001) at 391.

237 See OAG, *supra* note 11 at ss 5.18–5.19.

238 Canada Border Services Agency, Departmental Results Report 2016–2017, online: <https://www.cbsa-asfc.gc.ca/agency-agence/reports-rapports/dpr-rmr/2016-2017/ report-rapport-eng.html> (which inlcuded the budget for the 2017–18 fiscal year).

239 CBC Politics, online: <https://www.cbsa-asfc.gc.ca/agency-agence/reports-rapports/ dpr-rmr/2016-2017/report-rapport-eng.html>.

240 Public Safety Canada, "Security Certificates" (2015), online: Public Safety Canada <http://www.publicsafety.gc.ca/cnt/ntnl-scrt/cntr-trrrsm/scrt-crtfcts-eng.aspx> ["Security Certificates"].

241 Public Safety Canada, *Final Report: 2009–2010 Evaluation of the Security Certificate Initiative* (February 24, 2010) at 8, online: Public Safety Canada <http://www. publicsafety.gc.ca/cnt/rsrcs/pblctns/vltn-scrt-crtfct-2009-10/index-en.aspx> [*Final Report*].

242 See Michelle Shephard, "Last Security Certificate Detainee to Be Freed," *Toronto Star* (January 2, 2009), online: <http://www.thestar.com/news/canada/article/ 560982>. See also Public Safety Canada, *ibid*; and Canada Border Services Agency, "Quarterly Detention Statistics, 2018–2019, online: <https://www.cbsa-asfc.gc.ca/ security-securite/detent/qstat-2018-2019-eng.html>.

243 See Public Safety Canada, "Security Certificates," *supra* note 240; Government of Canada, News Release, "The Government of Canada Introduces Legislation to Improve Security Certificate Process" (October 22, 2007), online: Government of

Canada <http://www.canada.ca/en/news/archive/2007/10/government-canada
-introduces-legislation-improve-security-certificate-process.html>.

244 *Charkaoui, supra note 220.*

245 Martin Friedland, "Police Powers in Bill C-36" in Daniels et al, *supra* note 236 at
277.

246 *An Act to Enact the Security of Canada Information Sharing Act and the Secure Air
Travel Act, to Amend the Criminal Code, the Canadian Security Intelligence Service
Act and the Immigration and Refugee Protection Act and to Make Related and Consequential Amendments to Other Acts,* 2nd Sess, 41st Parl, 2015 (Bill C-51), online:
Parliament of Canada <http://www.parl.ca/DocumentViewer/en/41-2/bill/C-51/
royal-assent/page-155#42>. See also Department of Justice, "About the Anti_
terrorism Act, 2015," online: <https://www.justice.gc.ca/eng/cj-jp/ns-sn/ata15-lat15.
html>.

247 See Justin Ling, "New Powers to Combat Terrorism" (January 2014), online: Canadian Bar Association <http://nationalmagazine.ca/Articles/January-2014/New
-powers-to-combat-terrorism.aspx>.

248 On introduction of US security certificate regime after 9/11, see the section of this
chapter entitled "Preventive Detentions for Security Reasons: The US Position."
On the Canadian equivalent, see Pratt, *supra* note 9 at 43.

249 Pratt, *supra* note 9 at 43.

250 For example, with a rough average of 24,000 refugees (and their dependents)
accepted annually between 2005 and 2014, Canada detained a rough average of
5,000 refugees in each of the years between 2005 and 2011 (i.e., just under 21
percent of them each year). See Daniel Schwartz, "Canada's Refugees by the Numbers: The Data," *CBC News* (October 4, 2015), online: <https://www.cbc.ca/news/
canada/canada-s-refugees-by-the-numbers-the-data-1.3240640>, and Nakache, *supra*
note 13 at 41. With a rough average of 60,000 refugee arrivals in that country in
each year between 2007 and 2014, the United States detained a rough (widely
fluctuating) average of 30,000 refugees per year in the years between 2009 and
2011 (i.e., about 50 percent). See Kelly Jefferys, "Refugees and Asylees: 2006" (May
2007), online: DHS <https://www.dhs.gov/sites/default/files/publications/Refugees_
Asylees_2006.pdf> (citing 2004–06 acceptance figures); and Global Detention
Project, "United States Immigration Detention Profile" (updated May 2016), online:
Global Detention Project <http://www.globaldetentionproject.org/countries/
americas/united-states>. While it is quite difficult to find disaggregated figures
regarding the numbers of refugees detained in the United States, grassroots refugee
workers have estimated that roughly 50 percent of the 30,000 to 40,000 migrants
who have been typically detained at any time have been refugees. See Lauren Etter,
"Record Numbers of Undocumented Immigrants Being Detained in US," *Bloomberg
News* (November 10, 2016), online: <https://www.bloomberg.com/news/articles/
2016-11-10/record-numbers-of-undocumented-immigrants-being-detained-in-u-s>.
Apart from growing rapidly between 2013 and 2016 (during the Obama

Administration), this number also fluctuated between years. See Human Rights First, *Lifeline on Lockdown: Increased US Detention of Asylum Seekers* (New York/ Washington, DC: Human Rights First, July 2016) at 11, online: Human Rights First <http://www.humanrightsfirst.org/sites/default/files/Lifeline-on-Lockdown_0. pdf>. Note that these figures are all rough estimates, the best available evidence from the existing statistical data.

251 Zoe Lofgren, "A Decade of Radical Change in Immigration Law: An Inside Perspective" (2005) 16 Stan L & Pol'y Rev 349 at 354–65.

252 *Ibid* at 365–67.

253 See s 236(c) of the *INA* and 8 CFR s 236.1 (2001). See also Germain, *supra* note 187 at 515–16.

254 See 8 USC s 1225(b)(1)(B)(iii)(IV) (2005); 8 USC s 1225(b)(1)(B)(ii) (2005); Lofgren, *supra* note 251 at 365; and Shirin Sinnar, "Patriotic or Unconstitutional? The Mandatory Detention of Aliens under the USA PATRIOT Act" (2003) 55 Stan L Rev 1420 at 1426.

255 See 28 USC s 2241. See also Germain, *supra* note 187 at 516.

256 Germain, *ibid* at 505.

257 *Ibid*.

258 See 8 USC s 1226a(3).

259 See 8 USC 1226a(a)(1) [emphasis added]. See also Memorandum from James W. Ziglar, Commissioner of the US Immigration and Naturalization Service, to INS Regional Directors and Regional Counsel, "New Anti-Terrorism Legislation" (October 31, 2001) at 3 and 6–8.

260 Vergara, *supra* note 183 at 118–19.

261 Sinnar, *supra* note 254 at 1432. She cites *Re Anwar Haddam*, Suit No A22-751-813 (2000) BIA LEXIS 20 (Department of Justice, December 1, 2000). See also *Yusupov v Attorney General of US,* 518 F.3d 185 at 200 (3rd Cir 2008), where the Third Circuit Court stated that "[a]lthough we conclude that the statutory language does not demonstrate a clear congressional intent to adopt a probable cause standard, the Attorney General's adoption of a standard akin to probable cause in criminal cases is also reasonable, and thus 'a permissible construction of the statute.'"

262 For example, see *Cardoza-Fonseca v INS*, 480 US 421 (1987).

263 Germain, *supra* note 187 at 524.

264 Sinnar, *supra* note 254 at 1441–43.

265 *Ibid*.

266 Vergara, *supra* note 183 at 122–23.

267 *Carlson v. Landon*, 342 US 524 (1952).

268 Sinnar, *supra* note 254 at 1442–43.

269 See *Denmore v Kim*, 538 US 510 (2003); see also Taylor, *supra* note 186 at 161–64.

270 Vergara, *supra* note 183 at 126–27.

271 See 8 USC s 1226a; Sinnar, *supra* note 254 at 1432–33.

272 See 8 USC s 1226(b)(1) and 8 USC s 1226(b)(2)(A).

273 See 8 USC s 1226(b)(3).

274 See 8 USC s 1226(a)(7).

275 Harvard Immigration and Refugee Clinical Program, Press Release, "Refugee and Immigration Clinic Urges Canada to Accept Asylum Seekers Rejected by the US," online: <https://today.law.harvard.edu/harvard-releases-first-report-effect-trumps -executive-orders-asylum-seekers/> (Harvard Law School, February 8, 2017).

276 Harvard Immigration and Refugee Clinical Program, *supra* note 51 at 2.

277 Galloway, *supra* note 208 at 224.

278 *Ibid* at 222–25.

279 I reached this conclusion from reviewing the historical evidence regarding the arrests and detention of the roughly two dozen persons who have ever been named in a security certificate in Canada.

280 Pratt, *supra* note 9 at 45.

281 See s 82(1) of the *IRPA*, *supra* note 93.

282 *Charkaoui, supra* note 220; CCR, "Security Certificates: Next Steps" (June 6, 2007), online: CCR <http://ccrweb.ca/files/certificates07.pdf>; CCR, "Security Certificate Detention Conditions: Letter to Minister of Public Safety" (January 30, 2007), online: CCR <http://ccrweb.ca/en/security-certificate-detention-conditions> ["Detention Conditions"]. See also Standing Committee on Citizenship and Immigration, *Detention Centres and Security Certificates: Report of the Standing Committee on Citizenship and Immigration,* 1st Sess, 39th Parl (April 2007), online: Parliament of Canada <http://www.parl.gc.ca/content/hoc/Committee/391/CIMM/ Reports/RP2829796/cimmrp12/cimmrp12-e.pdf>.

283 *Charkaoui, supra* note 220 at paras 90–94, 139.

284 *Ibid* at para 189.

285 *Ibid*.

286 *Ibid* at para 137.

287 See CCR, "Detention Conditions," *supra* note 282.

288 Special Senate Committee on the Anti-Terrorism Act, *Fundamental Justice in Extraordinary Times: Main Report of the Special Senate Committee on the Anti-Terrorism Act* (February 2007), online: Government of Canada Publications <http://publications. gc.ca/collections/collection_2011/sen/yc2–2–0/YC2–2–0–391–3-eng.pdf>.

289 Frazier, *supra* note 137 at 1097–1103; Aldana-Pindell, *supra* note 187 at 988.

290 See *Bail Reform Act of 1984,* 18 USC s 3144 (1984).

291 Heidee Stoller et al, "Developments in Law and Policy: The Costs of Post 9/11 National Security Strategy" (2004) 22 Yale L & Pol'y Rev 197 at 199.

292 Chishti et al, *supra* note 133 at ii (of section A of the Appendix).

293 James Beckman, *Comparative Legal Approaches to Homeland Security and Anti-Terrorism* (Aldershot, UK: Taylor & Francis, 2007) at 33.

294 See Human Rights Watch, "Witness to Abuse: Human Rights Abuses under the Material Witness Law since September 11" (June 26, 2005), online: Human Rights Watch <http://www.hrw.org/report/2005/06/26/witness-abuse/human-rights -abuses-under-material-witness-law-september-11>.

295 *Ibid* at 219.
296 Chishti et al, *supra* note 133 at ii (of section A of the Appendix).
297 Stoller et al, *supra* note 291 at 200–2.
298 *Ibid*.
299 Friedland, *supra* note 245 at 276–77.
300 See Public Safety and Emergency Preparedness Canada, *Arrests without Warrants*, *supra* note 232 at 1.
301 See Department of Justice Canada, "The Anti-Terrorism Act: The ATA in Perspective," online: Department of Justice Canada <http://canada.justice.gc.ca/eng/antiter/act-loi/persp/persp_p3.html#sunsetting> (accessed June 15, 2004).
302 See Friedland, *supra* note 245 at 277. See also Laurie L. Levenson, "Material Witnesses," *National Law Journal* (October 31, 2001).
303 McLellan, *supra* note 151 at 5.
304 See *Bail Reform Act of 1984*, *supra* note 290.
305 See 8 USC s 1231(a)(1)(A) to (a)(2) (2001). See also 8 CFR s 241.4 (2008).
306 See 8 USC s 1231(a)(1)(A) to (a)(2) (2001). See also 8 CFR s 241.4 (2008).
307 See 8 USC s 1231(a)(6) (2001); 8 CFR s 241.4(a)(4) (2008); Megan Peitzke, "The Fate of 'Unremovable' Aliens before and after September 11, 2001: The Supreme Court's Presumptive Six Month Limit to Post-Removal-Period Detention" (2003) 30 Pepp L Rev 769.
308 See *Reno v Flores*, 507 US 292 (1993); *Zadvydas v Davis*, 533 US 678 (2001) [*Zadvydas*]. See also Sinnar, *supra* note 254 at 1430–31.
309 See *Zadvydas*, *ibid* at 19–20. See also Batoul Makki, "The United States Supreme Court Holds Indefinite Detention of Deportable Aliens to Be Unconstitutional: Where Do They Go from Here?" (2002) 79 U Det Mercy L Rev 479.
310 *Clark v Martinez*, *supra* note 34. As noted in c 2, n 208, the ratio of the *Nielsen v Preap* case does not really add all that much to the analysis here.
311 See 8 CFR s 241.14 (2001); *Continued Detention of Aliens Subject to Final Orders of Removal*, 66 Fed Reg 56967 (2001); and US, Office of the Chief Immigration Judge, Executive Office of Immigration Review, US Department of Justice, *Operating Policies and Procedures Memorandum 01–03: Continued Detention and Hearings* (November 19, 2001) (on file with the author).
312 K. Martin, *supra* note 175 at 24–25.
313 Vergara, *supra* note 183 at 120–21.
314 See Jim Edwards, "Rights Organizations Document Cases of Indefinite N.J. Detention of Aliens," *New Jersey Law Journal* (March 18, 2002) at 1.
315 *Ibid*.
316 Taylor, *supra* note 186 at 159–60.
317 OIG-DOJ, OIG Report, *supra* note 139 at 91–100.
318 Cole, *supra* note 40 at 1003–6.
319 OIG-DOJ, OIG Report, *supra* note 139 at 46.
320 *Ibid* at 51.

321 *Ibid* at 62–71.
322 USCIRF, *Asylum Report, supra* note 67 at 74.
323 OIG-DOJ, OIG Report, *supra* note 139 at 62–90.
324 D. Martin, *supra* note 107 at 310–11.
325 Office of the Inspector General of the US Department of Justice (OIG-DOJ), "OIG Analysis of Responses by the Department of Justice and the Department of Homeland Security to Recommendations in the OIG's June 2003 Report on the Treatment of September 11 Detainees" (nd) at 17 (on file with the author).
326 Immigration and Refugee Board of Canada, *Guidelines Issued by the Chairperson Pursuant to Section 65(4) of the Immigration Act: Guideline 2 – Guidelines on Detention* (March 12, 1998), No 2, online: Immigration and Refugee Board of Canada (on file with the author).
327 *Ibid*. See also *Charkaoui, supra* note 220.
328 Bagambiire, *supra* note 208 at 393–96, 401; Galloway, *supra* note 208 at 224.
329 Bagambiire, *ibid* at 298.
330 *Immigration Act*, RSC 1985, c I-2, s 103.1.
331 *Lin v Canada (Minister of Citizenship and Immigration)*, [2001] IAdjDD No 4, No A1-00224 (QL); *Canada (Minister of Citizenship and Immigration) v Liang*, [2000] IAdjDD No 7, No 99-00493 (A092) (QL). See especially, *Lin v Canada* at paras 10–12.
332 *Lin v Canada, ibid* at para 11.
333 *Canada v Liang, supra* note 331 at paras 1–3.
334 *Jaballah v Canada (Minister of Public Safety & Emergency Preparedness)*, 2007 FC 379, 63 Imm LR (3d) 60, 296 FTR 1, 156 ACWS (3d) 1143 (WLeC); *Mahjoub v Canada (Minister of Citizenship & Immigration)*, 2007 FC 171, 61 Imm LR (3d) 1, 309 FTR 72 (Eng) (WLeC).
335 See ss 55 and 81 of the *IRPA, supra* note 93.
336 *Ibid*, ss 57 and 82.
337 *Ibid*, s 82.
338 See CCR, "Detention" (nd), online: CCR <http://ccrweb.ca/en/issues/detention>. This fact is implied in this document.
339 See *Almrei (Re)*, 2009 CarswellNat 17, 2009 FC 3, 78 Imm LR (3d) 167, online: <http://cas-ncr-nter03.cas-satj.gc.ca/rss/DES-3-08%20Decision%20Jan2.pdf> (accessed December 5, 2009). See also Barbara Jackman, "Sustaining Investigations and Security Certificates through the Use of Profiles" in BCCLA (BC Civil Liberties Association), *Racial Profiling: A Special Report BCCLA Report on Racial Profiling in Canada* (Vancouver: BCCLA, 2010) at 69.
340 See *Almrei v Canada (Minister of Citizenship and Immigration)*, 2005 FC 1645 at para 249, online: Federal Court <http://decisions.fct-cf.gc.ca/en/2005/2005fc1645/2005fc1645.html>.
341 *Charkaoui, supra* note 220 at para 105.
342 See *Canadian Charter of Rights and Freedoms*, Part I of the *Constitution Act 1982*, being Schedule B to the *Canada Act 1982* (UK), c 11, ss 7, 12.

343 *Charkaoui, supra* note 220 at para 123 [emphasis in original].

344 For the view that indefinite detention is not practised in Canada, see Reg Whitaker, "Keeping Up with the Neighbours? Canadian Responses to 9/11 in Historical and Comparative Context" (2003) 41 Osgoode Hall LJ 241 at 261.

345 See *Alvin John Brown v Canada (Citizenship and Immigration),* 2017 FC 710.

346 *Ibid* at para 151.

347 K. Martin, *supra* note 175 at 25; Human Rights Watch, *supra* note 135 at 16–32; and Murray, *supra* note 130 at 55–57.

348 See *Center for National Security Studies, et al v United States Department of Justice,* Civil Action No 01-2500 (GK), 215 FSupp 2d 94 (2002), per Kessler J at 8 [*Center for National Security Studies*].

349 *Ibid.*

350 For example, see decision of New Jersey Superior Court Judge Arthur D'Italia in *American Civil Liberties Union of New Jersey v County of Hudson,* 2002 WL 1285110 (NJ Sup Ct App Div, 2002) (ordering the immediate public release of this information but staying his order until the determination of the Department of Justice's appeal against it). See also Jim Edwards, "Judge Orders End to Secret Detention of Federal Inmates in County Jails," *New Jersey Law Journal* (April 1, 2002) at 1 (of LexisNexis).

351 See *Center for National Security Studies, supra* note 348 at 14.

352 *Ibid* at 14–15.

353 *Ibid* at 15.

354 *Ibid* at 15–17 and 34–36.

355 *Ibid* at 20–24.

356 *Ibid* at 24.

357 *Ibid* at 24–27.

358 *Ibid* at 27.

359 *Ibid* at 33–34.

360 *Center for National Security Studies, et al v United States Department of Justice,* 331 F.3d 918 (DC Cir 2003).

361 *Ibid* at 937.

362 *Ibid* at 928–29.

363 *Ibid* at 937–52.

364 *Ibid* at 937.

365 *Ibid* at 943.

366 See Order List: 540 US (January 12, 2004) at 4 (on file with the author). See also *Center for National Security Studies, et al, Petitioners v Department of Justice,* 540 US 1104 (2004); 124 S Ct 1041; 157 L Ed 2d 888; 2004 US Lexis 46; 72 USLW 3446. The petition to the US Supreme Court for the grant of a writ of *certiorari* was denied.

367 The Constitution Society, *PATRIOT II: Analysis, supra* note 201 at 13–14.

368 Thomas Walkom, "Another Victim of Sept. 11," *Toronto Star* (April 11, 2007), online: <http://www.thestar.com/opinion/columnists/2007/04/11/another_victim_of_sept_11.html> (accessed November 9, 2007).

369   *Ibid.*

370   *Ibid.*

371   *Ibid.*

372   *Ibid.*

373   *Ibid.*

374   See *US v Benatta*, 2003 US Dist Lexis 16514. Quotation was also reproduced in Toronto Action for Social Change, "The Case of Benamar Benatta: Canada's First 9/11 Rendition to Torture" (July 20, 2007), online: Verbena-19 <http://verbena19. wordpress.com/2007/07/21/support-benamar-benatta-canadas-first-911-rendition -to-torture/>.

375   Commission of Inquiry into the Actions of Canadian Officials in Relation to Maher Arar, Dennis R. O'Connor, *Report on the Events Relating to Maher Arar, Factual Background*, vol 1 (2006), online: Library and Archives Canada <http://epe.lac-bac. gc.ca/100/206/301/pco-bcp/commissions/maher_arar/07–09–13/www.ararcom mission.ca/default.htm> [*Arar Report*].

376   For example, see Chishti et al, *supra* note 133 at 52–64; and Human Rights Watch, *supra* note 135 at 33–44 and 67–87.

377   Human Rights Watch, *ibid* at 67–87; Chishti et al, *ibid*.

378   OIG-DOJ, OIG Report, *supra* note 139 at 109–65.

379   See USCIRF, *Asylum Report, supra* note 67 at 189–90.

380   *Ibid* at 181.

381   *Ibid* at 185.

382   See "DOJ Detention Standards" (on file with the author). See also USCIRF, *Asylum Report, supra* note 67 at 182.

383   Department of Homeland Security, *Endgame, supra* note 202 at 2–9.

384   See USCIRF, Special Report, *supra* note 73 at 1.

385   *Ibid* at 184.

386   See USCIRF Report 2005, online: <https://www.uscirf.gov/reports-briefs/special -reports/report-asylum-seekers-in-expedited-removal>.

387   *Ibid* at 1.

388   Chishti et al, *supra* note 133 at 52–64; USCIRF, *Asylum Report, supra* note 67 at 186; and Human Rights Watch, *supra* note 135 at 69–73.

389   OIG-DOJ, OIG Report, *supra* note 139 at 112.

390   *Ibid* at 112.

391   *Ibid* at 142; Human Rights Watch, *supra* note 135 at 73–82.

392   OIG-DOJ, OIG Report, *supra* note 139 at 142.

393   *Ibid* at 143.

394   *Ibid* at 114.

395   *Ibid* at 116.

396   *Ibid* at 113.

397   USCIRF, Special Report, *supra* note 73 at 1–2.

398   OIG-DOJ, OIG Report, *supra* note 139 at 184–85.

399 *Ibid* at 165.

400 Pratt, *supra* note 9 at 28.

401 *Ibid*.

402 *Ibid* at 23–24.

403 Inter-American Commission on Human Rights, *Report on the Situation of Human Rights of Asylum Seekers within the Canadian Refugee Determination System* (2000) at para 134, online: <http://www.cidh.oas.org/countryrep/Canada2000en/canada.b.htm>.

404 *Gao v Canada*, [2000] OJ No 2784 at paras 4–13, [2000] OTC 581 (QL).

405 *Immigration Detention and Removal: Report of the Standing Committee on Citizenship and Immigration* (Ottawa: Standing Committee on Citizenship and Immigration, June 1998), online: Parliament of Canada <http://www2.parl.gc.ca/HousePublications/Publication.aspx?DocId=1031513&Language=E&Mode=1&Parl=36&Ses=1&File=2>.

406 Canada, *Government Response 1998, supra* note 55.

407 See CCR, "Comments on Detention and Removals Addressed to the Standing Committee on Citizenship and Immigration" (March 1998), online: CCR <http://ccrweb.ca/en/comments-detention-and-removals-addressed-standing-committee-citizenship-and-immigration>.

408 Nakache, *supra* note 13 at 73–80.

409 See *Toronto Star* (March 7, 2003).

410 See CCR, "Refugees and Non-Citizens in Canada: Key Concerns Regarding Canada's Compliance with the Covenant on Civil and Political Rights (CCPR)" (Submission to the UN Human Rights Committee, September 16, 2005) at 8 ["Refugees and Non-Citizens"], online: CCR <http://www.ccrweb.ca/ccpr2005.pdf>.

411 See *Almrei v Canada*, [2004] 4 FCR 327 at para 3.

412 *Ibid* at 7.

413 *Ibid* at paras 94–95; and *Jaballah v Canada*, [2005] OJ No 3681 at paras 35–40. See Fatima Najm, "Terror Suspect Says Life's Like Hell," *Globe and Mail* (September 8, 2004), online: <http://www.theglobeandmail.com/news/national/terror-suspect-says-lifes-like-hell/article4090638/>.

414 *Almrei v Canada* [2003] OJ No 5198 at paras 94–95, 133.

415 See Tim Groves and Ali Mustafa, "Still in Search of Justice: The Story of Security Certificate Detainee Mohammad Mahjoub," *Toronto Media Co-op* (June 26, 2012) online: <http://toronto.mediacoop.ca/story/still-search-justice-story-security-certificate-detainee-mohammad-mahjoub/11507>; and "Mohammad Mahjoub, Longest Held of Canada's Secret Trial Detainees, to Be Returned to His Family" (nd) *Homes not Bombs* (blog), online: <http://www.homesnotbombs.ca/mahjoubgetsbail.htm>. See also Najm, *supra* note 413.

416 Stock, *supra* note 67 at 106.

417 *Ibid*.

418 Aldana-Pindell, *supra* note 187 at 994–96.

419 Chishti et al, *supra* note 133 at 22.

420 American Immigration Lawyers Association, *Making the Case for Comprehensive Immigration Reform: Resource Guide* (February 27, 2007) at 90, online: American Immigration Lawyers Association <http://www.aila.org/resourceguide> at 90. On this issue, see also Justin Chasco, "Justice Alberto Gonzales? The Attorney General's Power to Overturn Board of Immigration Appeals' Decisions" (2007) 31 S Ill ULJ 363.

421 USCIRF, *Asylum Report, supra* note 67 at 89.

422 See American Immigration Lawyers Association, *Issue Packet on Comprehensive Immigration Reform* (February 24, 2004) at 30, online: American Immigration Lawyers Association <http://www.aila.org/>.

423 See, for example, Katherine E. Melloy, "Telling Truths: How the Real ID Act's Credibility Provisions Affect Women Asylum Seekers" (2007) 92 Iowa L Rev 637.

424 See Natsu Taylor Saito, "Symbolism under Siege: Japanese American Redress and the 'Racing' of Arab Americans as 'Terrorists'" (2001) 8 Asian LJ 1 at 3.

425 Chishti et al, *supra* note 133 at 99–104. Even the *PATRIOT Act* itself expressed the sense of Congress, *inter alia*, that "many Sikh-Americans ... have suffered both verbal and physical assaults as a result of misguided anger toward Arab-Americans and Muslim-Americans in the wake of the September 11, 2001 terrorist attack," and that "Congress is seriously concerned by the number of crimes against Sikh-Americans and other Americans all across the nation that have been reported in the wake of the tragic events that unfolded on September 11, 2001." See s 1002(a) of the *PATRIOT Act, supra* note 181.

426 Chishti et al, *supra* note 133 at 104–11.

427 *Ibid* at i of Appendix – Section A.

428 K. Martin, *supra* note 175 at 23.

429 Arnold, *supra* note 129 at 113–14.

430 USCIRF, "Report Card," *supra* note 84.

431 See Dave Boyer, "Obama: US Must Embrace Muslims to Defeat Terrorism," *Washington Times* (December 6, 2016), online: <http://www.washingtontimes.com/news/2016/dec/6/obama-us-must-embrace-muslims-defeat-terrorism/>; "'A Rollercoaster Ride': How Trump's Muslim Ban Has Affected Lives," *The Guardian* (May 24, 2017), online: <http://www.theguardian.com/commentisfree/2017/may/24/how-trumps-muslim-travel-ban-affects-us-panel>.

432 Sharryn Aiken, "Of Gods and Monsters: National Security and Canadian Refugee Policy" (2001) 14:2 RQDI 1, at 24.

433 *Department of Public Safety and Emergency Preparedness Act*, SC 2005, c 10 (assented to March 23, 2005).

434 See the *Convention on the Status of Refugees*, July 28, 1951, 189 UNTS 150, 19 UST 6259 (entered into force April 22, 1954); *International Covenant on Civil and Political Rights*, 1966, GA Res 2200A (XXI), 21 UN GAOR, Supp No 16, UN Doc A/6316 (1966); and *American Declaration of the Rights and Duties of Man*, 1948, OAS Res XXX (1948).

435 See "Advisory Opinion by the UNHCR Regional Representative in Washington DC (April 15, 2002), *supra* note 48. See also "Statement of Senator Edward Kennedy" in US, *The Detention and Treatment of Haitian Asylum Seekers, supra* note 27 at 2. This practice was also condemned by the Women's Commission for Refugee Women and Children, *Refugee Policy Adrift: The United States and Dominican Republic Deny Haitians Protection* (New York: Women's Commission for Refugee Women and Children, January 2003), online: Refworld <http://www.unhcr.org/refworld/docid/48aa82f00.html>. UNHCR Advisory Opinion on the Detention of Haitian Asylum Seekers in the US, 15 April 2002," reproduced in US, *The Detention and Treatment of Haitian Asylum Seekers, supra* note 27 at 108–10.

436 See Introduction to the *United Nations High Commissioner for Refugees (UNHCR) Guidelines on the Detention of Asylum Seekers,* online: <https://www.unhcr.org/publications/legal/505b10ee9/unhcr-detention-guidelines.html>, at para 5.

437 See *International Convention on the Elimination of All Forms of Racial Discrimination,* March 7, 1966, 660 UNTS 195 (entered into force January 4, 1969) at para 8.

438 See Preamble, at para (b).

439 See Introduction to the Guidelines, *supra* note 438 at para 1.

440 See Guidelines, *Ibid* at para 3(iv).

441 See Guidelines, *Ibid* at paras 5 and 10.

442 See Guidelines, *Ibid* at para 4.

443 See *IRPA, supra* note 93 a s 3(3)(f).

444 *Suresh v Canada (Minister of Citizenship and Immigration),* 2002 SCC 1, [2002] 1 SCR 3; *Baker v Canada,* [1999] SCR 817.

445 See CCR, "Refugees and Non-Citizens," *supra* note 410.

446 See UN Committee on the Elimination of Racial Discrimination (CERD), *UN Committee on the Elimination of Racial Discrimination: Concluding Observations, Canada* (May 25, 2007), CERD/C/CAN/CO/18 at para 18, online: Refworld <http://www.refworld.org/docid/465fe0082.html> [*Concluding Observations, Canada*].

447 See UN Commission on Human Rights, *Working Group on Arbitrary Detention Visit to Canada* (June 2005), E/CN.4/2006/7/Add.2 at paras 74 and 91 (on file with the author) [*Visit to Canada*].

448 See CERD, *Concluding Observations, Canada,* at para 14.

449 *Ibid.* See also CCR, "Brief," *supra* note 165 at 6.

450 This occurred in the case of Mahmood Jaballah. See Colin Perkel, "Court Finds Designation of Egyptian Man as Security Threat Unreasonable," *CBC News* (May 24, 2016), online: <http://www.cbc.ca/news/politics/mahmoud-jaballah-security-certificate-1.3598337>. It also occurred in the case of Hassan Almrei. See Michelle Shephard, "Court Strikes Down Almrei Security Certificate," *Toronto Star* (December 14, 2009), online: <http://www.thestar.com/news/canada/2009/12/14/court_strikes_down_almrei_security_certificate.html>.

451 International Commission of Jurists (ICJ), *Assessing Damage, Urging Action* (Geneva: ICJ, 2009) at 118–19.

452 Inter-American Commission on Human Rights, *supra* note 403 at paras 147–57. See also CCR, "Brief," *supra* note 165 at 5.

453 *Ibid*.

454 See UN Human Rights Committee (HRC), *UN Human Rights Committee: Concluding Observations, Canada* (April 20, 2006), CCPR/C/CAN/CO/5 at para 14, online: Refworld <http://www.refworld.org/docid/453777a50.html>; see also CERD, *Concluding Observations, Canada, supra* note 448 at para 18.

455 See CERD, *Concluding Observations, Canada, supra* note 448 at para 14.

456 See UN Commission on Human Rights, *Visit to Canada, supra* note 449 at 13–16; US, Department of State, *Country Reports on Human Rights Practices for 2015: Canada* (April 13, 2016) at 1–4, online: Department of State <http://www.state.gov/j/drl/rls/hrrpt/humanrightsreport/index.htm#wrapper>.

457 Even then, the scale and intensity of the application of this measure during this now-defunct regime was very mild compared with the US experience.

458 M. Cherif Bassiouni, "Don't Tread on Me: Is the War on Terror Really a War on Rights?" in E. Hagopian, ed, *supra* note 130 at 1; Human Rights Watch, *supra* note 135 at 9.

459 OIG-DOJ, OIG Report, *supra* note 139 at 111.

Chapter 3: Terrorism-Related Inadmissibility
Epigraph: US, *Oversight Hearing: US Refugee Admissions and Policy: Hearing before the Senate Judiciary Committee, Sub-Committee on Immigration, Border Security and Citizenship*, 109th Cong (2006) at 1 (The Hon. Patrick Leahy), online: US Senate <http://judiciary.senate.gov/hearings/testimony.cfm?id=2343&wit_id=3985> (accessed February 3, 2007).

1 See *Authority of the Secretary of Homeland Security, Delegations of Authority, Immigration Law*, 68 Fed Reg 10922 (March 6, 2003), 8 CFR s 1.1(o), 2.1, 103.1, and 239.1.

2 As in previous chapters, the term "refugees" will be used in the rest of this chapter to refer to both asylum seekers and accepted refugees.

3 See, e.g., Regina Germain, *A Practical Guide to US Asylum Law and Procedure* (Washington, DC: American Immigration Lawyers Association, 2007) at 113 [*Practical Guide*].

4 The concept of national security has been defined in such legislation as the *Classified Information Procedures Act*, Pub L No 96-456, 94 Stat 2025 (1980) (codified as 18 USC App Iii ss 1–16) at s 1(b) as "the national defense and foreign relations of the United States." Section 219(d)(2) of the *United States Immigration and Nationality Act*, 8 USC (1952) [*INA*], defines "national security" in much the same way, as "the national defense, foreign relations and economic interests of the United States." Yet even these commendable attempts to define this concept end up underlining the high level of vagueness associated with it. It is of course correct that case law has provided a slightly more detailed definition of the concept as denoting "any non-trivial risk to the Nation's defense, foreign relations, or economic interests."

For example, see *In Re A-H-, Respondent,* Interim Decision #3515, 23 I&N Dec 774 at para 4 (AG 2005). Yet even this more detailed definition provides almost as little specific guidance as the former one.

5 Won Kidane, "The Terrorism Exception to Asylum: Managing the Uncertainty of Status Determination" (2008) 41 U Mich JL Ref 669 at 689.

6 See Rene Bruin and Kees Wouters, "Terrorism and the Non-Derogability of Non-Refoulement" (2003) 15:1 Int'l J Refugee L 5 at 16.

7 See *Convention Relating to the Status of Refugees,* July 28, 1951, 189 UNTS 150, CTS 1969/6 (entered into force April 22, 1954, accession by Canada September 2, 1969) [*Refugee Convention*]. For some of the relevant US provisions, see *INA, supra* note 4 at s 241(b)(3)(B)(iii) (8 USC s 1231(b)(3)(B)(iii)) (serious non-political crimes); s 241(b)(3)(B)(i) (8 USC s 1231(b)(3)(B)(i)) (participation in the persecution of others); s 241(b)(3)(B)(ii) (8 USC s 1231(b)(3)(B)(ii)) (particularly serious crimes); and s 241(b)(3)(B)(iv) (8 USC s 1231(b)(3)(B)(iv)) (danger to the security of the United States). For some of the relevant Canadian provisions, see s 101(1)(f) of the *Immigration and Refugee Protection Act,* SC 2001, c 27 [*IRPA*]. See also Office of the UN High Commissioner for Refugees (UNHCR), "Guidelines on International Protection," HCR/GIP/03/05, September 4, 2003.

8 See the *Refugee Convention, ibid* at art 33(2). For some of the relevant US provisions, see *INA, supra* note 4, s 208(b)(2)(A)(iii) (8 USC s 1158(b)(2)(A)(iii)) (serious non-political crimes); s 208(b)(2)(A)(i) (8 USC s 1158(b)(2)(A)(i)) (participation in the persecution of others); and s 208(b)(2)(A)(ii) (8 USC s 1158(b)(2)(A)(ii)) (particularly serious crimes). For some of the relevant Canadian provisions, see *IRPA, ibid* at s 34(1)(c) (terrorism); s 34(1)(d) (danger to the security of Canada); and s 34(1)(f) (member of a terrorist organization).

9 See the *Illegal Immigration Reform and Immigrant Responsibility Act,* Pub L No 104-208, 10 Stat 3009–546 (1996); the *Anti-Terrorism and Effective Death Penalty Act,* Pub L No 104-132, 110 Stat 1214 (1996); and *INA, ibid.* See also Zoe Lofgren, "A Decade of Radical Change in Immigration Law: An Inside Perspective" (2005) 16 Stan L & Pol'y Rev 349 at 364–65. It must be noted that much, though not all, of the Attorney General's power under the *INA* was delegated by him to the Secretary of Homeland Security in March 2003. See *Authority of the Secretary of Homeland Security, Delegations of Authority, Immigration Law,* 68 Fed Reg 10922 (March 6, 2003), 8 CFR s 1.1(o), 2.1, 103.1, and 239.1.

10 Lofgren, *ibid* at 364–65.

11 See, for example: 1) the proposed *9/11 Recommendations Implementation Act of 2004,* Bill HR 10, 108th Cong, 2003–04, which passed the House of Representatives on October 8, 2004, but never became law. Section 3034 would have amended s 411 of the *PATRIOT Act* and thus modified the *INA*'s provisions with regard to TRI. This amendment would have made it easier to bar non-citizens, including refugees who are members of or who support any political organization that has used violence, regardless of its designation or otherwise as a foreign terrorist

organization. See "Letter from the American Immigration Lawyers Association
to US Senators and Representatives," reproduced in an email to the author from
Janet Dench on October 19, 2004; 2) the proposed *Securing America's Future through
Enforcement Reform (SAFER) Act of 2003*, Bill HR 3522, 108th Cong, 2003–04, which
was referred to a committee of the House of Representatives on December 10,
2003, but was never passed by the House and did not became law. This *Act* would
have provided increased authority to the relevant agencies to remove serious human
rights violators from the United States; 3) the proposed *Save America Comprehensive
Immigration Act of 2005*, Bill HR 2092, 109th Cong, 2005–06, which was referred
to a committee of the House of Representatives on January 20, 2006, but was never
passed and did not became law. This *Act* would, *inter alia*, have authorized the
Secretary of Homeland Security to adjust the status of certain non-citizens who
would otherwise be inadmissible, but would not have benefited those suspected
of TRI; and 4) the proposed *Border Protection, Antiterrorism, and Illegal Immigration
Control Act of 2005*, Bill HR 4437, 109th Cong, 2005–06, which passed the House
of Representatives on December 18, 2005, but never became law. This *Act* would,
among other things, have expanded the grounds for denying withholding of
removal to non-citizens who are deportable on grounds of terrorism, and would
have made this change retroactive.

12 *Uniting and Strengthening America by Providing Appropriate Tools Required to Intercept
and Obstruct Terrorism (USA PATRIOT) Act of 2001*, Pub L No 107-56, 115 Stat 272
(2001) *[PATRIOT Act]*; "REAL ID ACT of 2005," attached as Division B of the
*Emergency Supplemental Appropriation for Defense, the Global War on Terror, and
Tsunami Relief, 2005*, Pub L No 109-13, 119 Stat 231 *[REAL ID Act]*.
13 See Kidane, *supra* note 5 at 670.
14 See Regina Germain, "Rushing to Judgment: The Unintended Consequences of
the USA PATRIOT Act for Bona Fide Refugees" (2002) 16 Geo Immig LJ 505 at
508–9 ["Rushing"]; and Germain, *Practical Guide, supra* note 3 at 113. See also
Deborah E. Anker, *Law of Asylum in the United States* (Boston: Refugee Law Center,
1999) at 442–43.
15 See *Immigration Act of 1990*, Pub L No 101-649, 04 Stat 4798 (1990).
16 8 USC ss 1158(B)(2)(A)(v) and 1182(a)(3)(B)(i).
17 See Bruin and Wouters, *supra* note 6 at 14.
18 *Ibid* at 15.
19 See also Anker, *supra* note 15 at 444–45.
20 Margaret Stock, "Providing Material Support to a Foreign Terrorist Organization:
The Pentagon, the Department of State, the People's Mujahedin of Iran, and the
Global War on Terrorism" (2006) 11 Bender's Immigration Bulletin 521 at 523,
online: Bender's Immigration Bulletin <http://www.bibdaily.com/pdfs/Stock%20
PMOI%206-1-06bibfinal.pdf> (accessed May 16, 2007).
21 *Ibid* at 522. See also *Humanitarian Law Project v Reno*, 205 F.3d 1130 (9th Cir 2000)
(which was fought on the basis of this *AEDPA* provision).

22 See also Anker, *supra* note 14 at 445.

23 *Ibid.*

24 *PATRIOT Act, supra* note 12 at s 411(F); Germain, "Rushing," *supra* note 14 at 518–19.

25 See AILA (American Immigration Lawyers Association), "The Real ID Act of 2005: Summary and Selected Analysis of Provisions Included in the Emergency Supplemental Appropriations Package (H.R. 1268)" (May 4, 2005) at 4, online: AILA <http://www.aila.org/infonet/summary-and-Analysis-of-the-real-id-act-of-2005> ["Real ID Act of 2005"].

26 *Ibid.*

27 Kidane, *supra* note 5 at 676 and fn 48; Nancy Murray, "Profiled: Arabs, Muslims, and the Post-9/11 Hunt for the 'Enemy Within'" in Elaine Hagopian, ed, *Civil Rights in Peril: The Targeting of Arabs and Muslims* (Chicago: Haymarket Books, 2004) at 53.

28 See AILA, "Real ID Act of 2005," *supra* note 25 at 4.

29 See 8 USC s 1182(a)(3)(B)(iv)(IV).

30 See 8 USC s 1182(a)(3)(B)(iv)(VI).

31 See AILA, "Real ID Act of 2005," *supra* note 25 at 4.

32 See Kidane, *supra* note 5 at 690–91.

33 See *In Re S-K-,* Interim Decision #3534, 23 I&N Dec 936 (BIA 2006) at 948.

34 Melanie Nezer, "The Material Support Problem: Where US Anti-Terrorism Laws, Refugee Protection, and Foreign Policy Collide" (2006) 13 Brown Journal of World Affairs 177 at 179.

35 *Ibid* at 180.

36 *Ibid* at 178.

37 See Mark Fleming et al, eds, *Unintended Consequences: Refugee Victims of the War on Terror* (Washington, DC: Georgetown University Law Centre, Human Rights Institute, May 2006) at 21–26, online: <http://scholarship.law.georgetown.edu/cgi/viewcontent.cgi?article=1000&context=hri_papers>.

38 See Nezer, *supra* note 34 at 179. See also Fleming et al, *ibid* at 26–29.

39 See *In Re S-K-, supra* note 33 at 944–46.

40 *Ibid.*

41 See *Alturo v US Attorney General,* 716 F.3d 1310 (11th Cir 2013).

42 See *Singh-Kaur v Ashcroft,* 385 F.3d 293 (3d Cir 2004).

43 See Stock, *supra* note 20 at 3.

44 8 USC 1189.

45 See *Peoples Mojahedin Organization of Iran v US Department of State,* 337 US App DC 106, 182 F.3d 17, at 23 (DC Cir 1999) [*Peoples Mojahedin*].

46 See CRS (Congressional Research Service), "Immigration: Terrorist Grounds for Exclusion of Aliens" (March 2005) at 8 and fn 25 (on file with the author).

47 Stock, *supra* note 20 at 11.

48 US, *Oversight Hearing: US Refugee Admissions and Policy, Hearing before the Senate Judiciary Committee, Sub-Committee on Immigration, Border Security and Citizenship,*

109th Cong (2006) at 2 (The Hon. Patrick Leahy), online: US Senate <http://judiciary.senate.gov/hearings/testimony.cfm?id=2343&wit_id=3985> (accessed February 3, 2007) [*Oversight Hearing*].

49 Germain, *Practical Guide, supra* note 3 at 116–17; Germain, "Rushing," *supra* note 14 at 508.

50 Germain, *Practical Guide, ibid* at 116–17.

51 *Ibid* at 116.

52 See Kidane, *supra* note 5 at 704.

53 See *INA, supra* note 4 at s 212(a)(3)(B)(i)(VIII). See also AILA, "Real ID Act of 2005," *supra* note 25 at 4.

54 See Germain, "Rushing," *supra* note 14 at 520–21. See also US, Immigration and Naturalization Service (INS), "Memorandum for Regional Directors" (October 31, 2001) at 3 (on file with the author) ["Memo for Regional Directors"].

55 Germain, *Practical Guide, supra* note 3 at 116.

56 See Germain, "Rushing," *supra* note 14 at 520–21. See also INS, "Memo for Regional Directors," *supra* note 54 at 3.

57 See 8 USC s 1182(a)(3)(B)(i)(VII).

58 See *INA, supra* note 4 at s 212(a)(3)(B)(i)(IX). See also CRS, *supra* note 46 at i.

59 See *INA, ibid* at ss 212(a)(3)(B)(ii)(I) and 212(a)(3)(B)(ii)(II).

60 See CRS, *supra* note 46 at 4–5 and fn 16.

61 8 USC s 1227(a)(4)(B).

62 8 USC s 1182(a)(3)(B).

63 See CRS, *supra* note 46 at 4–5 and fn 16.

64 See the *Intelligence Reform and Terrorism Prevention Act of 2004*, Pub L No 108-458, 118 Stat 3638 (2004); CRS, *supra* note 46 at 4–5 and fn 16.

65 *Ibid*.

66 See US, Executive Order No 13769, *Protecting the Nation from Foreign Terrorist Entry into the United States*, 82 Fed Reg 8977 (January 27, 2017) at ss 3(c) and 5, online: The White House: <http://www.whitehouse.gov/the-press-office/2017/01/27/executive-order-protecting-nation-foreign-terrorist-entry-united-states>. This executive order was subsequently amended after being suspended/struck down by the courts. See US, Executive Order No 13780, *Protecting the Nation from Foreign Terrorist Entry into the United States*, 82 Fed Reg 13209 (March 6, 2017), online: The White House: <http://www.whitehouse.gov/the-press-office/2017/03/06/executive-order-protecting-nation-foreign-terrorist-entry-united-states>. This very similar second order was also struck down by the courts.

67 See the revised Executive Order, *ibid* at para 3; *Convention against Torture and Other Cruel, Inhuman or Degrading Treatment or Punishment*, December 10, 1984, 465 UNTS 85 (entered into force June 26, 1987).

68 See Adam Liptak, "Trump Loses Travel Ban Ruling in Appeals Court," *New York Times* (June 12, 2017), online: <http://www.nytimes.com/2017/06/12/us/politics/trump-travel-ban-court-of-appeals.html>.

69 See Michael D. Shear & Adam Liptak, "Supreme Court Takes Up Travel Ban Case, and Allows Parts to Go Ahead," *New York Times* (June 26, 2017), online: <http://www.nytimes.com/2017/06/26/us/politics/supreme-court-trump-travel-ban-case.html>. For the full text of this Supreme Court ruling itself, see *Donald J. Trump v International Refugee Assistance Project*, 582 US 1 (2017).

70 See *Trump, President of the United States, et al v Hawaii et al*, 585 US __ (2018), online: <http://www.supremecourt.gov/opinions/17pdf/17-965_h315.pdf>.

71 See *INA*, *supra* note 4 at s 212(a)(3)(B)(ii).

72 Germain, *Practical Guide*, *supra* note 3 at 115; Germain, "Rushing," *supra* note 14 at 519; and CRS, *supra* note 46 at 8.

73 See Nezer, *supra* note 34 at 179; Stock, *supra* note 20 at 10. It should be noted, though, that the Trump Administration was once considering abolishing this authority to grant TRI waivers; see Mica Rosenberg & Yeganeh Torbati, "Trump Administration May Change Rules That Allow Terror Victims to Immigrate to the US," *Reuters* (April 21, 2017), online: <http://in.reuters.com/article/usa-immigration-terrorism-exceptions-idINKBN17N130>. This change has not, however, come to pass.

74 See Federal Register (June 18, 2008) at 34, 770–77.

75 See US, Bill HR 2764, *Consolidated Appropriations Act of 2008*, 110th Cong, 2008, which became Pub L No 110-161. See also USCIS (US Citizenship and Immigration Services), "Fact Sheet: USCIS Implements Authority to Exempt Certain Persons Who Provided Material Support under Duress to the Revolutionary Armed Forces of Colombia (FARC)" (September 26, 2007), online: USCIS <http://www.uscis.gov/sites/default/files/USCIS/Humanitarian/Refugees%20%26%20Asylum/Asylum/MaterialSupportFS_26Sep07.pdf> [Fact Sheet: FARC]; USCIS, Memo from CIS Deputy Director to Associate Directors, "Withholding Adjudication and Review of Prior Denials of Certain Categories of Cases Involving Association with, or Provision of Material Support to, Certain Terrorist Organizations or Other Groups" (March 26, 2008), online: USCIS: <http://www.uscis.gov/files/nativedocuments/Withholding_26Mar08.pdf> (accessed November 29, 2008); USCIS, Update, "USCIS to Review Immigration Cases That Could Benefit from Consolidated Appropriations Act of 2008: Agency Will Hold Cases and Also Look at Denials or Referrals on or After Dec. 26, 2007" (March 27, 2008), online: <http://www.uscis.gov/files/article/CAA_27Mar08.pdf> (accessed November 29, 2008); and USCIS, Fact Sheet, "Department of Homeland Security Implements Exemption Authority for Certain Terrorist-Related Inadmissibility Grounds for Cases with Administratively Final Orders of Removal" (October 23, 2008), online: <http://www.uscis.gov/files/article/FACT%20SHEET%20DHS%20Exemption%20Authority%2020081023.pdf> (accessed November 29, 2008) [Fact Sheet: Exemption Authority].

76 For example, on April 27, 2007, pursuant to s 212(d)(3)(b)(i), DHS Secretary Michael Chertoff decided "to allow USCIS to provide exemptions to certain individuals who provided material support under duress to certain terrorist organizations

described in subsections 212(a)(3)(B)(vi)(I) and (II) (designated terrorist organizations that are often referred to as Tier I and Tier II organizations) if warranted by the totality of the circumstances." FARC was the first group identified as being exempt, in September 2007. See USCIS, Fact Sheet: FARC, *supra* note 75.

77 See 8 USC 1182(d)(3)(B)(i). See also USCIS Fact Sheet of 23 October 2008, *supra* note 75.

78 USCIS, Fact Sheet: Exemption Authority (October 23, 2008), *supra* note 75 at 3.

79 See *In Re S-K-*, *supra* note 33 at 948.

80 See Anker, *supra* note 14 at 443.

81 *Ibid.*

82 *Ibid.*

83 As stated by the court in *In Re A-H-*, *supra* note 4 at 789, the "reasonable grounds" standard is lower than the "preponderance of the evidence" standard applied in US civil law (which is the equivalent of the "balance of probabilities" in Canadian civil law), and is therefore far lower than the criminal burden of "proof beyond a reasonable doubt."

84 See *In Re U-H-*, Interim Decision #3469, 23 I&N Dec 355 at 356 (BIA 2002).

85 For example, the vast majority of designated foreign terrorist organizations as of April 30, 2008, were Arab or Muslim. It is difficult to accept that Arab/Muslim groups in reality constitute as high a percentage of the number of terrorist groups/armies that operate in the world. See US Department of State "Foreign Terrorist Organizations," online: <https://www.state.gov/foreign-terrorist-organizations/> (accessed August 22, 2019. The situation has not changed to date.

86 See Commission of Inquiry into the Actions of Canadian Officials in Relation to Maher Arar, *Report on the Events Relating to Maher Arar: Analysis and Recommendations* (Ottawa: Public Works and Government Services Canada, 2006) at 16–48, online: <http://www.sirc-csars.gc.ca/pdfs/cm_arar_rec-eng.pdf> (accessed December 17, 2006) [*Arar Commission Report*]. See also Erin Craddock, "Torturous Consequences and the Case of Maher Arar: Can Canadian Solutions 'Cure' the Due Process Deficiencies in US Removal Proceedings" (2008) 93:3 Cornell L Rev 621 at 634–37.

87 Human Rights First, "Denial and Delay: The Impact of the Immigration Law's 'Terrorism Bars' on Asylum Seekers and Refugees in the United States" (November 2009), online: Human Rights First <http://www.humanrightsfirst.info/pdf/RPP -DenialandDelay-FULL-111009-web.pdf> (accessed March 12, 2010) ["Denial and Delay"].

88 *Ibid* at 27–28.

89 *Ibid* at 29.

90 See Thomas Walkom, "US Security Trumps Freedom: Canadians Still in Need of Better Government Protection," *Toronto Star* (January 25, 2007), online: <http:// www.thestar.com/News/article/175534>.

91 See Craddock, *supra* note 86 at 649.

92 See *Peoples Mojahedin, supra* note 45. See also Germain, *Practical Guide, supra* note 2 at 115.

93 See Craddock, *supra* note 86 at 622, 640–41.

94 Stock, *supra* note 20 at 13.

95 *Ibid.*

96 See *In Re S-K-, supra* note 33 at 941 [emphasis added].

97 See Bruin and Wouters, *supra* note 6 at 15.

98 "Mandela Taken Off US Terror List," *BBC News* (July 21, 2008), online: <http://news.bbc.co.uk/go/pr/fr/-/2/hi/americas/7484517.stm>.

99 US, Bill HR 5690, *To Exempt the African National Congress from Treatment as a Terrorist Organization for Certain Acts or Events, Provide Relief for Certain Members of the African National Congress Regarding Admissibility, and for Other Purposes*, 110th Cong, 2008 (enacted as Pub L No 110-257). This two-section bill removed the ANC from the US terror watch list, such that ss (2)(A)(i)(I), (2)(B), and (3)(B) (other than clause (i)(II)) of s 212(a) of the *INA, supra* note 4 (8 USC s 1182(a)) would not apply "with respect to activities undertaken in association with the African National Congress in opposition to apartheid rule in South Africa."

100 See *In Re S-K-, supra* note 33 at 947.

101 "No Deportation for Cuban Militant," *BBC News* (September 28, 2005), online: <http://news.bbc.co.uk/2/hi/americas/4289136.stm>.

102 See *US v Posada Carriles*, 481 FSupp 2d 792 (WD Tex 2007).

103 See *US v Posada Carriles*, 486 FSupp 2d 599 (WD Tex 2007).

104 See *US v Posada Carriles*, 541 F.3d 344 (5th Cir 2008).

105 See John R. Crook, "Federal Jury Finds Alleged Anti-Castro Terrorist Not Guilty of Perjury Charges" (2011) 105 Am J Int'l L 601.

106 See Nezer, *supra* note 34 at 179.

107 *Ibid* at 182.

108 See Fleming et al, *supra* note 37 at 13.

109 *Ibid.*

110 *Consolidated Appropriations Act of 2008, supra* note 75 at s 691(b).

111 See US, *Oversight Hearing, supra* note 48 at 2.

112 Sharryn Aiken, "Manufacturing 'Terrorists': Refugees, National Security, and Canadian Law" (2001) 19:3 Refuge 54, at 60 ["Manufacturing 'Terrorists'"].

113 See Angus G. Grant, *Confronting (In)Security: Forging Legitimate Approaches to Security and Exclusion in Migration Law* (PhD Dissertation, Osgoode Hall Law School, 2016) at 80–82.

114 *Ibid* at 63–64.

115 See the *IRPA, supra* note 7, and the *Immigration and Refugee Protection Regulations*, SOR/2002-227 [*Regulations*].

116 The search for clarity here is not helped by the fact that there are a number of other grounds of security-related inadmissibility in s 34 of the *IRPA* that may encompass terrorist activities (for example, the expressions "engaging in subversion

by force," "danger to the security of Canada," and "engaging in acts of violence that would or might endanger the lives and safety of persons in Canada").

117 *Suresh v Canada (Minister of Citizenship and Immigration)*, 2002 SCC 1 at para 94, [2002] 1 SCR 3 at para 94 [*Suresh*]. For an Analysis and critique of this decision, see Obiora C. Okafor & Pius L. Okoronkwo, "Reconfiguring Non-refoulement? The Suresh Decision, Security Relativism and the International Human Rights Imperative" (2003) 15 Int'l J Refugee L 30.

118 See *IRPA, supra* note 7; and the *Regulations, supra* note 115. See also Audrey Macklin, "Borderline Security" in Ronald Daniels, Patrick Macklem, & Kent Roach, eds, *The Security of Freedom: Essays on Canada's Anti-Terrorism Bill* (Toronto: University of Toronto Press, 2001) 384 at 393.

119 See *Anti-terrorism Act*, SC 2001, c 41 [*ATA*]. The *ATA* was enacted into law in December 2001 and amended numerous laws: the *Criminal Code*, the *Canadian Human Rights Act*, the *Canadian Security Intelligence Act*, the *National Defense Act*, the *Federal Court Act*, the *Privacy Act*, and others. Although the *ATA* does not expressly refer to immigrants or refugees, some of its provisions have implications on the admissibility of certain categories of non-citizens.

120 *Suresh, supra* note 117; *R v Khawaja* (2006) CanLII 63685 (Ont SC) [*Khawaja*].

121 See *Khawaja, ibid* at para 64.

122 *ATA, supra* note 119 at 1. The portion of this definition enclosed in square brackets has been struck down by the courts. See the discussion of the *Khawaja* case in subsequent paragraphs.

123 For a thorough analysis of this provision, see Kent Roach, *September 11: Consequences for Canada* (Montreal/Kingston: McGill-Queen's University Press, 2003) at 29–45 [*September 11*].

124 *Ibid* at 29–36.

125 David Schneiderman & Brenda Cossman, "Political Association and the Anti-Terrorism Bill" in Daniels, Macklem, & Roach, *supra* note 118 at 173.

126 *Ibid* at 176.

127 *Ibid*.

128 See *Khawaja, supra* note 120 at paras 18–27.

129 *United States of America v Nadarajah* (2009), 95 OR (3d) 514 [*Nadarajah*].

130 See *Khawaja, supra* note 120 at para 7 [emphasis in original].

131 *Ibid* at para 58.

132 *Ibid* at paras 59–80.

133 *Ibid* at para 70.

134 *Ibid* at para 87.

135 *Suresh, supra* note 117 at para 96. See also the *International Convention for the Suppression of the Financing of Terrorism*, GA Res. 54/109, December 9, 1999, Annex.

136 *Ibid* at para 98.

137 *Ibid*.

138 See *Suresh, supra* note 117 at paras 13 and 100.

139 *Ibid* at para 100.

140 *Ibid* at para 108.

141 Roach, *September 11, supra* note 123 at 41.

142 See Kevin Davis, "Cutting Off the Funds to Terrorists: Whose Funds? Which Funds? Who Decides?" in Daniels, Macklem, & Roach, eds, *supra* note 118 at 314–15; and Roach, *September 11, supra* note 123 at 41–42.

143 See Roach, *ibid* at 39.

144 *Suresh, supra* note 117 at paras 109–10.

145 See Roach, *September 11, supra* note 123 at 39.

146 See *Toronto Coalition to Stop the War v Canada (Minister of Public Safety and Emergency Preparedness)*, 2009 FC 326, [2009] FCJ No 387.

147 *Criminal Code*, RSC 1985, c C-46, s 83.05(1), as amended by the *ATA, supra* note 119 at s 2.

148 *Ibid*. See also *Regulations Establishing a List of Entities*, SOR/2002-284.

149 See Public Safety Canada, "Currently Listed Entities" (December 2, 2015), online: Public Safety Canada <http://www.publicsafety.gc.ca/cnt/ntnl-scrt/cntr-trrrsm/lstd-ntts/crrnt-lstd-ntts-eng.aspx>; and Public Safety Canada, "Currently Listed Entities" (August 22, 2019), online: <https://www.publicsafety.gc.ca/cnt/ntnl-scrt/cntr-trrrsm/lstd-ntts/crrnt-lstd-ntts-en.aspx>.

150 In both *Thanaratnam v Canada (Minister of Citizenship & Immigration)*, [2004] 3 FCR 301, 2004 FC 349, reversed on other grounds, [2006] 1 FCR 474 (FCA), and *Sittampalam v Canada (Minister of Citizenship & Immigration)*, 2006 FCA 326, 56 Imm LR (3d) 161, 272 DLR (4th) 1, 354 NR 34, [2007] 3 FCR 198, the appellants submitted that "the lack of a statutory definition [of the word 'organization'] creates a danger of Courts over-reaching to cover the broadest range of criminal action that may appear to be taken in association with others," and argued that "for the purpose of paragraph 37(1)(a), an 'organization' must, at minimum, have a common criminal purpose and a sufficient structure to allow the benefits of its illegal conduct to be shared" (at para 34). The court rejected this argument, holding that "[t]hese criminal organizations do not usually have formal structures like corporations or associations that have charters, bylaws or constitutions. They are usually rather loosely and informally structured, which structures vary dramatically. Looseness and informality in the structure of a group should not thwart the purpose of IRPA. It is, therefore, necessary to adopt a rather flexible approach in assessing whether the attributes of a particular group meet the requirements of the IRPA given their varied, changing and clandestine character" (at para 39). While these cases concerned the definition of a criminal "organization" under s 37 of the *IRPA*, the same principles apply to the definition of a terrorist "organization," as noted in *Sittampalam* at paras 35–36.

151 *Nadarajah, supra* note 129 at paras 90–97.

152 See also Aiken, "Manufacturing 'Terrorists,'" *supra* note 112 at 62.

153 See Sharryn Aiken, "Of Gods and Monsters: National Security and Canadian Refugee Policy" (2001) 14:1 RQDI 7 at 26. See *Al Yamani v Canada (Solicitor General)*

(1996), 1 FC 174. See also the *Canadian Charter of Rights and Freedoms*, Part I of the *Constitution Act, 1982*, being Schedule B to the *Canada Act 1982* (UK), c 11.

154 See *Suresh, supra* note 117 at para 107.

155 See *Canada (Minister of Citizenship and Immigration) v Singh*, [1998] FCJ No 1147 (QL) at para 52, (1998) 151 FTR 101 (TD) [*Singh*]. See also Grant, *supra* note 113 at 106–14.

156 See *Poshteh v Canada (Minister of Citizenship & Immigration)*, 2005 FCA 85 at para 27, 331 NR 129 [*Poshteh*].

157 See *Immigration Act*, RSC 1985, c I-2.

158 *Singh, supra* note 155 at para 52.

159 *Poshteh, supra* note 156 at para 28.

160 *Ibid* at paras 33–35. The court concluded that an individual's status as a minor is relevant and there may be a distinction between a minor and an adult in the determination of whether the individual is a member of a terrorist organization under para 34(1)(f) of the *Act* if the minor provides evidence to support such a distinction. Relevant considerations would be matters such as whether the minor has the requisite knowledge or mental capacity to understand the nature and effect of his actions. Issues of duress or coercion may be relevant. The requisite knowledge or mental capacity should be viewed on a continuum; there is a presumption against the requisite knowledge or mental capacity in the case of young children, and a presumption that the closer the minor is to eighteen years of age, the greater the likelihood that the minor possesses the requisite knowledge or mental capacity.

161 See *Jahazi v Canada (Minister of Citizenship and Immigration)*, 2010 FC 242, [2010] FCJ No 271.

162 *Ibid* at para 48.

163 See *Ismael v Canada (Public Safety and Emergency Preparedness)*, 2010 FC 198, [2010] FCJ No 234 (QL).

164 See *Kanagendran v Canada*, 2014 FC 384.

165 See *Ezokola v Canada (Citizenship and Immigration)*, 2013 SCC 40, [2013] 2 SCR 678 [*Ezokola*].

166 See Grant, *supra* note 113 at 106–14.

167 See *Ezokola, supra* note 165 at para 77.

168 See *Joseph v Canada (Citizenship and Immigration)*, 2013 FC 1101 at para 14, [2013] FCJ 1171 (QL). See also Grant, *supra* note 113 at 113–14.

169 There is no specific offence of "mass murder" in the *Criminal Code*, nor was there such an offence before 9/11. This is a reference to s 22, "counseling a party," or s 464, "counseling an offence not committed," or s 231(3), "contracted murder," which includes "counseling" another person to commit murder.

170 *Tareen v Canada (Citizenship and Immigration)*, 2015 FC 1260.

171 See Davies Bagambiire, *Canadian Immigration and Refugee Law* (Aurora, ON: Canada Law Book, 1996) at 115. Contrary to the current legislation, s 11.4(1)(a) of the *Immigration Regulations, 1978*, SOR/78-172, explicitly provided that in order

to satisfy the landing requirements, a member of the (then) post-determination refugee claimants in Canada class could not be inadmissible under s 19 of the *Act, nor could any of their dependents be inadmissible* under s 19. As such, refugees were explicitly rendered inadmissible on the basis of an inadmissible family member (as defined in s 2(1) of the *Regulations, 1978*).

172 See *Khalil v Canada*, 2007 FC 923, [2008] 4 FCR 53. For a critique of this decision, see Reem Bahdi, "Re-imagining *Haj Khalil v Canada*" (2009) 27 Windsor YB Access Just 53.

173 See *Khalil v Canada*, 2009 FCA 66, 78 Imm LR (3d) 1.

174 See Jeremy Diamond & Kevin Liptak, "Trump Defends Travel Ban as Trudeau Looks On," *CNN Politics* (February 13, 2017), online: <http://www.cnn.com/2017/02/13/politics/donald-trump-justin-trudeau-white-house/>.

175 *Ibid.*

176 See *Suresh, supra* note 117 at para 110.

177 *Ibid.*

178 *Kablawi v Canada (Public Safety and Emergency Preparedness)*, 2008 FC 1011, [2008] FCJ No 1256.

179 *Chogolzadeh v Canada*, 2008 FC 405, [2008] FCJ No 544.

180 *Soe v Canada (Public Safety and Emergency Preparedness)*, 2007 FC 461, [2007] FCJ No 620 (QL).

181 See *IRPA, supra* note 7 at s 33 ("reasonable grounds to believe"). See also *Mugesera v Canada (Minister of Citizenship and Immigration)*, 2005 SCC 40 at para 114, [2005] 2 SCR 100 (explaining that "the 'reasonable grounds to believe' standard requires something more than mere suspicion, but less than the standard applicable in civil matters of proof on a balance of probabilities"). See also Emily Carasco et al, *Immigration and Refugee Law: Cases, Materials and Commentary* (Toronto: Emond Montgomery, 2007) at 670–71. The Canadian Council for Refugees (CCR) has described this standard of proof as an "extremely low" one. See CCR, "C-3 Submission" (November 26, 2007) at 10, online: CCR: <http://www.ccrweb.ca/documents/C-3submission.pdf>. The then chair of the UN Working Group on Arbitrary Detention once described this standard as amounting to "mere suspicion." See Dennis Bueckert, "UN Group Condemns Canada," *Canadian Press* (June 16, 2005), online: <http://cnews.canoe.ca/CNEWS/Canada/2005/06/15/1090106-cp.html> (accessed October 19, 2006).

182 See Reem Bahdi, "No Exit: Racial Profiling and Canada's War against Terrorism" (2003) 41 Osgoode Hall LJ 293; and Kathleen Harris, "Canadians Admit Racist Tendencies," *Toronto Sun* (January 15, 2007), online: No One Is Illegal <http://noii-van.resist.ca/?p=195>.

183 See Michelle Shephard, "Spy Agency Bungled Second Terror Case," *Toronto Star* (June 30, 2009), online: <http://www.thestar.com/news/canada/article/658621>; *(Re) Almrei*, 2009 FC 1263 at paras 157–58, 2009 CarswellNat 4286.

184 See Andrew Duffy, "Spy Agency Ordered to Turn over File on Harkat," *National Post* (May 28, 2009) A1; *Re Harkat*, 2009 FC 1050, 2009 CarswellNat 3192.

185 See *Arar Commission Report, supra* note 86.

186 See Roach, *September 11, supra* note 123 at 58.

187 See Schneiderman & Cossman, *supra* note 125 at 173.

188 See *Suresh, supra* note 117 at para 110.

189 See Tom Blackwell, "Former Journalist for the PLO Fights Immigration Ruling," *National Post* (June 4, 2004) A1.

190 See Lesley Ciarula Taylor, "Eritrean Minister Denied Canadian Visa," *Toronto Star* (September 13, 2008), online: <http://www.thestar.com/article/498645>.

191 See Deborah Summers, "George Galloway Banned from Canada," *The Guardian* (March 20, 2009), online: <http://www.theguardian.com/politics/2009/mar/20/george-galloway-banned-canada>.

192 *Ibid*.

193 See Blackwell, *supra* note 189.

194 See *Khalil v Canada*, 2011 FC 1332.

195 See *Canada v Khalil*, 2014 FCA 213, [2014] FCJ No 964 (QL).

196 See Summers, *supra* note 191.

197 Some of the aspects of this regime may not be discussed if there are no clearly identifiable international standards against which they may be assessed.

198 See *Refugee Convention, supra* note 7.

199 See Kidane, *supra* note 5 at 689. See also *Zrig v Canada*, [2003] FCJ No 565. Mohammed Zrig was accused of terrorism, but was deemed inadmissible under the *Refugee Convention* rather than the *IRPA* or the *Criminal Code*, as Canada's terrorism laws had not yet come into effect at the time he was deemed inadmissible. Thus, the Refugee Division concluded that Zrig was not a refugee within the *Refugee Convention* definition, being excluded under art 1F(b) and (c) as a person with respect to whom there are serious reasons for considering he has committed a serious non-political crime or is guilty of acts contrary to the principles of the United Nations. The Federal Court Trial Division upheld this decision. It held that it had to be concluded that the crimes attributed to the organization could be ascribed to Zrig as an accomplice by association. By performing his duties in the organization, the appellant knowingly tolerated – if not encouraged – the serious non-political crimes attributed to MTI/Ennahda since 1983.

200 See James Sloan, "The Application of Article 1F of the 1951 Convention in Canada and the US" (2000) 12 Int'l J Refugee L 222 at 222.

201 See UNHCR, "Advisory Opinion to Paul Engelmayer" (Washington, DC, January 6, 2006) at 3 (on file with the author) ["Advisory Opinion"]; and Bruin and Wouters, *supra* note 6 at 17.

202 See Volker Turk, "Forced Migration and Security" (2003) 15 Int'l J Refugee L 113 at 120.

203 See Inna Nazarova, "Alienating 'Human' from 'Right': US and U.K. Non-Compliance with Asylum Obligations under International Human Rights Law" (2002) 25 Fordham Int'l LJ 1335 at 1335–38.

204　See UNHCR, "Background Paper: Preserving the Institution of Asylum and Refugee Protection in the Context of Counter-Terrorism: The Problem of Terrorist Mobility" (Paper presented to the 5th Special Meeting of the Counter-Terrorism Committee with International, Regional and Subregional Organizations, Nairobi, Kenya, October 29–31, 2007) at 2 (on file with the author) ["Background Paper"].

205　See UNHRC (UN Human Rights Commission), *Report of the UN Special Rapporteur on the Promotion and Protection of Human Rights and Fundamental Freedoms while Countering Terrorism,* UN Doc A/62/263 (August 15, 2007) at 18 [*Report of UN Special Rapporteur*]. See also UNHCR, "Background Paper," *ibid* at 4.

206　See UNHRC, *Report of the UN Special Rapporteur, ibid* at 18.

207　See *In Re S-K-, supra* note 33 at 942 and fn 7.

208　See UNHCR, "Advisory Opinion," *supra* note 201 at 6.

209　See UNHRC, *Report of the UN Special Rapporteur, supra* note 205 at 19.

210　See UNHCR, "Addressing Security Concerns without Undermining Refugee Protection: UNHCR's Perspective" (Geneva, November 2001) at 4 (on file with the author).

211　See UN, Security Council, Subsidiary Organs, "The Consolidated United Nations Security Council Sanctions List," online: United Nations <https://www.un.org/securitycouncil/content/un-sc-consolidated-list>.

212　See Anya Bernstein, "The Hidden Costs of Terrorist Watch Lists" (2013) 61 Buff L Rev 461 at 462; and Justin Lin, "Revealed: Canada Uses Massive US Anti-Terrorist Database at Borders," *The Guardian* (June 21, 2018). See also *Abdelrazik v Canada,* [2010] 1 FCR 267 (offering some evidence of this interdependence); Reg Whitaker, "Securing the Ontario-Vermont Border: Myths and Realities in Post-9/11 Canadian-American Security Relations" (2004/2005) 60 Int'l J 53 at 64.

213　US, Department of State, "Foreign Terrorist Organizations" (June 12, 2016), online: Department of State <http://www.state.gov/j/ct/rls/other/des/123085.htm>; Public Safety Canada, "Currently Listed Entities" (June 12, 2016), online: Public Safety Canada <http://www.publicsafety.gc.ca/cnt/ntnl-scrt/cntr-trrrsm/lstd-ntts/crrnt-lstd-ntts-eng.aspx>. See also Public Safety Canada, "Currently Listed Entities" (August 22, 2019), online: https://www.publicsafety.gc.ca/cnt/ntnl-scrt/cntr-trrrsm/lstd-ntts/crrnt-lstd-ntts-en.aspx.

214　See Bernstein, *supra* note 212 at 462.

215　*Ibid* at 463–65; Lin, *supra* note 212.

216　The decision of the Court of Justice of the European Union in the *Kadi* case provides some guidance here. See *P. Kadi and Al Barakaat International Foundation v Council and Commission* [2008] ECR I-6351.

217　See UNHCR, "Advisory Opinion on the Extraterritorial Application of *Non-Refoulement* Obligations under the 1951 Convention Relating to the Status of Refugees and Its 1967 Protocol," online: UNHCR <https://www.refworld.org/docid/45f17a1a4.html>.

218　See *Suresh, supra* note 117 at paras 86–90.

219 See Germain, *Practical Guide, supra* note 3 at 112–13; and Anker, *supra* note 14 at 442–43.
220 See UNHRC, *Report of the UN Special Rapporteur, supra* note 205 at 18.
221 See Testimony of Ellen Sauerbrey in US, *Oversight Hearing, supra* note 48 at 2.
222 See Janet Dench, "Consequences on Citizenship, Immigration and Refugee Policies in Canada" (Presentation to the Forum of the International Civil Liberties Monitoring Group (ICLMG), February 17, 2004), online: CCR <http://www.ccrweb.ca/ICLMGforum.html#N_10_>.
223 *Ibid.*
224 See CCR, "Key Issues: Immigration and Refugee Protection" (March 2004), online: CCR <http://www.ccrweb.ca/keyissues.htm#N_2_>.
225 *Ibid.* See also *CBC News* (December 14, 2009), online: <http://www.cbc.ca/canada/story/2009/08/21/f-security-certificates.html> (accessed April 23, 2010) (reporting that "[s]ince 1991, at least 29 security certificates have been issued"); "Almrei Security Certificate Struck Down," *CBC News* (December 14, 2009), online: <https://www.cbc.ca/news/canada/toronto/almrei-security-certificate-struck-down-1.849196>; and Sharryn Aiken, "National Security and Canadian Immigration: Deconstructing the Discourse of Trade-Offs" in François Crépeau, ed, *The Complex Dynamics of International Migration* (Montréal: Presses de l'Université de Montréal, 2009) at 183, online: <https://papers.ssrn.com/sol3/papers.cfm?abstract_id=2494987> (reporting that fewer than thirty security certificates have been issued since 1991). All of these sources tend to support the statements made by the CCR and Janet Dench, and indicate that while the use of security certificates is increasing, it remains rare, and that the use of TRI legislation short of issuing a security certificate is likely increasing.

Chapter 4: The Canada-US Safe Third Country Measure
1 See Andrew F. Moore, "Unsafe in America: A Review of the US-Canada Safe Third Country Agreement" (2007) 47 Santa Clara L Rev 201 at 204–6. See also European Union Council Directive 2005/85/EC, December 1, 2005, Official Journal of the European Union, L/326/13; Tom Clark, "Human Rights in Asylum Sharing and Other Human Transfer Agreements" (2004) 22 Nethl QHR 217 at 218; Silvia Morgades, "The Externalization of the Asylum Function in the European Union," GRITIM Working Paper No 4 (2010) at 5; Chad C. Haddal, "Refugee and Asylum-Seeker Inflows in the United States and Other OECD Member States" (Congressional Research Service, Report to Congress, January 6, 2009) at 13; Michael John-Hopkins, "The Emperor's New Safe Country Concepts: A U.K. Perspective on Sacrificing Fairness at the Altar of Efficiency" (2009) 21 Int'l J Refugee L 218 at 219; and *European Parliament v Council of the European Union*, Case C-133/06, online: Official Journal of the European Union <http://eur-lex.europa.eu/LexUriServ/LexUriServ.do?uri=OJ:C:2008:158:0003:0004:EN:PDF>.
2 Moore, *ibid* at 205.

3   The definition of the term "safe" in this context will be considered in the section "Questioning the Agreement and Regimes."

4   *Agreement between the Government of Canada and the Government of the United States of America for Cooperation in the Examination of Refugee Status Claims from Nationals of Third Countries,* December 5, 2002, CTS 2004/2 (entered into force December 29, 2004), online: Citizenship and Immigration Canada <https://www.canada.ca/en/immigration-refugees-citizenship/corporate/mandate/policies-operational-instructions-agreements/agreements/safe-third-country-agreement/final-text.html> [*Agreement*].

5   See Cathryn Costello, "The Asylum Procedures Directive and the Proliferation of Safe Third Country Practices: Deterrence, Deflection and Dismantling of International Protection" (2005) 7 Eur J Migr & L 35 at 40; Rosemary Byrne & Andrew Shacknove, "The Safe Country Notion in European Asylum Law" (1996) 9 Harv Hum Rts J 185 at 185–86; and Moore, *supra* note 1 at 205–8.

6   *Ibid.*

7   See the *Convention Determining the State Responsible for Examining Applications for Asylum Lodged in One of the Member States of the European Communities,* June 15, 1990 (no longer in force) [*Dublin Convention*], online: Treaties Office Database <http://ec.europa.eu/world/agreements/prepareCreateTreatiesWorkspace/treatiesGeneralData.do?step=0&redirect=true&treatyId=7742> (this treaty has been replaced by the so-called Dublin II Regulation, February 18, 2003, Regulation (EC) No 343/2003); *Convention Applying the Schengen Agreement of 14 June 1985 between the Governments of the States of the Benelux, the Federal Republic of Germany and the French Republic on the Gradual Abolition of Checks at their Common Borders,* OJ L 239, 22.9.2000, 19–62, June 19, 1990 (entry into force September 1, 1993) [*Schengen Agreement*], online: <http://www.undp.md/border/ENG/Zona_Schengeneng.html> accessed October 29, 2004); Rosemary Byrne, Gregor Noll, & Jens Vedsted-Hansen, "Understanding Refugee Law in an Enlarged European Union" (2004) EJIL 355 at 360.

8   See Costello, *supra* note 5 at 37–39.

9   On amendments to the *Immigration Act* of 1976, see *Canadian Council for Refugees, Canadian Council of Churches, Amnesty International, & John Doe v Her Majesty the Queen,* [2008] 3 FCR 606 at para 8, (2007) FC 1262 [*Phelan Decision*]. On an attempt to introduce an STC measure, see Audrey Macklin, "Disappearing Refugees: Reflections on the Canada-US Safe Third Country Agreement" (2005) 36 Colum HRL Rev 365 at 370 ["Disappearing"].

10 Macklin, *ibid* at 370, 372–95. See also Howard Adelman, "Refugees and Border Security Post–September 11" (2002) 20 Refuge 5 at 9.

11 See Macklin, "Disappearing," *supra* note 9 at 394–95.

12 *Ibid.* See also Audrey Macklin, "Borderline Security" in Ronald Daniels, Patrick Macklem, & Kent Roach, eds, *The Security of Freedom: Essays on Canada's Anti-Terrorism Bill* (Toronto: University of Toronto Press, 2001) 384 at 387.

13 See Harvard Immigration Refugee Clinic, "Bordering on Failure: The US-Canada Safe Third Country Agreement Fifteen Months after Implementation" (Harvard Law School, March 2006) at 10 ["Bordering on Failure"].

14 See Macklin, "Disappearing," *supra* note 9 at 414.

15 *Ibid* at 414–16.

16 See CIC (Citizenship and Immigration Canada), "A Partnership for Protection: One Year Review," Executive Summary (November 2006) at 4 ["Partnership for Protection"].

17 *Ibid*.

18 *Ibid* at 5.

19 *Ibid* at 4.

20 *Ibid;* US, Department of Homeland Security, "US-Canada Smart Border/30 Point Action Plan Update" (December 6, 2002), at para 5 (on file with the author); Macklin, "Disappearing," *supra* note 9 at 381.

21 See Moore, *supra* note 1 at 202.

22 See Standing Committee on Citizenship and Immigration, *The Safe Third Country Regulations: Report of the Standing Committee on Citizenship and Immigration* (December 2002) at 6, online: Parliament of Canada <http://www.parl.gc.ca/content/hoc/Committee/372/CIMM/Reports/RP1032292/cimmrp01/cimmrp01-e.pdf>; and CCR (Canadian Council for Refugees), "Closing the Front Door on Refugees: Report on the Safe Third Country Agreement, Six Months after Implementation" (August 2005) at 6 ["Closing the Front Door"]. A recently released internal government memo backs up this point. See Amanda Connolly, "Safe Third Country Agreement 'No Longer Working as Intended,' Memo Reveals," *Global News*, March 14, 2019.

23 See CIC, "Partnership for Protection," *supra* note 16 at 5.

24 See *Convention Relating to the Status of Refugees*, July 28, 1951, 189 UNTS 137, CTS 1969/6 (entered into force April 22, 1954) [*Refugee Convention*]; *Convention against Torture and Other Cruel, Inhuman or Degrading Treatment or Punishment*, December 10, 1984, 1465 UNTS 85 (entered into force June 26, 1987) [*Convention against Torture*]; *Agreement, supra* note 4 at paras 1–3 of the Preamble. See also CIC, *ibid* at 5.

25 *Agreement, ibid* at para 6 of the Preamble; CIC, *ibid* at 5–6.

26 *Agreement, ibid* at art 4(1).

27 *Ibid* at art 1(1)(a).

28 *Ibid* at art 2.

29 *Ibid* at art 4(2)(d)(i).

30 *Ibid* at art 4(2)(d)(ii).

31 *Ibid* at arts 1(1)(f) and 4(2)(c).

32 *Ibid* at arts 1(1)(b) and 4(2)(a)&(b).

33 *Ibid* at art 6.

34 Macklin, "Disappearing," *supra* note 9 at 373.

35 *Ibid* at 373–74.

36 *Ibid* at 376.

37 See CCR, "Less Safe than Ever: Challenging the Designation of the US as a Safe Third Country for Refugees" (November 2006) at 8 and fn 6, online: CCR <http://ccrweb.ca/Lesssafe.pdf> ["Less Safe than Ever"].

38 See *Immigration and Refugee Protection Act (IRPA)*, SC 2001, c 27 (in force in its entirety since June 28, 2002), online: Justice Laws Website <http://laws-lois.justice.gc.ca/PDF/I-2.5.pdf>.

39 See the *Immigration and Refugee Protection Regulations*, SOR/2002-227, s 159.3, online: Justice Laws Website <http://laws-lois.justice.gc.ca/PDF/SOR-2002–227.pdf> [Canadian *Regulations*].

40 See CIC, *PP1: Processing Claims for Protection in Canada* (June 6, 2010) at 92, online: <http://overseastudent.ca/migratetocanada/IMMGuide/CICManual/pp/pp01-eng.pdf>.

41 For a list of the ports of entry in Canada, see Canadian *Regulations*, *supra* note 39 at schedule 1. See Macklin, "Disappearing," *supra* note 9 at 372.

42 Canadian *Regulations*, *ibid* at s 159.5(e). See, however, CCR, "Comments to the Standing Committee on Citizenship and Immigration on the Proposed Safe Third Country Regulations" (November 14, 2002) at 1 and 4, online: CCR <http://ccrweb.ca/en/comments-proposed-safe-third-country-regulations> ["Comments to the Standing Committee"].

43 Canadian *Regulations*, *ibid* at s 159.5(a)&(b). A United Nations High Commissioner for Refugees (UNHCR) report has found that Canada allows the immediate family members of a refugee claimant who has been found to meet an exception to accompany the claimant into Canada. See UNHCR, "Monitoring Report: Canada–United States 'Safe Third Country' Agreement" (June 2006) at 31, online: UNHCR <http://www.unhcr.org/455b2cca4.html>.

44 Canadian *Regulations*, *ibid* at s 159.5(c).

45 *Ibid* at s 159.5(d).

46 *Ibid* at s 159.5(f).

47 *Ibid* at s 159.5(g).

48 *Ibid* at s 159.5(h)(i).

49 *Ibid* at s 159.5(h)(ii).

50 *Ibid* at s 159.2.

51 *Ibid* at s 159.6.

52 See *IRPA*, *supra* note 38 at s 101(1)(e).

53 See Canadian *Regulations*, *supra* note 39 at s 159.4(1).

54 *Ibid* at s 159.4(2).

55 See CIC, "Minister Kenney Announces Removal of Exception Relating to Safe Third Country Agreement" (July 23, 2009), online: Market Wire <http://www.marketwired.com/press-release/minister-kenney-announces-removal-exception-relating-safe-third-country-agreement-1021464.htm> (accessed October 19, 2009).

56 *Ibid*. See also the refugee claims statistics for the year ending 2008 provided to the Canadian Council for Refugees, showing that in 2008, 61 percent of the persons exempted from the Canada-US safe third country measure were so exempt because of this now-rescinded exception for "moratorium countries." See email from Janet Dench, Executive Director of the CCR (February 20, 2009) (on file with the author).

57 For support for the statement that eligibility determinations at border posts in Canada are conducted by Canadian Border Services Agency (CBSA) officers, see CIC, "Partnership for Protection," *supra* note 16 at 2.

58 See also CCR, "Comments to the Standing Committee," *supra* note 42 at 2.

59 See "Procedural Issues Associated with Implementing the Agreement for Cooperation in the Examination of Refugee Status Claims from Nationals of Third Countries: Statement of Principles," reproduced in UNHCR, "Monitoring Report on the Canada–United States Safe Third Country Agreement, 29 December 2004–28 December 2005," app 4 at 104–5 ["Monitoring Report"].

60 *Ibid* at para 2.

61 See CIC, *PP1, supra* note 40 at para 18.4; Canada, *Government Response to the Report of the Standing Committee on Citizenship and Immigration: Safe Third Country Regulations* (May 2003) (on file with the author) at 5 [*Government Response*]. See also CCR, "Comments to the Standing Committee," *supra* note 42 at 2.

62 See CCR, "Refugees and Non-Citizens in Canada: Key Concerns Regarding Canada's Compliance with the Covenant on Civil and Political Rights (CCPR). Submission to the Human Rights Committee of the United Nations (September 16, 2005) at 4 ["Refugees and Non-Citizens"].

63 See *Implementation of the Agreement between the Government of the United States of America and the Government of Canada regarding Asylum Claims Made in Transit at Land Border Ports of Entry,* 69 Fed Reg 69480 (2004) (to be codified at 8 CFR pts 208, 212, 235), online: US Citizenship and Immigration Services (USCIS) <https://www.govinfo.gov/app/details/FR-2004-11-29/04-26239> and *Asylum Claims Made by Aliens Arriving from Canada at Land Border Ports-of-Entry,* 69 Fed Reg 69490 (2004) (to be codified at 8 CFR pts 1003, 1208, 1212, 1235, 1240), online: USCIS <https://www.federalregister.gov/documents/2004/11/29/04-26238/asylum-claims-made-by-aliens-arriving-from-canada-at-land-border-ports-of-entry>; Macklin, "Disappearing," *supra* note 9 at 377.

64 See US, *Immigration and Nationality Act,* s 208(a)(2)(A) INA, 8 USC 1158(a)(2)(A), online: <http://lib.store.yahoo.net/lib/aila/INASamplePages06.pdf>. See also Lynn S. Hodgens, "Domestic Silence: How the US-Canada Safe-Third-Country Agreement Brings New Urgency to the Need for Gender-Based-Asylum Regulations" (2006) 30 Vt L Rev 1045 at 1061.

65 See the *Illegal Immigration Reform and Immigrant Responsibility Act,* Pub L No 104-208, 110 Stat 3009-690 (2006) (entered into force April 1, 1997). See also CIC, "Partnership for Protection," *supra* note 16 at 3.

66 See especially 8 CFR s 208.30(e)(6).

67 *Ibid.* USCIS officers are part of the Department of Homeland Security.
68 See 69 Fed Reg 69490, *supra* note 63; and 69 Fed Reg 10622 (2004).
69 See 69 Fed Reg 10622, *ibid.*
70 See 8 CFR s 208.30(e)(6). See also Hodgens, *supra* note 64 at 1061.
71 See 8 CFR s 208.30(e)(6)(ii); and 69 Fed Reg 69490, *supra* note 63.
72 See 8 CFR s 208.30(e)(6)(i); and 69 Fed Reg 69490–91, *ibid.*
73 See 69 Fed Reg 69491, *ibid;* 8 CFR s 1240.11(g); and 8 CFR s 1208.4(a)(6).
74 See 8 CFR s 1208.4(a)(6); 8 CFR s 1240.11(g); and 69 Fed Reg 69491, *ibid.*
75 See 8 CFR s 1240.11(g)(2)(i)&(ii); 8 CFR s 1240.11(g)(3); 8 CFR s 1240.11(g)(4); and
    69 Fed Reg 69491–97, *ibid.*
76 See 8 CFR s 1240.11(g)(4); and 69 Fed Reg 69491, *ibid.*
77 In the United States, in practice, its implementation of its family unity principle
    has meant that if one member of a family meets an exception to the safe third
    country measure, then his or her spouse and any unmarried children under twenty-
    one years will benefit from that exception and be allowed to file their refugee
    claims in the United States. This is a more expansive reading of the "one family
    member in Canada" exception above. See CIC, "Partnership for Protection," *supra*
    note 16 at 5. In *US v Malenge*, 294 F App'x 642 (2nd Cir 2008), a Congolese claimant
    whose husband was already living as a refugee in the United States, had attempted
    to enter that country from Canada. She was arrested and prosecuted for attempting
    to enter the country with false documents. The US Court of Appeals for the Second
    Circuit held that the prosecution was fundamentally inconsistent with the obliga-
    tions of the US government to refugees and that, in any case, Ms. Malenge was,
    unknown to her, entitled to enter the United States legally under the "family
    member in the US" exception to the *Canada-US Safe Third Country Agreement.*
78 In *Nadarajah Viknesrajah v Officer Koson*, 2011 US Lexis 4374, the US District Court
    for the Western District of New York took note of the fact that the DHS had
    exercised its "public interest discretion" in favour of Mr. Viknesrajah in allowing
    him to apply for asylum in the United States even after having been rejected as a
    refugee in Canada, and having been removed to the United States from Canada.
79 The majority of the US Board of Immigration Appeals (BIA) held in *In Re R-D-,*
    Respondent, Interim Decision #3571, 24 I&N 221 (BIA 2007) at 221, that neither
    the *Agreement* nor US regulations mandate the status to be accorded in the United
    States to a non-permanent resident alien refugee claimant previously resident in
    the United States who is returned by Canada to the United States after an unsuccess-
    ful attempt to seek refugee status in Canada. In effect, the Board held that since
    such an alien is in law an "arriving" and not an "admitted" alien, he or she would
    still be subjected on arrival in the United States to a safe third country–based
    threshold screening interview by an asylum officer.
80 See 8 CFR s 208.30(e)(6)(iii).
81 See 8 CFR s 1240.11(g)(3).
82 See 8 CFR s 208.30(e)(6)(ii); and 69 Fed Reg 10623.

83 *Ibid.*
84 See UNHCR, "Monitoring Report," *supra* note 59 at 104 (Appendix 4, Procedural Issues Associated with Implementing the Agreement).
85 See 8 CFR s 208.30(e)(6)(i); and 8 CFR s 208.30(e)(7).
86 See CIC, "Partnership for Protection," *supra* note 16 at para V(B)(2)(iv).
87 See Penny Becklumb, "Canada's Inland Refugee Protection System" (Background Paper, BP 185E, nd) at 6, online: Library of Parliament <http://www2.parl.gc.ca/Content/LOP/ResearchPublications/bp185-e.htm#A-Eligibility> (accessed December 5, 2010). See also 8 CFR s 1003.42(h).
88 See 8 CFR s 1208.4(a)(6).
89 See 8 CFR s 1240.11(g).
90 One commentator has even argued that although the US system complies with international law, the Canadian regime tends to be significantly more liberal. See Patrick J. Glen, "Is the United States *Really* Not a Safe Third Country? A Contextual Critique of the Federal Court of Canada's Decision in *Canadian Council of Refugees et al v Her Majesty the Queen*" (2008) 22:4 Geo Immig LJ 587 at 614–19.
91 See Paulin Hountondji, "The Master's Voice – Remarks on the Problem of Human Rights in Africa" in UNESCO, ed, *Philosophical Foundations of Human Rights* (Paris: UNESCO, 1986) at 319.
92 For example, see CCR, "Brief to the Standing Committee on Citizenship and Immigration" (February 16, 2007) at 1–3, online: CCR <http://ccrweb.ca/SafethirdbriefSC.pdf> (accessed November 9, 2008); Moore, *supra* note 1 at 203; Harvard Immigration and Refugee Clinic, "Bordering on Failure," *supra* note 13 at 2, 11–15, 17–19; Macklin, "Disappearing," *supra* note 9 at 400–7; and Janet Dench, "America No 'Safe Haven' for Refugees," *Toronto Star* (February 6, 2007) at A17.
93 Government of Canada, "Regulatory Impact Analysis Statement [on the draft amendments to the *Immigration and Refugee Protection Regulations* to implement the Safe Third Country Agreement]," C Gaz 2002, II at 14.
94 See CCR, "Less Safe than Ever," *supra* note 37 at 1–6; and CCR, "Closing the Front Door," *supra* note 22 at 2–3.
95 See *Globe and Mail* (October 19, 2002) at A24. See also Amnesty International Canada's reaction at http://www.amnesty.ca/library/news/Arar02.htm (accessed March 14, 2005); and Commission of Inquiry into the Actions of Canadian Officials in Relation to Maher Arar, Dennis R. O'Connor, *Report on the Events Relating to Maher Arar* (2006), online: Library and Archives Canada <http://epe.lac-bac.gc.ca/100/206/301/pco-bcp/commissions/maher_arar/07–09–13/www.ararcommission.ca/default.htm>.
96 See *Washington Post* (December 26, 2002) at A01.
97 More than 1,000 people, most from Middle Eastern or Muslim countries, were arrested in the United States after 9/11." See the *Guardian*, "Lawsuit Brought by Muslims Rounded Up after 9/11 Gets Go-Ahead," online: <https://www.theguardian.com/us-news/2015/jun/21/lawsuit-muslims-september-11-roundup-abuse>.

98 See Nancy Murray, "Profiled: Arabs, Muslims, and the Post-9/11 Hunt for the 'Enemy Within'" in Elaine C. Hagopian, ed, *Civil Rights in Peril: The Targeting of Arabs and Muslims* (Chicago/London: Haymarket Books/Pluto Press, 2004) 27 at 45.

99 See Moore, *supra* note 1 at 261–62. For reporting on Obama's efforts to end renditions to torture as well as disturbing evidence that these practices continued even under his watch, see Scott Horton, "Target of Obama-Era Rendition Alleges Torture," *Huffington Post* (November 8, 2009), online: <http://www.huffingtonpost.com/2009/08/11/target-of-obama-era-rendi_n_256499.html>. For some evidence of the continued targeting of Arabs and Muslims as security risks, see US, House Committee on Homeland Security, *Committee Oversight Plan,* online: Department of Homeland Security <https://homeland.house.gov/files/CHS%20Oversight%20Plan%20112th%20Congress.pdf> (accessed March 21, 2014).

100 See, for example, Jonathan Martin & Alexander Burns, "Blaming Muslims after Attack, Donald Trump Tosses Pluralism Aside," *New York Times* (June 13, 2016), online: <http://www.nytimes.com/2016/06/14/us/politics/donald-trump-hillary-clinton-speeches.html?_r=0>.

101 See US, Executive Order No 13769, *Protecting the Nation from Foreign Terrorist Entry into the United States,* 82 Fed Reg 8977 (2017), online: The White House <http://www.whitehouse.gov/the-press-office/2017/01/27/executive-order-protecting-nation-foreign-terrorist-entry-united-states>. This Executive Order was subsequently amended after being suspended/struck down by the courts. See Executive Order No 13780, *Protecting the Nation from Foreign Terrorist Entry into the United States,* 82 Fed Reg 13209 (2017), online: The White House <http://www.whitehouse.gov/the-press-office/2017/03/06/executive-order-protecting-nation-foreign-terrorist-entry-united-states>. This second order has also been struck down by the courts. See Adam Liptak, "The Supreme Court's Options in the Travel Ban Case," *New York Times* (June 2, 2017), online: <http://www.nytimes.com/2017/06/02/us/politics/travel-ban-supreme-court-trump.html>.

102 See Moore, *supra* note 1 at 260–67; and CCR, "Supplementary Submission to Cabinet with Respect to the Designation of the US as a Safe Third Country for Refugees" (April 2007) at 2–3, online: CCR <http://ccrweb.ca/documents/safethirdapril07.pdf> ["Supplementary Submission to Cabinet"]; and CCR, "Less Safe than Ever," *supra* note 37 at 1–6.

103 See Harvard Immigration and Refugee Clinic, "Bordering on Failure," *supra* note 13 at 2, 17–19 (pointing out that Colombian refugee claimants, the group most affected by this material support bar in the United States, had low acceptance rates in that country, in the region of 45 percent for affirmative asylum claims and 28 percent before Immigration Judges, compared with 79–81 percent in Canada); *Arias v Gonzales,* 143 F App'x 464, 466 (3d Cir 2005) at 2; CCR, "Supplementary Submission to Cabinet," *ibid* at 3–4; and CCR, "Less Safe than Ever," *ibid* at 1–6.

104 See Harvard Immigration and Refugee Clinic, "Bordering on Failure," *ibid* at 2, 11–15; and Canada, *Government Response, supra* note 61 at 2.

105 See Hodgens, *supra* note 64 at 1048–49; and Moore, *supra* note 1 at 238–42.

106 See CCR, "Less Safe than Ever," *supra* note 37 at 14–15.

107 See Moore, *supra* note 1 at 255–60.

108 *Ibid* at 250–53. Moore also notes that, as one study has found, fully two-thirds of those who made their refugee claims in the context of removal procedures were not represented by legal counsel, something that is much rarer in Canada.

109 *Ibid* at 260–67. Although Moore is critical overall of the use of mandatory detention, he sought to provide a balanced assessment here.

110 See Canada, *Government Response, supra* note 61 at 2.

111 *Ibid*.

112 See Canada, *Safeguarding Asylum – Sustaining Canada's Commitment to Refugees: Report of the Standing Committee on Citizenship and Immigration*, 39th Parl, 1st Sess (May 2007) at 31, online: Government of Canada <http://publications.gc.ca/collection_2007/parl/XC64-391-1-1-02E.pdf>. Note, however, that the 2015 acceptance rates were a bit more disparate. Canada accepted 49 percent while the United States accepted 44.9 percent. See Daniel Schwartz, "Canada's Refugees by the Numbers: The Data," *CBC News* (October 4, 2015), online: <http://www.cbc.ca/news/canada/canada-s-refugees-by-the-numbers-the-data-1.3240640#IRBgraph>.

113 See Moore, *supra* note 1 at 259. Moore counters that this would be a strong argument save for the fact that the cases actually reaching the federal courts may only be the tip of the iceberg of both the total number of immigration cases in the United States and the total number of cases in which a miscarriage of justice has occurred.

114 See Government of Canada, "Report on the Review of the Designation of the United States as a Safe Third Country" (June 23, 2009) at 4 (on file with the author).

115 *Ibid* at 4.

116 *Ibid* at 5.

117 *Ibid* at 5–6.

118 *Ibid* at 6.

119 See *Phelan Decision, supra* note 9 at para 33.

120 See US, Executive Order No 13767, *Border Security and Immigration Enforcement Improvements*, 82 Fed Reg 8793 (2017), online: The White House <http://www.whitehouse.gov/the-press-office/2017/01/25/executive-order-border-security-and-immigration-enforcement-improvements>; and US, Executive Order No 13768, *Enhancing Public Safety in the Interior of the United States*, 82 Fed Reg 8799 (2017), online: The White House <http://www.whitehouse.gov/the-press-office/2017/01/25/presidential-executive-order-enhancing-public-safety-interior-united>. See also Michael Shear & Adam Liptak, "Supreme Court Takes Up Travel Ban Case, and Allows Parts to Go Ahead," *New York Times* (June 26, 2017), online: <http://www.nytimes.com/2017/06/26/us/politics/supreme-court-trump-travel-ban-case.html>.

For the full text of this Supreme Court ruling itself, see *Donald J. Trump v International Refugee Assistance Project*, 582 US 1 (2017).

121 See *Canadian Council for Refugees and others, Canadian Council of Churches, Amnesty International, & John Doe v Her Majesty the Queen*, 2006 FC 1046.

122 *Ibid* at para 1.

123 *Ibid*.

124 *Ibid* at paras 4–7.

125 *Ibid* at paras 13–19, 37–38.

126 *Ibid* at paras 22–31.

127 *Ibid* at paras 32–36 [emphasis in original].

128 See *Phelan Decision, supra* note 9.

129 *Ibid* at para 1–2.

130 *Ibid* at para 56–57.

131 *Ibid* at para 74.

132 *Ibid* at para 7.

133 The Court also noted that although the question of designating any country as a safe third country, especially "one with whom Canada has a close relationship, may be politically charged, the role of the Court is to assess the regulation and compliance from a legal perspective." *Ibid* at para 85.

134 *Ibid* at para 82. The court was also persuaded by a UK decision that reasoned that in reviewing whether the United States was a safe country for refugee claimants, consideration of its formal law alone was not enough. *Ibid* at para 129.

135 *Ibid* at paras 87–105.

136 *Ibid* at para 108.

137 *Ibid* at paras 143–216.

138 *Ibid* at para 256 [emphasis in original].

139 *Ibid* at para 333.

140 *Ibid* at para 281 [emphasis in original].

141 *Ibid* at para 333.

142 *Ibid* at paras 334–37. For a critical (albeit largely less than convincing) assessment of this decision from a US perspective, see Glen, *supra* note 90 at 611–19 (basically arguing that while the relevant Canadian standards may be more liberal, the United States does comply with the requirements of international law that are in his view less liberal than the Canadian ones; and sharply distinguishing – in my view quite wrongly – between the persons contemplated by art 1 of the 1951 *Refugee Convention* and those within the purview of art 33 of the same treaty).

143 See *Her Majesty the Queen v Canadian Council for Refugees, Canadian Council of Churches, Amnesty International, & John Doe* [2009] 3 FCR 136, 2008 FCA 229 (per Noel JA for the court) ["FCA Decision"]. The questions that were certified to the FCA by Phelan J concerned the appropriate standard of review of the Cabinet's decision to designate the United States as a safe third country; whether the *Regulations* implementing the *Agreement* are *ultra vires* and of no legal force and effect;

and whether the designation of the United States as safe for refugee claimants and/
or the ineligibility of claimants arriving in Canada from the United States to claim
refugee status in Canada violate the fundamental justice and equality provisions
of the *Canadian Charter of Rights and Freedoms* and are saved or not saved by s 1 of
the *Charter*. See "FCA Decision," *ibid* at para 27.

144 For the interlocutory decision staying the lower court's judgment, see 2008 FCA
40 (per Richard CJ).

145 See FCA Decision, *supra* note 143 at paras 44–46.

146 *Ibid* at paras 51–64, especially at 63–64.

147 *Ibid* at para 77.

148 *Ibid* at para 78.

149 *Ibid* at paras 70, 81, 87–88.

150 *Ibid* at para 82.

151 *Ibid* at paras 98–104, especially at 102 and 104.

152 For example, the Canadian Council for Refugees wrote a letter to the Canadian
government expressing its deep concern that removals to Somalia had not been
suspended as of early 2010. See Wanda Yamamato, CCR President, to Stephen
Rigby, President of the Canadian Border Services Agency (January 29, 2010), online:
CCR <http://ccrweb.ca/en/letter-withdrawal-temporary-suspensions-removal>.

153 *Ibid*.

154 *Ibid* (citing removals to Burundi, a country that had just ended a civil war and that
was not yet all that stable).

155 See *Canadian Council of Churches, et al v The Queen*, 2009 CanLII 4204 (SCC) (leave
application), online: Canadian Legal Information Institute <http://www.canlii.
org/en/ca/scc-l/doc/2009/2009canlii4204/2009canlii4204.pdf>; and CCR, "Supreme
Court Denial of Leave on Safe Third Regretted" (February 5, 2009), online: CCR
<http://ccrweb.ca/en/bulletin/09/02/05>. On the effort to relitigate, see Sonal Mar-
wah & Deborah Mebude, "The Legal Challenge to the Safe Third Country Agreement: What's at Stake?" online: <https://www.cpj.ca/legal-challenge-safe
-third-country-agreement-what-s-stake> (accessed February 19, 2016).

156 See CCR, "Comments to the Standing Committee on Citizenship and Immigration on the Proposed Safe Third Country Regulations" (November 14, 2002) at
4–5, online: CCR <http://ccrweb.ca/en/comments-proposed-safe-third-country
-regulations>.

157 See Canada, *Government Response, supra* note 61 at 4.

158 See 8 CFR s 208.30(e)(6)(iii).

159 *Ibid;* Hodgens, *supra* note 64 at 1068.

160 See Macklin, "Disappearing," *supra* note 9 at 373.

161 *Ibid*.

162 See Canada, *Government Response, supra* note 61 at 1; and Arthur C. Helton &
Dessie P. Zagorcheva, "Globalization, Terror, and the Movements of People" (2002)
36 Int'l Law 91 at 99.

163 See UNHCR, *UNHCR Global Trends 2010* (Geneva: UNHCR, 2011), online: <http://www.unhcr.org/statistics/country/4dfa11499/unhcr-global-trends-2010.html>.

164 See CIC, "Canada: A History of Refuge," online: CIC <https://www.canada.ca/en/immigration-refugees-citizenship/services/refugees/canada-role/timeline.html>.

165 See Michelle Zilio, "Canada on Track to Welcome More than 300,000 Immigrants in 2016," *Globe and Mail* (March 8, 2016), online: <http://www.theglobeandmail.com/news/politics/ottawa-seeks-to-bring-more-than-300000-newcomers-this-year/article29069851/>.

166 See Hodgens, *supra* note 64 at 1063; and CCR, "Closing the Front Door," *supra* note 22 at 3–4.

167 See Macklin, "Disappearing," *supra* note 9 at 373.

168 Regarding Canada, see Michael Bossin, "Bill C-31: Limited Access to Refugee Determination and Protection" (2001) 19:4 Refuge 55 at 55; and François Crépeau, Delphine Nakache, & Idil Atak, "International Migration: Security Concerns and Human Rights Standards" (2007) 44:3 Transcultural Psychiatry 311 at 319. With respect to the United States, see *Sale v Haitian Centers Council, Inc.*, 509 US 155 (1993); UNHCR, "Advisory Opinion on the Extraterritorial Application of *Non-Refoulement* Obligations under the 1951 Convention Relating to the Status of Refugees and Its 1967 Protocol" (January 26, 2007), online: UNHCR <http://www.unhcr.org/4d9486929.pdf> ["Advisory Opinion"]; and Glen, *supra* note 90 at 588. However, as events in Canada and the United States have shown, these interdiction measures are not wholly effective, as witness, for example, the docking of ships carrying Sri Lankan Tamils on Canada's west coast, and the arrival over the years of Cuban and Haitian "boat people" on US territorial waters or soil. See *Sale v Haitian Centers, ibid;* and Petti Fong, "Tamil Boat People in Good Health," *Toronto Star* (August 14, 2010), online: <http://www.thestar.com/news/canada/article/848057-tamil-boat-people-in-good-health>.

169 See Bossin, *ibid;* and UNHCR, "Advisory Opinion," *ibid.*

170 Macklin, "Disappearing," *supra* note 9 at 419. See also CCR, "Closing the Front Door," *supra* note 22 at 3–4; and CCR, "Comments to the Standing Committee," *supra* note 42 at 1.

171 See Canada, *Government Response, supra* note 61 at 3.

172 See CCR, "Refugees Entering from [the] US and Safe Third Country: FAQ" (February 2017), online: CCR <http://ccrweb.ca/en/print/26791>; Tavia Grant, "Are Asylum Seekers Crossing into Canada Illegally? A Look at the Facts behind the Controversy," *Globe and Mail* (August 1, 2018); and Harvard Immigration and Refugee Clinical Program to the Prime Minister of Canada and the Minister of Immigration (February 8, 2017) (on file with the author).

173 See Tavia Grant, *ibid;* and IRB (Immigration and Refugee Board of Canada), "Irregular Border Crosser Statistics," online: IRB <https://irb-cisr.gc.ca/en/statistics/Pages/Irregular-border-crosser-statistics.aspx>.

174 See Monique Scotti, "Over 26,000 People Have Crossed the Border Illegally since Last Year, but Only 1% Have Been Removed," *Global News* (May 7, 2018); Michelle

Zilio, "Canada, US in Talks to Close Loophole in Border Pact on Asylum Seekers," online: <https://www.theglobeandmail.com/politics/article-canada-in-talks-with -us-to-close-loophole-in-border-pact-on-asylum/> (March 17, 2019); and Connolly, *supra* note 22.

175   See CCR, "Closing the Front Door," *supra* note 22 at 16.

176   See CIC, "Partnership for Protection," *supra* note 16 at 8.

177   For instance, the 4,000 or so claims made at a Canadian land border post in 2005 by persons coming from the United States was only about half the number of claims made in the year before the *Agreement* was implemented. See CIC, "Partnership for Protection," *supra* note 16 at 7.

178   See TRAC Immigration, "Backlogs in Immigration Cases Continues to Climb" (March 11, 2011) online: TRAC Immigration <http://trac.syr.edu/immigration/ reports/225/>.

179   See TRAC Immigration, "Growing Backlog of Pending Cases in Immigration Courts" (nd), online: TRAC Immigration <http://trac.syr.edu/immigration/ reports/232/include/pendingG.html>.

180   See Schwartz, *supra* note 112; and Josh Wingrove, "Refugee Claims Hit 'Historic Low' as Ottawa's Policy Faces Fresh Criticism," *Globe and Mail* (January 22, 2014), online: <http://www.theglobeandmail.com/news/politics/refugee-claims-hit-historic -low-as-ottawas-policy-faces-fresh-criticism/article16461486/>.

181   For instance, the failure to fill vacancies at the Immigration and Refugee Board of Canada contributed to the backlog. See email from Janet Dench, Executive Director of the CCR (March 13, 2007) (on file with the author).

182   See Standing Committee on Citizenship and Immigration, House of Commons, "Evidence, CIMM 033, Testimony of Deborah Anker," 39th Parl, 1st Sess (February 8, 2007) at 9 (on file with the author) ["Anker Testimony"]; CCR, "Closing the Front Door," *supra* note 22 at 1; and Harvard Immigration and Refugee Clinic, "Bordering on Failure," *supra* note 13 at 15–16.

183   See CIC, "Partnership for Protection," *supra* note 16 at 7.

184   See Standing Committee on Citizenship and Immigration, "Anker Testimony," *supra* note 182 at 1.

185   Hodgens, *supra* note 64 at 1076.

186   *Ibid* at 5; and CIC, "Partnership for Protection," *supra* note 16 at 7.

187   See Standing Committee on Citizenship and Immigration, House of Commons, "Testimony of Francisco Rico-Martinez," 39th Parl, 1st Sess (February 8, 2007) at 3 (on file with the author) ["Rico-Martinez Testimony"]. See also CIC, "Partnership for Protection," *supra* note 16 at 21–23.

188   *Ibid*.

189   See Standing Committee on Citizenship and Immigration, "Anker Testimony," *supra* note 182 at 9.

190   *Ibid* at 2; Harvard Immigration and Refugee Clinic, "Bordering on Failure," *supra* note 13 at 2.

191   See CIC, "Partnership for Protection," *supra* note 16 at 13.

192 *Ibid.*

193 *Ibid.*

194 CCR, "Closing the Front Door," *supra* note 22 at 23.

195 *Ibid.*

196 *Ibid.*

197 *Ibid.* See also CCR, "Refugees and Non-Citizens in Canada," *supra* note 62 at 2.

198 See Reem Bahdi, "Before the Law: Creeping Lawlessness in Canadian National Security" in Vida Bajc & Willem de Lint, *Security and Everyday Life* (New York: Routledge, 2011) 143 at 145–46 and 154–55.

199 See Standing Committee on Citizenship and Immigration, "Rico-Martinez Testimony," *supra* note 187 at 7; CIC, "Partnership for Protection," *supra* note 16 at 3.

200 See Standing Committee on Citizenship and Immigration, "Anker Testimony," *supra* note 182 at 1. This issue is more of a worry in Canada mainly because, as we have seen, the Canada-US refugee claimant traffic is heavily oriented toward the Canadian side of the border.

201 See Harvard Immigration and Refugee Clinic, "Bordering on Failure," *supra* note 13 at 22.

202 See Standing Committee on Citizenship and Immigration, "Rico-Martinez Testimony," *supra* note 187 at 4.

203 See CIC, "Partnership for Protection," *supra* note 16 at 10–11.

204 See Nicholas Keung, "Asylum-Seekers Rush the Border," *Toronto Star* (September 24, 2007), online: <https://www.thestar.com/news/canada/2007/09/24/asylum_seekers_rush_the_border.html> (reporting that human smugglers were helping undocumented migrants find unguarded or lightly guarded crossings into Canada). See also email from Janet Dench, Executive Director of the CCR, September 24, 2007 (on file with the author).

205 See Harvard Immigration and Refugee Clinic, "Bordering on Failure," *supra* note 13 at 22.

206 See CBC News, "Canada-US Border Security 'Unacceptably Ineffective': Report," *CBC News* (February 1, 2011), online: <http://www.cbc.ca/politics/story/2011/02/01/canada-us-border-security.html>. See also US Government Accountability Office, "Border Security: Enhanced DHS Oversight and Assessment of Interagency Coordination Is Needed for the Northern Border" (Report to Congressional Requesters, December 2010) at 36, online: US Government Accountability Office <http://www.gao.gov/new.items/d1197.pdf> at 36.

207 See CBC News, "22 Refugees Entered Manitoba near Emerson Border Over the Weekend," *CBC News* (February 6, 2017), online: <http://www.cbc.ca/news/canada/manitoba/22-refugees-enter-manitoba-1.3969874> ["22 Refugees"].

208 *Ibid.*

209 See CIC, "Partnership for Protection," *supra* note 16 at 10–13.

210 *Ibid* at 14. See also UNHCR, "Monitoring Report," *supra* note 59 at 50.

211 CIC, *ibid* at 9.

212 See UNHCR, "Monitoring Report," *supra* note 59 at 53–54.

213 For example, see Andrew Cohen, "Extraordinary Rendition," *CBS News* (February 18, 2005), online: <http://www.cbsnews.com/stories/2005/02/18/opinion/courtwatch/main674973.shtml>.

214 See Byrne & Shacknove, *supra* note 5 at 186; Costello, *supra* note 5 at 47.

215 See CIC, "Partnership for Protection," *supra* note 16 at 3.

216 See Moore, *supra* note 1 at 218–19.

217 *Ibid*.

218 See UNHCR, "UNHCR's Guidelines on Applicable Criteria and Standards Relating to the Detention of Asylum Seekers" (February 26, 1999), online: Refworld <http://www.unhcr.org/refworld/docid/3c2b3f844.html>.

219 *Ibid* at 4 (introduction).

220 For example, see *ibid* at 218–20; and Costello, *supra* note 5 at 40.

221 UNHCR, *ibid* at 219.

222 Costello, *supra* note 5 at 219.

223 See Byrne & Shacknove, *supra* note 5 at 190–91 and fn 22. See also Executive Committee of the High Commissioner's Program, Conclusion No 58 (XL) (1989).

224 See Executive Committee of the High Commissioner's Program, Conclusion No 15 (XXX) (1979); and Macklin, "Disappearing," *supra* note 9 at 393.

225 *Ibid*.

226 See UNHCR, "UNHCR Comments on the Draft Agreement between Canada and the United States of America for 'Cooperation in the Examination of Refugee Status Claims from Nationals of Third Countries'" (July 26, 2002) at 1, online: Refworld <http://www.refworld.org/docid/3d4e69614.html> ["Comments on the Draft"]; and Macklin, "Disappearing," *supra* note 9.

227 For example, see Moore, *supra* note 1 at 218–19; Costello, *supra* note 5 at 40; Byrne & Shacknove, *supra* note 5 at 186–91; and Macklin, "Disappearing," *supra* note 9 at 393.

228 See Costello, *supra* note 5 at 40.

229 See Moore, *supra* note 1 at 218–21.

230 See Standing Committee on Citizenship and Immigration, "Anker Testimony," *supra* note 182 at 8.

231 See UNHCR, "Comments on the Draft," *supra* note 227 at 1–6; and Macklin, "Disappearing," *supra* note 9 at 407–8.

232 See UNHCR, *ibid* at 2.

233 See art 3 of the *Agreement*.

234 UNHCR, "Monitoring Report," *supra* note 59 at 24–25, 50.

235 See Standing Committee on Citizenship and Immigration, "Rico-Martinez Testimony," *supra* note 187 at 7. See also UNHCR to Canadian Border Services Agency (per Jahanshah Assadi), May 1, 2007, cited in email from Janet Dench, Executive Director of the CCR, October 10, 2007 (on file with the author).

236 See UNHCR to Canadian Border Services Agency, *ibid*.

237 *Ibid.*
238 See UNHCR, "Monitoring Report," *supra* note 59 at 24–25.
239 See UNHCR, "Comments on the Draft," *supra* note 227 at 1.
240 See Moore, *supra* note 1 at 267–70.
241 See OAS, Inter-American Commission on Human Rights, *Report on Immigration in the United States: Detention and Due Process,* OEA/Ser.L/V/II./Doc. 78/10 (December 30, 2010), online: OAS <http://cidh.org/countryrep/USImmigration/TOC.htm>.
242 *Ibid.*
243 UNHCR, "Monitoring Report," *supra* note 59 at 53–54.
244 *Ibid* at 49.
245 *Ibid.*
246 *Ibid* at 22.
247 *Ibid* at 28.
248 See CIC, "Partnership for Protection," *supra* note 16 at 2.
249 See Hodgens, *supra* note 64 at 1059; UNHCR, "Revisiting the Dublin Convention: Some Reflections by UNHCR in Response to the Commission Staff Working Paper" (January 2001), online: UNHCR <http://www.unhcr.org/43662b3e2.pdf>; and Costello, *supra* note 5 at 42.
250 For example, see Standing Committee on Citizenship and Immigration, "Anker Testimony," *supra* note 182 at 9; Macklin, "Disappearing," *supra* note 9 at 372–73. See also *Phelan Decision, supra* note 9 at para 8.
251 See Macklin, *ibid.*
252 See Reg Whitaker, "Keeping Up with the Neighbours? Canadian Responses to 9/11 in Historical and Comparative Context" (2003) 41 Osgoode Hall LJ 241 at 253–59; and Kent Roach, *September 11: Consequences for Canada* (Montreal/Kingston: McGill-Queen's University Press, 2003) at 126.
253 Kent Roach, *September 11: Consequences for Canada* (Montreal/Kingston: McGill-Queen's University Press, 2003) at 372–73.
254 *Ibid.*
255 See Government of Canada, *supra* note 93 at 3242. See also CIC, "Partnership for Protection," *supra* note 16 at 5.

Conclusion: Refugee Law, Security Relativism, and National Self-Image in Canada and the United States after 9/11

1 See Lauren Gilbert, "National Identity and Immigration Policy in the US and the European Union" (2007) 14 Colum J Eur L 99 at 100.
2 See Kent Roach, *September 11: Consequences for Canada* (Montreal/Kingston: McGill-Queen's University Press, 2003) at 5 [*September 11*].
3 *Ibid* at 5.
4 *Ibid* at 3.
5 *Ibid* at 13–14.

6 See Kent Roach, "Uneasy Neighbours: Comparative American and Canadian Counter-Terrorism" (2012) 38 Wm Mitchell L Rev 1701 at 1702 ["Uneasy Neighbours"].

7 Roach, *September 11, supra* note 2 at 126 and 133.

8 Reg Whitaker, "Keeping Up with the Neighbours? Canadian Responses to 9/11 in Historical and Comparative Context" (2003) 41 Osgoode Hall LJ 241 at 264 ["Neighbours"]. See also Roach, *ibid* at 6.

9 See the US, Library of Congress, *Nations Hospitable to Organized Crime and Terrorism: A Report Prepared by the Federal Research Division, Library of Congress* (October 2003) at 146, online: Library of Congress <https://www.loc.gov/rr/frd/pdf-files/ Nats_Hospitable.pdf> [*Nations Hospitable to Organized Crime*].

10 *Ibid* at 145.

11 See Roach, *September 11, supra* note 2 at 5.

12 *Ibid* at 126.

13 *Ibid*.

14 *Ibid* at 3–4.

15 *Ibid*.

16 The attempt to deport Mr. Manickavasagam Suresh from Canada led to the important Supreme Court decision in *Suresh v Canada*, 2002 SCC 1, [2002] 1 SCR 3 [*Suresh*]. See also Stewart Bell, "Federal Court Upholds Deportation of Tamil Tigers Fundraiser Who Has Fought to Stay in Canada for 22 Years," *National Post* (January 16, 2017), online: <http://news.nationalpost.com/news/canada/federal-court-upholds -deportation-of-tamil-tigers-fundraiser>.

17 See Craig S. Smith & Dan Levin, "As Canada Transforms, an Anti-Immigrant Fringe Stirs," *New York Times* (January 21, 2017), online: <http://www.nytimes. com/2017/01/31/world/americas/canada-quebec-nationalists.html>.

18 *Ibid*.

19 See Peter Zimonjic, "Tory Leadership Candidate Kellie Leitch Wants Immigrants to Be Asked: 'Are Men and Women Equal?'" *CBC News* (March 7, 2017), online: <http://www.cbc.ca/news/politics/leitch-immigrants-canadian-values-1.4012764> (reporting on a key Conservative Party leadership candidate's pledge to screen immigrants to Canada for "Canadian values"). See also Andre Domise, "The Rise of an Uncaring Canada," *Macleans*, April 21, 2019, online: https://www.macleans. ca/news/canada/the-rise-of-an-uncaring-canada/.

20 See Patrick Brethour, "Harper Finally Wins Majority as NDP Surges into Opposition," *Globe and Mail* (May 2, 2011), online: <http://www.theglobeandmail.com/ news/politics/harper-finally-wins-majority-as-ndp-surges-into-opposition/ article597814/>; and Jay Makarenko, "2008 Canadian Federal Election: Results and Summary," *Mapleleafweb* (October 21, 2008), online: <http://www.mapleleafweb. com/features/2008-canadian-federal-election-results-and-summary.html>.

21 In Canada, the Liberal Party, the New Democratic Party, the Bloc Québécois, and the Green Party are all left-of-centre to left-leaning parties. See "Paul Martin's

Balancing Act," *The Economist* (December 18, 2003), online: <http://www.economist.com/node/2303353>; and Alex Ballingall, "Amid Leadership Race, NDP Finds Itself at a Crossroads – Again," *Toronto Star* (March 11, 2017), online: <http://www.thestar.com/news/canada/2017/03/11/amid-leadership-race-ndp-finds-itself-at-a-crossroads-again.html>.

22 See Isabel Wallace, "Canada's Long Tightening of Refugee Policy," *Ottawa Citizen* (July 14, 2014), online: <http://ottawacitizen.com/news/national/canadas-long-tightening-of-refugee-policy>.

23 See Roach, *September 11, supra* note 2 at 13–17.

24 See Hon. Anne McLellan, "Reviewing the Anti-terrorism Act" (Speech to the Sub-Committee on Public Safety and National Security, March 22, 2005) at 4 (on file with the author). As we saw in Chapter 4, this *Act* has had significant implications for the post-9/11 protection of refugee rights in Canada, or the lack thereof.

25 See "Anti-Terrorism Act Has Sparked Legal, Political Challenges," *CBC News* (June 23, 2008), online: <http://www.cbc.ca/news/canada/anti-terrorism-act-has-sparked-legal-political-challenges-1.751694> (noting that "in a nod to civil libertarians, the original bill contained a five-year 'sunset clause' on some of its more controversial elements, meaning those sections would have to be reviewed by Parliament, which would decide whether or not to extend them after five years").

26 See Canada: A People's History, "The October Crisis" (nd), online: CBC Learning <http://www.cbc.ca/history/EPISCONTENTSE1EP16CH1PA4LE.html>.

27 See Hon. Anne McLellan, *supra* note 24 at 4.

28 See *Suresh, supra* note 16; *Ahani v Canada*, 2000 SCC 2, [2002] 1 SCR 72.

29 See Roger Karapin, "The Politics of Immigration Control in Britain and Germany: Subnational Politicians and Social Movements" (1999) 31:4 Comparative Politics 423 at 426–29, 437–39.

30 In 2011, the foreign-born population (many of whom hail from the Global South) constituted 20.6 percent of the total Canadian population. As a comparator, only 12.9 percent of the US population was foreign-born that year. More importantly, in that same year, 19.1 percent of Canada's population were visible minorities, i.e., immigrants from the Global South and their offspring. See Statistics Canada, "Immigration and Ethnocultural Diversity in Canada" (September 15, 2016), online: Statistics Canada <http://www12.statcan.gc.ca/nhs-enm/2011/as-sa/99-010-x/99-010-x2011001-eng.cfm>. In Toronto, the proportion of visible minorities approached 50 percent. See Statistics Canada, "Table 2, Visible Minority Population and Top Three Visible Minority Groups, Selected Metropolitan Areas, Canada, 2011" (April 13, 2016), online: Statistics Canada <http://www12.statcan.gc.ca/nhs-enm/2011/as-sa/99-010-x/2011001/tbl/tbl2-eng.cfm>. This proportion has continued to grow since then and is expected to continue to grow. For example, according to a 2017 Statistics Canada report, immigrants and their offspring are likely to constitute about half the total Canadian population by 2036, and over one-third of the working-age population (a large majority of voters) is likely to be visible minority

by that same year. See Statistics Canada, "Study: A Look at Immigration, Ethno-cultural Diversity and Languages in Canada up to 2036, 2011 to 2036" (January 25, 2017), online: Statistics Canada <http://www.statcan.gc.ca/daily-quotidien/170125/dq170125b-eng.htm>.

31 For example, see Anna M. Paperny, "Ridings with Most Immigrants Voted Liberal by a Landslide – and Other Things We Learned from Federal Election Results," *Global News* (March 7, 2016), online: <http://globalnews.ca/news/2291301/immi-grants-voted-liberal-by-a-landslide-and-other-things-we-learned-from-the-federal-election-results/>.

32 See Stewart Bell, "Canada Revokes Citizenship of Toronto 18 Ringleader Using New Anti-Terror Law," *National Post* (September 26, 2015), online: <http://news.nationalpost.com/news/canada/canada-revokes-citizenship-of-toronto-18-ringleader> (on the revocation of citizenships); and John Barber, "Canada's Con-servatives Vow to Create 'Barbaric Cultural Practices' Hotline," *The Guardian* (October 5, 2015), online: <http://www.theguardian.com/world/2015/oct/02/canada-conservatives-barbaric-cultural-practices-hotline> (on the now-defunct "barbaric practices hotline").

33 See Andrew Griffiths, "Seeing Red: Visible Minority Votes Flock to Liberals," *Policy Options* (October 23, 2015), online: <http://policyoptions.irpp.org/2015/10/23/21408/> .

34 See, for example, David Hodari, "Main Suspect behind 1996 Bombing of US Mil-itary Base Residence in Saudi Arabia Arrested," *Telegraph* (August 26, 2015), online: <http://www.telegraph.co.uk/news/worldnews/middleeast/saudiarabia/11825664/Main-suspect-behind-1996-bombing-of-US-military-base-residence-in-Saudi-Arabia-arrested.html>.

35 For example, see *AILA's Issue Packet,* online: <http://www.aila.org/>. American Immigration Lawyers Association, *Issue Packet on Comprehensive Immigration Reform* (February 24, 2004) at 30, online: American Immigration Lawyers Association <http://www.aila.org/>.

36 For example, a 2007 Pew poll found that about two-thirds of Americans shared this view. See Peter Dizikes, "Understanding Anti-Immigrant Sentiment," *MIT News* (February 19, 2010), online: <http://news.mit.edu/2010/anti-immigrant-sentiment-0219>. See also US, Library of Congress, *Immigration: Challenges for New Americans* (Teacher's Guide: Primary Resource Set), online: Library of Congress <http://www.loc.gov/teachers/classroommaterials/primarysourcesets/immigration/pdf/teacher_guide.pdf>.

37 See Catherine Rampell, "Why Republicans' New Anti-Immigrant Platform Likely Spells Doom for Them," *Washington Post* (July 14, 2016), online: <http://www.washingtonpost.com/opinions/why-republicans-new-anti-immigrant-platform-likely-spells-doom-for-them/2016/07/14/4a40f204-49fc-11e6-bdb9-701687974517_story.html?utm_term=.e987751da014>.

38 See Nacha Cattan & Eric Martin, "'I Feel the Hatred.' Mexicans Reel in Shock after Trump Victory," *Bloomberg News* (November 9, 2016), online: <http://www.

bloomberg.com/news/articles/2016-11-09/-i-feel-the-hatred-mexicans-reel-in-shock-after-trump-victory>.

39 See Muzaffar Chishti, Sarah Pierce, & Jessica Bolter, "The Obama Record on Deportations: Deporter-in-Chief, or Not?" *Migration Information Source* (January 26, 2017), online: Migration Policy Institute <http://www.migrationpolicy.org/article/obama-record-deportations-deporter-chief-or-not>.

40 See Adam Serwer, "Can Trump Bring Back Torture?" *The Atlantic* (January 26, 2017), online: <https://www.theatlantic.com/politics/archive/2017/01/trump-torture/514463/>.

41 See the earlier discussion in this section.

42 See Thomas Holbrook, "Here's a Close Look at How Immigrant Voters Could Affect the 2016 US Election," *The Guardian* (June 26, 2016), online: <https://www.washingtonpost.com/news/monkey-cage/wp/2016/06/26/heres-a-close-look-at-how-immigrant-voters-could-affect-the-2016-election/> (noting that the vast majority of persons of colour, which most immigrants to the United States are, did not vote for Donald Trump in 2016).

43 See "Permission Slip," Clip of the 2004 State of the Union Address, *C-SPAN* (January 20, 2004), online: <http://www.c-span.org/video/?c4485601/permission-slip>.

44 I first used the term "security relativism" in Obiora C. Okafor, "Globalism and Memory in Post-9/11 Human Rights and National Security Argumentation" (2006) Proceedings of the Raoul Wallenberg International Human Rights Symposium 69 at 71. It should be noted that despite my relatively recent usage of this term, the phenomenon that it denotes has been with us for a very long time. See Roger Daniels, *Guarding the Golden Door: American Immigration Policy since 1882* (New York: Hill & Wang, 2004) at 82–83.

45 Jack Donnelly, "Human Rights: Both Universal and Relative (A Reply to Michael Goodhart)" (2008) 30 Hum Rts Q 194 at 195.

46 *Ibid*.

47 As Volker Turk has insightfully noted, it is often unclear exactly whose security the dominant concept of national security accommodates, and whether this concept includes the security of refugees themselves, i.e., their need to become secure in the very state of refuge that all too often seeks to expel them. See Volker Turk, "Opinion: Forced Migration and Security" (2003) 15 Int'l J Refugee L 113 at 113–14. This is a very different kind of securitization of refugee discourse than is usually the case. The dominant form of this move is to make adverse inferences and deductions for national security from attempts to protect refugees. This is well noted in the literature. For example, see Joanne van Selm, "Refugee Protection in Europe and the US after 9/11" in Niklaus Steiner, Mark Gibney, & Gil Loescher, eds, *Problems of Protection: The UNHCR, Refugees and Human Rights* (New York: Routledge, 2003) at 238.

48 Upendra Baxi, *The Future of Human Rights* (Delhi: Oxford University Press, 2002) at 113.

49 Jack Donnelly, *Universal Human Rights in Theory and Practice* (Ithaca, NY: Cornell University Press, 2003) at 89–90. See also Jack Donnelly, "Cultural Relativism and Universal Human Rights" (1984) 6 Hum Rts Q 400 at 401 ["Cultural Relativism"].

50 Jack Donnelly, "The Relative Universality of Human Rights" (2007) 29 Hum Rts Q 281 at 295.

51 Donnelly, "Cultural Relativism," *supra* note 49 at 401.

52 See Okafor, *supra* note 44 at 71.

53 See Richard Posner, *Not a Suicide Pact: The Constitution in a Time of National Emergency* (New York: Oxford University Press, 2006) at 41. See also Bernard E. Harcourt, "Judge Richard Posner on Civil Liberties: Pragmatic Authoritarian Libertarian" (2007) 74 U Chicago L Rev 1723 at 1723–24.

54 See Alan M. Dershowitz, *Why Terrorism Works: Understanding the Threat, Responding to the Challenge* (New Haven, CT: Yale University Press, 2002) at 159.

55 Michael Ignatieff, *The Lesser Evil: Political Ethics in an Age of Terror* (Toronto: Penguin, 2004) at vii–viii, 23–24.

56 Arthur Helton & Dessie Zagorcheva, "Globalization, Terror, and the Movements of People" (2002) 36 Int'l Law 92 at 99–100.

57 See Mordechai Kremnitzer & Liat Levanon, "Not a Suicide Pact: A Comment on Preventative Means in General and on Torture in Particular" (2009) 42:2 Isr LR 248 at 253–74.

58 See *Suresh, supra* note 16.

59 See Catherine Dauvergne and Wesley W. Pue, "Editors' Introduction: Challenging Nation" (2004) 8 Law Text Culture 1; and Ruth Buchanan & Sundhya Pahuja, "Law, Nation and (Imagined) International Communities" (2004) 8 Law Text Culture 137 at 137–40; and Benedict Anderson, *Imagined Communities: Reflections on the Origin and Spread of Nationalism* (London: Verso, 1983) at 133. It is recognized that there is a rich sociological literature on this concept, and the contributions to that literature canvassed in this section are only a representative sample.

60 Dauvergne & Pue, *ibid* at 2–3.

61 John R. Morss, "Heteronomy as the Challenge to Nation: A Critique of Collective and of Individual Rights" (2004) 8 Law Text Culture 167 at 167–68.

62 See Stephen Clarkson, *Uncle Sam and Us: Globalization, Neoconservatism, and the Canadian State* (Toronto: University of Toronto Press, 2003) at 12, 427.

63 See Evan Potter, "Canada and the New Public Diplomacy Essay" (2003) 58 Int'l J 43 at 57.

64 See *Securing an Open Society: Canada's National Security Policy* (Ottawa: Privy Council Office, April 2004) at 5, online: Government of Canada <http://publications.gc.ca/collections/Collection/CP22-77-2004E.pdf>.

65 *House of Commons Debates*, 009 (October 26, 2007) at 459 (Dave Mackenzie).

66 See Right Honourable Justin Trudeau, Prime Minister of Canada, "Diversity Is Canada's Strength" (Address, November 26, 2015), online: Prime Minister of Canada <http://pm.gc.ca/eng/news/2015/11/26/diversity-canadas-strength>.

67   James E. Cameron & John W. Berry, "True Patriot Love: Structure and Predictors of Canadian Pride" (2011) 40:3 Canadian Ethnic Studies 17.

68   David Hornsby, "Changing Perception into Reality: Canada in Africa" (2014) 69 Int'l J 334; Bernard Duhaime, "Canada and the Inter-American Human Rights System: Time to Become a Full Player" (2012) 67 Int'l J 639 at 654.

69   Roach, "Uneasy Neighbours," *supra* note 6 at 1704.

70   Roach, *September 11, supra* note 2 at 163.

71   For instance, see *Securing an Open Society, supra* note 64 at 45.

72   Will Kymlicka, "Marketing Canadian Pluralism in the International Arena" (2004) 59:4 Int'l J 829.

73   See Shibao Guo & Lloyd Wong, "Revisiting Multiculturalism in Canada: An Introduction" in *Revisiting Multiculturalism in Canada: Theories, Policies and Debates,* ed. Shibao Guo & Lloyd Wong (Rotterdam: Sense Publishers, 2015) at 1–16.

74   See *Securing an Open Society, supra* note 64 at 45; and Tavia Grant, "Canadians Still Pro-Immigration, but Souring on United States: Survey," *Globe and Mail* (May 8, 2017), online: <http://www.theglobeandmail.com/news/national/canadians-still -pro-immigration-souring-on-united-states-survey/article34916205/>.

75   Whitaker, "Neighbours," *supra* note 8 at 266; Roach, *September 11, supra* note 2 at 898; and Clarkson, *supra* note 62 at 358–59, 427.

76   Roach, *September 11, supra* note 2 at 897.

77   *Ibid* at 124.

78   See *The Daily* (Statistics Canada) (April 30, 2007) at 5.

79   See IpsosReid.Com, "Canada: A Land of Immgrants Becomes More Positive about Immigration," *CanWest News Service* (June 16, 2007), online <https://www.ipsos. com/en-ca/canada-land-immigrants-becomes-more-positive-about-immigration>.

80   See Library of Congress, *Nations Hospitable to Organized Crime, supra* note 9; and Standing Committee on Citizenship and Immigration, House of Commons, "Evidence, CIMM 033, Testimony of Deborah Anker," 39th Parl, 1st Sess (February 8, 2007) at 2 (on file with the author).

81   See *The Daily* (Statistics Canada) (December 4, 2007); and Statistics Canada, "Some Facts about the Demographic and Ethnocultural Composition of the Population" (nd), online: Statistics Canada <http://www.statcan.gc.ca/pub/91-003-x/ 2007001/4129904-eng.htm>.

82   *Ibid.*

83   See Government of Canada, "How Does Canada Respond to Humanitarian Crises?" (June 7, 2016), online: Government of Canada <http://international.gc.ca/world -monde/issues_development-enjeux_developpement/response_conflict-reponse_ conflits/about_humanitarian-a_propos_humanitaire.aspx?lang=eng>.

84   See *Baker v Canada*, [1999] SCR 817, 1999 CanLII 699 (SCC).

85   *House of Commons Debates, supra* note 65 at 459.

86   See CCR (Canadian Council for Refugees), "Brief to the House of Commons Subcommittee on Public Safety and National Security of the Standing Committee

on Justice, Human Rights, Public Safety and Emergency Preparedness: Anti-Terrorism Act Review" (September 8, 2005) at 1–2, online: CCR <http://www.ccrweb.ca/ATAcomments.pdf>.

87 Reem Bahdi, "No Exit: Racial Profiling and Canada's War against Terrorism" (2003) 41 Osgoode Hall LJ 293 at 296.

88 See *Toronto Sun* (January 15, 2007).

89 See *Ottawa Sun* (January 17, 2007).

90 See Duncan McCue, "Racism is Still an Uncomfortable Truth in Canada," *CBC News* (November 12, 2014), online: <https://www.cbc.ca/news/canada/racism-still-an-uncomfortable-truth-in-canada-duncan-mccue-1.2831066>. See also Josh K. Elliot, "Nearly 50% of Canadians Think Racist Thoughts Are Normal: Ipsos Reid Poll," *Global News* (May 21, 2019), online <https://globalnews.ca/news/5262461/canadian-racism-ipsos-poll/>.

91 Bahdi, *supra* note 87 at 317.

92 See US, *Hearing before the Subcommittee on Immigration, Senate Committee on the Judiciary*, 107th Cong (April 4, 2001) S.HRG 107-249 at 1 (Sam Brownback, US Senator from Kansas) (quoting President Ronald Reagan).

93 See *Cuban American Bar Association v Christopher*, 43 F.3d 1412 (11th Cir 1995) at 14.

94 Helton & Zagorcheva, *supra* note 56 at 93.

95 Krissy A. Katzenstein, "Reinventing American Immigration Policy for the 21st Century" (2008) 41 Vand J Transnat'l L 269 at 271.

96 See ABA-CI & LCCR, *American Justice through Immigrants' Eyes* (Washington, DC: ABA-CI & LCCR, 2004) at 109.

97 Brandon E. Davis, "America's Immigration Crisis: Examining the Necessity of Comprehensive Immigration Reform" (2008) 54 Loy L Rev 353 at 354.

98 See US, *Hearing before the Subcommittee on Immigration, Border Security and Citizenship, Senate Committee on the Judiciary*, 111th Congress (April 30, 2009) at 2 (Jeff Moseley), online: US Senate <http://www.judiciary.senate.gov/meetings/date-change_-comprehensive-immigration-reform-in-2009-can-we-do-it-and-how>.

99 See Priscilla Huang, "Anchor Babies, Over-Breeders, and the Population Bomb: The Reemergence of Nativism and Population Control in Anti-Immigration Policies" (2008) 2 Harv L & Pol'y Rev 385; and US, *Hearing before the Subcommittee on Immigration, Border Security and Citizenship, Senate Committee on the Judiciary*, 111th Congress (April 30, 2009) at 3 (Doris Meissner, Director of the US Immigration Policy Program, Migration Policy Institute), online: US Senate <http://www.judiciary.senate.gov/meetings/date-change_-comprehensive-immigration-reform-in-2009-can-we-do-it-and-how>.

100 See Library of Congress, *Nations Hospitable to Organized Crime, supra* note 9 at 146; and Roach, "Uneasy Neighbours," *supra* note 6 at 1704.

Index

9/11 Recommendations Implementation Act of 2004 (Bill HR 10) (US), 73; and border with Canada, 58; and deportations to torture, 22, 23, 50, 51; and expedited removal, 73; and pre-trial detention of suspected terrorists, 96; s 3007, 73; s 3032, 22, 23, 50, 51; s 3142, 96

124, 126–27; and inadmissibility
of spouses and children, 177; and
indefinite detention, 125–26; *IRPA*
and, 126; and "irregular arrivals," 126;
and length of detention, 125–26,
128; and mandatory detention,
128; and membership in terrorist
organizations, 175–76; military
training from terrorist organizations
and, 176; and national self-image,
242, 243, 244; and preventive
detention, 125, 127; provision of
material support to terrorism in,
174; and racial/ethnic/country
profiling, 124, 127; and right to seek
asylum, 68; and roundups/dragnets,
124–25, 127; and safe third country
agreements, 214–15; and security
certificates, 127–28; terrorism-related
inadmissibility in, 172–79; terrorist
activity in, 173–74; and US refugee
law, 196–97
Iraq, US invasion of, 57, 77
irregular crossings. *See* clandestine/
irregular crossings
Ismael v Canada, 162–63

Jaballah, Mahmoud, 108
Jaballah v Canada, 119
Jahazi v Canada, 162
Jama v INS, 34
Jamshid (refugee from Afghanistan),
147
Juma, Monica, 8
Justice, Department of (US): and
Abu Ghraib prison scandal, 19–20;
and conditions of detention, 117;
Guidance on Racial Profiling, 78;
and Haitian refugees, 66; and "hold
until cleared" detention, 85; and
length of detention, 106–7; and
refugee detention, 67; and roundups

of Muslim and Arab males, 75–76;
on severe interrogation methods,
19–20; *Statistical Yearbook,* 53–54; and
Voluntary Interview Project, 77; and
waivers, 151

Kablawi v Canada, 168
Kagwanja, Peter, 8
Kamalthas v INS, 36
Kanagendran v Canada, 163
Karen National Union, 145
Karnes County Civil Detention
Center, 71
Karzai, Hamid, 147
Katzenstein, Krissy, 246
Kennedy, Edward, 67
Khalil, Hawal Haj, 171, 172
Khalil v Canada, 166, 172
Khawaja, R v, 152, 153–54, 155
Khouzam v Ashcroft, 31, 32
Kidane, Won, 132
Krasner, Stephen, 6
Krome detention facility (FL), 65
Kymlicka, Will, 242

Laoye v Attorney General US, 39
Laval Detention Centre, 118
Leahy, Patrick, 55, 61, 131
length of detention: for Almrei,
109–10; in *Alvin John Brown v
Canada,* 111; before asylum hearing,
71; Attorney General (US) and,
104–5; in Canada, 107–11; in Canada
vs. US, 111; *Canadian Charter of
Rights and Freedoms* and, 107, 110;
dangerousness and, 109; expedited
removal and, 68; FBI investigation/
clearance and, 106; flight risk and,
104, 108; for foreign nationals vs.
permanent residents, 109; Haitian
refugee, 67; history of, 64; under
IIRIRA, 105; under *Immigration*